Competition Policy and the Control of Buyer Power

NEW HORIZONS IN COMPETITION LAW AND ECONOMICS

Series Editor: Steven D. Anderman, *Department of Law, University of Essex, UK*

This series has been created to provide research based analysis and discussion of the appropriate role for economic thinking in the formulation of competition law and policy. The books in the series will move beyond studies of the traditional role of economics – that of helping to define markets and assess market power – to explore the extent to which economic thinking can play a role in the formulation of legal norms, such as abuse of a dominant position, restriction of competition and substantial impediments to or lessening of competition. This in many ways is the *new horizon* of competition law policy.

US antitrust policy, influenced in its formative years by the Chicago School, has already experienced an expansion of the role of economic thinking in its competition rules. Now the EU is committed to a greater role for economic thinking in its Block Exemption Regulations and Modernisation package as well as possibly in its reform of Article 102. Yet these developments still raise the issue of the *extent* to which economics should be adopted in defining the public interest in competition policy and what role economists should play in legal argument. The series will provide a forum for research perspectives that are critical of an unduly-expanded role for economics as well as those that support its greater use.

Titles in the series include:

Collective Dominance and Collusion
Parallelism in EU and US Competition Law
Marilena Filippelli

Cartels, Competition and Public Procurement
Law and Economic Approaches to Bid Rigging
Stefan Weishaar

The Chinese Anti-Monopoly Law
New Developments and Empirical Evidence
Edited by Michael Faure and Xinzhu Zhang

Standardization under EU Competition Rules and US Antitrust Laws
The Rise and Limits of Self-Regulation
Björn Lundqvist

Joint Research and Development under US Antitrust and EU Competition Law
Björn Lundqvist

Monopolies and Underdevelopment
From Colonial Past to Global Reality
Calixto Salomão Filho

Resale Price Maintenance and Vertical Territorial Restrictions
Theory and Practice in EU Competition Law and US Antitrust Law
Barbora Jedličková

Competition Policy and the Control of Buyer Power
A Global Issue
Peter C. Carstensen

Competition Policy and the Control of Buyer Power

A Global Issue

Peter C. Carstensen

Fred W & Vi Miller Chair in Law Emeritus, University of Wisconsin Law School, Senior Fellow, American Antitrust Institute, USA

NEW HORIZONS IN COMPETITION LAW AND ECONOMICS

Edward Elgar PUBLISHING

Cheltenham, UK • Northampton, MA, USA

Published by
Edward Elgar Publishing Limited
The Lypiatts
15 Lansdown Road
Cheltenham
Glos GL50 2JA
UK

Edward Elgar Publishing, Inc.
William Pratt House
9 Dewey Court
Northampton
Massachusetts 01060
USA

A catalogue record for this book
is available from the British Library

Library of Congress Control Number: 2017939799

This book is available electronically in the **Elgar**online
Law subject collection
DOI 10.4337/9781782540588

FSC
www.fsc.org
MIX
Paper from
responsible sources
FSC® C013056

ISBN 978 1 78254 057 1 (cased)
ISBN 978 1 78254 058 8 (eBook)

Typeset by Servis Filmsetting Ltd, Stockport, Cheshire
Printed and bound in Great Britain by TJ International Ltd, Padstow

Contents

Acknowledgments

Many people have contributed to the work on this book. None of them should be regarded as responsible for any of its defects, but they can jointly and severally take credit for any virtues the reader may find.

First and foremost are my research assistants. They were Jose Castro, Eric Eisenheim, Christopher Snyder and Elaine Xu. In addition, the editors of the *Antitrust Bulletin*, the *William and Mary Business Law Review*, and the *University of Pennsylvania Business Law Review* published articles that have provided important bases for this book. They all earned my appreciation for their diligent editorial contribution.

I had the privilege of presenting parts of this work at the Law and Society Association meeting in Honolulu in 2012 and at the Conference on Buyer Power in Competition Law sponsored by the University of Oxford Centre for Competition Law and Policy also that year. In addition, I have drawn on my presentation at the American Antitrust Institute's symposium on buyer power held in Washington, DC in 2007. The comments and suggestions from those meetings were very helpful.

Several scholars, without in any way agreeing with my positions and analysis, have been generous enough of their time to read and comment on parts of this work. They were Fred Carstensen, Daniel Gifford, John Kirkwood and Kyle Steigert. In addition, I have benefitted greatly from conversations too numerous to catalogue with antitrust lawyers and scholars about the issues surrounding buyer power.

I have benefited from financial support from the University of Wisconsin Graduate School, the Food Systems Research Project, the Quarles & Brady Summer Research Fellowship of the University of Wisconsin Law School and the Law School's own research fund. That support was most welcome and greatly facilitated the completion of this project.

Finally, but most importantly to the final version of this work, I have great debt to Amy Fine who provided extraordinary editorial advice and counsel to make this project as coherent as it is.

1. Buyer power: a pervasive challenge to competition policy

Every economy faces the challenge of creating and maintaining a workable system for producing and allocating goods and services as well as providing incentives and rewards for innovation. The resulting economic order must be resilient and respond positively to change because economies are inherently dynamic. Since the end of World War II, and even more since the collapse of the Soviet system, a nearly global consensus has emerged that economies should be based on market processes. The degree of reliance on markets and the rules defining or constraining their structure and use vary. Nevertheless, the core recognition is that market processes, with appropriate oversight of the conduct of the participants, are central to achieving socially desirable economic results both in the short term and the long term. Thus, competition policy broadly defined is itself an essential feature in every such economic system.

Conventional thinking about competition policy has emphasized the market distortion of seller power, resulting in harm to consumers and to the dynamics of markets. Less appreciated, but potentially even more harmful, is the exploitation of buyer power. A central claim of this book is that abuse of buyer power is a threat at least as serious to the competitive process as the abuse of seller power. The abuse of buyer power is often more embedded in the market process than abuse of seller power. Because it can result in lower input prices, which in turn may contribute to lower final prices to consumers, exploitation of buyer power can take on a superficial, pro-consumer character, making its harmful characteristics less visible. Standard ideology in competition policy emphasizes a single-minded pursuit of 'consumer welfare', which further obscures the harm to competition from abuse of buyer power. Moreover, its impact is often dispersed over a wide range of stakeholders, further decreasing awareness of its impact. Thus, it has been politically and ideologically challenging for those competition law enforcers inclined to pursue a more active policy.

Many commentators hold the erroneous belief that the risks of buyer power are limited to contexts in which there are many producers and few buyers. Such markets include agriculture, retail commodities and employment. In fact, the risks of buyer power are likely to exist in any buying market in which a buyer has substantial power. Unfortunately, only limited data and examples illustrate that broader problem because of the failure of most competition authorities and scholars of competition issues to focus on it. Certainly, the potentially abusive use of buyer power is highest when the buyer is a relatively large firm and the producers from which it buys are comparatively small. Indeed, there are many examples from retailing in which even firms of substantial size have been subject to abusive buying practices. Parity of size in a market reduces some of the risk of abuse, but a producer with market power that sells to a buyer with market power is likely to have upstream buyer power by virtue of that relationship. The harmful consequences of, for example, a merger that enhances the power of a buyer may well be felt by the upstream suppliers of any producer that deals directly with that buyer.

This combination of economic, ideological and political characteristics has resulted in an underappreciation of the risks buyer power poses. It also has resulted in only a modest, but growing, amount of useful economic theorizing and modeling. The existing empirical and theoretic analyses, however, demonstrate that different metrics and measures are necessary to determine when the use of buyer power, which is a common aspect of many market relationships, becomes or should become a source of competitive policy concern. This book joins a short, but growing, list of efforts to contribute to a better conceptualization of the competitive issues and the formulation of standards and criteria for judging the merits of buyer conduct.

At the outset it is important to stress the pervasiveness of the problems that buyer power causes for market economies. Commentators have observed that 'monopsony is far more prevalent than many have recognized', citing recent American examples including bid rigging in auctions for things ranging from antiques to treasury bonds, collusive practices involving financial aid to college students, salary setting for professional athletes, restrictions on college athletic scholarships and coaches, collusion to restrict competition for various kinds of technically skilled employees and restraints in agricultural product markets.[1]

Illustrative of the long-run harm in the United States is the transformation of rural America. The historical record clearly shows that farmers have gotten less and less of the food dollar as large buyers have increasingly dominated the buying of agricultural commodities.[2] When large

[1] Roger Blair and Jeffrey Harrison, *Monopsony in Law and Economics* (Cambridge University Press, Cambridge 2010) 1–14.

[2] The National Farmers Union reports that, as of October 2014, farmers and ranchers received a little less than 16 cents of every dollar spent on food. See National Farmers Union (31 October 2014), 'Farmer's Share of Retail

grocery retailers demand lower prices, the processors in turn drive down the prices they pay for the inputs from the farm. This exploitation of buyer power has sapped the economic viability of America's farmers, especially those operating small to mid-sized farms.[3] The consequences are visible in the overall decline of rural America and in the fact that the average age of American farmers is now in the late 50s.[4] There has been a steady exit from farming of the children of farmers and little new entry by others. Farmers serving commercial poultry processors are subject to such comprehensive controls that an Attorney General of Oklahoma once opined that the contracts made them employees of the processor.[5] But, of course, these farmers get none of the benefits accorded employees. Their treatment indeed makes them more like serfs than traditional farmers.

Buyer exploitation of farmers is not limited to the United States. Various commentators have expressed concern over the ways in which the large global buyers of agricultural commodities exploit their ability to drive down farm gate prices.[6] In many countries agriculture is highly

---

Food Dollar', available at http://www.nfu.org/images/103114_Farmers_Share.pdf.

[3] For more detailed examinations of the impact of buyer power on American agriculture see Christopher Leonard, *The Meat Racket* (Simon and Schuster, New York 2014) and Wenonah Hauter, *Foodopoly* (The New Press, New York 2013). A counterargument praising the restructuring of the meat processing industries is found in Maureen Ogle, *In Meat We Trust: An Unexpected History of Carnivore America* (Houghton Mifflin Harcourt, Boston 2014).

[4] According to the United States Department of Agriculture, '[i]n 2012, the average age of principal farm operators was 58.3 years, up 1.2 years since 2007, and continuing a 30-year trend of steady increase. The older age groups all increased in number between 2007 and 2012.' US Department of Agriculture (February 2014), *2012 Census of Agriculture, US Farms and Farmers*, available at http://www.agcensus.usda.gov/Publications/2012/Preliminary_Report/Highlights.pdf.

[5] Oklahoma Attorney General Opinion No. 01-17 (11 April 2001), available at http://www.oscn.net/applications/oscn/DeliverDocument.asp?CiteID=212530. See also Leonard, *supra* note 3, at 231–3.

[6] See, eg, Olivier De Schutter (2010), 'Addressing Concentration in Food Supply Chains: The Role of Competition Law in Tackling the Abuse of Buyer Power', available at http://www.srfood.org/images/stories/pdf/otherdocuments/20101201_briefing-note-03_en.pdf (hereinafter De Schutter, 'Concentration'); Olivier De Schutter (2009), 'Report of the Special Rapporteur on the Right to Food 5' ('Concentration in buying markets is particularly worrying, and even more so than concentration in selling markets, because dominance in buying markets can be achieved with a relatively small market share . . .'), available at http://www2.ohchr.org/english/bodies/hrcouncil/docs/13session/A-HRC-13-33.pdf (hereinafter De Schutter, 'Report'); Traidcraft and South Centre (2008), 'Rebalancing the Supply Chain: Buyer Power, Commodities and Competition Policy', available at http://unctad.org/Sections/ditc_ccpb/docs/ditc_ccpb0009_en.pdf.

dependent on export markets. In cocoa and bananas, the highly concentrated buying markets have resulted in long-term exploitation of producers.[7] Historically, these countries also had monopsonistic, state-run buying agencies that further exploited producers. Over the last 30 years those agencies have largely disappeared, but the results for farmers have not always been significantly better.[8]

In 2010, Olivier De Schutter, United Nations Special Rapporteur on the Right to Food, published a short discussion of the role of buyer power in the food chain with a specific focus on developing countries.[9] He reported that:

> [J]ust four firms carry out 45% of all coffee roasting, and only four firms carry out 40% of all international coffee trading. Similarly, just three companies control over 80% of the world's tea markets, and four companies control 40% of international trading in cocoa, 51% of cocoa grinding and 50% in confectionary manufacturing.[10]

Thus, both developed and less developed countries experience pervasive buyer power in agriculture.

Another classic example of buyer power's harmful consequences is the exploitation of workers. Employers can and do drive down wages even when the employer is profitable if market conditions support such exploitation. Moreover, there is often a downward 'ratchet', through which competing employers exercise their power over their workers to further depress wages and other workplace investments in order to offer greater discounts to the powerful buyers they supply. The consequence of lower wages is less capacity for workers to buy goods and services. This kind of exploitation transfers wealth from poor workers to wealthy owners. Those with modest incomes spend most of that income on goods and services, but the wealthy have a lower consumption function.[11] Hence, the

---

[7] See, eg, Bananalink, *The Problem with Bananas*, available at http://www.bananalink.org.uk/the-problem-with-bananas (last visited 10 March 2016); UN Conference on Trade and Development (2008), 'Cocoa Study: Industry Structures and Competition', available at http://unctad.org/en/Docs/ditccom20081_en.pdf. See generally Agricultural Accountability Initiative, 'Power Buyers, Power Sellers: How Supermarkets Impact Farmers, Workers and Consumers—and How We Can Build a Fairer Food System', available at http://www.ase.tufts.edu/gdae/pubs/rp/aai_issue_brief_3.pdf.

[8] An exception is the Ghana Cocoa Marketing Board. See Ghana Cocoa Board, https://www.cocobod.gh/index.php (last visited 3 March 2016).

[9] De Schutter, 'Concentration', *supra* note 6.

[10] *Ibid* at 2 (footnotes omitted).

[11] Economists generally assume that when income increases the recipient spends less than all of the increase. See, eg, Don Patinkin, *Money, Interest, and*

macroeconomic implication of such a wealth transfer, whether within a single country or from developing to developed countries, is that aggregate demand for many goods and services declines even if there is some growth in luxury goods markets. Depressed wages, therefore, greatly increase the probability that an economy will stagnate. Demand drives investment and economic growth, but when the majority of wage earners face flat or declining wages there is little room for increased demand.

The effect of buyer power on workers is evident worldwide. In the United States, there have been several conspiracies to reduce wages for nurses.[12] A number of major technology companies in Silicon Valley entered into a conspiracy not to compete for each other's employees. When sued by the Department of Justice, the companies agreed not to engage in such conduct in the future.[13] Their employees brought a major class action suit,[14] in which the judge initially concluded that the proposed $325 million payment was inadequate.[15] Subsequently, the court approved a $415 million settlement.[16] There is a long history of employer collusion back to the post-Civil War era, when plantation owners agreed not to compete with each other for sharecroppers. In effect, this imposed a new kind of economic slavery on the recently freed slaves.[17]

In the case of developing countries, global buyers victimize employers and their employees. They use their buyer power to drive down prices to the point that employers are unable to pay adequate wages or make the necessary investment in facilities that will provide a safe working environment. The collapse of entire factories and the catastrophic fires resulting from inadequate safety are recurring events in Pakistan and Bangladesh.[18] The buying practices of the large multinational enterprises that buy most

---

Prices (Harper and Row, New York 2nd edn 1965) 206 ('marginal propensity to demand commodities out of real income is assumed positive, but less than unity').

[12] See *Fleischman v Albany Med. Ctr.*, 728 F. Supp. 2d 130 (N.D.N.Y. 2010); *Reed v Advocate Health Care*, 268 F.R.D. 573 (N.D. Ill. 2009); *Cason-Merenda v Det. Med. Ctr.*, 862 F. Supp. 2d 603 (E.D. Mich. 2012).

[13] See Final Judgment, *United States v Adobe Sys.* (D.C.N. Cal. 2011), available at http://www.justice.gov/atr/cases/f272300/272393.htm.

[14] In re *High-Tech Emp. Antitrust Litig.*, 856 F. Supp. 2d 1103 (N.D. Cal. 2012) (upholding the complaint against a motion to dismiss).

[15] In re *High-Tech Emp. Antitrust Litig.*, 2014 WL 3917126 (N.D. Cal. Aug. 8, 2014) (denying proposed settlement as inadequate).

[16] In re *High-Tech Emp. Antitrust Litig.*, 2015 WL 5159441 (N.D. Cal. Sept. 2, 2015) (final approval of revised settlement).

[17] Darrell Miller, 'The Thirteenth Amendment and the Regulation of Custom' (2012) 112 *Columbia Law Review* 1811, 1833.

[18] See Aravind R Ganesh, 'The Right to Food and Buyer Power' (2010) *German Law Journal* 1190; Editorial, 'Fire Safety in Garment Factories' *New York Times*

export commodities is a continuing source of concern to human rights advocates concerned with developing countries.[19]

Farmers and workers are not the only victims of buyer power. Its abuse is a recurring concern in retail sales relationships for branded and generic goods. Whenever there are relatively few outlets for consumer goods, a retailer will have significant buyer power that it can exploit in a variety of ways that harm the producers and ultimately the economy generally by causing dynamic distortion, limiting consumer choice and transferring to the retailer wealth that ought to go to producers. Walmart is an example of this exploitation of producers.[20] Amazon, because of its dominance of the e-book business, has imposed price and non-price burdens on book publishers in the United States, Germany and globally.[21] Both Walmart and Amazon justify their exploitation by pointing to their low prices, but sharing the gains of abusive buying practices is not a legitimate defense for anticompetitive conduct.

Other examples of misuse of buyer power show the range of contexts in which it occurs. Through its ownership of two large chains of eyeglass retailers in the United States, Luxottica was able to limit Oakley's access to the market and ultimately forced it to sell out, further entrenching Luxottica's control of supply.[22] As a result consumers ultimately faced

---

(10 December 2012) at A26, available at http://www.nytimes.com/2012/12/10/opinion/fire-safety-in-garment-factories.html.

19 See, eg, Traidcraft (2014), 'Cashing in on Cashews', available at http://www.traidcraft.co.uk/media/3bed9565-4d1b-4ccc-a76e-3381b986c9c4.

20 See Hauter, *supra* note 3, at 68–73; United Food and Commercial Workers (2010), 'Ending Walmart's Rural Stranglehold', available at https://grist.files.wordpress.com/2010/09/ag_consolidation_white_paper2.pdf?. *Cf* Tom Angotti, Brian Paul, Tom Gray and Dom Williams (2010), 'Wal-mart's Economic Footprint: A Literature Review Prepared by Hunter College Center for Community Planning and Development and New York City Public Advocate Bill De Blasio', available at http://www.hunter.cuny.edu/ccpd/repository/files/walmart.pdf.

21 John B Kirkwood, 'Collusion to Control a Powerful Customer: Amazon, E-Books, and Antitrust Policy' (2014) 69 *University of Miami Law Review* 1, 8–9; Markus Brauck, Wolfgang Höbel and Claudia Voigt, 'An Amazon Problem: The Book Is Dead, Long Live the Book' *Spiegel Online International* (15 March 2013), available at http://www.spiegel.de/international/zeitgeist/rise-of-amazon-and-ebooks-force-german-publishers-to-reinvent-selves-a-888679.html.

22 See 'Oakley Settles Suits Against Luxottica' *Bloomberg News* (22 May 2003), available at http://articles.latimes.com/2003/may/22/business/fi-oakley22 (reporting that Oakley settled its patent infringement case with Luxottica). Three years later Oakley sold out to Luxottica after Luxottica excluded its lines from its retail outlets. See Olivia Fleming, 'Why DO Designer Glasses Cost More than an iPad? The Eyewear Company with "Total Domination" Setting Astronomical Prices' *Daily Mail* (9 October 2012), available at

both higher prices and reduced choice. In markets with high concentration on both the buying and selling side, the abuse of buyer power can occur even if the courts regard such conduct as irrational and implausible.[23] Smaller motion picture chains still face exclusionary use of buyer power by major chains—a problem of long standing.[24]

Perhaps the most visible context in which buyer power issues have arisen is in grocery retailing. The rapid expansion of high volume grocery supermarkets combined with significant mergers has resulted in many countries having highly concentrated grocery retailing markets from the buying side, even if consumers have two or three choices. A number of national competition authorities have belatedly discovered that buyer-side concentration creates significant problems for producers and ultimately is reflected in limited consumer choice and reduced competition in the supply markets. From the United Kingdom to Norway and Finland to Australia and South Africa the recognition of the threats to competition in food supply markets has generated a number of responses aimed at regulating in some way the conduct of large grocery buyers.[25] Interestingly, the

---

http://www.dailymail.co.uk/femail/article-2215287/Luxottica-The-eyewear-company-total-domination-setting-astronomical-prices.html.

[23] See *Adaptive Power Sols. v Hughes Missile Sys.*, 141 F.3d 947, 952–3 (9th Cir. 1998) (the only two buyers of a missile part colluded to refuse to deal with one of the two manufacturers, but the court of appeals held that the claim made 'no economic sense' and refused to impose liability). See also Christopher Leslie, 'Rationality Analysis in Antitrust' (2010) 158 *University of Pennsylvania Law Review* 263, 334–6 (2010) (criticizing the decision in *Adaptive Power* for ignoring the rational gains to the buyers of establishing a willingness to destroy suppliers).

[24] The older cases include *United States v Griffith*, 334 U.S. 100 (1948) (use of buyer power to exclude competition by bundling movie license locations); *Shine Chain Theaters v United States*, 334 U.S. 110 (1948) (same facts as *Griffith*); recent examples of the same conduct include *Cobb Theatres III v AMC Entm't Holdings, Inc.*, 101 F. Supp. 3d 1319 (N.D. Ga. 2015) (upholding complaint charging a conspiracy to exclude a smaller theater chain from the market by exclusive dealing contracts with a competing major chain). See also Jared Klaus and Jay Levine (3 June 2015), 'Antitrust Probe of Movie Theater Chains Enters Next Act' *Antitrust Law Source*, available at http://www.antitrustlawsource.com/2015/06/antitrust-probe-of-movie-theater-chains-enters-next-act/; Eriq Gardner, 'AMC Can't Escape Antitrust Lawsuit Over Distribution of Studio Movies' *Hollywood Reporter* (23 March 2015), available at http://www.hollywoodreporter.com/thr-esq/amc-cant-escape-antitrust-lawsuit-783762.

[25] See, eg, United Kingdom (2009), 'The Groceries Supply Code of Practice', available at https://www.gov.uk/government/publications/groceries-supply-code-of-practice. The Australian Competition and Consumer Commission has interpreted the Australian Consumer Law to authorize challenges to unconscionable conduct by major buyers. See Press Release (22 December 2014),

focus is often narrowly on grocery buying rather than the more general questions raised by concentrated retailing markets and their impact on upstream suppliers.

Indeed, the same risks of buyer exploitation arise in markets for a wide variety of components for assembly into more complex products or supplies to manufacturers. Buyers are often explicit in the strategy of creating a dependent relationship with key suppliers, that is, being the most important customer of that supplier.[26] Walmart has a similar record, including driving some of its suppliers into bankruptcy.[27] Boeing drove its suppliers' prices down by 15 percent and then increased the lag in paying for inputs from 30 days to 120 days.[28]

Buyer power arises in markets in which producers have few options for the sale of their products and lack the capacity either to reduce production efficiently or transfer their facilities to other products. Larger producers, however, may be able to diversify their product lines.[29] By reducing its dependency on any particular product line, even if most products have only a few buyers, an enterprise can survive and have a more effective bargaining position. It can refuse to produce at all if the terms are unsatisfactory. Of course, this is likely to impose significant costs on employees and the broader community in which a plant is located. In addition, the pressure on suppliers to diversify in turn drives mergers, which further concentrate the market structure and increase the resulting firm's potential upstream buyer power.

The harms resulting from buyer power abuse spread from the initial victims and affect the wealth of the communities in which the producers operate. The suppliers to the input producer lose sales, and they too reduce

---

'Court Finds Coles Engaged in Unconscionable Conduct and Orders Coles Pay $10 Million Penalties', available at https://www.accc.gov.au/media-release/court-finds-coles-engaged-in-unconscionable-conduct-and-orders-coles-pay-10-million-penalties.

[26] Walmart is the largest buyer for a number of major brands and has shown the capacity to force its suppliers to do its bidding, including absorbing many transaction costs without price increases. See Hauter, *supra* note 3, at 68–73.

[27] See *ibid* at 71.

[28] See Alwyn Scott and Tim Hepher, 'Boeing Slows Payments to Suppliers as It Accelerates Cost Cutting' *Reuters* (7 July 2016), available at http://www.reuters.com/article/us-boeing-suppliers-idUSKCN0ZN1GG.

[29] Suppliers with sufficient resources often acquire firms in related fields to diversify the risks they face. See Harriet Jones, 'Connecticut Aerospace Companies Face Technological Leap' *WNPR* (7 May 2014), available at http://wnpr.org/post/connecticut-aerospace-companies-face-technological-leap (supplier of parts to United Technologies had acquired five other businesses within the past year as part of its effort to increase its size).

employment and squeeze their vulnerable suppliers. Thus, the harm flows through the entire economy and is most hurtful when the economy injured is remote from any benefit that might accrue to the abusive buyer, its employees and customers. This is most obvious in export industries, where the exporting country suffers the losses and the importing countries enjoy the benefits. It is also apparent in American agriculture, where farmers bear the costs and urban consumers may get benefits. The capacity to transfer much of the economic risk to third parties is another aspect of buyer power that makes it both more pernicious than seller power and harder for competition authorities to deal with because of the dispersed nature of its impact.[30]

The traditional mantra of competition law has been that mere wealth transfer away from producers is not a competitive concern.[31] Hence, much of the exploitation resulting from buyer power was and still is ignored. Indeed, using a short term, neo-classical model to look for harm to 'consumer welfare', or even total welfare, limits the enforcement agenda for competition authorities, and the competition enforcement agencies globally have been slow to react to the problems that buyer power can present. Public awareness and concern with the evident harm to the competitive process have resulted in an increasing number of regulatory responses. These often involve legal regimes beyond those envisaged in conventional competition policy. US competition law enforcers, those in the European Union (EU) and in a number of its Member States, the Russian Federation, Japan, the Republic of Korea, Taiwan (China), Canada, South Africa, Australia and a number of other countries, started to address buyer power

---

[30] In American poultry production, the grower must have expensive buildings for raising the birds. A buyer can vary its output in response to market conditions by controlling when it takes delivery of flocks of birds without incurring the fixed costs of the vast complex of facilities necessary for raising them. In a more competitive market, growers would demand assurances that their fixed costs would be covered as a condition of incurring the initial investment. See generally Leonard, *supra* note 3, at 23–5, 67–8, 71.

[31] Others, including Robert Lande, have argued that maximizing total surplus is not the overarching goal of antitrust law and that the law should seek to prevent firms from achieving market power without justification or by taking the wealth of consumers or small producers. See Robert H Lande, 'Wealth Transfers as the Original and Primary Concern of Antitrust: The Efficiency Interpretation Challenged' (1982) 34 *Hastings Law Journal* 65; Robert H Lande and John B Kirkwood, 'The Fundamental Goal of Antitrust: Protecting Consumers, Not Increasing Efficiency' (2008) 84 *Notre Dame Law Review* 192. As discussed in Chapter 2 this position confuses rather than clarifies the goals of competition law because it starts from an economic theoretical perspective but then qualifies it with a market process concern.

issues at the start of the twenty-first century.[32] In 2008, the Organisation for Economic Co-operation and Development (OECD) held a conference to discuss these issues.[33] In 2013, the EU issued a Green Paper that reported the experience and substantial concerns of the Member States' competition authorities with various 'unfair' trade practices.[34] The paper suggests that the EU itself should consider developing uniform regulations designed to control such practices.[35] The EU's competition authority also created a panel that focused on issues related to food retailing, including problems with buyer power.[36] But, adhering to the consumer welfare definition of competition law policy, the inquiry resulted in no change or improvement in EU enforcement with respect to buyer power.[37] The United Kingdom, Russia, Norway, Finland, Australia, Japan and the Republic of Korea have established rules that treat abusive buyer exploitation of sellers as unconscionable conduct. In doing so, these laws seek to provide suppliers with a 'voice' because the option of an 'exit' is no longer available.[38]

Only in 2010 did the American antitrust authorities include an explicit section in their merger guidelines discussing the buyer-side merger analysis.[39] From a historical perspective, this belated acknowledgement of the

---

[32] See OECD, 'Policy Roundtable: Monopsony and Buyer Power' DAF/COMP(2008) 38, 141–301, available at http://www.oecd.org/dataoecd/38/63/44445750.pdf.

[33] *Ibid.*

[34] European Commission, *Green Paper on Unfair Trading Practices in the Business-to-Business Food and Non-Food Supply Chain in Europe*, COM(2013) 37 final, available at http://eur-lex.europa.eu/legal-content/EN/TXT/PDF/?uri=CELEX:52013DC0037&from=EN.

[35] *Ibid* at 12–14, 16–17.

[36] Competition Committee, *Roundtable on Competition Issues in Food Chain Industry* 6–8, DAF/COMP/WD(2013)105, available at http://ec.europa.eu/competition/international/multilateral/2013_oct_food_chain_industry_en.pdf; European Commission (2014), 'The Economic Impact of Modern Retail on Choice and Innovation in the EU Food Sector', available at http://ec.europa.eu/competition/publications/KD0214955ENN.pdf.

[37] European Commission, *Tackling Unfair Trading Practices in the Business-to-Business Food Supply Chain* 2, COM(2014) 472 final, available at http://ec.europa.eu/internal_market/retail/docs/140715-communication_en.pdf ('This Communication does not foresee regulatory action at EU level . . .').

[38] See generally Albert O Hirschmann, *Exit, Voice, and Loyalty: Responses to Decline in Firms, Organizations, and States* (Harvard University Press, Cambridge, MA 1970) (when groups can no longer exit from a relationship they will seek to have a voice in it).

[39] Federal Trade Commission and Department of Justice (2010), 'Horizontal Merger Guidelines', available at https://www.ftc.gov/sites/default/files/attachments/merger-review/100819hmg.pdf.

importance of buyer power analysis is striking; farm groups were primary advocates for the original American antitrust laws because of the exploitation of farmers in the sale of their commodities and livestock.[40]

Despite a gradual expansion of concern about buyer power in both economics and law, there remains a relative dearth of comprehensive evaluations of the unique characteristics of the buying side of the market. Few books have focused on buyer power, and none has examined the range of responses to buyer power that are emerging around the world. This book undertakes to link an analysis of the major competitive issues that arise from the use and abuse of buyer power to the responses of competition agencies, courts and scholars around the world. The focus is on the policy and legal issues in this field, although there must necessarily also be a substantial discussion of the economics. Indeed, the discussion will at least explore, even if it cannot definitively resolve, the questions of identifying the market structures and contexts in which buyer power is most likely to have adverse effects on the competitive process.

The contemporary literature on the legal policy issues that buyer power raises is not yet substantial, but it is growing in response, no doubt, to the increased focus on these issues by enforcement authorities.[41] However, much of the work has focused on specific contexts, such as loyalty programs and slotting allowances, without a full recognition of the buyer power nexus involved in the topics under review. Moreover, there are deep divides among commentators with respect to the economic and the policy issues.[42] One of the central issues is the degree of threat and potential for harm that comes from the abuse of buyer power. This study has a clear position that buyer power is both a serious and pervasive problem

---

40 Thomas J DiLorenzo, 'The Origins of Antitrust: An Interest-Group Perspective' (1985) 5 *International Review of Law and Economics* 75.

41 See, eg, Ariel Ezrachi and Maria Ioannidou, 'Buyer Power in European Union Merger Control' (2014) 10 *European Competition Journal* 69; Kirkwood, *supra* note 21; Maurice Stucke, 'Looking at the Monopsony in the Mirror' (2013) 62 *Emory Law Journal* 1509; 'Symposium: Buyer Power and Antitrust' (2005) 72 *Antitrust Law Journal* 505. My own contributions include 'Buyer Power, Competition Policy, and Antitrust: The Competitive Effects of Discrimination among Suppliers' (2008) 53 *Antitrust Bulletin* 271; 'Buyer Cartels versus Buying Groups: Legal Distinctions, Competitive Realities, and Antitrust Policy' (2010) 1 *William and Mary Business Law Review* 1; and 'Buyer Power and the Horizontal Merger Guidelines: Minor Progress on an Important Issue' (2012) 14 *University of Pennsylvania Business Law Journal* 775.

42 See, eg, Richard Scheelings and Joshua D Wright, '"Sui Generis"?: An Antitrust Analysis of Buyer Power in the United States and European Union' (2006) 39 *Akron Law Review* 207.

globally. It requires much more attention from competition authorities and policy makers generally than it has received.

Roger Blair and Jeffrey Harrison wrote an important book in 1993[43] that focused on the economics of buyer power with American antitrust law applications, and another in 2010.[44] Especially in the more recent book, they take a relatively sanguine view of buyer power in many circumstances. A group of European agricultural economists have also produced a very useful book on food retailing and buyer power in the EU.[45] Again, that book attempts to make the case that, although in some circumstances buyer power may contribute positively to economic welfare, in many other circumstances the likely impact is adverse. Neither of these works, nor the several books focused on labor issues, including those dealing with the monopsony issues in professional sports,[46] focuses on the range of competition policy issues. These works have made important contributions, but a policy-oriented book with an international focus on competition law and policy provides a significant addition to the modest current literature.

The central thesis of this book, in contrast to Blair and Harrison, is that undue buyer power is a serious threat to the long-run achievement of a workable competitive economic process, but its abuse is inherently more difficult to control. At the very least, it is as serious a problem as seller power and even, I will contend, more serious. This is true despite some considerations that arguably induce buyers to be moderate in their exploitation of their suppliers.[47]

The goal of competition policy should be to define rules and standards

---

[43] Roger Blair and Jeffrey Harrison, *Monopsony: Antitrust Law and Economics* (Princeton University Press, Princeton, NJ 1993).

[44] Blair and Harrison, *supra* note 1.

[45] Roger Clarke, Stephen Davies, Paul Dobson and Michael Waterson, *Buyer Power and Competition in European Food Retailing* (Edward Elgar Publishing, Cheltenham, UK and Northampton, MA, USA 2002).

[46] Alan Manning, *Monopsony in Motion: Imperfect Competition in Labor Markets* (Princeton University Press, Princeton, NJ 2003); Roger Noll (ed), *Government and the Sports Business* (The Brookings Institute, Washington, DC 1974). See also Gerald Scully, 'Pay and Performance in Major League Baseball' (1974) 64 *American Economic Review* 915.

[47] See John M Crespi, Tina L Saitone and Richard J Sexton, 'Competition in Farm Product Markets: Do Long-Run Incentives Trump Short-Run Market Power?' (2012) 34 *Applied Economic Perspectives and Policy* 669 (contending that the long-run interest of buyers will keep them from exploiting suppliers). Although 'excessive exploitation' is unlikely if buyers take a long-run perspective and see no likely replacement for the exploited supplier, it is not obvious that buyers as a class have or even can have such a well-informed, long-run, non-strategic vision and commitment.

that can effectively minimize exploitation and facilitate, over time, a desirable competitive process. Inherent institutional and economic characteristics, however, make it difficult to identify which controls over abusive buying practices by individual firms will produce the market incentives necessary to constrain buyer power. Hence, the appropriate legal standards for directly controlling unilateral abuse of buyer power are perhaps even more elusive than those for controlling monopolistic behavior. The difficulty with effectively identifying and implementing direct controls reveals the extraordinary challenges competition law has in dealing in a predictable and consistent way with unilateral buyer conduct that harms the competitive process.

Because of the explicit policy focus of the subsequent discussion, it is also important at the outset to identify the policy goals that will inform the subsequent analysis. This task requires an analysis of the contending claims for different goals as the primary purpose of competition law and policy. This topic will be addressed in Chapter 2 because it has particularly important implications for policy toward buyer power. When goals are framed in narrow, conventional economic-theoretical terms, the resulting policy implications downplay or ignore many competitively relevant aspects of buyer power. Chapter 2 provides both an analysis of competition policy goals generally and also focuses on the relevance of different ultimate goals for the framing of public policy with respect to buyer power.

Chapters 3 and 4 provide an economically oriented analysis of buyer power. Chapter 3, which draws on the work of Blair and Harrison, provides a deeper understanding of why buyer power is not the 'mirror image' of seller power. Indeed, the 'mirror image' metaphor is another of the obstacles to getting competition policy better oriented toward the risks that buyer power can present to the competitive process. Chapter 4 then examines how buyer power can affect competition adversely. The central premise is that exploitation of suppliers, and the resulting ripple effects on broad segments of society, is a primary competitive harm. It is particularly difficult to control exploitation directly in ways consistent with workably competitive markets. The difficulty stems from the need to balance control of abusive conduct with the recognition that some of the same conduct is important to the short-run and long-run achievement of an effective competitive process. Indeed, that tension concerning the use of buyer power creates the difficulty in framing useful rules of general application to control its abuse. This chapter also explains why overcoming buyer power is likely to be more difficult than overcoming seller power.

The next four chapters provide a comprehensive assessment of the options available to competition policy to deal with abuses, actual or potential, of buyer power. Chapter 5 examines competition policy options for controlling directly the unilateral abuse of buyer power. It evaluates the rules that can control both exploitative and exclusionary use of buyer power as well as the potential to impose structural remedies when such conduct occurs. This chapter is central to the thesis of this book that exploitation of buyer power is more difficult to control than abuse of seller power even as it is as pervasive as, or more pervasive than, seller power.

Chapter 6 evaluates the use of market regulations outside conventional competition law to minimize the harms that buyer power can cause. Such regulations are common responses in many market-oriented economies and seem particularly common for addressing the abuse of buyer power. But such regulations, especially as they focus on specific business relationships, carry risks to the competitive process because they can rigidify markets and undermine the valuable dynamics that come from innovation. Any specific regulation invites evasion and so may have only limited utility; moreover, such regulations tend to invite those who gain advantage from them to lobby for their enhancement and expansion beyond what is needed to protect the competitive process itself.

Chapter 7 reviews the law and policy governing buying cartels and buyer groups, and Chapter 8 provides a similar analysis of the standards used when mergers lead to significant buyer power. In combination these two chapters show that it is feasible to have competition policies that control the creation of buyer power by clear and consistent structural standards and specific prohibitions on certain kinds of buying arrangements. By controlling the creation of undue buyer power, the problems identified in Chapters 5 and 6 with directly regulating the unilateral abuse of such power are avoidable in significant part.

Chapter 9 concludes that the best policy for dealing with buyer power is to control its creation rather than to rely on rules to regulate its use. But because buyer power can and does exist in ways that are not parallel with seller power, different metrics, measures and criteria need to be used to ensure that the competitive process on the buying side of the market works fairly and equitably. Chapter 9 also considers how the globalization of markets creates issues for the enforcement of rules against buyer power abuse. Conduct in developed countries can cause serious harm in developing countries that may leave competition authorities in both jurisdictions unable to respond effectively.

This overview should end with a couple of caveats. First, despite the resolute effort to take a global perspective on the issues of buyer power, there is an unavoidable emphasis on the American experience. This emphasis derives, first, from the author's own background, which is in American competition policy issues generally and buyer power issues in particular. Second, American competition policy has addressed some issues of buyer power for well over a century. Indeed, a major element in the agitation that led to the Sherman Act was the concern of farmers with the buyer power of meat packers, grain elevator operators and other downstream buyers. As a result, there is a longer and broader experience with buyer power and its control in America than in any other country.

The second caveat is that any effort to synthesize a great range of materials and observations carries a tendency to abstract and generalize in ways that may gloss over important qualifications and limitations of the analysis. The reader should know that the author is aware of the problem and that every effort has been made to acknowledge the limits of the claims and the proposed analyses. The thesis of this book is that buyer power creates pervasive and serious risks to the competitive process, but the overall effect may be to suggest that any exercise of buyer power is somehow anticompetitive and undesirable. Again, every effort is made to qualify such a tone. Still, the cautious reader may want to keep a salt shaker at hand.

Finally, there is no question that competition policy overall must address both buyer and seller power. I contend, however, that there is already in place a vigorous and effective competition policy to control undue seller power. Therefore, this book addresses the need to do the same for buyer power.

2. The goals of competition policy

The ultimate goals of public policy in any legal domain are important. Their selection underlies the choices of specific policies and the resulting standards or rules that govern policy implementation. Hence, any analysis and critique of public policy should be based on the goals that are or should be the objectives of that policy.

In the case of competition policy, and especially with respect to buyer power, contending goals sometimes point in different policy directions. Moreover, the choice of overall goal will in many circumstances have an outcome-controlling effect on the assessment of the merits of the specific policies that emerge from the analysis. If the economic theory of maximizing consumer welfare is the primary goal of competition policy, then many of the adverse effects on producers will not be a source of concern because there is no immediate effect on consumers. But if the applicable goal is maximizing aggregate welfare, then adverse effects on producer surplus would be of concern, but the use of aggregate welfare analysis produces ambiguous results. A fairness goal, like a concern for aggregate welfare (indeed, the two goals may be synonymous), will take harm to producers seriously, but it too lacks a coherent means of identifying the specific policies that will accomplish it. If preserving and enhancing the competitive process is the primary goal of competition policy, then harm to producers is as relevant as harm to consumers. The fundamental objective of such a policy is to define efficient, equitable and enforceable standards compatible with market dynamics to govern all marketplace participants.

To the majority of commentators and competition agencies, the goal of competition law is the maximization of consumer welfare or aggregate welfare or some other economic abstraction.[1] However, a long-standing

[1] See, eg, Federal Trade Commission (2015), 'Statement of Enforcement Principles Regarding "Unfair Methods of Competition" Under Section 5 of the FTC Act', available at https://www.ftc.gov/public-statements/2015/08/statement-enforcement-principles-regarding-unfair-methods-competition; European Commission, Directorate-General for Competition (2012), 'Delivering for Consumers', available at http://bookshop.europa.eu/en/delivering-for-consumers-eu-competition-policy-pbKD3212085/;pgid=Iq1Ekni0.1lSR0OOK4MycO9B0000qh4MZmxm;sid=mzYGeHoKnzoGeCzdsnSY3xgvOfV6KDdphUQ=?Catalog

strand of competition policy analysis, which draws on frequent judicial expression, is that the goal of competition law is to promote and protect the competitive process.[2] To justify the choice of one goal over the others, it is necessary to critically evaluate the options in both practical and normative terms. This chapter examines the alternative goals of competition policy and develops a critique of each to determine which is the best guide for defining appropriate competition policies, rules and regulations. Each of the three possible goals—those based on economic theory, fairness and the promotion of the competitive process—will be evaluated in turn against the criteria of normative justification and practicality.

The normative argument for selecting among the various goals is central to the final conclusion of this chapter that preserving and enhancing the competitive process is the preferable fundamental goal for competition policy because it provides more guidance with which to frame specific policies and standards. For that reason, this book proceeds from that policy perspective. The subsequent chapters that address specific areas of competition policy toward buyer power will show that using this goal as the underlying guide to policy can lead in some important contexts to different, and normatively better, standards and rules than either economic welfare-based or fairness goals. Those comparisons also ensure that it will be possible to identify the different policy outcomes that different goals require. In that way, it is possible to avoid letting a specific goal overwhelm the more general analysis of buyer power standards.

I. GOALS BASED ON ECONOMIC THEORY

We are regularly told that competition law is moving away from fixed rules and toward an open-ended inquiry into the merits of specific acts and practices.[3] Indeed, some commentators, such as Blair and Sokol, have advocated legality for some cartels because they are 'likely' to improve

---

CategoryID=iuoKABstTO0AAAEjtZAY4e5L ('Consumer interests are thus at the core of competition policy'). See generally 'Symposium: Antitrust's Pursuit of Purpose' (2013) 81 *Fordham Law Review* 2151.

[2] See, eg, *Brown Shoe Co. v United States*, 370 U.S. 294, 320 (1962) (antitrust is concerned with '*competition*, not *competitors*'); Case C-8/08, *T-Mobile Netherlands BV v Raad van bestuur van de Nederlandse Mededingingsautoriteit*, [2009] ECR I4529 ¶ 31 ('[I]n order for a concerted practice to be regarded as having an anti-competitive object, it is sufficient that it has the potential to have a negative impact on competition').

[3] See, eg, Carl Shapiro, 'The 2010 Horizontal Merger Guidelines: From Hedgehog to Fox in Forty Years' (2010) 77 *Antitrust Law Journal* 49.

aggregate welfare.[4] The approach broadly is to examine the costs and benefits of specific practices in specific cases to determine whether or not, on balance, there are likely to be adverse effects on either aggregate welfare or consumer welfare. Economists and antitrust academics disagree about which of these two economic abstractions is the better criterion.[5] Both are goals derived from economic theory and so can be examined together.

In one of the first sustained analyses of competition policy using economic criteria, Turner and Kaysen identified four distinct goals for antitrust law: efficiency, progressiveness, stability and fairness.[6] Three of the four are explicitly economic. Only fairness falls outside conventional economic criteria. But Turner and Kaysen also demonstrated that, depending on which economic goal is given primacy, different policies emerge as appropriate guidance for competition law enforcers. Thus, policies that best serve the goal of stability point toward protecting incumbent firms from 'excessive' competition, but that is likely to conflict with the goals of efficiency and progressiveness. Indeed, there is a real tension between an interest in efficiency (an immediate economic effect) and progressiveness (improved economic results over time resulting from innovation and change).[7] Efficiency focuses on static, short-run economic welfare while progressiveness identifies market dynamics as the dominant concern for competition policy. Even if there was agreement that economic criteria are the best way to define the goals of antitrust, there is an inherent tension among the goals.

Current academic thinking about competition policy tends strongly to identify some form of economic welfare as the basic goal of competition policy.[8] Articles, judicial expressions and policy declarations from law enforcers both in the United States and the rest of the world reflect this.[9] This 'consensus' conceals a great deal of inconsistent and undertheorized applications of economic models. In particular, significant assumptions constrain the applicability of all the models, but those limits are recognized only in some situations.

The conventional category of economic welfare contains three distinct

---

[4] Roger Blair and Daniel Sokol, 'The Rule of Reason and the Goals of Antitrust: An Economic Approach' (2012) 78 *Antitrust Law Journal* 471, 492–7.

[5] See, eg, 'Symposium', *supra* note 1.

[6] Donald Turner and Carl Kaysen, *Antitrust Policy: A Legal and Economic Analysis* (Harvard University Press, Cambridge, MA 1959) 11–18.

[7] This tension is explored in Peter C Carstensen, 'Antitrust Law and the Paradigm of Industrial Organization' (1983) 16 *UC David Law Review* 487, 496–500.

[8] See 'Symposium', *supra* note 1; Blair and Sokol, *supra* note 4.

[9] See sources cited *supra* note 1.

economic abstractions: consumer welfare, producer welfare and aggregate (total) welfare. The three types of welfare are parts of what Turner and Kaysen labeled 'efficiency'. Each concept or combination of concepts has supporters as the best definition of the primary goal for competition law and policy.[10] But all of these concepts suffer from serious inherent limitations when used as the primary goal for competition policies.

These models of welfare had their origin as part of the neo-classical price theory model, which demonstrated that, holding everything else constant, competitive markets were more desirable than monopoly markets. Moving out from that basic demonstration, microeconomics has sought to evaluate the mix of contexts that in some abstract way might be said to make individuals, whether producers or consumers, better off.

These concepts originally defined a static, short-term optimization of production. The models also assumed rational self-interested economic actors with complete knowledge of supply and demand conditions. Although these assumptions are manifestly unrealistic, they provided a basis for examining how, under those conditions, markets would, in the short term, maximize the welfare of producers and consumers. The most general model, aggregate welfare, sought to identify the mix of goods and services, including the costs of distribution, that maximized the combined welfare of producers and consumers (assuming that market values are a complete measure of welfare). In the Pareto formulation, there is some distribution that is 'optimal', and no change can improve the total welfare of the community.[11] Interesting, but largely ignored, is the observation that there are multiple optimal points depending on the initial endowments of various market participants.[12]

The less demanding Kaldor-Hicks measure asks whether those who gain from some change in the market could compensate those who have lost as a result of that change and still have a net gain.[13] When no such

---

[10] See, eg, John Kirkwood and Robert Lande, 'The Fundamental Goal of Antitrust: Protecting Consumers, Not Increasing Efficiency' (2008) 84 *Notre Dame Law Review* 191; Blair and Sokol, *supra* note 4; 'Symposium', *supra* note 1.

[11] An allocation of goods and services in an economy is optimal if there is no reallocation that would leave everyone better off. This result can arise from a number of alternative initial allocations. See Jeffrey L Harrison, *Law and Economics in a Nutshell* (West Publishing, Eagan, US 1995) 30–3.

[12] See Amartya Sen, 'The Possibility of Social Choice' (1999) 89 *American Economic Review* 349 (mathematical demonstration of socially questionable but Pareto-optimal outcomes).

[13] JR Hicks, 'The Foundations of Welfare Economics' (1939) 49 *The Economic Journal* 696; Nicholas Kaldor, 'Welfare Propositions of Economics and Interpersonal Comparisons of Utility' (1939) 49 *The Economic Journal* 549.

transactions are possible, then the economy is operating at the optimal level. Again, there can be more than one optimal point.

As applied to competition policy, these total welfare measures require that the gains to some consumers and producers be summed and offset by the losses incurred by other producers and consumers. A policy that creates the potential for a positive net result is desirable in this framework because it increases the total value to society of economic activity. The implication is that a cartel or a monopoly may be preferred to a competitive market because the 'value' to society is higher than under the comparable situation in which there is more competition, higher volume, lower price, but less abstract consumer value.

In the debate surrounding vertical restraints in distribution, including resale price maintenance (RPM), two articles demonstrated that infra-marginal consumers were subsidizing marginal consumers.[14] When product differentiation gave a seller power over access to retailers, some consumers paid more than they should have compared to the resources used to serve them, so that the seller could serve higher-cost customers and increase the output of its product. Taking a broader view of the product category, total consumption could have been negatively affected if most of the producers of alternatives engaged in similar tactics and raised the average price of all products in the category. Thus, expanding individual firm output is not the same as expanding output of a more broadly conceived set of related products. Indeed, this example highlights one of the problems with using a firm-specific aggregate welfare analysis as a guide to competition policy. As applied, it fails to use the inclusive perspective inherent in the theory and instead looks at specific transactions, which are isolated from the broader market context.

More to the point, it is impossible in real-world terms to calculate the total costs and benefits of any state of the world, especially when the analysis moves from monetary values to the overall utility that parties receive.[15] Indeed, value itself is subjective; one can argue that any existing state of the world is optimal because, by definition, economic actors have chosen it. The practical implication of using maximizing total welfare as the goal of competition policy is to inhibit robust competition law enforcement. No

---

[14] William Comanor, 'Vertical Price Fixing, Market Restrictions, and the New Antitrust Policy' (1985) 98 *Harvard Law Review* 983; FM Scherer, 'The Economics of Vertical Restraints' (1983) 52 *Antitrust Law Journal* 687.

[15] This point is made indirectly in Maurice Stucke, 'Reconsidering Antitrust's Goals' (2012) 53 *Boston College Law Review* 551 (hereinafter Stucke, 'Reconsidering'), and 'Should Competition Policy Promote Happiness?' (2013) 81 *Fordham Law Review* 2575 (hereinafter Stucke, 'Happiness').

agreement, merger or dominant firm conduct is prima facie undesirable. Every situation requires a comprehensive review of the gains and losses to the economy before it can be condemned. Carried to its logical extreme, no cartel, no monopoly, no merger can be invalidated without an intensive review of the potential gains and losses. But such a review is impossible not only because of the lack of data, but even more fundamentally, it is impossible because the economy is always changing. Demand shifts and products change; comparing the situation under review to a static equilibrium yields little realistic information that is relevant to the future.

Blair and Sokol's argument for use of aggregate welfare as a basic policy goal for competition law illustrates several of its problems.[16] They demonstrate that, given a set of assumptions about bargaining outcomes based on economic theory, in a static world, under some circumstances, buyer cartels and mergers to monopoly are better for aggregate welfare than a competitive and competitively structured buying market facing a concentrated supply market.[17] They argue for a rule of reason with respect to buyer cartels when such firms face a concentrated supply market and for allowing mergers among buyers that substantially increase market power if counterbalancing seller power creates some overall welfare gain.[18] The same arguments can be and have been made for seller cartels when buyers are concentrated.[19]

The unexpressed but central assumption in these claims is that the market facts are given and immutable. But the analysis ignores time and the potential for change. Indeed, if either of the Blair and Sokol options were lawful, the long-term structure of the affected market would change. New entrants on the buying side would be even further deterred because the upstream and downstream monopolists would have a mutual interest in protecting their market control.[20] A buyers' cartel could similarly deter entry into production because of the risks to an entrant of exploitation by such buyers. Thus, these short-term remedies for producer power become

---

16 Blair and Sokol, *supra* note 4, at 473–4.

17 *Ibid* at 492–7.

18 *Ibid.*

19 See, eg, John B Kirkwood, 'Collusion to Control a Powerful Customer: Amazon, E-Books, and Antitrust Policy' (2014) 69 *Miami Law Review* 1, 51–64.

20 Business historian Tom McCraw has shown how General Electric worked with large department stores to enforce RPM, which created barriers to entry at both the production and retail levels. Thomas K McCraw, 'Competition and Fair Trade: History and Theory' (1996) 16 *Research in Economic History* 185.

probable longer term harms to the market and are likely to result in adverse effects on aggregate welfare in the future.

Overall, because of the uncertainty of the effect of any particular intervention, the use of aggregate welfare as a goal becomes an argument for a limited competition policy. The lack of certainty, unavoidable given the impossibility of collecting, processing and interpreting the relevant data, means that the underlying normative perspective of the advocates of the use of this goal is that competition law should be minimally invasive in the market.

The primary alternative among the economic models is consumer welfare, which focuses on the gains or losses to consumers as a result of some competitive practice or the impact of a market structure, such as a merger that increases concentration.[21] The argument here is that the goal of competition law is to protect consumers. Therefore, the appropriate focus is on the consequences to them regardless of whether the losses suffered by producers are greater than the gains to consumers (that is, a change that would not satisfy either the Pareto or Kaldor-Hicks utility criteria).

In the American context the argument for this position rests in part on the legislative history of the Sherman Act and, to a lesser extent, the Clayton Act. Lande has argued that the central concern of the relevant legislators was harm to consumers.[22] Certainly, the Clayton Act with its condemnation of any result that 'may substantially . . . lessen competition or tend to create a monopoly'[23] is more consistent with a consumer welfare approach than with an aggregate welfare approach. The Federal Trade Commission (FTC) Act is explicit: both unfair methods of competition and unfair or deceptive acts or practices are unlawful.[24] The FTC's authority to enforce the prohibition against unfair or deceptive acts or practices is limited, however, to those acts and practices that 'cause[] or [are] likely to cause *substantial injury to consumers. . . .*'[25] If this limit applies only to unfair acts and practices, then by inference the policy goal advanced by the prohibition on unfair competition has been left undefined. But the FTC has aligned itself exclusively with the consumer welfare goal.[26]

---

[21] Steven C Salop, 'Question: What Is the Real and Proper Antitrust Welfare Standard? Answer: The True Consumer Welfare Standard' (2010) 22 *Loyola Consumer Law Review* 336.

[22] Robert Lande, 'Wealth Transfers as the Original and Primary Concern of Antitrust: The Efficiency Interpretation Challenged' (1982) 34 *Hastings Law Review* 65.

[23] 15 U.S.C. § 14 (2016).

[24] *Ibid.* § 45(a)(1).

[25] *Ibid* § 45(n) (emphasis added).

[26] In 2015, the FTC issued a statement of its enforcement policy with respect to 'unfair competition' that commits it to limiting the use of that provision to

Like aggregate welfare, the initial problem with use of consumer welfare is that it involves the comparison of two states of the world at a time when everything else is held constant. On that basis, if the prices to consumers go up, and the quantity supplied goes down or choices are limited, then the conduct or structure has a negative effect on consumer welfare. But that statement is too inclusive because in the real, dynamic world, there are a variety of reasons why a price would go up or down and quantities would increase or decrease.

Moreover, some argue that constant or even increasing demand for a product following a price increase shows that consumers are getting greater value. Hence, consumer welfare is being enhanced and not diminished. This argument creates confusion when the policy goal is the maximization of consumer welfare. The debate about RPM is a telling example. RPM's effect is to increase prices to a level higher than those that would otherwise be charged. If it does not have that effect, it is pointless. Defenders, using consumer welfare as the goal of policy, argue that the increased price is necessary to cover the costs of product demonstration or other investments that are vulnerable to free riding or that it is necessary to provide assurance to customers that they are getting high-value goods. This latter argument is particularly interesting—the consumer pays an overcharge, beyond the costs of production and distribution, to enable the manufacturer and retailer to preserve the reputation of the good. The overcharge is presumably shared between the manufacturer and the retailer, but the buyer gets 'greater value' by paying the higher price. Thus, successfully imposing a higher price is itself deemed to be evidence that consumer welfare is enhanced, even though the same good with the same services could have been provided at a lower price leaving the consumer free to buy other goods or services. The irrationality of blindly equating price with quality undermines the central assumption of rational acting by consumers.[27]

Like its cousin, aggregate welfare, consumer welfare does not provide a useful goal on which to base competition policy. Without a great deal of interpretation based on assumptions of various kinds, this economic model does not provide a sufficiently clear direction for competition policy.

---

conduct that harms 'consumer welfare'. FTC (2015), 'Statement of Enforcement Principles Regarding "Unfair Methods of Competition" Under Section 5 of the FTC Act', available at https://www.ftc.gov/public-statements/2015/08/statement-enforcement-principles-regarding-unfair-methods-competition.

[27] See Warren Grimes, 'Spiff, Polish, and Consumer Demand Quality: Vertical Price Restraints Revisited' (1992) 80 *California Law Review* 815.

The last form of economic theory analysis is producer welfare, which reflects the difference between the costs of producing a good or service and the price paid for that good or service. Profit maximization is, of course, a basic and fundamental goal of business. But it does not provide a generally useful guide to policy. Indeed, no scholar seems to advocate that producer welfare should be a primary goal of competition policy. At the same time, depriving a producer of legitimate gains from its economic activity undermines the market process, which makes producer surplus relevant in the computation of aggregate welfare. Further, some observers recognize that conduct that reduces producer welfare below its presumed level in a more competitive market should provide a basis for concern under certain circumstances.[28] In general, however, a goal of maximizing producer welfare would lead to policies contrary to conventional notions of a workable market. To some degree, the views of the Federal Circuit on patent rights reflect a producer welfare goal for the protection of inventors.[29] These results have been criticized.[30]

Some advocates of the consumer welfare goal recognize that competition policy should take account of some abuses of producers. Thus, Kirkwood, while adhering generally to a consumer welfare goal, also advocates that producer welfare should be a concern when the producers are small enterprises subject to harm by powerful buyers.[31] In such circumstances, the goal of competition law should be to ensure that sellers receive a fair price (that is, one that approximates what the sellers would have received if the buying market were workably competitive) and are not subject to other constraints inconsistent with the sellers' self-interest.[32]

---

[28] John B Kirkwood, 'The Essence of Antitrust: Protecting Consumers and Small Suppliers from Anticompetitive Conduct' (2013) 81 *Fordham Law Review* 2425; Warren Grimes, 'Buyer Power and Retail Gatekeeper Power: Protecting Competition and the Atomistic Seller' (2005) 72 *Antitrust Law Journal* 563; see also William K Jones, 'Concerted Refusals to Deal and the Producer Interest in Antitrust' (1989) 50 *Ohio State Law Journal* 73, 88 ('[I]t is plain that the antitrust laws were intended to promote and preserve competitive markets; and the beneficiaries of such competition were to be producers as well as consumers').

[29] See, eg, *Intergraph v Intel Corp.*, 195 F.3d 1346 (Fed. Cir. 1999); *CSU, LLC v Xerox Corp.*, 203 F.3d 1322 (Fed. Cir. 2000); *LG Elecs., Inc. v Bizcom Elecs., Inc.*, 453 F.3d 1364 (Fed. Cir. 2006), rev'd sub nom. *Quanta Computer, Inc. v LG Elecs., Inc.*, 553 U.S. 617 (2008).

[30] See generally Robin Feldman, *Rethinking Patent Law* (Harvard University Press, Cambridge, MA 2012); Herbert J Hovenkamp and Christina Bohannan, *Creation without Restraint: Promoting Liberty and Rivalry in Innovation* (Oxford University Press, Oxford 2012).

[31] Kirkwood, *supra* note 28.

[32] *Ibid* at 2455–6; see also Grimes, *supra* note 28, at 574–5.

The problems with the use of any of these economic abstractions as a goal for competition policy are several. First, they are essentially static concepts. When the world changes, as it does continuously, these models cannot determine whether the result is optimal or not. If competition policy has only a very short-term concern for momentary prices and output, then these concepts at least fit. But this approach would require policy makers to deny that which is most obvious. The technologies of supply and distribution as well as consumer tastes are continuously changing. New products enter the market and displace old ones. The narrow, static theory that underlies these concepts has no application to dynamic markets, no matter how many policy advocates urge that some measure of welfare is the appropriate guide to policy.

Second, neither consumer welfare nor total welfare provides reliable guidance in a variety of circumstances. Taken literally, a consumer welfare goal would condemn any restraint that causes prices to increase even if the increase is justified. Conversely, if maximizing aggregate welfare is the goal of competition policy, then as long as those who gained value could, in theory, pay those who lost, the conduct or structure makes the economy better off overall.[33]

The starkest example comes from the analysis of cartels. A cartel that eliminated the need to engage in costly competition for consumers could, in theory, lower prices and at the same time earn monopoly profits.[34] Thus, under both a consumer welfare and an aggregate welfare goal, the cartel is excusable because it results in lower consumer costs compared to the prior competitive environment. Of course, the context will be hard to identify, but, if the goal is some measure of welfare, the defendant in a cartel case should be allowed to offer such a defense. In the one American case in which such a defense was implicitly suggested, the Supreme Court by a four to three vote rejected the claim and condemned the agreement.[35] Thus, a consumer welfare goal, like an aggregate welfare goal, would seem to require an ad hoc review of each event to determine its economic effect.

The foregoing is not to argue that economic analysis based on both theory and empirical work is irrelevant to the definition of goals for competition policy. Rather, the argument here is that using economic models

---

33 Blair and Sokol, *supra* note 4, at 487–90.

34 *Cf* Oliver Williamson, 'Economics as an Antitrust Defense: The Welfare Tradeoffs' (1968) 58 *American Economic Review* 18 (arguing that a merger that increases monopoly power may also achieve efficiencies; the static welfare tradeoff suggests that from a total welfare perspective the transaction is economically desirable).

35 *Arizona v Maricopa Med. Found.*, 457 U.S. 332 (1982).

of welfare as the goal of public policy toward competition misdirects the inquiry and mires it in an intractable set of assumptions. The theory of the second best forcefully illustrates the fundamental weakness of economic welfare concepts as policy goals.[36] The theory teaches that unless all elements of the economy are optimal, a movement toward optimality in a particular element will have consequences for the rest of the system, making it impossible to tell whether overall the situation is better or worse. In the real world, this results in a reiterative process of incremental decision making in which the consequences of change induce further regulatory and market responses in an unending dynamic process.[37]

The theory of the second best underscores the fundamental fact that economic activity is never in equilibrium and is always changing. Hence, a static goal of optimization of welfare ignores vital parts of the basic market process. Once dynamics are introduced, the result for an economic theory of conduct and its consequences is highly contingent on its assumptions and gives no consistent guidance.

II. FAIRNESS

Advocates of economic welfare as the goal of competition law often suggest that the only other option is some form of 'fairness'—the protection of small and other favored competitors from the rigors of the market.[38] It is open to significant question whether American antitrust policy was ever grounded on the notion of fairness even though some individuals, such as Louis Brandeis, certainly held that view.[39] Moreover, some Supreme Court opinions have been read as consistent with that goal. But the oft-quoted statement from *Trans-Missouri Freight* about 'small and worthy' businesses needing protection from large enterprises, for

---

[36] RG Lipsey and Kelvin Lancaster, 'The General Theory of Second Best' (1956) 24 *Review of Economic Studies* 11.

[37] Charles Lindblom, 'The Science of "Muddling Through"' (1959) 19 *Public Administration Review* 79.

[38] Robert H Bork, *The Antitrust Paradox: A Policy at War with Itself* (Basic Books, New York 1978) 5–8; Richard Posner, *Antitrust Law* (University of Chicago Press, Chicago 2nd edn 2001) 23–8, 35; Sandeep Vaheesan, 'The Evolving Populisms of Antitrust' (2014) 93 *Nebraska Law Review* 370.

[39] Thomas McCraw, 'Rethinking the Trust Question' in Thomas McCraw (ed.), *Regulation in Perspective* (Harvard University Press, Cambridge, MA 1981) 25–55 (a critical analysis of Brandeis's views on competition and protection of small business).

example, is taken totally out of context.[40] The decision, written by Justice Peckham, one of the stronger social Darwinists of the Court, accepts that in a market economy, inefficient small businesses will fail, but insists on the right of all businesses to have markets free from cartels and monopolies.[41] The context of the statement makes it clear that the focus of concern should be only those anticompetitive exclusionary practices that distort the market process.

Isolated statements from judicial opinions do not necessarily identify the guiding policy goal. Although the position of some justices, especially Brandeis, a former cartel manager,[42] was certainly consistent with the idea that antitrust law should protect small business from large enterprise, even Brandeis rested his position on the proposition that large enterprises were inherently inefficient and so undesirable.[43]

RPM has a similarly confusing story. For 30 years Congress authorized the states to impose RPM.[44] It is commonly thought that Congress's motivation for authorizing RPM was to protect small retailers from the 'unfair' rigors of competition that resulted from the courts' interpretation of the Sherman and Clayton Acts.[45] Congress later repealed that authority because it concluded that the gains in 'fairness' did not justify the costs to consumers.[46] But the Supreme Court then restored the right of businesses to engage in RPM, but rested its decision on notions of economic welfare.[47]

Certainly, some court decisions invoke analyses that seem to resonate more with notions of fairness than with either economic analysis or the

---

[40] *United States v Trans-Missouri Freight Ass'n*, 166 U.S. 290, 324 (1897) (it is 'unfortunate for the country . . . depriving it of the services of a large number of small but independent dealers . . .').

[41] *Ibid* at 323 ('In any great and extended change in the manner or method of doing business it seems to be an inevitable necessity that distress, and, perhaps, ruin, shall be its accompaniment, in regard to some of those who were engaged in the old methods.'); see also Peter C Carstensen, 'Lost in (Doctrinal) Translation: The Misleading Retelling of the Supreme Court's Antitrust Decisions on Restraints of Trade' (2009) 62 *SMU Law Review* 525, 528–39.

[42] McCraw, *supra* note 39, at 38.

[43] Louis Brandeis, *Other People's Money and How the Bankers Use It* (Bedford/St Martins, Boston, MA 1995 edn (1914)).

[44] Miller-Tydings Act of 1937, ch. 690, 50 Stat. 693 (1937).

[45] See Roger L Blair and David L Kaserman, *Antitrust Economics* (Oxford University Press, New York 2nd edn 2009) 384 ('The purpose of this legislation generally has been to protect small merchants who are threatened economically by mass merchandisers').

[46] Consumer Goods Pricing Act of 1975, Pub. L. 94-145, 89 Stat. 801.

[47] *Leegin Creative Leather Prods., Inc. v PSKS, Inc.*, 551 U.S. 877 (2007).

promotion of competition. One such analysis is found in the *Brown Shoe* decision, in which the Court concluded that the efficiencies Brown Shoe Co. would achieve from vertical integration were anticompetitive.[48] On its face, this seems a perverse analysis, but it is consistent with the notion of fairness as involving the protection of small, inefficient businesses. However, from an economic perspective this analysis might be read as saying that if there were real efficiencies, then firms should vertically integrate through de novo expansion upstream or downstream rather than buying market position. That would produce a true market test of the efficiency hypothesis.

Moreover, while the government was arguing that the asserted efficiency made the merger anticompetitive, the defendants were arguing that the merger had no efficiency effect![49] This assertion by the defendants would suggest that the merger was irrational and therefore a bad business decision. The Court's conclusion would imply that the merger was not economically irrational even if, in the context of the arguments before it, this left the Court agreeing with the government. Ultimately, however, it appears the defendants were in fact correct. There turned out to be no cognizable economies to vertical integration beyond some specialized shoe manufacturers. The 'efficiencies' that the government identified are consistent with the exclusionary consequences of raising rivals' costs.[50] Thus, in hindsight, the government may have mischaracterized its concern with the potential competitive effect of the merger.

Several scholars have sought to resurrect the fairness concept as a central goal for competition policy.[51] These scholars often start with the new behavioral and evolutionary economic models and supporting empirical research that show that economic actors, both consumers and producers, operate with bounded rationality, often respond to situations with altruistic motives and do not behave in practice as rational profit maximizers in any narrow sense. These scholars also offer a strong critique of the conventional economic goals as too limited and unresponsive to important values that competition law historically has served.[52] Another

---

[48] *Brown Shoe Co. v United States*, 370 U.S. 294, 326 (1962).

[49] Compare Brief for Appellant at 193–9, *Brown Shoe Co. v United States*, 370 U.S. 294 (1962) (No. 4), with Brief for Appellee at 120–2, 133–7, *Brown Shoe*, 370 U.S. 294 (1962) (No. 4).

[50] See Thomas G Krattenmaker and Steven C Salop, 'Anticompetitive Exclusion: Raising Rivals' Costs to Achieve Power over Price' (1986) 96 *Yale Law Journal* 209.

[51] See, eg, Thomas Horton, 'Fairness and Antitrust Reconsidered: An Evolutionary Perspective' (2013) 44 *McGeorge Law Review* 823; Stucke, 'Happiness', *supra* note 15; Stucke, 'Reconsidering', *supra* note 15.

[52] See Horton, *supra* note 51; Stucke, 'Happiness', *supra* note 15; Stucke, 'Reconsidering', *supra* note 15.

stream of commentary has emphasized the social and political interests that underlie competition law.[53] Indeed, FM Scherer, one of the leading economists in the field, has asserted that the primary reason for competition law is the political value to democracy of controlling concentrations of economic power.[54] Similarly, Charles Lindblom has demonstrated that there is a link between the reliance on market mechanisms for organizing an economy and the strength of democratic institutions.[55]

These perspectives are important for understanding the relationship between robustly competitive markets and the broader social and political needs of democratic societies. They also identify some of the central weaknesses of the conventional narrow economic goals used to define competition policy. But, fairness and its related political values do not provide useful templates for concrete policies. Horton, for example, suggests that cases should go to juries because juries will do the right thing.[56] Stucke suggests that competition policy, if it is to promote total well-being, cannot maximize one narrow dimension.[57] These positions do not represent coherent policies and rules that can be explained to and followed by business executives in making decisions. The lack of definition becomes a serious drawback to adhering to a fairness goal as the basis for policy.

There is a rough analogy between the concept of fairness, as elaborated by Stucke and Horton, and a concept of aggregate welfare that is expanded to include non-market values. Both approaches suggest that sometimes less competition is better than more, but neither has an explicit process for making that decision with any consistency. For these reasons, although fairness has a normative value, its use in providing a criterion for specific competition policies is of limited value. This is not to say that ideas of fairness play no role in competition policy. Indeed, in popular and political discourse the idea of a fair competitive environment is a powerful rhetorical device. But as the primary goal of competition policy, it cannot provide useful guidance unless its operational characteristics incorporate either economic or competitive process standards.

---

53 Robert Pitofsky, 'The Political Content of Antitrust' (1979) 127 *University of Pennsylvania Law Review* 1051; Harry First and Spencer Weber Waller, 'Antitrust's Democracy Deficit' (2013) 81 *Fordham Law Review* 2543.

54 FM Scherer and David Ross, *Industrial Market Structure and Economic Performance* (Houghton Mifflin, Boston, MA 3rd edn 1990) 18–19.

55 Charles E Lindblom, *Politics and Markets: The World's Political-Economic Systems* (Basic Books, New York 1977).

56 Horton, *supra* note 51, at 854–5.

57 Stucke, 'Reconsidering', *supra* note 15, at 624.

III. PROMOTING AND PROTECTING COMPETITION AS A PROCESS

The third option for a policy goal is the promotion and protection of market competition. The role of the market is both economic and political. Scherer and Ross observe that the most powerful arguments for competition law are in fact political and not economic.[58] Indeed, competitive markets over time achieve both economic and political goals—efficiency, progressivity and limits on economic power. A market system decentralizes the allocation of goods, services and income, which contributes to limiting both economic power and the role of government. In contrast, state-managed economies such as socialism or communism or those built on state-authorized cartels[59] use centralized systems to allocate economic benefits. These systems tend to be antidemocratic and authoritarian. The goal of preserving and promoting the market process explicitly incorporates some of the rationale for using fairness as a guide to policy. But it focuses on the establishment of rules that govern the process of competition much as traffic safety rules define how drivers are to conduct themselves on the highway.

Designating the promotion and protection of market competition as the central objective of competition law and policy does not negate the relevance of economic analysis and models or fairness considerations to determining when conduct or structure adversely affect competition, but the policy focus is the market process, which guides the development of rules and presumptions. The fundamental point of comparative statics in price theory is that competitive markets are generally preferable to monopolistic ones. The related welfare analyses show that society is better off overall with workably competitive markets. Both provide important justifications for policies that maintain and enhance the competitive process and a lens for critically evaluating the specific rules that are designed to implement the goal.

Finally, at this level of abstraction, considerations of fairness enter into the definition of the competitive process through rules that forbid false advertising, consumer deception, physical attacks on, or other overt predation against, competitors. Normative values that recognize that only

---

58 Scherer and Ross, *supra* note 54, at 18–19.

59 Tony Freyer, *Antitrust and Global Capitalism, 1930–2004* (Cambridge University Press, New York 2006) (tracing the history of market policy in the United States, European Union, Australia and Japan and showing the post-World War II transformation of these economies to reliance on markets and competition policy).

some kinds of competition are economically and socially useful also guide the definition of the competitive process.

Even this policy goal can lead to quite a wide range of policy outcomes depending on how inherently robust the market process is understood to be. One strand of analysis conceives of markets as strong, self-governing, self-correcting systems.[60] The market process will overcome market failure and other problems because it is an inherently powerful mechanism that drives out undesirable behavior and remedies inefficient structure. This conception of the market process, which serves as a good basis for understanding the Chicago school of competition policy, leads to the policy conclusion that competition law should be narrowly confined to cartels and mergers that create significant, unjustified concentration. Competition policy should also prevent rent-seeking by special interests that disguise their real objectives under a cloak of 'public interest' claims.[61] Broader rules are deemed to pose the risk of disrupting the natural functioning of the market.[62] This position is often associated with a general concern over the role of the government in the economy.

The contrasting perception of markets is that they are less inherently robust and potentially subject to significant and durable disruptions and failures. There is an inherent tension between the objective of any enterprise operating in a market economy that seeks to maximize its long-run profits and the goal of competition, which is to ensure that the market remains workably competitive. As result, markets can and do fail for a variety of reasons; the legal framework must police both conduct and structure to ensure as far as possible that markets are, remain or become workably competitive.

The global embrace of competition law, with its prohibition of cartels, sanctions against monopolistic conduct, review of the competitive implications of a variety of contracts and restrictions on mergers and acquisitions that are anticompetitive, is, on its face, inconsistent with the naïve view

---

[60] Werden, for example, a senior economic counsel at the Antitrust Division of the Department of Justice, argues that competition is the goal of American competition law, but takes a very conservative view of the scope of the resulting standards that should apply. Gregory J Werden, 'Antitrust's Rule of Reason: Only Competition Matters' (2014) 79 *Antitrust Law Journal* 557.

[61] For an exposition of the public choice perspective, see Fred S McChesney and William F Shughart II (eds), *The Causes and Consequences of Antitrust: The Public-Choice Perspective* (University of Chicago Press, Chicago 1995).

[62] Judge Easterbrook is a leading advocate of this perspective. See Frank H Easterbrook, 'Limits of Antitrust' (1984) 63 *Texas Law Review* 1.

that markets are self-correcting.[63] Indeed, almost all those who believe in the robustness of the market accept the need for some regulation. The real debate is over the scope of market regulation necessary to protect and promote workably competitive markets.

The advantage of using the goal of enhancing and protecting the competitive process as the basis for policy is that it focuses explicitly on the adverse effects on both producers and consumers that can and do result from market failure. It fits more comfortably with the position advanced by Kirkwood that consumer interests should dominate competition policy but sellers need protection from undue exploitation.[64]

Competition as a process also recognizes the importance of protecting the dynamics of markets even if conventional price theory does not offer much guidance to explain or model these contexts. Moreover, when more complex economic models, such as those involving game theory, are employed they produce ambiguous results. The theory of the second best demonstrates that unless all markets are optimally competitive, the longer term implications for changing conduct in any market are unknowable because of the impact on other markets.[65] Proponents of economic welfare goals tend to ignore this theory, but it is consistent with an ongoing policy of responding to changing competitive conditions by continually seeking to maximize the competitive character of each market.

Indeed, if one approaches market regulation from the Lindblom perspective of incremental decision making,[66] it is not surprising that there will be unintended consequences. They result from the continual adjustments that go on in markets as the legal regime, technology, demand and all other underlying conditions change. The dynamic nature of markets is one of their strongest social and economic advantages. They are not constrained by state planning or other external controls that limit their ability to respond to changing circumstances. But the ways that market actors respond can facilitate workable competition or frustrate it. Hence, the ongoing need for oversight and policies that restrict anticompetitive conduct and structure.

A competition policy that promotes, protects and enhances socially and economically desirable competition must be forward-looking and work to retain options for both producers and consumers. Operationally, this

---

[63] It should be acknowledged that the public-choice concerns with the potential for the manipulation of any government mandate for the benefit of insiders reflect real and serious risks.

[64] Kirkwood, *supra* note 28; see also Kirkwood and Lande, *supra* note 10.

[65] See Lipsey and Lancaster, *supra* note 36.

[66] Lindblom, *supra* note 37.

means that more market participants are better than fewer. Structure is a continuing concern, therefore, because of its long-run impact on all dimensions of competition. The rationale for condemning cartels, contrary to the ambiguous conclusion drawn from welfare economics, is that a naked restraint, conduct that restricts competition and nothing more, is inherently bad when carried out by private parties.[67] Such conduct directly conflicts with the fundamental concept of a market—a process in which participants have the right to compete on terms of their choosing.

In the paradigm of Calabresi and Melamed, the freedom to compete is itself an inalienable right, but an individual can accept limits in connection with a lawful transaction.[68] Indeed, restrictions on the freedom to compete are unavoidable in a variety of transactions. Some transactions carry inherent restraints, such as forward-looking agreements setting price and quantity. Other restraints are functional accompaniments necessary to define the transactional relationship or address some avoidable risk that would otherwise undermine the transaction's business utility. For all restraints, including mergers, the tests should be whether the transaction or venture has a legitimate business justification and whether the restraint is no more restrictive than necessary to accomplish its legitimate goal.[69]

Competition policy can flesh out these basic criteria with presumptions that enable many restrictive terms to be presumed to be lawful. The extensive regulations of the European Union set forth categories of exempt transactions,[70] while the American model uses judicial interpretation

---

67 See *Vancouver Malt & Sake Brewing Co. v Vancouver Breweries* [1934] UKPC 9 (Privy Council reversing enforcement of a naked restraint on competition on the basis that such contracts are inherently unreasonable); see also Restatement (Second) of Contracts § 187 (1981) (declaring contracts imposing naked restraints on competition to be invalid).

68 Guido Calabresi and Douglas Melamed, 'Property Rights, Liability Rules, and Inalienability: One View of the Cathedral' (1972) 85 *Harvard Law Review* 1089. One cannot sell oneself into slavery, but one can agree to an employment contract that imposes limits on one's freedom to compete.

69 These standards have ancient roots. See *Mitchel v Reynolds* [1711] 24 Eng. Rep. 347 (Kings Bench) (upholding a covenant not to compete that was ancillary to a lease of property); *United States v Addyston Pipe & Steel Co.*, 85 F. 271 (6th Cir. 1898) (adopting ancillary restraint analysis for the meaning of the rule of reason for American antitrust law); *cf* C Scott Hemphill, 'Less Restrictive Alternatives in Antitrust Law' (2016) 116 *Columbia Law Review* 927.

70 See generally European Commission (2013), 'Rules Applicable to Antitrust Enforcement: General Block Exemption Regulations and Guidelines', available at http://ec.europa.eu/competition/antitrust/legislation/handbook_vol_2_en.pdf.

linked to strict review of the merits of claims at an early stage.[71] In the case of cartels and other naked restraints on competition, the burden of justification falls squarely on the parties to such an agreement, and the permissible justifications are few. The only successful justifications in the United States require a demonstration of public authority to engage in the relevant conduct.[72]

Clearly at this stage of policy implementation there are significant choices for the extent of intervention in business transactions. If policy makers believe that the competitive process is robust and resilient, negative presumptions can be narrowed or abandoned. Indeed, large areas of questionable conduct might even be presumed legal or exempted from any review. If there is greater concern for the risks to competition, then a negative presumption can be strengthened or created. For many years, American merger law effectively presumed mergers to be unlawful if they resulted in a significant increase in market concentration.[73] That presumption has been weakened despite significant evidence of the harmful results of increased concentration.[74] The European merger system requires positive approval before major mergers can proceed.[75] Although denials and approvals are subject to judicial review, the European Commission's veto power makes it possible to implement stricter controls over mergers subject to the Commission's review. But here, too, actual enforcement policy has varied over time.

In the case of an existing monopoly, the concerns are first with

---

[71] Compare *Leegin Creative Leather Prods., Inc. v PSKS, Inc.*, 551 U.S. 877 (2007) (RPM presumed lawful unless challenger shows its use is unreasonable), with *FTC v Ind. Fed. of Dentists*, 476 U.S. 447 (1986) (agreement not to provide information presumptively illegal) and *Polygram Holdings v FTC*, 416 F.3d 29 (D.C. Cir. 2005) (agreement between joint venturers to regulate competition in products that competed with their joint product presumed illegal).

[72] Peter C Carstensen and Bette Roth, 'The Per Se Legality of Some Naked Restraints: A [Re]Conceptualization of the Antitrust Analysis of Cartelistic Organizations' (2000) 45 *Antitrust Bulletin* 349 (some naked restraints are lawful if imposed within the scope of explicit or implied authorization and conducted consistent with the process required by such authorization).

[73] Peter C Carstensen, 'The *Philadelphia Bank* Presumption: Merger Analysis in a Dynamic Economy' (2015) 80 *Antitrust Law Journal* 219 (data support the conclusion that most major mergers are of doubtful economic merit and so a strong presumption against mergers affecting competition is warranted).

[74] See *ibid* at 236–41; John Kwoka, *Mergers, Merger Control, and Remedies: A Retrospective Analysis of US Policy* (MIT Press, Cambridge, MA 2015).

[75] Council Regulation 139/2004 on the Control of Concentrations between Undertakings, 2004 O.J. (L 24) 1, available at http://ec.europa.eu/competition/mergers/legislation/regulations.html.

legitimacy and second with remediability. Mere possession of monopoly is not in itself inconsistent with the competitive process. Schumpeter's concept of creative destruction makes monopoly a part of the dynamic competitive process.[76] But when a monopoly arises from or entrenches itself through anticompetitive means that undermine the competitive process, it harms the very market dynamic that Schumpeter identified. Exploitation or exclusion by conduct that lacks a legitimate non-monopoly explanation creates an additional distortion to the competitive process.[77] The proper goal of intervention based on competitive process goals is to facilitate restoration or creation of competition. Hence, the focus is predominantly on exclusionary practices, but remedying unreasonable exploitation is a feature of some competition policies. In addition, where there is persistent but remediable market failure that allows monopoly to retain dominance, concern for the competitive process would call for structural remedies despite the lack of unlawful exclusionary conduct.[78]

In contrast to the hands-off version of policy to protect the competitive process, this book proceeds from the premise that competition is vulnerable to disruption and that market failure is a serious risk. A strong policy against any conduct that is likely to have a significant impact on competition is appropriate and necessary. The risk of irreversible harm to the competitive process resulting from allowing conduct or structure that possesses significant risks to the preservation of competition provides the rationale for rules that require justification for such effects and imposes the burden of justification on those seeking to engage in such conduct or create or retain such structures. Such rules ensure the continued viability of the competitive process even if in specific instances they may impose burdens that seem unnecessary, even 'unfair'.

---

[76] Joseph Schumpeter, *Capitalism, Socialism and Democracy* (Harper and Row, New York 1942).

[77] See Pinar Akman, *The Concept of Abuse in EU Competition Law: Law and Economic Approaches* (Hart Publishing, Oxford 2012) (arguing that both exclusion and exploitation are comparable abuses).

[78] The claim rests on the initial Supreme Court decisions in *Standard Oil Co. v United States*, 211 U.S. 1 (1911), and *United States v American Tobacco Co.*, 211 U.S. 106 (1911). See Peter C Carstensen, 'Remedies for Monopolization from *Standard Oil* to *Microsoft* and *Intel*: The Changing Nature of Monopoly Law from Elimination of Market Power to Regulation of Its Use' (2012) 85 *Southern California Law Review* 815.

IV. BALANCE

The three goals for competition law and policy will yield similar policies for many situations. This is particularly likely when the economic goals are defined in longer term, dynamic ways. But as discussed above, the economic criteria tend to be agnostic with respect to how an economically desirable result is achieved. Using those criteria, a goal of maximizing short-run aggregate welfare would not necessarily deem certain kinds of anticompetitive conduct, especially cartels, absolutely objectionable. But competition policy in practice has consistently concluded that cartels are inherently objectionable unless directly regulated by public authorities. As discussed earlier, the narrowly oriented consumer welfare version of economic efficiency ignores important elements of cost and competition. The results-oriented focus of economic goals is inconsistent with a process-oriented goal for competition policy.

The fairness goal is also, overall, not a useful guide to policy. Fairness criteria may produce results similar to those produced by the economic and competition-promoting criteria for many issues of competition policy. Indeed, some doctrines such as the prohibition on tying may well draw considerable strength from notions of fairness. But more generally, fairness criteria are ambiguous and do not, like the economic goals, provide a basis on which to condemn all cartels or monopoly in general. Fairness can excuse conduct that is done 'fairly' and in ways perceived as serving some legitimate public goal. Thus fairness allows its proponents to excuse some cartels as desirable, which implies that all cartels should be entitled to offer such an excuse. Implicitly the advocates of fairness seem to be arguing for a policy goal of facilitating a socially and economically useful competitive process.

Maintaining competition as a process provides a preferable policy goal because it focuses on the operation of markets, which are preferred for both economic and political reasons. Nevertheless, carrying out the goal implies choosing among a range of policies because of the varied perspectives on the robustness of the market process itself when faced with market failure. But the policy options to implement this goal themselves reflect a core empirical and theoretical understanding of markets and the risks they confront. This study takes as its starting point that market failure is a pervasive risk and that regulation of markets is essential to achieving the overall, long-term benefits, economic and political, of a workably competitive market system. The description in Chapter 1 of the many and persistent buyer side market failures around the world provide the empirical predicate for this position.

In explaining why antitrust employed rules that condemned certain kinds of conduct without inquiry into the merits of specific violations, Justice Stevens analogized the rules of competition to the rules of the road that, for example, limit speed regardless of the specific risks created by the speeder. He noted that 'every speeder . . . poses some threat to the community. . . So it is with boycotts and price fixing. Every such horizontal agreement among competitors poses some threat to the free market.'[79] Rules of the road exist to ensure the safe use of the roads, which in turn is likely to serve other social interests. So, too, the rules of competition serve the goal of facilitating workably competitive markets. Such markets will over time and in general achieve greater economic welfare than other systems of market organization and do so in ways that most observers and participants are likely to regard as fairer than any other way of allocating economic gains.

---

[79] *FTC v Superior Court Trial Lawyers Ass'n*, 493 U.S. 411, 433 (1990).

3. Buyer power: its definition and measurement

This chapter examines the definition and measurement of buyer power. Section I examines the conventional theories of monopsony and buyer power and challenges the notion that there is a distinction between 'monopsony' and 'buyer power' that is relevant to competition policy. Rather, there is a continuum of buyer power from modest to substantial whose interaction with supply will vary depending on a number of factors. Those factors affect the kind and quality of competitive risks that producers may face, but it is a mistake to premise competition policy on a dichotomous theory of buyer power.

It is commonly said that monopsony is the 'mirror image' of monopoly.[1] This may be true from the perspective of some model building exercises, but it is not an accurate depiction of the reality of the economic world. Litigation, studies and observed business behavior consistently show that potentially malevolent buyer power exists at lower market shares than is traditionally associated with seller power. There are also important differences between buying-side and selling-side power with respect to the kinds of responses that competitors are likely to make. Finally, the disparity between buyers (relatively few) and producers (relatively many) has more impact on the immediate risks of abusive use of buyer power than do comparable disparities on the risks of abuse of seller power. Sections II and III demonstrate that buyer power must be examined using distinct and relevant criteria.

Section II examines the two related contexts in which significant buyer power can exist: the production of components sold for final assembly into products and the distribution of branded consumer goods. Significant buyer power exists whenever producers lack readily accessible alternative outlets for their productive capacity and lack substantial seller power.

---

[1] See, eg, Note by the United States, OECD, 'Policy Roundtable: Monopsony and Buyer Power', DAF/COMP(2008)38, available at https://www.ftc.gov/sites/default/files/attachments/us-submissions-oecd-and-other-international-competition-fora/monopsony.pdf ('In important respects, monopsony is the mirror image of monopoly').

Despite the similarity of the underlying competitive effects, the configuration of the competitive issues and definition of relevant market contexts are different. Moreover, the level of concentration that gives rise to buyer power concerns is lower in the case of branded consumer goods than in the case of general input markets. However, in both contexts, buyer power issues can arise at lower market shares and with a larger number of competitors than conventional seller side theory would regard as creating significant competitive concerns.

Section III identifies three factors that increase the relative power of buyers but which are not currently emphasized in the literature. First, powerful buyers are the primary decision makers in many transactions. This explains, in part, why buyer power may exist at relatively low levels of overall market concentration. Second, arbitrage among sellers is difficult and unlikely; therefore, buyers face less constraint on the discriminatory exploitation of their power. Third, significant institutional and incentive barriers inhibit and deter the market processes that might otherwise overcome the exploitation of buyer power. For these reasons, abuse of buyer power is as serious a competitive concern as abuse of seller or monopoly power.

Finally, section IV reviews the criteria that identify markets particularly susceptible to significant buyer power and its abuse and proposes ways to ameliorate the risks of such abuse. In combination, these criteria should guide policy makers and law enforcers in identifying where the risks of anticompetitive harms are most likely.

I. THE MEANING OF BUYER POWER AND THE IRRELEVANCE OF THE MONOPSONY–BUYER POWER DICHOTOMY

Buyer power poses the greatest risk of harm to competition in markets in which a buyer uses intermediate goods or services as inputs into a product or service that it will resell. Any buyer or group of buyers can have and exercise buyer power if the purchases are substantial with respect to a particular seller.[2] Buyer power exists whenever a buyer has the ability to compel a seller to accept a lower price for its product than it would

[2] Final consumers, as a group, have not been deemed to raise competitive policy concerns. Courts often regard consumer boycotts, which are an exercise of buyer power, as falling outside the scope of antitrust law. See, eg, *Missouri v Nat'l Org. for Women Inc.*, 620 F.2d 1301 (8th Cir. 1980). If such a boycott involves threats of violence, then other law may apply. See *NAACP v Claiborne Hardware*

have received under ideal competitive conditions or compel a producer to accept some other burdensome limitation on its competitive discretion. Use of buyer power in ways that unduly exploit or unreasonably constrain the competitive conduct of a producer is harmful to the competitive process and should be a source of concern to competition policy.

A. Conventional Models of Monopsony

Monopsony is the ability to impose a price on a producer that is below its marginal cost. The standard model assumes a uniform price for the input; when a buyer reduces the price it pays, the producer responds by reducing the quantity provided. Assuming the buyer is a price taker (a competitor without any market power) in the market in which it resells the product that incorporates the monopsonized input, it generates a higher profit on those sales only because of its lower input cost.[3] Assuming a uniform input price, the model also shows that increasing the price to increase the supply of the input results in a sizeable increase in the total cost of inputs to the monopsony buyer relative to its gains. Because the price increase applies to all of the input, including the portion that would have been supplied at a lower price, the buyer must expect a substantial gain from the marginal units to justify paying the higher price for all units. The profit on those added units must cover the increase in its total input cost. Conventional economic theory models this interaction as shown in Figure 3.1. The marginal product of the incremental unit shown in line *MRP* reflects the assumption that the price paid for all units will increase in order to obtain the marginal unit. Hence, the benefit of the marginal unit must equal that entire expense.

Another way to conceive of the impact of a change in input cost under these assumptions is to use a numeric example, as shown in Table 3.1.[4] The buyer has sufficient monopsony power (perhaps as the dominant buyer in a region) to force the price of input *A* down by five percent from the competitive price, but this results in a reduction of supply by five percent. Either some producers exit the market or all reduce production by the same amount in response to the lower price. Further, the example assumes

Co., 458 U.S. 886 (1982) (consumer boycott lawful to enforce constitutional rights unless implemented by threats of violence to compel individuals to refuse to buy).

3 In the case of a final consumer with buyer power, the lower price enhances the consumer surplus of the buyer and increases its capacity to buy other goods and services with the cost savings.

4 *Cf* Cory Capps, 'Buyer Power in Health Plan Mergers' (2010) 6 *Journal of Competition Law and Economy* 375, 377 tbl.1.

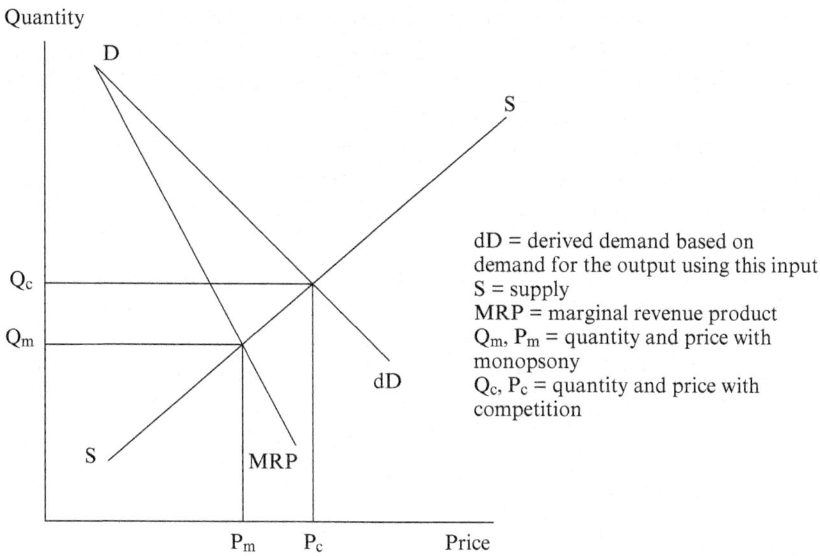

Figure 3.1 *Basic monopsony*

Table 3.1 *Monopsony and Profits*

	Input A Price Per Unit	Total Cost A+Other Element	Price of Final Product	Total Product Produced	Profit Margin Total
Competitive	$100	$200	$210	500,000	$5,000,000
Monopsony	$95	$195	$210	475,000	$7,125,000

that the downstream market is fully competitive, and the buyer's reduced production has no upward impact on the final price. Even so, the buyer's profits increase by more than 40 percent over what it would have earned if it had to buy input *A* in a workably competitive market. Therefore, a monopsonist can increase its profit margin even if it suffers some loss in total income.[5]

The conditions for exploitation based on the monopsony model are

[5] Had the buyer used an all-or-nothing contract (see *infra* text accompanying notes 6–7), its gain would have been even more substantial because it would not have suffered any reduction in the quantity of input *A* that it received.

stringent. The producers must have increasing marginal costs (so that reducing output will reduce total producer cost by more than the revenue lost from reducing output), and the price paid per unit must be the same for all units. Hence, either every producer reduces its output to achieve lower costs or producers with the highest costs below the competitive price exit the market. Thus cabined, monopsony can be marginalized as a rare phenomenon limited largely to employment and agricultural commodities. These are not, of course, trivial segments of the economic order, but the implication is that most other markets are not likely to exhibit monopsony characteristics.

The assumptions of uniform price, increasing marginal cost and the producer's ability to decide how much to supply are central to the output results of the model. If, however, the buyer employs an all-or-nothing approach to its buying, it can extract the same quantity of output that would have been produced at a competitive price without paying that price.[6] An efficient producer, that is, one whose average per unit cost is less than the prevailing market price, with an upward sloping cost curve, has a marginal cost that exceeds average cost. An all-or-nothing contract requires a set quantity at a set price or there is no sale. The producer that accepts this contract can be compelled to produce a volume at which marginal cost exceeds the price received, but the price per unit approximates the average cost of producing that unit, as shown in Figure 3.2. The quantity equals what a competitive market price ($Q_c = Q_{anc}$) would yield, but the producer receives a price (P_{anc}) below the competitive price (P_c). Thus, the buyer appropriates the inframarginal gains of the producer and at the same time acquires the competitive level of production.[7]

From the perspective of the ultimate consumer, this is merely a wealth transfer between a producer and a buyer that has no effect on the ultimate price or quantity of the final good. But from the perspective of the producer, the wealth transfer is significant. It means that efficiency, keeping cost below the market price, is no longer rewarded. This in turn will discourage investment and innovation in the producer's market. It also

---

[6] See Roger D Blair and Jeffrey L Harrison, *Monopsony in Law and Economics* (Cambridge University Press, Cambridge 2010) 83–5; C Robert Taylor, *Monopsony and the All-or-Nothing Supply Curve: Putting the Squeeze on Suppliers* (Auburn University Working Paper ES.6, 2003).

[7] An inframarginal producer earns Ricardian economic rents—the difference between the market price for the commodity and the lower costs an efficient producer incurs. Because its costs are below the competitive market price, it receives a supracompetitive return. The buyer, by using an all-or-nothing contract, can appropriate this 'surplus' without losing volume. See Roger G Noll, '"Buyer Power" and Economic Policy' (2005) 72 *Antitrust Law Journal* 589, 593, 596–600.

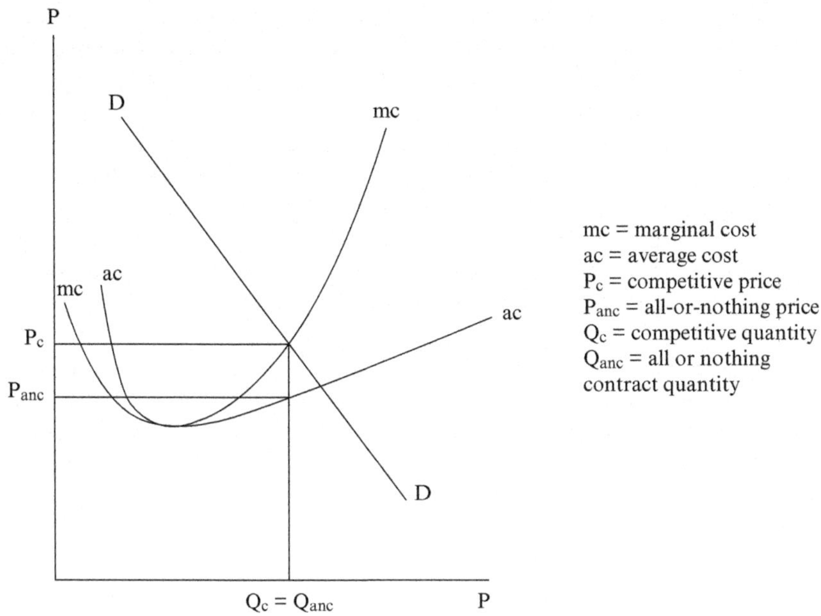

Figure 3.2 All-or-nothing contracts

deprives the efficient producer of a reward for efficiency, which ought to be the hallmark of workable competition. Ultimately, because the producer has less incentive to be efficient and innovative, a buyer may find it necessary to instruct the producer in ways to enhance efficiency for the benefit of the buyer.[8]

B. Conventional Understanding of Buyer Power

In contrast, buyer power is said to exist when producers do not face significantly increasing marginal costs.[9] If the producer operates in a region

---

[8] This can in part explain why powerful buyers impose very detailed requirements on their suppliers. See, eg, Christopher Leonard, *The Meat Racket* (Simon and Schuster, New York 2014) 20–34, 115–31 (describing Tyson's regulation of its chicken farmers); Wenonah Hauter, *Foodopoly* (New Press, New York 2013) 62–73 (describing Walmart's imposition of significant controls on its suppliers).

[9] See Roger Clarke, Stephen Davies, Paul Dobson and Michael Waterson, *Buyer Power and Competition in European Rood Retailing* (Edward Elgar Publishing, Cheltenham, UK and Northampton, MA, USA 2002) 9–44; Zhiqi

of declining marginal cost, reducing output will result in increased per unit costs as economies of scale are lost. The rational producer will not respond to a lower price by cutting production. If marginal costs are relatively constant, then the quantity produced is largely independent of price. As long as the price is above marginal cost, the producer will produce as much as necessary to meet demand. Theoretically, it will exit the market if the price is below its cost of production. Proceeding from these insights, this model suggests that buyers and sellers bargain over price and other conditions but that the quantity purchased is independent of these considerations. The buyer would take as much of the input as it can use for its downstream market needs.

The prevailing theory is that this use of buyer power, because it does not affect price, will not have any impact on output and so cannot constitute an inherently anticompetitive act. But there are a number of ways in which a buyer can in fact distort competition by the terms and conditions it imposes on its supplier.[10] Although this difference may have some relevance to abstract economic models, it does not meaningfully distinguish among the cases from a competition policy perspective.

This conclusion draws additional strength from the fact that in business, in contrast to economic theory, the price-cost relationships that are most relevant often have nothing to do with the marginal or incremental costs of production. For example, if a firm has taken on a substantial quantity of debt, it must pay the principal and interest on that debt or face bankruptcy. By diminishing the quantity it takes, a buyer can push a

Chen, 'Buyer Power: Economic Theory and Antitrust Policy' (2007) 22 *Research in Law and Economics* 17, 19–20.

[10] A buyer might use its bargaining power to seek commitments to refuse to deal with competitors of the buyer or for some other exclusionary action. For example, Toys 'R' Us induced its major suppliers to refuse to sell key products to its competitors. *Toys 'R' Us, Inc. v FTC*, 221 F. 3d 928 (7th Cir. 2000). Other examples include imposing costs or risks on suppliers. See, eg, *Been v O.K. Indus., Inc.*, 398 Fed. App'x 382, 2010 WL 3995981 (10th Cir. 2010, unpublished) (varied quantities of chickens delivered to growers shifting risk to them from the processor or 'integrator'). For a discussion of the United Kingdom's regulation of major grocery chains, see Groceries Supply Chain Practices Market Investigation Order 2009, available at https://www.gov.uk/government/publications/groceries-supply-chain-practices-market-investigation-order. For a discussion of Japanese control over abusive contract terms, see Masako Wakui and Thomas K Cheng, 'Regulating Abuse of Superior Bargaining Position under the Japanese Competition Law: An Anomaly or a Necessity' (2015) 3 *Journal of Antitrust Enforcement* 302, 308–14 (describing cases and illustrating the risk transfer process).

supplier closer to default.[11] The producer can then be compelled to provide discounts or absorb additional expenses in order to retain the volume it needs even if its profit level is reduced.

Alternatively, such a supplier might well agree to engage in various exclusionary practices in return for a slightly better return. A producer with relatively constant long-run costs still can face significant transition costs if it has to reduce its production by a non-trivial amount. If it operates multiple plants, it will likely have to close or mothball one or more operations, which will require adjusting delivery and input purchase commitments. If the firm has a declining cost curve or if its costs are close enough to the point at which it would face diseconomies from a reduction of output, any buyer that can push the producer back up its cost curve possesses substantial leverage.[12] It follows that the consequences for competition are the same as those that result from the coercion of a firm with increasing costs. Thus, if a buyer with the capacity to inflict significant economic harm demands a lower price, wants the producer to provide additional services at no charge, proposes to shift risks to the producer without compensation or insists that the producer impose higher prices on, or refuse to deal with, less significant customers, such a producer is very likely to be compelled to accept such conditions.

An all-or-nothing contract is not a useful tool against producers with either constant or declining costs, but such producers face both short-run adjustment costs and potentially significant long-run diseconomies if they lose a significant buyer and cannot readily replace it. Such a producer may instead accept prices that leave some costs uncompensated. To recover these costs, it may exploit further any buyer power it has upstream with respect to its suppliers—including its employees.[13] This

---

[11] See *Been*, 398 Fed. App'x 382 (poultry integrator that paid farmers by the flock to raise its chickens reduced the number of flocks provided to its farmers causing them economic distress).

[12] Many observers speculate that firms are likely to have L-shaped cost curves. If true, although expanding production past the point of minimum efficient scale will not generally yield extensive costs savings, any loss of volume that reduces total output below the minimum efficient scale would confront a producer with serious cost consequences. See Edith Penrose, *The Theory of the Growth of the Firm* (Oxford University Press, Oxford 1959) 55–6, 128–9, 189–90, 198.

[13] Intermediate-level producers often assert that downstream buyers are forcing them to cut wages or reduce prices paid for inputs. See, eg, United Food & Commercial Workers (2010), 'Ending Walmart's Rural Stranglehold', available at https://grist.files.wordpress.com/2010/09/ag_consolidation_white_paper2.pdf?CFID=10082208&CFTOKEN=55376804 (describing the impact of Walmart on upstream producers and their employees); Northwest Arkansas Workers' Justice

can have long-run adverse effects by reducing supply and causing some upstream suppliers to exit the market, but it remains a potential short-run response. Indeed, for those highly dependent on income from a single crop or from employment, depressed income can have the perverse result of inducing greater production; the producer requires a basic level of income and must therefore produce (or work) more in order to achieve the same level of income.[14]

An alternative for some producers is the so-called waterbed effect, that is, increasing prices to other buyers to compensate for the lost revenue.[15] If the previous prices were optimal, then this tactic will create long-run adverse effects on both the disfavored customers and the producer. The disfavored customers face higher costs that adversely affect their capacity to compete in the market, leading to reduced sales volume. The producer itself will then face reduced sales to these customers and may see some of them exit the market over time. A further and competitively more serious problem exists when the disfavored customers compete directly with the favored customer in the downstream market. In that case, the waterbed effect creates an explicit 'raising of rivals' costs' that allows the favored buyer either to reap a greater margin or to undercut the prices of its downstream competitors.[16] Either way, the long-term consequence is harmful to competition.

The elasticities of supply and demand are central to the exploitation of buyer power regardless of the producer's cost curve. In the monopsony model developed by Blair and Harrison, the relevant considerations for a

---

Center (2016), 'Wages and Working Conditions in Arkansas Poultry Plants', available at http://www.uusc.org/updates/report-wage-violations-poor-working-conditions-at-arkansas-poultry-plants (describing poor working conditions and low wages for employees).

[14] See, eg, Brian O'Keefe, 'Bitter Sweets' *Fortune* (March 2016) at 55 (describing how reduced payments to cocoa producers has resulted in widespread use of child labor and other harms).

[15] Paul W Dobson and Roman Inderst, 'The Waterbed Effect: Where Buying and Selling Power Come Together' 2008 *Wisconsin Law Review* 331; see also David E Mills, 'Buyer Power and Industry Structure' (2010) 36 *Review of Industrial Organization* 213, 219–21 (describing various ways in which buyer power can result in waterbed effects).

[16] Thomas G Krattenmaker and Steven C Salop, 'Anticompetitive Exclusion: Raising Rivals' Costs to Achieve Power over Price' (1986) 96 *Yale Law Journal* 209, 214; see also Benjamin Klein, 'The "Hub-and-Spoke" Conspiracy that Created the Standard Oil Monopoly' (2012) 85 *Southern California Law Review* 459 (showing how the Standard Oil monopoly used its power as a buyer of railroad services to demand rebates from the railroads even on its competitors' shipments thus doubly raising its rivals' costs).

buyer seeking to exploit producers are whether there are other buyers who can absorb the potential supply at the prevailing market price (elasticity of demand) or whether producers can vary output without any significant variance in per unit costs (elasticity of supply) or both.[17] Output variation includes the capacity to switch production facilities to other product lines without significant reconstruction of the facility and with the capacity to market the resulting goods easily. The greater either elasticity, the more limited the buyer's power. But if other buyers cannot take up the potential surplus output, and if the producers have less ability to vary output, then the buyer has more power.

The Blair-Harrison model employs the standard assumptions about monopsony, that is, that price is uniform and producers' marginal costs increase with expanded production. But the model's central insight is more general. The more options a producer has to sell to other buyers or to control its own volume—regardless of whether it has increasing, decreasing or constant costs—the less power any particular buyer will have. This more general insight draws strong support from a study of auctions, which demonstrated that price will approximate the optimal level only when there are a significant number of non-collusive bidders.[18]

The distinction between buyer power and monopsony also assumes that buyer power involves a negotiated price and quantity. A producer presumably can bargain effectively with a buyer to set a price and other conditions. Indeed, implicit bargaining occurs even when a buyer deals with many small producers if those producers have the ability either to switch at low cost to other buyers or can change their product line when faced with low prices. But a small producer, even if it has declining costs, may have little bargaining power if the buyer, regardless of its downstream market position, is the only or one of very few customers of that producer.

A producer that supplies a substantial share of a buyer's demand for an input is likely to have a strong bargaining position.[19] However, if

---

[17] Blair and Harrison, *supra* note 6, at 64.

[18] Robert Marshall and Michael Meurer, 'Bidder Collusion and Antitrust Law: Refining the Analysis of Price Fixing to Account for the Special Features of Auction Markets' (2004) 72 *Antitrust Law Journal* 83.

[19] Farmers raising chickens under contract are invariably small relative to the total demand of their processors, and the processors often exploit them. See Leonard, *supra* note 8, at 17–113. In contrast, some large hog-raising operations in the United States also rely on contracts with processors. But large scale, capital-intensive operations make economic sense to investors and lenders only if the producer has sufficient bargaining capacity to ensure its economic viability. Some scholars have argued that all contractual relationships are likely

both the producer and the buyer are dominant in their respective selling markets, the resulting bargaining will be a version of bilateral monopoly negotiation. Economic models suggest that the price and output results of bargaining between an upstream monopolist selling to a downstream monopsonist is likely to be better than that which would result if one side was workably competitive and the other side was monopolistic. However, this is static analysis. For the reasons explained below, buyers are more likely to overcome the effects of monopoly than producers are to successfully resist monopsony. Dynamic analysis suggests that bilateral monopoly can and often does result in the expansion of market power to other markets.[20]

When either the monopolistic producer has upstream buyer power or the monopsony buyer has downstream monopoly power, the resulting bargain involves finding the quantity of production that maximizes the monopoly-monopsony profits and allocates those profits between the two parties.[21] This is hardly a pro-competitive outcome. Moreover, it creates incentives to engage in mutual entrenchment in the market, thereby strengthening the undesirable structure.[22]

The continuum of buyer power is a function of the following factors:

(1) the buyer's market options for its output;
(2) the producer's ease of switching outlets or product lines;

---

to produce positive results for farming enterprises. See Michael K Adjemian et al, *Thinning Markets in U.S. Agriculture: What Are the Implications for Producers and Processors?* (Economic Information Bulletin No. 148, US Department of Agriculture Economic Research Service, 2016), available at http://www.ers.usda.gov/media/2030725/eib148.pdf. In fact, the benefits of contractual relationships will vary greatly.

[20] See Kalman J Cohen and Richard M Cyert, *Theory of the Firm: Resource Allocation in a Market Economy* (Prentice Hall, New Jersey, NJ 1965) 274–77; Noll, *supra* note 7, at 602–10.

[21] For example, a study of New England milk prices found that, as a result of concentration in the processing and retailing sectors of the market, prices to farmers declined and prices to consumers increased. How the two concentrated intermediate levels allocated the resulting profits is less clear. See *Monopsony Issues in Agriculture: Buying Power of Processors in Our Nation's Agricultural Markets, Hearing before the S. Comm. on the Judiciary*, 108th Cong. (2003) (submission of Ronald W Cotterill, Adam N Rabinowitz and Li Tian, 'Milk Market Channel Structure: Its Impact on Farmers and Consumers, and the Inadequacies of Antitrust Enforcement as a Foundation for Dairy Policies: Evidence from the Northeast Dairy Industry'), available at http://www.fmpc.uconn.edu/research/milk/Testimony103003.pdf.

[22] See sources cited *supra* note 16.

(3) the quantities that the buyer takes from any one producer as a percentage of its purchases of that input; and
(4) the percentage of its own output that a producer sells to a single buyer.

Thus, the scale and options available to producers can attenuate the power of buyers; but such attenuation is a function of a variety of factors that do not correlate strongly with the cost functions of the producer, which is the conceptual basis for the buyer power–monopsony distinction.

C. Abuse of Monopsony or Buyer Power Harms the Competitive Process

The distinction between monopsony and buyer power from a competitive process perspective rests on an implicit value judgement. Monopsony is—almost without exception—competitively undesirable, while some uses of buyer power are regarded as competitively useful. It is true that 'power buyers' can constrain the market power that results from concentration in an upstream input market.[23] For the purposes of this book, however, the term connotes something more ambiguous. The evolution in buyer power analysis has shown that the positive effects of the use of such power require specific kinds of market reactions that are theoretically plausible, but not necessarily strategically likely.[24]

In addition, a reduction of input prices through buyer power will advance the parochial interests of consumers only if the buyer reduces the prices of its output. This can be a myopic view of underlying economic reality. To the extent that producers are undercompensated, their ability to participate in the economy is impaired.[25] Moreover, such wealth transfers mean that those who bear the burdens are not those who gain the benefits. Thus, abuse of buyer power can create harmful externalities.

---

[23] See, eg, US Department of Justice and FTC (2010), 'Horizontal Merger Guidelines' § 8 (mergers among firms facing powerful buyers may not raise competitive concerns).

[24] Either all buyers must get similar prices (hence the powerful buyer directly lowers prices for all buyers) or there must be some feedback effect in the market so that less powerful buyers are able to get the benefit of the lower price. These results are the exact opposite of the waterbed effect discussed earlier.

[25] Amy J Cohen, 'Supermarkets in India: Struggles over the Organization of Agricultural Markets and Food Supply Chains' (2013) 68 *University of Miami Law Review* 19 (arguing that, because the majority of consumers in India are still farmers or small shopkeepers, vertical integration by supermarkets that results in buyer power threatens to impose serious costs on these individuals in their roles as both producers and consumers).

Overall, society suffers a net loss when one sector receives less than its reasonable share of compensation for the value it has created. Thus both buyer power and monopsony can harm the competitive process and have long-run effects on the economy as whole.[26]

One example of the long-run effect of such exploitation is the aging of America's farmers. The current average age of farmers in the United States is over 50,[27] and exploitation in American agriculture makes farming increasingly unattractive to their children. In developing countries such as Bangladesh, low wages and unacceptable working conditions are the result of buyer power that drives down wages and forces manufacturers to avoid health and safety investments that would drive up their costs relative to those of their less scrupulous competitors.[28] In India, farmers are resisting the rise of grocery supermarkets because their buyer power will result in harsher conditions.[29] The decline of farm income in African cocoa growing regions is directly related to the increased buying power of the chocolate processor oligopoly.[30] A similar analysis applies to bananas, which are dominated by oligopsony.[31]

It should be acknowledged that some bargaining power on the part of buyers is important to the competitive process. Buying in large volume

---

26 See generally Stephen Devadoss and Wongun Song, 'Oligopsony Distortions and Welfare Implications of Trade' (2006) 14 *Review of International Economy* 452 (oligopsony results in a variety of anomalies for the market including deterioration of the terms of trade).

27 US Department of Agriculture (February 2014), *2012 Census of Agriculture, U.S. Farms and Farmers*, available at http://www.agcensus.usda.gov/Publications/2012/Preliminary_Report/Highlights.pdf ('In 2012, the average age of principal farm operators was 58.3 years, up 1.2 years since 2007, and continuing a 30-year trend of steady increase. The older age groups all increased in number between 2007 and 2012').

28 Ian Urbina and Keith Bradsher, 'Linking Factories to the Malls, Middleman Pushes Low Costs' *New York Times* (8 August 2013) at A1; Steven Greenhouse, 'Europeans Fault American Safety Effort in Bangladesh' *New York Times* (19 November 2013) at B3; Steven Greenhouse, 'Major Retailers Agree to Inspection Standards in Bangladesh' *New York Times* (21 November 2013) at B3.

29 Cohen, *supra* note 25, at 40.

30 See O'Keefe, *supra* note 14; Alexei Kireyev, *Export Tax and Pricing Power: Two Hypotheses on the Cocoa Market in Côte d'Ivoire* (IMF Working Paper 10/269, 2010), available at https://www.imf.org/external/pubs/ft/wp/2010/wp10269.pdf.

31 See Fair Trade Foundation (2014), 'Britain's Bruising Banana Wars: Why Cheap Bananas Threaten Farmers' Futures', available at http://www.fairtrade.org.uk/~/media/fairtradeuk/what%20is%20fairtrade/documents/policy%20and%20research%20documents/policy%20reports/britains%20bruising%20banana%20wars.ashx; see also Steve Hannaford, *Market Domination!: The Impact of Industry Consolidation on Competition* (Praeger, Westport, CT 2007) 30.

creates an incentive on the part of a buyer to be more attentive to and search more diligently for the relevant input. There are, as a result, identifiable economies of scale and scope as well as transaction cost savings in the buying process itself. The volume of a purchase can create additional economies for producers, including longer production runs and more intensive use of productive capacity. Hence, the buyer is in a position to bargain for a share of the efficiency gains that the seller will realize from those sales. When both buyer and seller have other viable options, the result is a bargaining process that represents workable competition. Because there is no inherently 'correct' price for inputs, the parties can reasonably bargain within the range of plausible prices.

Some commentators contend that there is little or no risk of abusive buyer power because supply expands and contracts without any change in costs. For example, Jacobson asserts that the supply curve 'at prevailing levels of production . . . [is] typically flat',[32] and therefore a producer can increase or decrease output without facing any increase in unit costs. He cites Scherer and Ross for this proposition.[33] But what those authors actually report is that, assuming there is fairly full use of the firm's productive capacity, the U-shaped cost curve has a flat middle section, which connotes full use of inputs to production. If demand declines significantly for any reason, short-run and potentially longer run per unit costs will go up. A ten percent or greater drop in demand can impose very serious costs on a producer, even if it can adjust output without a significant increase in per unit production costs. This would be especially true if the producer has high fixed costs, such as for debt service, relative to its operating expenses. Scherer and Ross also explain that diseconomies of scale can occur as well.[34] Jacobson additionally relies on several other authors whose actual statements do not support his position.[35] In fact, substantial buyers, that

---

[32] Jonathan M Jacobson, 'Monopsony 2013: Still Not Truly Symmetric' (December 2013) *Antitrust Source* 1, 4, 11, available at http://www.americanbar.org/content/dam/aba/publishing/antitrust_source/dec13_jacobson_12_18f.authcheckdam.pdf; see also Jonathan M Jacobson and Gary J Dorman, 'Joint Purchasing, Monopsony and Antitrust' (1991) 36 *Antitrust Bulletin* 1, 12.

[33] FM Scherer and David R Ross, *Industrial Market Structure and Economic Performance* (Houghton Mifflin, Boston, MA 3rd edn 1990) 97–107.

[34] *Ibid* at 104–05.

[35] Of the other citations, only Dennis W Carlton and Jeffrey M Perloff, *Modern Industrial Organization* (Pearson, Boston, MA 4th edn 2005) 40 (reporting that empirical studies tend to show L-shaped cost curves) arguably supports Jacobson's position, but even this is weak support for the reasons set forth in the text. The remaining references do not provide empirical support for the claim. See George Stigler, *The Theory of Price* (Macmillan, London 3rd edn 1966) 182

is, those taking more than ten percent of a firm's output, can exercise significant power over a supplier through the disruption and diseconomies they can impose, regardless of the shape of the supplier's cost curve. (Of course, if the buyer is dependent on that supplier for a substantial share of its need for that input, the producer has an offsetting power that might equalize the parties' bargaining positions. But that possibility is highly dependent on the options available to each side.)

The central conclusion from the foregoing discussion is that buyer power—with monopsony as the extreme case—creates the potential for harm to the competitive process in both the short run and the long run. The attempt to divide buyer power into two distinct categories is not helpful in developing competition policies whatever utility it might have in building economic models.

II. THE TWO TYPES OF BUYER POWER: INPUT BUYING AND MARKETING OF BRANDED CONSUMER GOODS

Buyer power creates problems for competition in two specific, but related, circumstances: the sale of inputs and the marketing of branded goods. This section describes the sources of buyer power in both cases and the relevant market characteristics that define its scope.

A producer that supplies intermediate goods to a buyer for assembly into final or other intermediate goods may be subject to the exercise of buyer power, especially if the producer has relatively few outlets for its production. The larger the buyer relative to the producers the greater the potential level of power.

Producers of branded or specialized consumer goods sold through a retailer face somewhat different buyer power issues. These retailers provide the essential conduits through which goods must pass to reach the

---

(a theoretical discussion arguing that the structure of production is efficient); William R Baumol, 'On the Proper Tests for Natural Monopoly in a Multiproduct Industry' (1977) 67 *American Economic Review* 809, 814, 818–19 (a theoretical model explaining natural monopoly); John B Kirkwood, 'Powerful Buyers and Merger Enforcement' (2012) 92 *Boston University Law Review* 1485, 1496 (merely citing Carlton and Perloff, *supra* note 35, and Jacobson and Dorman, *supra* note 32); and John McGee, 'Efficiency and Economies of Size', in H Goldschmidt, HM Mann and JF Weston (eds), *Industrial Concentration: The New Learning* (Little Brown and Company, New York 1974) 58, 67, 72, 81 (arguing that large firms are large because they have economies of scale).

final consumer. Hence, even fairly large producers are vulnerable to buyer power. The second part of this section provides an analysis of the special buyer power attributes facing such producers.

In both contexts, a key variable is the capacity of the seller to find alternative buyers for its products or shift its production without undue delay, risk or switching costs. Thus, in addition to conventional market shares, an estimate of actual buyer power requires attention to the structural and institutional characteristics of the market in which the buyer buys. The following two subsections elaborate on the distinctions between the two contexts with respect to the sources of power, market definition and the thresholds at which buyer power is likely to pose competitive risks.

A. Buyer Power in Input or Component Markets Generally

Buyer power is a significant issue for producers of inputs used in the production of final products. These producers range from employees to farmers to a myriad of input suppliers for all kinds of manufactured products.

1. The sources of buyer power

A producer that sells directly to a buyer on a repeat basis will face certain costs if it switches to another customer. The costs start with the investment of time and effort necessary to locate an alternative buyer. Next the seller must determine whether its product fits the buyer's needs. In many cases, the price and other terms for the purchase of the goods will be negotiated. All of this investment will be wasted effort if the producer cannot make the sale. The producer may well stay with his original buyer because the costs of seeking alternative output channels outweigh the perceived potential gains, even if the buyer imposes a reduced price or other conditions on the seller.

If a buyer learns that one of its suppliers has been seeking other customers, it may be less willing to continue to use that supplier. This can be a serious problem for a producer who 'defects' to a new customer and then regrets that decision. It will frequently have a difficult time returning to its old buyer who will, in all probability, have developed a new source of supply in the interim. If there are few buyers overall, that risk will be a substantial deterrent to looking for an alternative outlet, even if the current buyer imposes substantial burdens on the producer. Thus, the costs and risks of switching increase as the number of potential buyers declines.

These costs and risks also vary with the quantity and proportion of the producer's output that the buyer takes. If the buyer takes all or a substantial part of a producer's output, the difficulties associated with finding an alternative buyer will increase. The other side of this relationship is also relevant. If the buyer gets a substantial part of its total requirements of the input from the producer, then it too can face significant adjustment costs if the relationship is broken. The greater the resulting interdependence the more the parties are likely to respect each other and resolve any issue by agreement.

One classic example of a one-sided relationship is human labor. An employee usually sells all or most of her labor to a single buyer. Economic models of labor markets show that, as a matter of theory, employers often have buyer power even if there are many of them, and various empirical studies confirm this.[36] The degree of 'lock-in' is a function of the transferability of the skills of the worker and the worker's knowledge of and access to other employment opportunities. The same considerations would apply to any other input market with similar characteristics. When a buyer buys the same input from a number of different suppliers, each of whom sells all or most of its output to that buyer, each such supplier has much less capacity to bargain effectively. If the buyer refuses to buy, the seller faces a potentially serious problem because of its dependence on that specific buyer, but the buyer does not face the same potential dislocations of its business if it terminates any specific supplier.

Further support for the need of sellers to have access to multiple buyers comes from a model Jeremy Sandford developed to examine the incentives of sellers to provide quality in goods or services.[37] His model assumed that customers were concerned with the quality of service but had no reliable information prior to making their purchases. The questions he asked were whether and when it would be rational for sellers to invest in providing good service. He found that when customers had a significant number of choices available to them (that is, lower switching costs), the incentives for producers to provide better service increased because of the

---

[36] See Orley C Ashenfelter, Henry Farber and Michael R Ransom, 'Modern Models of Monopsony in Labor Markets: Tests and Estimates' (2010) 28 *Journal of Labor Economics* 203; see also Council of Economic Advisers (October 2016), 'Labor Market Monopsony: Trends, Consequences, and Policy Responses', available at https://www.whitehouse.gov/sites/default/files/page/files/20161025_monopsony_labor_mrkt_cea.pdf (analysis of the harm to workers from employer monopsony power and suggesting various policies to reduce those harms).

[37] Jeremy Sandford, 'Competition and Endogenous Impatience in Credence-Good Markets' (2013) 169 *Journal of Institutional and Theoretical Economics* 531; see also Peter A Diamond, 'Mobility Costs, Frictional Unemployment, and Efficiency' (1981) 89 *Journal of Political Economy* 798; Peter A Diamond, 'Aggregate Demand Management in Search Equilibrium' (1982) 90 *Journal of Political Economy* 881.

risk of loss of customers. The model is consistent with the ordinary intuition that a buyer will be reluctant to return to his old supplier, especially if the relationship is at all personal, and so will want to have many choices available before deciding to exit.

Although Sandford's model focused on the question of when a powerless consumer can induce desirable conduct by producers, its basic insight is that switching in concentrated markets when an actor has limited or imperfect knowledge is inherently risky because of the limited options. Often the specifics of price and other elements of the buying relationship, especially when the transaction involves some indeterminate elements, such as quantity or forward prices, are not fully disclosed. Hence, producers face transaction costs and risks in seeking alternative outlets, and those costs and risks increase as the number of potential buyers declines. If producers have a number of choices open to them, buyers will have more incentive to pay reasonable prices and adopt other terms of trade that satisfy the seller. This result is a restatement of the basic concept of how a competitive market *should* work.

Robert Lande has shown that a significant source of market power on the selling side arises from market failure.[38] He looked to consumer protection law to illustrate the kinds of conduct (such as misleading information, in the form of false advertising, and concealed information) and other market defects that cause consumers to make unnecessarily costly choices. Firms that operate in such markets have a power over price that comes from these market failures. Lande urged that such markets either be narrowly defined or that the market share necessary to indicate market power be reduced.

These same market failures, in part already discussed, are particularly apparent in the analysis of buyer power. In American livestock markets, for example, confidentiality surrounds the specific terms of contractual relations between buyers and sellers. The fact that details are secret increases the bargaining power of the buyers because farmers cannot easily compare the options that might be available. By increasing search costs, the buyers increase their buyer power. In addition, the secrecy of these contracts means that buyers can make different deals with different producers and face little or no hostility from buyers as a group. This also increases their relative power.

Although labor and farm commodities are two well-known examples

---

[38] See Robert Lande, 'Market Power Without a Large Market Share: The Role of Imperfect Information and Other "Consumer Protection" Market Failures' (American Antitrust Institute Working Paper No. 07-06, 2007).

of buyer power, it should be obvious that in any context in which the input producer has a major buyer and faces any significant impediment to switching to another buyer, the buyer will have power. Many small to mid-sized firms have only a few major customers. Consider a firm that specializes in providing technical services to the hog industry. It will necessarily have a limited set of major customers because of the concentrated nature of that market. Moreover, it is highly unlikely that such a firm can transfer its productive facilities to some other use easily and quickly. Even if it deals with several of the major buyers, it faces buyer power from each. Only if the firm diversifies to produce services for different markets, and especially if it can use the same facilities to produce inputs for those different markets, will it have some capacity to resist unreasonable demands.

Central to the power of the buyer in these contexts is the fact that it assembles a large number of components of various kinds to produce the goods or services it sells. This creates an all but insuperable barrier for individual component makers that want to vertically integrate into the buyer's downstream market. Therefore, if major buyers decline to continue to buy, the producer must find other outlets for its production or reduce production. The same basic situation almost always confronts an employee. A single worker cannot expect, except in very limited situations, to be able to establish a business comparable to that of her employer. Alternative employment is the only plausible option.

2. Defining buyer side input markets

To determine whether a buyer has significant buyer power in an input market, the market must be defined with respect to the producer's options for both products and geography.

Many input producers are highly specialized. Cattle feed lots have only one use. The same is true for chicken houses or cocoa trees. Specialized manufactured products may also require significant investment in facilities having few alternative uses. On the product market side, therefore, the definitional question is what range of goods or services can a producer offer?

The second issue is the geographic scope of actual and potential sales. Some products, such as live chickens, cannot travel great distances. Other components, such as vitamins, can be shipped long distances. Combining the potential outputs and the scope of the geographic area within which it is feasible to sell these products, it is possible to define the market accessible to a producer. The resulting market may well be very different from the downstream markets in which the products manufactured from the components are sold. Hence, the buyers' selling side markets can be either over- or under-inclusive of the upstream input markets. If the downstream markets of some buyers are themselves concentrated, buyers will have an additional incentive to exercise upstream power because that can yield even greater profits and provide a means of excluding potential downstream competition.

Within a buying market, the next crucial question is the number and size of potential buyers. The resulting measure of buyer concentration provides an important indicator of the risks of undue buyer power. But the level of concentration that should trigger concern is significantly lower than that usually considered relevant to seller side analysis. This is a significant reason to reject the mirror image metaphor.

How the specific market operates is also important. If a public commodity market provides the primary forum for the sale of the input, the risks of buyer power are limited as long as there are a reasonable number of buyers. The key considerations would be the extent to which the public market is the primary market for transactions and whether some buyer, or small group of buyers, takes such a large proportion of the sales that they have an incentive to manipulate prices. If the commodity market serves as a residual market, creating a base price for transactions that result from direct dealing, then the risk of market price manipulation increases even if the buying side of the market is less concentrated.

When buyers deal directly with suppliers in the absence of any public commodity market, there will be some buyer power inherent in the transactions. Moreover, the more specialized the input, the greater the potential for buyer power because switching costs are likely to be substantial even if there are a number of potential buyers.[39] The ease and speed with which a producer can switch to other products or adapt its product to satisfy another buyer will determine the extent of these costs.

Another relevant factor is whether the producer regularly sells to several buyers at once. This effectively diversifies the risks of lost sales and reduces the dependency of the producer on any one buyer. In contrast, when a producer sells all or most of its production to a single buyer, that buyer is much more likely to acquire at least some power even if there are other buyers in the market. In that situation the switching costs, including the risk that the alternative buyer is not satisfactory, will be much more substantial, and the producer will be more vulnerable to coercive power.

---

[39] The assumption is that specialized inputs are likely to be custom-made, so the loss of that customer would create significant risks and switching costs.

3. Thresholds for concern with buyer power in input markets

If producers face high switching costs, there is an even greater need for a large number of potential buyers to ensure effective competition on the buying side. Sandford's work implies that a workable selling market requires that producers have access to at least five and probably more potential buyers.[40] The auction literature (discussing formal multi-party buying markets) strongly supports the conclusion that at least five or six relatively significant buyers are the minimum necessary.[41] Moreover, any buyer with a market share over 20 percent (a single-firm Herfindahl-Hirschman Index (HHI) above 400) is likely to have buyer power regardless of the overall HHI of the market, although this would depend on the structure of the supply side. The more producers outnumber buyers, the greater the potential for exploitation because the buyers will at any point be buying from more than one producer. Under those circumstances, the threat of cutting off a single producer is much more credible.

Also relevant are the elasticity of supply on the part of the producers and the elasticity of demand from the remainder of the buyers.[42] The producers' ability to reduce output at low cost when confronted with low prices or other unacceptable burdens will be a significant check on the exercise of buyer power. Similarly, if other buyers have the capacity, interest and ability to increase their purchases quickly and substantially, then a reduction in price or other adverse conduct by a substantial buyer is likely to result in producers switching sales to other input buyers.

B. Branded Consumer Goods

The second context in which buyer power is common arises in sales of branded consumer goods.[43] Most relevant are goods that must be sold in stores that carry a wide variety of goods. The manufacturer of such goods needs a substantial number of geographically dispersed retail outlets in order to have access to enough potential final consumers to sell a sufficient

---

40 See Sandford, *supra* note 37.

41 See Marshall and Meurer, *supra* note 18; *cf*, DeeVon Bailey, B Wade Brorsen and Chris Fawson, 'Buyer Concentration at Feeder Cattle Auctions' (1993) 15 *Review of Agricultural Economics* 103.

42 Blair and Harrison, *supra* note 6, at 58.

43 Although the following discussion emphasizes the issues related to branded consumer goods in both groceries and other mass retail markets, the same issues arise in unbranded food products such as meat, poultry, and dairy products. In those lines, the challenge for the volume producer is to have sufficient access to retail outlets to maintain efficient production. Geographic dispersion is less central, however, as there is no advertising investment to amortize.

quantity of its products. Thus retailers are 'gate keepers' between the producer and the consumer seeking its products. Some manufacturers have product lines that allow them to franchise dealers or even vertically integrate into retailing. Others may be able to use the internet to make direct sales of sufficient volume that they are less dependent on retail outlets.[44] Hence, as with component producers and their buyers, the importance of access to retail outlets varies across the many types of branded consumer goods.

The competitive issues arising from retailer power are objects of concern among competition authorities globally, including those in the United Kingdom, Finland, Australia, Japan and the Republic of Korea. Indeed, some countries have adopted the position that even retail grocery chains with 30 percent or less of the relevant buying market can still hold a 'dominant' position, making their unilateral conduct subject to oversight by the competition authority.[45] This level of concentration is lower than that usually considered relevant to seller side analysis—further evidence that the mirror image metaphor is an inaccurate basis for competition policy with respect to buyer power.

The analytic problems for identifying buyer power in branded goods markets include explaining the nature of the buyer power (the access issue), defining the relevant markets and determining the market shares on the buying side that can create such power. Enterprises that produce generic consumer goods face the same buyer power issues as any other input supplier. They do not, however, incur the special risks that branded goods producers face.

1. Access to retail outlets

The challenge of distribution for producers of branded consumer goods is to get a sufficient volume of goods into a sufficiently large number of retail

---

[44] See 'Invasion of the Bottle Snatchers' *Economist* (9 July 2016) at 53 (study by the Boston Consulting Group and IRI finding that dominant firms in consumer packaged goods were losing market share globally because of changes in marketing and consumer access to information).

[45] See Mika Oinonen, 'The New 30% Rule: A Viable Solution to Detrimental Buyer Power in the Finnish Grocery Retail Sector?' (2014) 10 *European Competition Journal* 98; Law on Competition, art 3, as amended (1999) (Lithuania), available at http://kt.gov.lt/en/index.php?show=antitrust&antitrust_doc=law_competition (standard of 30 percent); Latvia has an even more expansive definition. See Competition Law § 13(2) (2009), available at http://www.kp.gov.lv/en/dominant-position-in-retail-trade ('A company that is in a dominant position in retail trade has the ability to impose unfair transaction terms or payments on suppliers, yet contrary to the classic dominant position, they do not have the ability to act completely independently of consumers or competitors').

outlets that the resulting sales can support an efficient level of production. Like the component manufacturer, the producer of consumer goods and grocery products is unlikely to be able to integrate forward into large-scale retailing.[46] Whenever the distribution goes through large volume retailers, the need for access creates power on the buying side.[47]

Moreover, Robert Steiner long argued that, because there is competition at the point of sale between a branded good and a retailer's house brand or a generic good, the retailer is both a customer and competitor, which creates even more incentive for the use of buyer power.[48] Because consumers can choose between branded goods and house brands or generics, a buyer can put pressure on the suppliers of all three categories of goods. In addition, as house brands play an increasingly significant role in retail sales, volume buyers have even more opportunity to discriminate among suppliers and exploit both the producers of house brands and those who produce trademarked goods.[49]

The branded product producer's ultimate goal is the customer that seeks out its branded product. Hence, it will directly promote the product or assist retailers in doing so. Further, because no single outlet or, except

---

[46] The exceptions include high-end clothing and accessory producers with a diverse line of products. Indeed, some of these firms have their products produced by others and are essentially only retailers. The limits to such integration are manifest—even Procter & Gamble or Kraft could not stock a full-line grocery store.

[47] See Paul Dobson, 'Exploiting Buyer Power: Lessons from the British Grocery Trade' (2005) 72 *Antitrust Law Journal* 529, 534. This relative power issue may explain why cars are sold through dealerships that are subject to significant geographic limitations. Automakers do not want to face powerful dealers who might impose their will on the manufacturer's design or pricing decisions. Dealers in turn have used the political process to gain some protections. See Stewart Macaulay, *Law and the Balance of Power* (Russell Sage Foundation, New York 1966) (studying how dealers and manufacturers sought to develop law to protect their respective interests); *cf Exxon Corp. v Maryland*, 437 U.S. 117 (1978) (Maryland prohibition on gasoline refiners owning service stations upheld as constitutionally permitted).

[48] For a comprehensive review and analysis of Steiner's work, see 'Special Issue: The Implications of the Work of Robert Steiner' (2004) 49 *Antitrust Bulletin* 821.

[49] A manufacturer of generic goods is like any other component producer. It has to find one or more outlets for its products. As such a producer becomes more specialized, either voluntarily or in response to pressure from its major customer, it too will be subject to the kind of buyer power discussed previously. Indeed, it is frequently said that retailers like to concentrate their orders on a relatively small number of producers. This undoubtedly creates some economies of scale and scope, but it also creates buyer power as the supplier becomes more dependent on the specific buyer for a large proportion of its sales.

rarely, set of outlets owned by a single retailer will produce a sufficient volume of sales for a branded product line, its producer must have access to shelf space in a number of retail outlets and reach a number of distinct retail markets. Therefore, every retailer that buys a significant portion of a manufacturer's branded product has independent leverage over that manufacturer. The threat of termination of any one of those supply contracts confronts the manufacturer with the risk of a permanent loss of sales. This risk differs from the risk of a loss of sales to a component producer because branded product manufacturers need a geographically dispersed distribution system.

If the manufacturer has a dominant brand, it can partially insulate itself from this coercion because the retailer is likely to feel compelled to carry the product. Retailers may treat 'must-carry' products differently from those that have a significant presence but are not so important that the retailer feels obligated to stock them. Even so, the retailer has a great deal of discretion as to how it displays and promotes a product; even a major brand producer may have an incentive to placate the interests of a substantial retailer.

Both stocking fees and category captains reflect in part the power of the downstream retailer. The stocking fee is the most obvious strategy by which a retailer puts a price on access to its shelves.[50] Those who defend this practice as efficiency-enhancing argue that the retailer is in effect selling access to a scarce commodity—its shelf space.[51] The buyer willing to pay the most has the greatest expectation of market response, which in turn argues that this is the highest and best use of that space. Indeed, in a non-strategic world in which shelf space was subdivided into modest units, there is a plausible theoretical argument that the retailer could be a largely passive lessor of access.

In reality, a retailer needs to develop an overall mix of goods that targets its customer base at a range of prices and quality. Therefore, it is not a passive actor. In addition, large retailers have an incentive to invest in the exclusion of smaller and newer rivals to protect their market position. They can employ their buying power to that end. Indeed, there can be a symbiotic relationship between the large retailer and the large producer of consumer goods. The producer also wants to limit new competition, and limiting access to shelf space can be an important weapon. Hence, a dominant producer is also paying for exclusion. Stocking fees do no more

---

[50] Joshua Wright, 'Slotting Contracts and Consumer Welfare' (2007) 74 *Antitrust Law Journal* 439.

[51] *Ibid* at 448.

than transfer surplus from producer to retailer only if analyzed as a matter of economic welfare—assuming that smaller and newer options are less desirable because they cannot or will not pay more for access. But from a competitive process standpoint, the use of buyer power to exploit access creates serious competitive concerns exactly because it undermines the dynamics of the market and makes new entry and expansion by marginal producers much more difficult.

Category captains constitute a more subtle use of buyer power. A dominant firm in a category undertakes to act as category captain and incur the costs and burdens of managing the category for the retailer, such as stocking shelves and allocating space among different brands.[52] Those managerial costs are shifted from the retailer to the supplier.[53] The captain must then find ways to coordinate the sale of the products within the category to yield higher revenue for the retailer. Thus viewed, the gain to the retailer reflects its power as a buyer. The captain's benefit is its enhanced ability to control competition with its product lines.

The large retailer and large branded product supplier may well share an interest in reducing or eliminating actual or potential competition at both levels. Each faces the risk that competition will force prices down and lead to reduced market share. If a large brand name manufacturer raises its price, or provides less service, to new entrants and marginal competitors,[54] the market position of the dominant retailer will be protected. Reciprocally, the dominant manufacturer benefits when the large retailer refuses to buy from new entrants or marginal producers that

---

52 Leo S Carameli, 'The Anti-Competitive Effects and Antitrust Implications of Category Management and Category Captains of Consumer Products' (2004) 79 *Chicago-Kent Law Review* 1313; see *Conwood Co. v U.S. Tobacco Co.*, 290 F.3d 768 (6th Cir. 2002) (US Tobacco used its position as the category manager to undermine its competitor).

53 Several studies from the United Kingdom's Competition Commission provide insight into how this process reduces retailer costs and increases the costs of producers. See, eg, *Supply Chain Practices and the Supermarkets Code of Practice* (UK Competition Commission, Working Paper, 2007); *Primary Production and the Grocery Supply Chain* (UK Competition Commission, Working Paper, 2007); and *Category Management* (UK Competition Commission, Working Paper, 2007), available at http://webarchive.nationalarchives.gov.uk/20110315081651/http://www.competition-commission.org.uk//inquiries/ref2006/grocery/further_working_papers.htm.

54 For example, Clorox refuses to sell the largest containers of its products to smaller retailers despite their desire to carry them. This protects Clorox's relationship with its largest volume customers such as Costco and Walmart. *Woodman's Food Mkt. v Clorox Co.*, 2015 WL 420296 (W.D. Wis. 2015) (holding this refusal an unlawful discrimination), rev'd, 2016 WL 4254935 (7th Cir. 2016).

compete with its favored source of supply. McCraw examined this symbiotic relationship in the case of General Electric's support for resale price maintenance (RPM), which advanced the interests of its high-volume retail clients who in turn focused their purchases on General Electric's products.[55] Ultimately, new entry at both the production and retailing levels resulted in the death of the RPM strategy.[56]

Retail outlets are not fungible for branded good distribution. The manufacturer needs to have as many outlets as possible and in as wide a geographic distribution as possible in order to achieve and retain a high volume of sales. Unlike an input supplier, the branded product manufacturer's switching costs involve retaining access to the ultimate consumer. When a retailer excludes a product line, the manufacturer must both find a new outlet and induce customers to come to the new retailer. Customers rarely go to a store to buy a single branded product, so the termination may cut the producer off from its established customer base. Even if it can replace the outlet with another, the manufacturer must attract the loyalty of the customers in the new outlet, whose preferences in that category may already be set. Indeed, in some situations, if there is no alternative high-volume outlet, the manufacturer may be unable to replace the excluded retailer's lost sales. This is especially true if most other retailers in that market already stock the product.

The dynamics of advertising increase the pressure on branded goods' producers to have regional or national distribution. The economies of scale of national product promotion accrue only if the product line is available nationally. For many producers of such goods, there is no benefit to substituting outlets in one region for those in another. The producer needs coverage in all regions, so substantial retailers in each

---

[55] Thomas K McCraw, 'Competition and "Fair Trade": History and Theory' (1996) 16 *Research in Economic History* 185.

[56] *Ibid* at 213–14. The symbiotic relationship between manufacturers and retailers is also seen in *NicSand, Inc. v 3M Co.*, 507 F.3d 442 (6th Cir. 2007) (en banc). A multiline manufacturer made such substantial front-end payments to retailers that its single-line smaller competitor was forced to withdraw from the market, leaving the successful producer as a monopolist. By 'coordinating' on a single supplier, the retailers avoided any risk of price competition from different brands, and the manufacturer ensured that at least one potential competitor for one of its related products, conventional sandpaper, was no longer in the market. The defeated firm alleged that, after the small firm was forced out, the buyers raised the price of the product by 70 percent. (If, as is likely, the barriers to entry are low for the production of sandpaper designed for use on cars, the successful dominant firm will have to continue to make substantial payments to retain its dominant position.)

region have significant power over the producer even if they do not take a very large percentage of its goods. Concentration in either a regional or national market for the purchase of a specific class of branded consumer good is likely to enhance the buyer power of the retailer. The power derives from the volume of goods the retailer purchases from the manufacturer and is largely independent of that possessed by other buyers. The branded goods' producer needs the volume necessary to sustain its production. Hence, it is vulnerable to the demands of every substantial buyer. Indeed, some producers have explicitly stated that they want to avoid having any buyer take more than a modest share of their total output.[57]

2. Defining markets in retail distribution

The geographic markets for the purchase of branded consumer goods by retailers are usually very broad, broader than the retail markets in which the goods are resold. The branded goods' producer needs many outlets to achieve its required volume and wide geographic coverage to ensure that its products reach a sufficiently large customer base. The branded goods' producer also needs coverage over entire regions or nations to make efficient use of advertising and product promotion. Hence, the geographic market in which buyers buy and sellers sell branded goods is likely to be national or even global. The need for regional coverage may, however, narrow the definition of the geographic market.[58] If buyers in a region are highly concentrated, but economies of scale in advertising or other product promotion require that producers include that region in their total sales area for a product, a dominant buyer may be able to use its control over access to that region to impose burdens that extend beyond the boundaries of that region alone. This power will, of course, have limits

---

[57] See US Department of Justice and US Department of Agriculture, Public Workshops Exploring Competition Issues in Agriculture 276–77 (25 June 2010) (testimony of Louise Hemstead, Chief Operating Officer, Organic Valley Cooperative), available at https://www.justice.gov/sites/default/files/atr/legacy/2011/01/12/wisconsin-agworkshop-transcript.pdf (explaining why they dropped Walmart as a customer).

[58] The EU cases involving grocery chain mergers emphasized national markets (that is, EU regions). See, eg, Case M-784, *Kesko/Tuko*, 1997 O.J. (L 174) 1; Case COMP/M.1684, *Carrefour/Promodes*, 2000 O.J. (C 164) 5 (identifying market shares of slightly more than 20 percent in national markets as creating the potential for buyer dominance). See also Chloé Benet, *Buyer Power in EU Competition Law* 177 n.564 (May 2014) (Ph.D. dissertation, Université Catholique de Louvain) (French competition authority concluding that 20 percent is the level at which a retailer would have a dominant position with respect to its suppliers).

as a producer is likely to forgo the benefits of access if the costs are excessive and if it retains access to other regions with sufficient volume of sales. Producers serving specialized regional tastes will similarly find that they have geographically narrower markets.

Product market definition, however, should look at the options producers have for retaining a sufficient volume of sales. If a producer can employ its facilities to produce several distinct products, then it may be able to adjust the output of any particular branded product in response to changes in buyer demand. But in most cases, production facilities are devoted to a specific product or product group. The relevant product market is that product or class of products, even if other products may have similar uses. Thus, although butter and margarine may be substitutes at the dinner table, they are manufactured by very different means. A margarine producer needs to sell margarine and is vulnerable to buyer power whenever a buyer takes a sufficiently large volume and the producer has limited alternative outlets for its product.

Overall, the markets for branded goods are likely to have broad geographic boundaries but relatively narrow product dimensions because the focus should be on the options available to producers. Hence, the key issue will be the number of buyers and the relative quantities of the product that they buy.

3. Thresholds for concern about retailer buyer power

The striking thing about some of the cases involving access to retail outlets is the relatively modest market share needed to enable a buyer to exercise significant power. In *Toys 'R' Us*, the chain bought about 20 percent of all toys sold in the United States, sufficient for it to have substantial power over its suppliers.[59] Paul Dobson reports that in the United Kingdom the data show that retailers buying ten percent of the total sales of a product line have substantial buyer power over its producer.[60] In evaluating a retail merger, the EU competition authority concluded (based on a substantial market survey) that a buyer that takes 22 percent or more of a producer's goods has substantial buyer power.[61] Moreover, in several Member States a low level of buyer concentration can support a finding of unilateral market dominance.[62]

A variety of sources suggest that buyer power arises from a volume

---

59 *Toys 'R' Us v FTC*, 221 F.3rd 928 (7th Cir. 2000).
60 Dobson, *supra* note 47, at 534–5.
61 See *supra* note 58.
62 See *supra* note 45.

of purchases substantially less than that conventionally associated with significant power on the selling side of the market. As emphasized earlier, the key for buyer power is that the buyer takes a significant aggregate quantity of the consumer good at issue and that access to that buyer is itself important or even essential to the efficient operation of a producer of branded goods.[63] This combination of conditions, which are similar to those examined earlier in the section on buyer power in the input markets, gives the buyer substantial leverage in negotiating with the seller. The buyer has better options, and therefore more leverage, than the seller.[64]

In the case of branded goods, as many as nine or ten substantial buyers, with market shares of about ten percent, may be necessary for workable competition. Any retailer with a share above ten percent of the buying market may have sufficient power to impose unjustified burdens on branded good producers. Once a buying market concentrates to six substantial competitors, the potential for abusive buyer power is significant. Certainly when a retailer exceeds a 20 percent share of the relevant buying market, it is likely to have buyer power regardless of the structure of the rest of the market. It is important to remember that, if the branded producer can ship its products at an efficient cost, this concentration is measured in geographically broad markets. These structural considerations once again demonstrate that the mirror image metaphor is inapplicable.

III. THREE FACTORS THAT INCREASE THE RELATIVE POWER OF BUYERS

Three aspects of the roles of buyers and sellers have the potential to increase the relative power of buyers in ways that make buyer power plausible at smaller than expected market shares and harder to overcome by ordinary market responses. These are (1) the primacy of the buyer in one-on-one transactions (the buyer as 'decider'); (2) the inherent limits on arbitrage among producers; and (3) the market's difficulty in overcoming buyer power.

---

63 The sentence states the general condition, but any specific producer of branded goods is subject to a retailer's power only if that retailer sells a significant quantity of the producer's lines.

64 A producer that expands its portfolio of popular brands can increase its ability to resist unjustified demands by buyers by making a credible threat to withdraw all of its brands from the retailer.

A. The Buyer as Decider

Any buyer that is not a pure price taker has some buyer power. Even an individual customer at an auto dealership has the power to negotiate a lower price. The power of the buyer comes from a central economic fact of the market process: the buyer is the 'decider' with respect to whether and how much to purchase of any particular commodity or input. Moreover, the buyer also decides from whom to make the purchase. The resulting discretion is central to the potential for substantial buyer power. The potential seller must accept the offer or wait for another buyer to come along. As the costs and risks to the producer of delay and uncertainty increase, including whether other buyers exist, the buyer's leverage increases. Thus, the fact of decisional power differentiates buyers from sellers and substantially explains why buyers can have significant power even when they do not dominate the buying side of the market in ways comparable to those associated with seller power.[65]

An important element in this power differential is direct purchase by the buyer. Whenever transactions are negotiated directly, every buyer who has any significant buying capacity has the ability to affect its suppliers. The effect is strongest when the buyer deals with a number of suppliers of the same input or suppliers face switching costs significantly greater than those the buyer would face. Indeed, such buyers may be able to extract substantial concessions with only a modest degree of buyer power.

The fact that buyers gain a negotiating advantage from direct purchase helps to explain the decline of commodity exchanges. Historically in the United States, public markets existed for grain, livestock and other commodities. These markets provided important protections for producers, who could avoid being tied to any particular buyer. As long as a producer delivered a generic commodity that satisfied specific standards, the buyer was indifferent as to its source.[66] Prices could vary with each transaction.

---

[65] Some producers have seller power, that is, the capacity to refuse to deal. This power is greatest in consumer goods when the producer has a branded product with a downstream demand and few competitors. Component part producers can have seller power from patents or barriers to entry and limited numbers of competitors. As discussed earlier, when powerful sellers and buyers interact, the result can be a bilateral monopoly or oligopoly, in which the parties are likely to collaborate to exploit both upstream suppliers and downstream customers. See *supra* text accompanying notes 20–21.

[66] For example, an effort by Chicago grain merchants to boycott rural cooperative grain elevators failed because the grain arrived in Chicago as a generic commodity. As long as some traders would sell it and others buy it, there could be no effective boycott. See Peter C Carstensen, 'The Content of the Hollow Core

When these markets operated efficiently, the marginal value of the product as an input matched its current price. Moreover, the producer effectively diversified its sales through the commodity market. There was no direct link between any specific buyer and seller, and an efficient quantity level and price for products ensured that sellers were not exploited. Of course, if there were few buyers, these results were less likely.[67]

For a variety of reasons, the use of commodity markets has declined markedly in the United States over the last 50 years. The increased use of contracts and direct purchases has efficiency explanations.[68] But large buyers also gain a bargaining advantage from direct purchases; repeat business ties the producer to the buyer increasing the buyer's leverage over the producer.[69] It is likely that modernizing commodity exchanges could make them as efficient as direct contracting, but the capacity to bring about such reforms is lacking.[70] Smaller buyers and producers would face significant collective action problems if they sought to reform public markets to adapt them to changing market conditions. In addition, dominant buyers would use their political and economic muscle to resist such reforms. As a result, public markets have become residual outlets for

---

of Antitrust: The *Chicago Board of Trade* Case and the Meaning of the "Rule of Reason" in Restraint of Trade Analysis' (1992) 15 *Research in Law and Economics* 1, 33.

67 The Packers and Stockyards Act of 1921, 7 U.S.C. §§ 181–229b (2016), was a response to buyer abuse of livestock markets. See *Stafford v Wallace*, 258 U.S. 495 (1922) (upholding the constitutionality of the statute and describing the concerns about buying practices).

68 See GIPSA Livestock and Meat Marketing Study, Vol. 3 (2007), 'Fed Cattle and Beef Industries: Final Report' (intensive review of markets for cattle and beef showing the growth of contracting), available at https://www.gipsa.usda.gov/psp/publication/livemarketstudy/LMMS_Vol_3.pdf.

69 See GIPSA Livestock and Meat Marketing Study, Vol. 4 (2007), 'Hog and Pork Industries: Final Report' (showing evidence of significant buyer power in hog contracting); see also Xiaowei Cai, Kyle W Stiegert and Stephen Koontz, 'Regime Switching and Oligopsony Power: The Case of U.S. Beef Processing' (2011) 42 *Agricultural Economics* 99 (recurring tacit collusion among cattle buyers).

70 See Cohen, *supra* note 25, at 38–9 (evidence in West Bengal, India, that vertically integrated food processors were no more efficient in getting fresh food to the final consumer than the traditional wholesale market system). A requirement that certain commodities be purchased only through public market systems would create the incentive for all stakeholders to participate in the development of efficient market systems that serve both buyer and seller interests. But the political power necessary to induce such a radical change is nonexistent, at least in the United States, and for many commodities and inputs, a public market system may not be practical. In India, the state has mandated a public market process and restricted the ability of buyers to use direct contracting. *Ibid* at 21.

many commodities. Indeed, in the case of American poultry, buyers contract to hire farmers to raise flocks of the buyer's birds at compensation not directly related to the market price of the commodity produced. The public wholesale market in live poultry has totally disappeared.

The purchase and sale of any commodity not totally integrated in the manner of the US poultry industry requires a pricing mechanism that assigns a value to the product produced. Therefore, the residual public market can provide a benchmark price for the vastly larger volume of private transactions. If there is sufficient participation by buyers and sellers, the results can provide a useful basis for direct negotiations. But those negotiations, even when informed by reasonable competitive prices, still provide a buyer with the kind of discretion that can result in significant competitive harm.

The public market price can be an unreliable basis for contract prices when buyers get a substantial part of their supplies through direct contracts with producers. If the contract price is based on the public price combined with premiums or other incentives, buyers will look for ways to reduce the reference price in order to reduce the ultimate contract price.[71] The problem is compounded if the contract price uses the buyer's contemporary price as the reference point. Moreover, competing buyers are likely to have the same incentives and so downward price manipulation can become endemic. Even when not manipulated, residual market prices are likely to fluctuate significantly because of limited volume, which increases sensitivity to small changes in demand.

The buyer, therefore, is the dominant decision maker in many circumstances. In most contemporary markets, inputs are sold on a direct, one-on-one basis, which creates a greater potential for the exercise of buyer power. In that context, the buyer can select among potential sellers

---

[71] One well-documented example is the cheese market in the United States. In the 1990s, Kraft Foods purchased about 30 percent of all cheese sold in the country. But it was a net seller on the one public commodity market for cheese. Kraft benefited because the modest dollar amount of its commodity market sales depressed prices for a large number of its off-exchange purchases. The effect of those sales was to retard price increases and accelerate price declines. See Willard F Mueller, Bruce W Marion, Maqbool H Sial and FE Geithman (1996), 'Cheese Pricing: A Study of the National Cheese Exchange', available at https://www.aae.wisc.edu/pubs/misc/docs/cheese.pdf. In 2015, Kraft was charged with manipulating the futures' market price for wheat in order to drive down the price it paid in off-exchange transactions. Complaint, *Commodity Futures Trading Comm'n v Kraft Foods Group Inc.* (No. 1:15-cv-02881, N.D. Ill. 2015), available at http://www.cftc.gov/idc/groups/public/@lrenforcementactions/documents/legalpleading/enfkraftcomplaint040115.pdf.

in addition to deciding whether to buy the input at all. This capacity to decide gives the buyer an inherent negotiating advantage, especially when the buyer takes a significant percentage of the producer's output and the producer is one of several suppliers of the same input to the buyer.

B. The Limited Effectiveness of Producer Arbitrage

Arbitrage is generally recognized as an important way to limit discrimination and exclusion on the seller side of the market. Favored buyers of a commodity can resell it to those who are disfavored. This constrains the capacity of a monopolist to impose different prices or other conditions on specific buyers. In addition, buyers have an incentive to obtain volume discounts even if that requires buying more than they need. Reselling some of the commodity is necessary to achieve the economic advantage. Buyers can arbitrage the difference between the discounted price they pay and the full price that would be paid to the producer by smaller buyers by selling the commodity to the smaller buyers at some price in between. The smaller buyers might then pay less than full price, but the producer suffers with respect to both sets of buyers—receiving discounted prices from large buyers losing sales to small ones. In other cases, buyers set up buying groups to obtain the benefit of such discounts.[72]

But it is difficult for a producer to engage in arbitrage the way a buyer can. When a buyer buys directly from a producer, it can insist that the producer provide the input itself, to prevent the producer from delivering to the buyer substitute commodities from another, disfavored producer. Indeed, for reasons of quality control and source verification, even buyers without significant buyer power may insist on such terms. A public commodity market provides an alternative to arbitrage because inherently no producer is favored over any other.

Moreover, a producer with a favorable selling price and available production capacity has little incentive to supplement its production by buying from a disfavored producer. Only if the favored producer has over-promised on quantity or encountered production problems is it likely to look to others for the commodity it can profitably produce itself, making producer arbitrage unlikely.

Therefore, when buyers and producers deal directly with each other and not through a commodity market, it is relatively easier for buyers to discriminate among their suppliers than for sellers to discriminate among their customers. Buyers can negotiate different terms with each supplier

72 The competitive implications of this strategy are analyzed in Chapter 7.

and often require producers to keep terms secret, which enhances further their ability to differentiate.[73] In a case involving American cattle, a jury determined that the ability to offer individual contracts, combined with secrecy, resulted in a multibillion dollar reduction in revenue for disfavored sellers, but the courts refused to impose liability for the discrimination.[74]

C. The Market's Inherent Difficulty in Overcoming Buyer Power

In the *Standard Oil* decision, the US Supreme Court famously observed that the 'centripetal and centrifugal' forces of the market will ordinarily remedy monopoly.[75] Monopoly profits attract entry. Buyers paying monopoly prices have incentives to look for alternative sources or even sponsor entry into the market. The Schumpeterian model of creative destruction similarly postulates that monopoly will induce responsive innovation.[76] The US Supreme Court has even endorsed monopoly as a reward for innovation with the implicit notion that the same reward awaits the next innovator.[77]

But the incentives for both the producers and the competitors of the buyer are qualitatively different under monopsony. Producers receive below-market prices or accept uncompensated risks or other burdens, but their options for escaping this situation require either significant investment or collective action. One response is to vertically integrate into the market level where the monopsonist operates. This is likely to be costly, and the integration must be sufficient to reach a downstream market. There are examples of such efforts. In the early 1900s, privately owned grain elevators often paid monopsonistically low prices to wheat and corn

---

73 See Carole Morison, 'Contract Poultry Farming' (November 2001) *American Agriculture Movement Newsletter*, available at http://www.aaminc.org/newsletter/v7i4/v7i4p4.htm ('The pay for a contract farmer is based on what growers call "artificial competition shrouded in secrecy."'); see generally Susan Stokes (2013), 'The Dilemma of Contracting: Risk Management or Risky Business?', available at http://www.flaginc.org/wp-content/uploads/2013/03/CLE_SES.pdf; see also Packers and Stockyards Act of 1921, 7 U.S.C. § 229(b) (2016) (authorizing farmers to discuss contract terms with advisors).

74 *Pickett v Tyson Fresh Meats, Inc.*, 315 F. Supp. 2d 1172 (M.D. Ala. 2004), aff'd, 420 F. 3d 1272 (11th Cir. 2005) (denying liability despite the plaintiffs' losses).

75 *Standard Oil v United States*, 221 U.S. 1, 62 (1911).

76 See Joseph A Schumpeter, *Capitalism, Socialism, and Democracy* (Harper Perennial, New York 3rd edn 2008).

77 *Verizon Commc'ns Inc. v Law Offices of Curtis V. Trinko*, 540 U.S. 398, 407 (2004) ('charging . . . monopoly prices . . . is not only not unlawful; it is an important element of the free-market system').

farmers.[78] Because of the costs of hauling grain at that time, competition was rare. But farmers could organize to create a cooperatively owned elevator, which would give them access over rail lines to many markets and lead to competitive prices. In addition, the co-op elevators were large, which ensured that they could store sizeable volumes of crops.[79] Although advantageous, these ventures face significant collective action problems, as described below. Only if the number of participants required is not overwhelming will the latter problem be manageable.[80]

Another option is to create a producers' cartel that negotiates prices with buyers. In the United States, such agreements would be illegal unless exempted from competition law. In 1922, Congress authorized farm groups to establish cooperatives that negotiated prices that buyers would pay participants,[81] enabling farm cooperatives to engage in a range of activities that enhanced returns to producers.[82] Industry-wide labor agreements had been a target of antitrust litigation until 1935, when Congress legalized industry-wide collective bargaining, thus conferring the implied exemption.[83] But these options require collective action, which may be difficult to achieve, especially when producers have different incentives and interests.

Even if there are no legal impediments, the challenges to collective action associated with creating a cartel are substantial. The buyer will immediately be aware of the effort and will adopt responsive strategies. One such strategy would be to offer premiums to some of the colluding sellers. If they accept, the cartel will be destroyed and the buyer can at some future date return to its earlier exploitive practices. Moreover, any buyer that buys in multiple input markets can refuse to deal for a period of time in the market where it faces organized resistance. Unless the producers have either alternative outlets or the financial capacity to withstand a significant lull in sales, their ability to resist will quickly collapse. The history of unionization in the United States provides illustrations of the weakness of such efforts absent strong governmental support. Indeed, the continued decline of unions in this country suggests the great challenges that collective action faces.

---

78 See Carstensen, *supra* note 66, at 32.

79 See *ibid* (citing an FTC study of grain markets).

80 In the case of the early grain cooperatives, a trading company on the Chicago Board of Trade provided support for the development of the cooperatives whose trades it then handled. See *ibid* at 29.

81 Capper-Volstead Act, 7 U.S.C. §§ 291–2 (2016).

82 Peter C Carstensen, 'Agricultural Cooperatives and the Law: Obsolete Statutes in a Dynamic Economy' (2013) 58 *South Dakota Law Review* 462.

83 See National Labor Relations Act, 29 U.S.C. §§ 151–69 (2016).

A study of West Bengal, India, vegetable farmers found that, as a group, they strongly preferred the existing wholesale market system over the proposed use of contracts.[84] But individually, each would be powerless to resist such a change and the resulting enhanced buyer power. The laws of West Bengal strongly supported the retention of the wholesale market system. This has resolved much of the collective action problem. But as major buyers become more active in the market, the question remains whether individual farmers looking at higher immediate prices will retain their loyalty to the current market system.

In American agriculture, there is no public wholesale market for chickens or turkeys. Instead, a poultry processer, or integrator, pays farmers to raise the flocks that the integrator owns by use of a 'tournament' system. The process compares the efficiency of all farmers whose flocks are delivered to a processing facility in a set time period and adds or subtracts from a base price based on the comparative efficiency of the producer. This allows the processor to retain a constant average cost of production and shifts the risks of lower quality birds, disease and other losses onto the farmers. Although this system has some efficiency justifications, it also allows the processor to shift a great many risks onto the farmers.[85] Hogs and cattle are also predominantly marketed through contract systems.[86] A number of independent feeders remain in both the hog and cattle sectors. Nevertheless, market prices usually provide the basis for most cattle and many hog contracts despite the thin and manipulable nature of those markets.

Farmers may recognize that it is in their collective interest to retain a strong transactional market, but individual operators face significant pressure to accept contracts.[87] For example, in the cattle industry, open market

---

[84] Cohen, *supra* note 25, at 62.

[85] For a fuller exposition of the problems that result from this system, see Leonard, *supra* note 8, at 105–06, 114–17, 120–25.

[86] Adjemian et al, *supra* note 19, at 18 (more than 90 percent of hogs and more than 70 percent of beef cattle are now sold using some form of forward contract).

[87] See Lynn Hunnicutt, DeeVon Bailey and Michelle Crook, 'Rigidity in Packer-Feedlot Relationships' (2004) 36 *Journal of Agricultural and Applied Economics* 627 (feed lots have a strong tendency to look to the same buyers over time). This author observed discussions among some major feeders several years ago, and the general view was that the price advantage from contracts would disappear if all feedlots had access to this option and that the cattle buyers would then abandon the system. Contractual discrimination allowed the buyers to obtain a substantial gain by price manipulation. See *Pickett v Tyson Fresh Meats, Inc.*, 420 F.3d 1272 (11th Cir. 2005) (despite significant price discrimination resulting in lower payment to those who sold on the public market, no violation of law found as to the buyer).

prices are consistently below contract prices.[88] Hence, a feedlot operator is better off with a contract even if the resulting prices are below that which a fully functional transactional market would have produced. In hogs, there is often a shortage of slaughter capacity. Contract hogs will have priority in such situations. Hence, hog raisers have an incentive to enter into contractual relationships that assure an outlet for their production.

The evolution of the American markets for poultry and livestock illustrate the process by which buying markets in which buyers are powerful and sellers dispersed and not well-organized move toward organizational structures that maximize the power of buyers and minimize the capacity of producers to develop alternative systems that would move market prices closer to a competitively optimal price.[89] These forces then work to reinforce and increase buyer power over time. Absent very self-conscious resistance by producers, these buyer interests will dominate the continuing evolution of these markets. The West Bengal example described earlier illustrates the importance of a political-economic response that limits the creation of undue buyer power. But the need for ongoing collective action by producers makes the long-run success of such responses tenuous.

On the demand side, the incentive structure also works against overcoming monopsony or buyer power. Buyers seeking entry must be able to offer a premium and a durable commitment in order to capture the commodity and remain in the market. Both considerations create barriers to entry.

Bidding up an input price will depress the margin that a buyer can get in the downstream market in which it sells its product. This follows even if the downstream market in which the potentially competing buyer sells is different in location or product from that in which the firm with buyer power sells. By definition, the new buyer is challenging a dominant buyer, which can retaliate by bidding up the price in the short run, making it even more costly for the entrant to compete. If the dominant buyer has locked up a share of the supply through long-term contracts with set prices, it can

---

[88] The more contract cattle taken in a week, the lower the demand for open market cattle, which in turn depresses the market price. That price also serves as the benchmark for contract prices. Thus, both prices are depressed but the contract price still exceeds the market price.

[89] The growth of Uber as a ride service provider offers an illustration. In San Antonio, Texas, there were a number of independent, upscale 'town car' service providers. Some of those owner-drivers signed onto Uber, but although they added more buyers, they lost their unique clientele. As a result, by 2016, they claimed that Uber controlled their access to their old customers and the pay that they could receive. See Alan Feuer, 'The Uber Drivers' Rebellion' *New York Times* (21 February 2016) at A26.

even more effectively bid up the price it will pay to other producers, still at less overall cost to itself, and force up the competing buyer's total costs.[90]

In addition, the entering buyer faces the problem of establishing its durability as a buyer. A producer that shifts its sales to the new entrant may have a hard time finding an outlet for its products if that entrant subsequently fails. Its former buyer, the dominant firm, may well choose to punish it by either refusing to buy at all or imposing onerous conditions. Because producer arbitrage is difficult, the incumbent, dominant buyer has the capacity to discipline any particular defecting producer.

Furthermore, established competing buyers have a similar incentive to avoid any conduct that raises input prices or shifts risks back to them, either of which would improve the terms of their transactions for producers. Hence, all buyers in the same market have a shared interest in avoiding price competition for inputs unless there is an acute shortage.[91]

IV. CONCLUSION: LOCATING AND OFFSETTING BUYER POWER

This chapter has discussed the definition and measurement of buyer power, analyzed buyer power in the input and branded goods markets, and identified factors that increase the power of buyers. It has also demonstrated the fallacy of the oft-repeated assertion that monopsony and buyer power are the mirror images of monopoly and seller power.

The analysis demonstrates the potential for buyer power whenever a producer has limited options for the sale of its output. Thus, buyer-market structure is a central consideration. In an assessment of buyer power in general input markets, the first point of inquiry should be the number of significant buyers. The fewer the number of potential buyers, the greater the power of those who are in the market. The second and related question is the number of producers serving the market, because buyer power is prevalent in situations in which producers significantly outnumber buyers.

---

[90] This was probably the factual situation in *Weyerhaeuser Co. v Ross-Simmons Hard-Wood Lumber Co.*, 549 U.S. 312 (2007). See Michael E Haglund, '*Weyerhaeuser*'s Aftermath: Increased Vulnerability of Resource-Based Input Markets to Monopsony' (2008) 53 *Antitrust Bulletin* 411 (in the various cases remanded as a result of the decision, plaintiffs obtained financial settlements, but the rule of the case may permit future harmful conduct).

[91] Empirical work on cattle buying shows that the price pattern is one of recurring interdependent prices despite the occasional period of short supply with relatively competitive prices. See Cai, Stiegert and Koontz, *supra* note 69.

In those cases, a buyer purchases its input from several producers, which increases the buyer's power over any one producer. In the case of branded products, the producer may be a substantial enterprise, but still dependent on a handful of major buyers. If there are reasonable numbers of both, then the risks of buyer power are reduced.

The extent of buyer power is also subject to the degree to which a producer is dependent on a particular buyer. Based on the observed cases, it appears that an input buyer that takes 20 percent or more of a producer's output in direct purchases has the potential to wield significant power over that producer. In the case of retailing, buyer power appears to arise at an even lower share of sales and even when conventional market analysis based on the seller-side experience would suggest that there should be little or no power. Thus producers of branded consumer goods face somewhat greater barriers to workable buyer competition than do producers of other kinds of inputs.[92]

As discussed in section I.B of this chapter, the loss of a significant share of sales volume has the potential to be catastrophic for a producer. Most production schedules are keyed to expected sales volume. Facilities, input commitments and employment are linked. This is particularly true when the facility is in whole or in part dedicated to the buyer's specific requirements. Moreover, if the capital structure of an enterprise includes substantial fixed costs for debt, its need for revenue may well remain unchanged.

In some situations the risks of buyer power can be offset. Again, as discussed in section I.B of this chapter, the elasticity of both supply and demand are important factors in this analysis. The more producers can either easily sell their products to other buyers or alter the mix of what they produce, the less the capacity of even a substantial buyer to exercise power over them.

A producer that supplies a substantial share of a buyer's requirements of an important input will have some countervailing bargaining power. If a buyer has limited alternative sources of supply, the producer's bargaining power will be even greater. This is more likely in input markets than in retailing—as noted earlier, a retailer combines a large number of products on its shelves and can usually offer generic or other branded alternatives.

---

[92] In some non-grocery product lines, such as appliances and electronics, internet sales opportunities may diminish the capacity of high-volume retailers to exercise power unless they have a more substantial market share. But as *Toys 'R' Us* and *Klor's, Inc. v Broadway-Hale Stores, Inc.*, 359 U.S. 207 (1959) (dominant appliance retailer allegedly induced suppliers to refuse to supply competitor of dominant buyer) illustrate, the market share necessary for buyer power is still significantly below that which is normally associated with seller-side market power.

Even so, some items are heavily promoted 'must-have' products that the retailer will want to carry, although it may be able to impose other burdens on an uncooperative supplier.

Some producers may be able to avoid undue buyer power under more limited circumstances, such as those that might, at low cost, be able to switch production at their facilities to another product line with a readily available market. This option is more likely to be available to input suppliers than to branded product producers.[93] Other producers might be able to reduce their production. As an example, when poultry integrators faced falling demand, they were able to cut production because of their own buyer power over the farmers that raised the poultry.[94] By reducing the number or size of the flocks, the integrators could reduce output at relatively low cost. As explained earlier, however, farmers with large fixed costs bore the brunt of this risk transfer.

Buyers of inputs do have a long-term interest in access to high-quality supplies. As long as a buyer takes the long view (the future casting a shadow over the present[95]), it has an incentive to treat suppliers reasonably.[96] But, of course, part of the long-run interest of buyers is the exclusion of competition. Therefore, their incentive to treat suppliers reasonably holds only as long as those suppliers assist in minimizing or eliminating the risks of entry or competition in the buyer's downstream

---

[93] Presumably, the alternative market yields lower revenue or is otherwise less attractive, or the producer would already have been active in it.

[94] See, eg, *Been v O.K. Indus., Inc.*, 398 Fed. App'x 382, 2010 WL 3995981 (10th Cir. 2010, unpublished) (upholding claims of loss resulting from reduction in the provision of poultry to growers).

[95] See Robert Axelrod, *The Evolution of Cooperation* (Basic Books, New York 1984) (showing that in reiterated prisoners' dilemma games, cooperation is preferable to betrayal so long as the players foresee that they will continue to interact in the future). For a discussion of this insight as it relates to antitrust see Peter C Carstensen, 'While Antitrust Was Out to Lunch: Lessons from the 1980s for the Next Century of Enforcement' (1995) 48 *SMU Law Review* 1881, 1886–93.

[96] See Adjemian et al, *supra* note 19 (arguing that even in markets with few buyers, farmers will be adequately compensated because of the buyer's long-run interest in a viable supply); John M Crespi, Tina L Saitone and Richard J Sexton, 'Competition in Farm Product Markets: Do Long-Run Incentives Trump Short-Run Market Power?' (2012) 34 *Applied Economics Perspectives and Policy* 669 (the authors contend that the long-run interest of buyers will keep them from exploiting suppliers). But see Harwood D Schaffer and Daryll E Ray, 'Which Will Increase the Most after the Brazilian Beef Agreement, Beef Exports or Imports?' (19 August 2016) 37 *Mid America Farmer Grower*, available at http://www.agpolicy.org/weekcol/837.html (a US-Brazilian agreement will increase imports more than exports and give American meat packers another source for cattle).

market. Moreover, when short-term economic needs dominate, a buyer may well use its power to exploit. That exploitation may in turn cause the producer to engage in upstream exploitation of its own vulnerable suppliers, especially if it has multiple suppliers of the same input who sell all or most of it to the producer.

The evidence so far suggests that if a producer is a large enterprise and one of only a few suppliers, the immediate effects of buyer power are likely to be limited. But the mutual need to exclude competition in both the upstream market (the producer's interest) and the downstream market (the buyer's interest) means that the market process is likely to be impaired and made more rigid with increased but avoidable barriers to entry. The usual market forces are unlikely to undo such power. The current state of empirical research does not provide much basis for a more precise description of when the offsetting power of buyers and sellers will result in a workably competitive market with no significant adverse upstream or downstream effects. Hence, generalizing from the examples on which the foregoing analysis rests is problematic. The better approach, given the demonstrable risks of undue buyer power demonstrated in those examples, is not to rely on the beneficence of powerful buyers but to identify durable market characteristics that will diminish or limit the incentives to cause adverse competitive effects despite apparently concentrated buying. In a market with those characteristics, the risk to the competitive process from buyer power would be limited. But only when competition authorities and scholars take the risks of buyer power more seriously and focus their attention on the buying side of the market will those characteristics become evident. Therefore, the creation, enhancement and exploitation of buyer power ought to be a major concern of competition authorities.

4. The potential competitive harms from the existence and abuse of buyer power

This chapter describes the potential adverse exclusionary and exploitive competitive effects of buyer power and examines the factors that make buyer power a durable threat to competition and a significant risk even at relatively low market shares. The contention here is that abuse of buyer power is as serious and arguably a more serious threat to the competitive process than is abuse of seller power or monopolization. The analysis also shows that, with respect to the abuse of buyer power, exploitation is a more serious risk than exclusion. The stage is then set for evaluating the different mechanisms by which competitive law and policy can try to limit or avoid these harmful effects.

These adverse effects should be balanced against the potential of buyer power to facilitate a positive aspect of competitive markets—the buyer's vigorous search for better prices and products. Price discrimination, for example, when a buyer pays different sellers different prices for similar goods, can be harmful to competition, but it also reflects the flexibility and ongoing adjustment to changes in supply and demand that are central to the effective functioning of the market. This dichotomy, as discussed in Chapters 5 and 6, means that workable remedies to alleviate the harm of unilateral abuse of buyer power ought not disrupt the competitive process itself.

I. EXPLOITATION OF PRODUCERS

Seller exploitation of producers leads to two types of harm: (1) harm to a producer's other customers; and (2) harm to the producer itself. Therefore, the harmful effects can, and often do, impact third parties as much as the initial victim.

A. Prices Below the Competitive Market Price

Buyers exercise their market power most directly by driving the price paid to a producer to a point below the level that would prevail in a competitive market. As shown in Chapter 3, the effect is reduced income to the producer and, based on the standard economic model of monopsony, reduced total economic output. This has two direct adverse effects on the competitive process. First, those producers remaining in the market will produce at a less than optimal level, which reduces their incentive to invest in improved production and encourages market exit over time as fixed investments are consumed and not replaced. Second, at the margin, suppliers that 'ought' to have entered or remained in the market are excluded from it. At best, the assets and employees of those firms are transferred to competitively less desirable uses and aggregate economic welfare decreases.

Buyers may be able to both retain the same level of inputs and exploit suppliers with lower prices. First, if the buyer can buy in two markets—one a competitive supply market and one in which it has monopsony power—it can reduce the price it pays in the market it controls and expand its purchases in the competitive market, thereby gaining monopsony profits without reducing its total purchases and consequent sales volume. Using a dual input price system, the buyer will be able to engage in overt price discrimination against the producers in the monopsony market.[1] This discrimination disfavors the efficient producer in the monopsony market and substitutes purchases from a less efficient producer in the competitive market. This distortion of the incentives for growth and investment among producers in both markets is harmful to the competitive process.

Second, a buyer may be able to use an all-or-nothing strategy to insist on output comparable to that which would occur in competition, while forcing down the price paid to the supplier.[2] Buyers in both input and retail markets can employ this strategy. In the case of inputs, all-or-nothing contracts are a common feature of many American livestock and

---

[1] This pattern describes the market for hogs in the United States, where there is a competitive market in the Midwest but an oligopsony that has become, essentially, a monopsony in the Southeast. A firm buying in both regions can exploit suppliers in the Southeast, even if this results in suboptimal production, while retaining its total input volume by increasing purchases in the competitive Midwest market.

[2] See Chapter 3, text accompanying notes 5–7, for a fuller explanation of the all-or-nothing contract.

all commercial poultry buying arrangements.[3] In retail markets, a buyer can force a seller to reduce its price in order to retain volume and access to shelf space.

But even if there were no immediate distortions to downstream competition, the implications for the dynamics of the producers' market are negative. The all-or-nothing contract penalizes the efficient producer thereby eliminating the incentive to operate efficiently. The buyer may then impose additional requirements in order to compel efficient conduct. This increases transaction costs, which is itself an inefficiency. Moreover, and of even greater long-run concern, the inability to capture gains from innovative contributions to efficiency in production creates a disincentive to enter, expand or innovate within the production sector. If there are substantial sunk costs in specialized assets, however, the producers may remain in place for a long period of time. This is even more likely if a government loan-guarantee program meant lenders did not critically evaluate risks.[4] Eventually exploited producers will exit and not be replaced, leading buyers to look to other sources of inputs—often second- or third-best sources.

If a major buyer imposes prices that are below average total cost, the producer must recover the lost revenue somehow to survive.[5] Thus,

---

[3] Poultry raising contracts tie farmers to an exclusive buyer. The buyer determines how many chickens it will place with the farmer. The quantity will vary depending on the buyer's needs. Hence, it has the ability to vary its output without incurring higher or lower unit prices, shifting the risk of changing demand to the producers. See, eg, *Been v O.K. Indus., Inc.*, 398 Fed. App'x 382, 2010 WL 3995981 (10th Cir. 2010, unpublished) (buyer shifted risk of decreased demand to its growers by decreasing the number of flocks provided, causing growers significant economic harm). See generally Randi Ilyse Roth, 'Redressing Unfairness in the New Agricultural Labor Arrangements: An Overview of Litigation Seeking Remedies for Contract Poultry Growers' (1994–95) 25 *University of Memphis Law Review* 1207.

[4] In the case of poultry, integrators have worked to bring in new groups of farmers, including recent immigrants, such as Laotian refugees. Christopher Leonard, *The Meat Racket* (Simon and Schuster, New York 2014) 45–6, 113–39. Moreover, the United States Department of Agriculture has provided guarantees to the banks that lend money to these and other farmers to buy, build or renovate chicken houses without any review of the risks of failure that these loans create. Hence, the important market process of risk assessment that should constrain risk transfers did not work. *Ibid* at 141–5.

[5] A producer with relatively high fixed costs may receive prices above its average variable cost but below its average total cost, which will eventually cause it to fail. But if the fixed investments consist of sunk costs (that is, facilities that have no other use), the producer is likely to stay in production for an extended period of time.

logically, such a producer may seek to exploit further its suppliers, or if it supplies more than one customer, it may raise prices to its less powerful buyers to cover its costs. This is the so-called waterbed effect.[6] The disfavored buyers facing input costs that are higher than those imposed on the favored buyer are at a competitive disadvantage if they compete directly with the favored buyer and are denied the advantage of lower cost goods if they compete in some other market. Any of these results will distort the overall competitive market process and over time are likely to reduce total demand for the input produced in the affected market.

There is, however, an important counterargument in favor of buyer power in the context of price. Powerful buyers can disrupt seller power that is either collusive or unilateral, moving concentrated seller markets toward greater competitiveness. A large retailer can use buyer power to break a producer cartel by threatening to reduce or eliminate its support (in the forms of advertising and shelf location for example) for the branded good unless it gets price concessions. Price concessions to one buyer can then spread both directly, as other substantial buyers demand similar treatment, and indirectly, as competing producers respond with price cuts of their own.[7] If either tacit collusion or monopolistic competition in the upstream branded goods market results in above-cost pricing, the power of buyers to insist on selective price cuts or other limits on pricing power may undermine and limit the producer's anticompetitive conduct.[8]

A positive competitive process outcome requires that the successful buyer pass on at least some of the reduced price to the next level of consumer.[9] Price cutting disadvantages the direct competitors of the favored

---

[6] See Paul W Dobson and Roman Inderst, 'The Waterbed Effect: Where Buying and Selling Power Come Together' 2008 *Wisconsin Law Review* 331. See also Chapter 3, text accompanying note 15, for further discussion of the waterbed effect.

[7] See John Kirkwood, 'The Robinson-Patman Act and Consumer Welfare: Has Volvo Reconciled Them?' (2007) 30 *Seattle University Law Review* 349.

[8] Some economists are skeptical that increased buyer power will have these positive effects. See Dennis W Carlton, Mary Coleman and Mark Israel, 'Buyer Power in Merger Review', in Roger D Blaire and D Daniel Sokol (eds), *Oxford Handbook of International Antitrust Economics* (Oxford University Press, Oxford 2015) 529, 540–1.

[9] A buyer with downstream seller power and a producer with upstream buyer power will engage in a bilateral negotiation seeking optimal monopoly and monopsony prices with an allocation of the resulting supranormal profits between the two levels. There is some evidence that this has happened in the New England fluid milk market. See *Monopsony Issues in Agriculture: Buying Power of Processors in Our Nation's Agricultural Markets, Hearing before the S. Comm. on the Judiciary*, 108th Congress (2003), available at http://www.fmpc.uconn.edu/

buyer. In theory, those competitors in the downstream market then have an incentive to put pressure on their suppliers to reduce prices, leading to a general price reduction that gets passed on to the next level of consumer. To be plausible, this scenario requires that the other buyers take a high enough volume of the same goods to make credible demands on the producer. If that is not the case, the favored buyer has lower input costs while its competitors face the higher oligopoly or monopoly price.[10] This is also a form of the waterbed effect.

Buyers can use all-or-nothing contracts to force down prices by threatening to take nothing and potentially creating a major hole in suppliers' expected sales. These contracts can also provide a way of dealing with the risk of 'double marginalization' that arises when a downstream monopolist buys from an upstream monopsonist.[11] If the seller imposes a full monopoly charge on the buyer who then imposes its own monopoly charge before reselling the product, the monopoly overcharge would be doubled and substantially reduce total demand by inflating the price of the final good beyond the optimal monopoly price.

This model, therefore, assumes a great deal of myopia on the part of both the buyer and the seller. Indeed, observation suggests that the results of such dealings are likely to be prices somewhat below the optimal monopoly price rather than above it.[12] The real business problem is to split the potential monopoly profits between the two levels in some acceptable way.[13] One way to avoid the problem is to use a contract technique that requires more or less set production and purchases at, or even slightly greater than, the optimal monopoly production level. Other contracting

---

research/milk/Testimony103003.pdf (submission of Ronald W Cotterill, Adam N Rabinowitz and Li Tian, 'Milk Market Channel Structure: Its Impact on Farmers and Consumers, and the Inadequacies of Antitrust Enforcement as a Foundation for Dairy Policies: Evidence from the Northeast Dairy Industry').

[10] As discussed in Chapter 7, one potential response by smaller buyers is to pool their purchases and to create collective buying power. Although potentially solving the price discrimination problem, buying groups may create new upstream and downstream competitive risks.

[11] See Roger D Blair and Jeffrey L Harrison, *Monopsony in Law and Economics* (Cambridge University Press, Cambridge 2010) 123–45.

[12] See, eg, Richard Friedman, 'Antitrust Analysis and Bilateral Monopoly' 1986 *Wisconsin Law Review* 873, 910.

[13] This point is frequently made by economists and some sophisticated legal observers. See, eg, *ibid*; Roger D Blair, David L Kaserman and Richard E Romano, 'A Pedagogical Treatment of Bilateral Monopoly' (1989) 55 *Southern Economic Journal* 831. See also Jonathan B Baker, Joseph Farrell and Carl Shapiro, 'Merger to Monopoly to Serve a Single Buyer: Comment' (2008) 75 *Antitrust Law Journal* 637; Blair and Harrison, *supra* note 11 (providing economic models of pricing).

strategies also exist to deal with the problem. From the perspective of this discussion, in any such case both the buyer and the seller would have substantial power in their respective markets. This yields net negative results for the competitive process and for consumer welfare. The resulting price and quantity reflect a joint effort to achieve an optimal monopoly outcome rather than the competitive one.

One econometric study found that the primary impact of horizontal mergers was a reduction in the price of inputs.[14] In part, buying larger volumes may reduce transaction costs and create economies of scale. But it is also probable that a volume buyer has the capacity to bargain for better prices. Producers, on the other hand, have no initial incentive to give discounts across the board. Such price discrimination can further marginalize smaller firms and reinforce downstream concentration, which then has a further feedback effect on supply markets.

But if competition or other law required uniform pricing, producers, especially large ones, would be more inclined to resist demands for discounts, even when they were cost-justified. Moreover, if the upstream supply market is at all oligopolistic, a required uniform price would facilitate tacit collusion. Also, large buyers would have greater assurance that their competitors faced the same prices. Such input price stability could further facilitate tacit overcharges in oligopolistic downstream markets.

In sum, when buyer power is used to leverage lower prices from suppliers, the results of any analysis of the likely effects on the competitive process will be ambiguous. Moreover, it is difficult to categorize any given price as being inherently desirable or undesirable. The evaluation is context-specific. In general, however, as buyer power increases, the risk that a buyer will exploit that power also increases. Consequently, one can, as a general rule, conclude that if the buying side of the market is workably competitive and producers have alternative sources of demand, the risk of highly abusive ad hoc uses of power to drive down prices below a competitive level will be constrained.

B. Seller Access

A second harmful use of buyer power, which is common in agricultural and retail markets, but observed in many other markets, is discriminatory

---

[14] C Edward Fee and Thomas Shawn, 'Sources of Gains in Horizontal Mergers: Evidence from Customer, Supplier, and Rival Firms' (2004) 74 *Journal of Financial Economics* 423; see also Sugato Bhattacharyya and Amrita Nain, 'Horizontal Acquisitions and Buying Power: A Product Market Analysis' (2011) 99 *Journal of Financial Economics* 97.

or total denial of access to the buying market. The buyer can privilege one set of suppliers and exploit another set if it has sufficient buyer power.[15] This power is pervasive because, as Chapter 3 demonstrated, arbitrage is harder to accomplish on the supply side. Except in public commodity markets, buyers deal directly with sellers and can impose different requirements on each without much risk of the disfavored seller being able to get access to the favored seller's option.

In the American beef market, buyers exercise discretion as to whom they will buy from, and favored feeders get contracts that provide them with a price advantage over the open market price. Disfavored feeders do not. In *Pickett v Tyson's Fresh Meats,*[16] plaintiffs proved that the disfavored producers received consistently lower prices.[17] Thus, variable levels of supplier access to contracts resulted in significant price discrimination. Other forms of selective exploitation or exclusion exist in poultry and other agricultural commodity contracts.[18] The all-or-nothing contract also facilitates this kind of access limitation. The input seller has to accept exclusive dealing and cannot shop its services to other buyers. Moreover, the incumbent buyer can use the offer of access, as well as the capacity to exclude, to enforce its all-or-nothing demands as well as to extract price concessions.

The core of the access issue in input markets is that the buyer has the

---

[15] For example, in 2014, YouTube's subscription music service paid much lower rates to independent record labels than to major labels such as Universal, Sony and Warner. Ben Sisario, 'Independent Record Labels Waging a Battle with YouTube' *New York Times* (16 May 2014) at B6.

[16] *Pickett v Tyson Fresh Meats, Inc.*, 420 F.3d 1272 (11th Cir. 2005) (independent feeders challenged the practices of major cattle buyers as discriminatory under the Packers and Stockyards Act, 7 U.S.C. §§ 181–229b (2016), but the court rejected the claim, despite proof of a substantial adverse effect, because the buyers had a 'legitimate' business reason to use the contracts and the potential for less harmful contractual processes was not relevant).

[17] C Robert Taylor, 'Proving Anti-Competitive Conduct in the U.S. Courtroom: Economic Issues with the Courts' Opinions in *Pickett v Tyson Fresh Meats, Inc.*' (2006) 4 *Journal of Agricultural and Food Industrial Organization* 9.

[18] See Roth, *supra* note 3; Neil D Hamilton, 'Broiler Contracting in the United States—A Current Contract Analysis Addressing Legal Issues and Grower Concerns' (2002) 7 *Drake Journal of Agricultural Law* 43; Glenn A Hegar, Jr, 'Adhesion Contracts, Debt, Low Returns and Frustration—Can America's Independent Contract Farmer Overcome the Odds?' (1998) 22 *Hamline Law Review* 213; see also *Been v O.K. Indus., Inc.*, 398 Fed. App'x. 382, 2010 WL 3995981 (10th Cir. 2010, unpublished) (buyer shifted risk of decreased demand to its growers by decreasing the number of flocks provided, causing growers significant economic harm).

discretion to buy or not buy from any particular supplier. When there are few buyers, and especially if a buyer will take a substantial part of the total production of an individual producer, the power of selection is very significant. As noted earlier, even though public commodity markets might provide equally efficient sources of inputs, buyers are likely to favor direct purchases because of the discretionary power such relationships create. In the case of cattle, meat packers vigorously resisted a proposal that would have required them to make an open offer for future delivery of cattle meeting their specifications.[19]

The harm to competition stems not from contracting itself but from the power of the buyer to impose unfair and unreasonable contract terms, as well as to discriminate unfairly between producers. Reasonable contracts can be an effective means of allocating risk and providing guarantees for long-term investments. Thus, a long-term poultry contract guaranteeing a reasonable volume and minimum price for chickens over a period of years would provide the kind of protection a rational lender would expect absent a government loan guarantee.[20] More generally, in many circumstances contracts can provide more efficient outcomes than conventional commodity markets.[21] Wisconsin has a workably competitive market for vegetables to be used in commercial canning and freezing. In the 1990s, representatives of farmers and processors revised and updated the contracting process. The results were imbedded in a state administrative rule that constrains the discretion of all parties.[22] Moreover, affected farmers can look to the state to enforce these rules. But when buyers are few and producers have limited alternatives, contracting can create substantial dependency and the opportunity for exploitation.

In retailing, the same access problem arises when retailers refuse to carry competing product lines. In the Beechnut-Heinz merger case, for

---

[19] See Western Organization of Resource Councils, 'Petition for Rule-making on Captive Supply Procurement Practices under the Packers and Stockyards Act' (8 October 1996), available at https://www.gipsa.usda.gov/psp/publication/worc_petition/petition.pdf.

[20] See Leonard, *supra* note 4, at 141–5 (discussing the long-term risks to chicken farmers and the role of government loan guarantees in eliminating lender surveillance of risk).

[21] Michael K Adjemian et al, 'Thinning Markets in U.S. Agriculture: What Are the Implications for Producers and Processors?' (Economic Information Bulletin No. 148, US Department of Agriculture Economic Research Service, 2016), available at http://www.ers.usda.gov/media/2030725/eib148.pdf. This report did not consider, however, whether reorganizing commodity markets could achieve comparable efficiency and avoid some of the risks of dependency arising from buyer power.

[22] Wisconsin Admin Code ATCP §§ 101.01–101.07 (2011).

example, the evidence showed that retailers would carry only one of those two brands as well as the dominant brand.[23] Although producers do not need to have their goods in every store in the country, when there is a dominant supplier in a category, sufficient access to retailers can be a difficult challenge for the remaining competitors.

A category captain may be able to use its status to limit or exclude its competitors.[24] Stocking fees and slotting allowances are also examples of buyer power that can result in significant foreclosure of smaller producers.[25] The large producer can buy access to a number of stores, arguably paying in part for the exclusion of its rivals. The small producer lacks the resources and the potential volume to justify paying for access to a large number of stores. The result is foreclosure of such producers from access to all of the retailer's stores. This foreclosure primarily affects competitors of the favored supplier, but their existence stems from the retailer's buyer power.

The risk to the competitive process, however, of restricting a buyer's discretion to select its supplier is market system rigidity. If a seller has some guarantee that the buyer must take its goods, its incentives to pursue efficient production and quality may be impaired, especially if the buyer is unable to switch to better options. Thus, the assessment of the merits of refusals to deal is necessarily situation-specific.

C. Market Information Distortion

Another competitive risk in some input markets involves the insistence on confidentiality for contracts and other agreements as well as restricted and distorted information disclosure. Buyers often seek to treat their contracts as confidential so that producers are unable to compare their relative treatment or ascertain the contract terms offered to competing

---

23 *FTC v H.J. Heinz Co.*, 246 F.3d 708, 718 (D.C. Cir. 2001).

24 See Chapter 3, text accompanying notes 50–51, for an explanation of category captains. See also Debra M Desrochers, Gregory T Gundlach and Albert A Foer, 'Analysis of Antitrust Challenges to Category Captain Arrangements' (2003) 22 *Journal of Public Policy and Marketing* 201; *Conwood Co. v United States Tobacco Co.*, 290 F.3d 768 (6th Cir. 2002) (upholding a $1 billion judgment against the monopolist of chewing tobacco that had used its position as category captain to exclude its smaller rival).

25 But see Joshua Wright, 'Slotting Contracts and Consumer Welfare' (2007) 74 *Antitrust Law Journal* 439 (arguing for the desirability of such contracts); see also Federal Trade Commission (2003), 'Slotting Allowances in the Retail Grocery Industry: Selected Case Studies in Five Product Categories', available at http://www.ftc.gov/os/2003/11/slottingallowancerpt031114.pdf.

suppliers.[26] This increases the buyer's ability to impose differential and discriminatory terms.

The reasons for confidentiality include claims that the buyer wants to avoid collusion among buyers or sellers and that the exact terms are confidential business information. But the primary effect of confidentiality is to deny producers access to important information about their treatment relative to others. Even faced with a monopsonist, a producer might have an incentive to bargain for favorable terms it knew other sellers were getting. Alternatively, a seller that realizes it is disfavored might exit the market, even though exit is likely to be costly. Restricting suppliers' access to information is one of the factors leading to market failure and market power, even if several competitors exist in the market, as highlighted, in different ways, by Lande and Sandford.[27]

A second manipulative device that aids discrimination in input markets is a buyer's possession of substantial but undisclosed information about its short-term demand for inputs. This problem occurred when the US Department of Agriculture introduced a reporting system on cattle prices that contained a consistent error on prices. Buyers recognized the error but did nothing to correct it because it enabled them to negotiate favorable prices in their purchase contracts. When the error was finally revealed, the buyers faced no liability for their misleading conduct because the court held that the law regulating the market did not prohibit such exploitation.[28]

Kraft's manipulation of cheese prices[29] led to potential liability to

---

[26] The opposite is true in public commodity markets where prices and other terms must be disclosed.

[27] See Robert Lande, 'Market Power Without a Large Market Share: The Role of Imperfect Information and Other "Consumer Protection" Market Failures' (American Antitrust Institute, Working Paper No. 07-06, 2007) (market failures of various kinds confer power on sellers); and Jeremy Sandford, 'Competition and Endogenous Impatience in Credence-Good Markets' (2013) 169 *Journal of Institutional and Theoretical Economics* 531 (when quality of goods is not obvious, producers will have greater incentive to enhance quality if consumers have more options to choose from).

[28] The Eighth Circuit held that the buyers' exploitation of the incorrect pricing information did not violate the Packers and Stockyards Act, 7 U.S.C. §§ 181–229b (2016), because the buyers did not 'intend' to exploit the sellers. *Schumacher v Cargill Meat Solutions Corp.*, 515 F.3d 867, 872 (8th Cir. 2008). The decision held that the law required specific intent rather than the broader and customary use in such statutes of general intent—the awareness of the consequences of one's actions (here paying a price based on price reports known to be false). See *United States v U.S. Gypsum Co.*, 438 U.S. 422 (1978) (general intent is sufficient for antirust criminal liability).

[29] See *infra* text accompanying notes 51–2 for the details of this conduct.

California dairy farmers under California law,[30] but Wisconsin's courts found no liability by invoking an expansive definition of the filed rate doctrine.[31] In 2015, the Commodity Futures Trading Commission charged Kraft with manipulating the price of wheat futures to drive down its input costs.[32]

These cases highlight how the legal system can create incentives that encourage anticompetitive price manipulation by buyers. If the buyer faces no liability for its strategic conduct, there is no economically rational reason not to pursue it. In United States livestock and milk markets, important decisions have effectively legalized price manipulation. By insulating such conduct from liability, the courts increase the probability that large buyers will engage in price manipulation. So far, courts have not recognized the incentive effects of their decisions.[33]

There are, however, dangers in disclosing detailed, contemporaneous market information in concentrated markets. Such information can result in tacit coordination among buyers on prices. For the reasons set forth in Chapter 7, there is a basis for concern that tacit collusion based on information disclosure can be more pervasive on the buying side of the market because of the nature of buyers' incentives. Solving the information problem has benefits in some circumstances, but may be counterproductive in others.

---

30 *Knevelbaard Dairies v Kraft Foods, Inc.*, 232 F.3d 979 (9th Cir. 2000).

31 *Servais v Kraft Foods Group, Inc.*, 2001 WI App 165, aff'd by an equally divided court, 252 Wis. 2d 145, 643 N.W.2d 92 (2002). The appeals court, despite noting several times that the federal milk order prices were minimum prices and did not set prices of the sort called for by conventional filed rate doctrine, nonetheless held the prices to be 'filed rates' under Wisconsin antitrust law. Therefore, plaintiffs could not predicate their claim for damages on the difference between what they were paid and what they would have been paid had the defendants not manipulated cheese prices, with the consequent effect on the price paid for milk. One federal court has reached a contrary result holding that milk order prices are not 'filed rates' under federal antitrust law. *Ice Cream Liquidation, Inc. v Land O'Lakes, Inc.*, 253 F. Supp. 2d 262 (D. Conn. 2003).

32 Complaint, *U.S. Commodity Futures Trading Comm'n v Kraft Foods Group*, CA No. 15-2881 (N.D. Ill. 2015), available at http://www.cftc.gov/idc/groups/public/@lrenforcementactions/documents/legalpleading/enfkraftcomplaint040115.pdf. See also Press Release, Commodity Futures Trading Comm'n, 'CFTC Charges Kraft Foods Group, Inc. and Mondelēz Global LLC with Manipulation of Wheat Futures and Cash Wheat Prices' (1 April 2015), available at http://www.cftc.gov/PressRoom/PressReleases/pr7150-15.

33 *Cf* Benedict Carey, 'Study Links Punishment with an Ability to Profit' *New York Times* (7 April 2006) at A22 (punishment of those who violate group norms is a factor in allowing groups to be profitable and economically efficient).

D. Buyer Incentives to Coordinate Locations

Input buyers have an incentive to engage in geographic differentiation whenever there are substantial transportation costs associated with a costly input. By locating at a distance from the next comparable buyer or by acquiring the most proximate competing facilities, a buyer will have much greater power over its suppliers. In poultry, for example, the pattern of new plant development in the United States has increasingly created a geographic separation among buyers that reduces the capacity of farmers to seek alternative outlets for their services.[34] In a broad sense, there is tacit collusion among buyers to allocate geographic markets, giving each a position of dominance within its territory.

This dominance, combined with the capacity to discriminate among producers, creates a substantial barrier to entry to new competitors seeking to obtain the same costly input. An entrant's potential suppliers can be diverted one by one to an incumbent that does not have to pay all its suppliers the enhanced prices it pays each target.[35] Once regional allocation exists, the resulting capacity to discriminate makes it very difficult to move the market for inputs toward a more competitive outcome.[36] Any rational buyer would look for a different geographic location in which to open its business. Thus, inherent barriers to entry make it difficult to break up established regional buyer power.

The American pork industry illustrates both sides of this process. Two major processors dominated the American Southeast. Smithfield developed that region and faced only one major competitor. No other entry occurred despite the fact that the region had a very large capacity to

---

[34] Leonard points out that Tyson was very active in acquiring regional chicken processing operations in areas where it already had operations. Leonard, *supra* note 4, at 81–111, 174–7.

[35] Thus, the Supreme Court got the substantive analysis wrong in *Cargill, Inc. v Monfort of Colo., Inc.*, 479 U.S. 104 (1986). The Court rejected as implausible Monfort's challenge to a merger of beef packers that resulted in a multimarket buyer overlapping Monfort's primary operation in Greeley. Monfort's claim was that the merger would result in the strong potential for a supply squeeze. Having lost the case, Monfort quickly sold out to another multimarket processor rather than remain vulnerable to the exclusionary tactics available to its direct competitor in buying cattle. *Cf* Keith Hylton, 'Weyerhaeuser, Predatory Bidding, and Error Costs' (2008) 53 *Antitrust Bulletin* 51 (such squeezes are rational ways to create monopsony power even though the author concludes that the risks of error are such that very restrictive standards should apply to claims of overbidding).

[36] The basic model from which policy is derived assumes uniform prices for inputs, but as the analysis in Chapter 3 and empirical evidence demonstrate, buyers can often offer different prices to different suppliers.

produce hogs. Smithfield ultimately acquired its only regional competitor, reducing even more the options for any producer in the region.[37] It is plausible that no other processor will attempt to make entry in that region.

In contrast, in the Midwest (consisting of Iowa, Minnesota, Missouri, Illinois, Indiana, Michigan, Ohio, South Dakota and Nebraska), there are a number of competing pork processors. There has also been entry in this region and the establishment of new facilities.[38] Incumbent buyers will be less able to target even those producers that plan to deal only with the entrant, because any increase in price is likely to create a competitive war among the remaining buyers. The existence of multiple buyers also makes entry easier on the supply side, which in turn, of course, stimulates further entry on the buyer side. In contrast, regional specialization among competing producers leads to exploitation of producers and labor by the buyer.[39]

For retailers, regional diversification may be an important buyer strategy. By operating in multiple markets with a significant market share, the retailer makes itself into an increasingly important outlet for producers

---

[37] A major empirical study of the American pork industry found that, prior to this merger, buyers had substantial buying power and that this power increased as concentration increased. GIPSA Livestock and Meat Marketing Study, Vol. 4: 'Hog and Pork Industries: Final Report' (2007), available at https://www.gipsa.usda.gov/psp/publication/livemarketstudy/LMMS_Vol_4.pdf. The Antitrust Division apparently ignored this data in approving Smithfield's acquisition. However, the statement of the Antitrust Division justifying its refusal to sue claimed that sellers retain substantial options and the merged firm would not have substantially increased buyer power. See Press Release, US Department of Justice, 'Statement of the Department of Justice Antitrust Division on its Decision to Close its Investigation of Smithfield's Acquisition of Premium Standard Farms Inc' (7 May 2007), available at https://www.justice.gov/archive/atr/public/press_releases/2007/223077.pdf.

[38] See, eg, Press Release, Cooper Farms, 'Cooper Farms Joins Eight Hog Farms and Clements Food Group to Build Fresh Pork Processing Plant in Michigan' (2016), available at http://www.cooperfarms.com/OurCompany/MediaCenter/News/tabid/147/ArticleId/100/COOPER-FARMS-JOINS-EIGHT-HOG-FARMS-AND-CLEMENS-FOOD-GROUP-TO-BUILD-FRESH-PORK-PROCESSING-PLANT-IN-MI.aspx; 'Huge New Pork Processing Plant Planned for Iowa' *Wisconsin Agriculturalist* (15 May 2015), available at http://farmprogress.com/story-huge-new-pork-processing-plant-planned-iowa-9-127838; 'Big Pork Processing Plant Planned for Mason City', *Wallaces Farmer* (25 March 2016), available at http://farmprogress.com/story-big-pork-processing-plant-planned-mason-city-9-139258.

[39] See Leonard, *supra* note 4, at 314–18 (data on counties with major Tyson facilities showed slower growth than counties without such facilities); see also Northwest Arkansas Workers' Justice Center (2016), 'Wages and Working Conditions in Arkansas Poultry Plants', available at http://nwawjc.org/poultry-report/.

of branded consumer goods. Loss of a major retailer requires a producer to assemble a more dispersed set of replacement outlets to maintain its volume of sales and get full advantage of any national advertising. The potential increase in buyer power resulting from the combination of retailers in different regions is a consideration that has rarely been recognized in retail merger analysis to date.

These location-dependent buyer strategies underscore the point that different buyers will take account of different considerations in deciding where to locate. Moreover, those considerations are quite distinct from the locational factors considered by sellers. Ultimately, the choice of location has to balance both buying and selling considerations.

E. Risk and Cost Transfers

Detailed UK buyer behavior studies appear to show that, in addition to bargaining over price, dominant buyers can impose on producers a variety of other burdens that transfer costs from the retailer to the producer without adding to the producer's compensation.[40] In one example, a buyer required a producer to make payments to it, including one for £100,000, which the producer did without complaining 'for fear of "upsetting the relationship".'[41] Additionally, producers had to do some or all of the stocking and provide other related inventory services.[42] These activities may enhance efficiency, but without compensation, they drive up the costs of the producer and reduce the operating expenses of the buyer-retailer. As a result the retailer has both lowered its own operating costs and forced the producer to absorb an increase in its costs without a commensurate increase in income.

A study of Walmart showed that it imposed major costs on its suppliers by forcing them to change their methods of coding products. Walmart saved millions of dollars, but its suppliers paid all the costs.[43] Moreover, those suppliers unable or unwilling to make Walmart's 'suggested

---

40 See Competition Commissionn (UK) (2000), 'Supermarkets: A report on the Supply of Groceries from Multiple Stores in the United Kingdom' [hereinafter 'Supermarkets'], available at http://webarchive.nationalarchives.gov.uk/20140402141250/http://www.competition-commission.org.uk/rep_pub/reports/2000/fulltext/446c11.pdf.

41 *Ibid* at 234.

42 See Paul Dobson, 'Exploiting Buyer Power: Lessons from the British Grocery Trade' (2006) 72 *Antitrust Law Journal* 529, 558–9 (summarizing 52 practices found in 'Supermarkets', *supra* note 40).

43 See Wenonah Hauter, *Foodopoly* (The New Press, New York 2012) 70–1.

improvements' paid penalties in the form of reduced payments for their products. Similar practices occur in Japan, where powerful buyers have been sanctioned for imposing a variety of undue burdens on their suppliers.[44] Australia's competition authority has challenged similar risk shifting as 'unconscionable' conduct.[45]

Some buyers defer paying their suppliers, which is the equivalent of forcing the supplier to make a loan to the buyer. In 2015, there were reports that some major food processors were delaying payments to their suppliers for up to 120 days after receiving goods.[46] The buyer gets the advantage of an interest-free loan for the period of the delay, while the producer must directly or indirectly cover the cost of the deferred compensation.

F. Buyer-induced Bundling

Buyers can also bundle their input purchases in ways that both yield pecuniary gains to them and harm the competitive process overall. For example, by insisting on bundling inputs subject to a high level of competition with those over which the producer has significant market power, the buyer may be able to negotiate a favorable price for the package. Certainly, this strategy occurs when sellers have power in some markets

---

[44] During 2013, Japan's Fair Trade Commission imposed one cease and desist order and issued 58 warnings concerning 'abuse of a superior bargaining position'. See Japan Fair Trade Commission, 'Enforcement of the Antimonopoly Act in FY2013 (Summary)', available at http://www.jftc.go.jp/en/pressreleases/yearly-2014/may/AMAinFY2013_Summary.html. For a summary of the cases, see Masako Wakui and Thomas K Cheng, 'Regulation Abuse of Superior Bargaining Position under the Japanese Competition Law: An Anomaly or a Necessity?' (2015) 3 *Journal of Antitrust Enforcement* 302.

[45] See Peter Strong, 'Unconscionable Behavior Demonstrates Need for Cultural Change' *Newdaily* (22 December 2014), http://thenewdaily.com.au/money/2014/12/22/supermarket-chains-must-change-culture/. See also Press Release, Australian Competition and Consumer Commission, 'Court Finds Coles Engaged in Unconscionable Conduct and Orders Coles Pay $10 Million Penalties' (22 December 2014), available at https://www.accc.gov.au/media-release/court-finds-coles-engaged-in-unconscionable-conduct-and-orders-coles-pay-10-million-penalties.

[46] Stephanie Strom, 'Giant Food Companies Pay Later, Squeezing Their Suppliers' *New York Times* (8 April 2015) at B-1. Similarly, Boeing has extended its payment schedule from 30 to 120 days. See Alwyn Scott and Tim Hepher, 'Boeing Slows Payments to Suppliers as It Accelerates Cost Cutting' *Reuters* (7 July 2016), available at http://www.reuters.com/article/us-boeing-suppliers-idUSKCN0ZN1GG.

but not in others.[47] Similar conduct by major buyers and buying groups has been observed in the purchase of hospital supplies.[48]

Bundling denies suppliers that operate only in the competitive input market the opportunity to make sales. This creates a further barrier to effective competition in specific product markets and can entrench the dominant multi-product upstream producer. Despite the possibility of increased seller power, powerful buyers may favor this system because it can stabilize the upstream market and reduce the risk that a competitive input source will disrupt tacitly collusive downstream competition. This is especially true if the downstream market has inelastic demand and informational or other asymmetries that result in prices above current costs. Limiting entry into the upstream input market would serve the interests of downstream buyers because it would reduce the risk of price or product competition.

G. Upstream Effects—Passing on Buyer Power Pressure

A secondary effect that harms the market process, but which is not usually included among the panoply of competitive effects in competition analysis, is the distortion of the overall economy that results from the reduction in income to the exploited producer. When its revenue declines, a producer will have less to spend. Even if the loss re-emerges as a gain elsewhere in the economy, the exploited producer will buy less. Sellers of goods and services to these producers will have lower sales volumes. This in turn will result in less employment for workers in those businesses at those locations. There are recurring examples of these deleterious consequences. The exploitation of cocoa, coffee and banana producers results in malnutrition, exploitation of child labor and general impoverishment.[49] Buyer power drives prevailing market prices in the garment

---

[47] See, eg, *LePage's Inc. v 3M*, 324 F.3d 141, 156 (3rd Cir. 2003).

[48] See, eg, Einer Elhauge (25 June 2002), 'The Exclusion of Competition for Hospital Sales Through Group Purchasing Organizations', available at http://www.law.harvard.edu/faculty/elhauge/pdf/gpo_report_june_02.pdf; Mary Williams Walsh, 'New Scrutiny Directed at Bundled Sale of Hospital Supplies' *New York Times* (17 July 2003), available at http://www.nytimes.com/2003/07/17/business/new-scrutiny-directed-at-bundled-sale-of-hospital-supplies.html.

[49] See, eg, Bananalink, 'The Problem with Bananas', available at http://www.bananalink.org.uk/the-problem-with-bananas (last visited 10 March 2016); UN Conference on Trade and Development (2008), 'Cocoa Study: Industry Structures and Competition', available at http://unctad.org/en/Docs/ditccom20081_en.pdf. See generally Agricultural Accountability Initiative, 'Power Buyers, Power Sellers: How Supermarkets Impact Farmers, Workers and Consumers—And How We

industry to suboptimal levels, resulting in terrible working conditions and exploitatively low wages in the countries where such production occurs.[50] The fact that American or European consumers may get slightly less expensive food or clothing, assuming some of the underpayment is passed on to them (that is, global aggregate welfare is arguably unaffected and consumer welfare is advanced), does not offset the harm to the producers. Thus, exploitation of buyer power that results in prices below the competitive level broadly distorts the market process.

One striking illustration of this process comes from the cheese industry. For a period of years Kraft, the largest buyer of cheese in the United States, was a major seller of cheese on the Green Bay Cheese Exchange, the price-making market for cheese. Very little cheese was sold through the exchange, however. The vast majority was sold directly. By driving down the price on the exchange though a very limited number of sales, Kraft manipulated downward the price of all the cheese it bought directly.[51] The cheese producers in turn lowered the price they paid for milk, the largest component in the cost of cheese. The deleterious effects of Kraft's price manipulations came to rest on the dairy farmers who produced the milk rather than the cheese companies.[52] In addition, this affected the price of all milk because that price is largely shaped by the price of cheese and its milk components. As a result, all dairy farmers had less disposable income and faced greater risk of bankruptcy as well as a general reduced capacity to buy goods and services, adversely affecting their entire community. Thus there is negative upstream feedback when buyers force down the price paid to the supplier because the supplier imposes reductions on its producers in order to reduce its costs and retain its prior level of profitability.

As discussed earlier, a primary effect of mergers between competing

---

Can Build a Fairer Food System', available at http://www.ase.tufts.edu/gdae/pubs/rp/aai_issue_brief_3.pdf.

[50] See Editorial, 'Fire Safety in Garment Factories' *New York Times* (9 December 2012), available at http://www.nytimes.com/2012/12/10/opinion/fire-safety-in-garment-factories.html; Ian Urbina and Keith Bradsher, 'Linking Factories to the Malls, Middleman Pushes Low Costs' *New York Times* (8 August 2013) at A1; Steven Greenhouse, 'Europeans Fault American Safety Effort in Bangladesh' *New York Times* (19 November 2013) at B3; Steven Greenhouse, 'Major Retailers Agree to Inspection Standards in Bangladesh' *New York Times* (21 November 2013) at B3.

[51] Willard F Mueller, Bruce W Marion, Maqbool H Sial and Frederick E Geithman (1996), 'Cheese Pricing: A Study of the National Cheese Exchange', available at http://www.aae.wisc.edu/fsrg/finalFolder/All%20Chapters%20File.pdf.

[52] See *Knevelbaard Dairies v Kraft Foods, Inc.*, 232 F.3d 979 (9th Cir. 2000).

firms is a reduction in input costs.[53] Although the producer faces a more concentrated buying market with its consequent enhanced buyer power, it also receives the benefit of fewer competitors on the selling side thereby increasing its buying power.[54] Such a producer has an incentive to exploit its expanded buyer power in order to restore its margins. Moreover, all-or-nothing contracts allow the producer to retain the same quantity of its input supply as before, while reducing the total paid for that supply. The passing back of buyer power is likely to have long-run negative implications for the producer that engages in such conduct. Reduced earnings will in turn induce upstream suppliers to exit the market, and entry will be less likely as potential earnings are reduced. This is not to say that pass-backs will necessarily happen, but only that a producer facing increased buyer power has an increased incentive to look for ways to reduce its costs by exercising its power in any component market in which it *can* use its leverage, even if this has negative long-run implications for both the buyer and its suppliers.

H. Competitive Policy Analysis of Supplier Exploitation

The extent to which competition policy should be concerned about exploitation of suppliers depends, in part, on which fundamental goal of competition policy is used for the analysis. As a general rule, prices below competitive levels, and the other harmful competitive effects of supplier exploitation examined above, distort the market process, but the different policy goals lead to varying levels of competitive concern. If total economic welfare is the basis for policy, exploitation of buyer power should cause concern. In that framework, however, the overall short-term welfare consequences of exploitation can be ambiguous. Various kinds of buyer conduct may have no effect or even a positive effect on short-run aggregate welfare. Hence, use of aggregate welfare as the fundamental goal of policy leads to a much weaker concern with buyer conduct—in the short run the conduct affects only suppliers, even though it directly harms the competitive process. A competition policy based on fairness would have the same disadvantage, merely weighing the effects on various parties to determine whether a specific exploitation was 'fair' or 'unfair'.

If consumer welfare is the primary goal, the need for competitive

[53] See Fee and Shawn, *supra* note 14, at 425 (as horizontal mergers concentrate the buying side the number of suppliers falls).

[54] *Ibid* at 430–1 (noting that the number of suppliers declines as concentration increases).

concern will be dependent on two conditions. First, the buyer can have only one source of input so that its output declines as result of the lower price paid. Second, even then, harm to consumers will result only if the buyer also has power in the selling market. If there is substantial competition from other sellers in the downstream market, the buyer's reduced output will not noticeably affect the volume or price.[55] The buyer will transfer wealth from the producer to itself, but it will not affect consumers significantly. Only if the buyer has enough downstream market power to raise the price of goods to its customers will there be immediate harm to consumer welfare. Therefore, if consumer welfare is the primary goal of competition policy, only a limited set of situations would create enforcement concerns. Most exploitation would fall into the category of 'mere' wealth transfers.

If competition policy has as its fundamental goal the promotion and protection of the competitive process, then the use of buyer power to exploit upstream producers will be a subject of serious concern. The competitive process perspective will result in greater concern with buyer conduct than either welfare goal because it recognizes a broader range of competitive harm that the unreasonable use of buyer power can create. Moreover, only a process perspective can support competition policies that condemn purely monopsonistic conduct, all buyer cartels, and mergers that affect only upstream producers.

The focus of section I has been on the adverse competitive effects of exploiting buyer power, but it has also identified the potential positive effects of using buyer power to reduce input or differentiated good prices that have been inflated through seller collusion or oligopoly conduct. Also relevant is the point made earlier that, in many markets, price differentiation can more efficiently match the price of each unit of input to the value it adds and therefore should not be universally condemned. Prices will change over time, but the effect is to allow supply and demand to adjust continuously. Similarly, other exploitive conduct, such as restricted access to favorable buying options, bundling of purchases, limits on disclosure of market information, and even risk or cost transfers can have legitimate business justifications, and so can more easily be analyzed with reference to the existence and strength of a non-exclusionary justification for the specific practice.[56]

---

[55] This point is illustrated in Chapter 3, Table 3.1.

[56] As suggested in section II, this analysis needs to look critically at both the merits of the justification and whether less restrictive options could achieve the legitimate needs of the parties.

The most perplexing element of this mixed analysis is that justifiable conduct may also have adverse impacts on producers and their suppliers. Similarly, the unavoidable market divisions that can occur when buyers focus on substantial inputs that are not geographically mobile are likely to result in increased exploitation of producers, but are themselves the unavoidable consequence of rational individual firm decisions.

II. THE USE OF BUYER POWER TO EXCLUDE COMPETITION

Conventional competition policy has long identified the potential risks of powerful buyers excluding competition with a variety of strategies. This section will review those strategies and their implications for the competitive process. Jonathan Baker has argued that exclusion is as harmful to the competitive process as naked exploitive restraints.[57] In the context of buyer power, as Chapters 5 and 6 will demonstrate, unilateral exclusion by buyers violates conventional competition law only under limited circumstances, and non-competition-law market regulation is also not very effective in addressing these problems. Moreover, with the exception of naked agreements among buyers that require producers to refuse to deal with the buyers' competitors (a topic examined in Chapter 7), competition law itself is unduly deferential to joint buyer conduct that excludes competition in the buying market directly or indirectly.

A. Exclusive Buying

Dominant input buyers can insist that their suppliers refuse to deal with competing buyers. This use of buyer power can preclude or limit competition in the downstream markets in which the buyer sells by denying the buyer's competitors access to essential inputs. Indeed, a buyer might even pay a slight premium for exclusive access to the supplier's inputs.[58] The exclusionary effect occurs if the buyer's competitors are unable to find alternative sources of input.

Foreclosure may be more feasible for popular, branded consumer

---

[57] Jonathan Baker, 'Exclusion as a Core Competition Concern' (2013) 78 *Antitrust Law Journal* 527.

[58] See, eg, *JTC Petroleum v Piasa Motor Fuels*, 190 F.3d 775 (7th Cir. 1999) (cartel of highway pavers plausibly could have paid a premium to suppliers of paving material in return for suppliers' refusing to deal with a price-cutting competitor).

goods than for generic component inputs. Producers need many outlets for branded products as well as desirable shelf space and possibly in-store promotion. They are vulnerable to demands by high volume retailers that they not deal with smaller outlets or that they do so only on less favorable terms. General Electric's use of resale price maintenance suggests that it sought to ensure favorable treatment for its household small appliances by assuring large department stores that it would not allow any buyer to engage in price competition. The department stores reciprocated by focusing their sales on General Electric products. This created a double, simultaneous barrier to entry at both the production and retail levels.[59]

The use of exclusive dealing arrangements can foreclose competition in downstream product markets. For example, Mylan contracted with all the potential suppliers of a key input to a drug, which was not otherwise protected from competition.[60] Mylan also agreed to share its profits with its suppliers.[61] The contracts for the input enabled Mylan to achieve market dominance in the market for the drug and exclude competition. It was then able to raise the price of the drug dramatically. Thus, when an input is relatively specialized or can be obtained only from limited sources, a dominant buyer can secure powerful exclusionary effect by obtaining an exclusive buying right. Similarly, a lawsuit involving a post-patent effort to exclude competition in the single-serving coffee machine market also included the claim that the buyer had agreed to share its monopoly profits with a key input supplier in return for an exclusive right to its product.[62] These cases usually involve a buyer with downstream power that uses its buyer position to entrench and protect itself from threats of competition from marginal firms or potential entrants. Thus, control of the supply side in such circumstances can be a powerful weapon to protect the monopoly.

There are legitimate business reasons, however, for a buyer to ask for some form of exclusive dealing or full supply commitment from any supplier of key inputs. The buyer might be uncertain as to the quantity it will require or seek to ensure the availability of a sufficient supply for its production needs. The mere existence of such an arrangement is not per se evidence of an anticompetitive objective, even though the result may cause an adverse effect on competition. The more difficult ques-

---

[59] See Thomas K McCraw, 'Competition and "Fair Trade": History and Theory' (1996) 16 *Research in Economic History* 185.

[60] *FTC v Mylan Labs, Inc.*, 62 F. Supp. 2d 25 (D.D.C. 1999).

[61] *Ibid* at 34.

[62] Complaint at 37–43, *Treehouse Foods Inc. v Green Mountain Coffee Roasters, Inc.*, No. 14 Civ. 905 (S.D.N.Y. 2014) (on file with author). The complaint sets forth a series of claims about agreements that foreclosed access to key equipment.

tion is whether the legitimate gains to the parties offset the competitive harm. Absent buyer power, it is reasonable to assume that the parties find the cost savings worth the restrictions on their competitive freedom. But when significant buyer power is present, the presumption ought to be reversed—there should be convincing justification that the restraint limiting access by others is the least invasive way to protect a compelling efficiency interest.[63]

B. Inducing a Supplier Refusal to Deal

Using an approach closely related to exclusive dealing, buyers have unilaterally or in combination coerced their suppliers, especially those of modest size, to refuse to deal with competitors of the buying group. In the United States, the reported cases extend back to the early 1900s.[64] The Supreme Court restated the rule against such practices in *Klor's v Broadway-Hale*,[65] and the Seventh Circuit upheld the FTC's challenge to *Toys 'R' Us*'s use of this same tactic.[66]

Australia has at least two comparable cases. In one, a major retailer sought to require its suppliers to agree that they would not give discounts to any other customer that were greater than those given to the dominant buyer.[67] In another case very similar to *Toys 'R' Us*, a dominant buyer of cans for beer sought to compel its supplier to refuse to sell cans to a discounting competitor.[68]

These cases illustrate how buyer power can be used to restrict access to inputs for competitors. As discussed earlier, American courts have taken the view that such agreements may not be unduly harmful when undertaken in pursuit of a legitimate business objective.[69] This has created a legal context in which such foreclosure is often deemed unobjectionable.

---

63 This framework draws on the 'quick look' approach used in some American cases in which the conduct is facially anticompetitive but might be justified. See, eg, *Polygram Holding, Inc. v FTC*, 416 F.3d 29 (D.C. Cir. 2005).

64 *Montague v Lowry*, 193 U.S. 38 (1904); *E States Retail Lumber Dealers Ass'n v United States*, 234 U.S. 600 (1914).

65 *Klor's, Inc. v Broadway-Hale Stores, Inc.*, 359 U.S. 207 (1959).

66 *Toys 'R' Us v FTC*, 221 F.3d 928 (7th Cir. 2000).

67 *Austl. Competition & Consumer Comm'n v Australian Safeway Stores Pty Ltd.* [2003] FCAFC 149.

68 *TPC v Carlton United Breweries Ltd.* (1990) 24 FCR 532 (Austl.).

69 The discussion in *NYNEX Corp. v Discon, Inc.*, 525 U.S.128 (1998), illustrates this. The Supreme Court rejected the application of per se illegality to a scheme in which a seller bribed a buyer to refuse to deal with a lower-priced service provider. The Court was concerned that such a standard would unduly interfere

On the other hand, the emerging rules governing abuse of buying power by retailers in Japan, the United Kingdom and other countries suggest the growing awareness of the competitive risks of these restrictions.

C. Most Favored Nation and Most Favored Nation Plus Contracts

Most favored nation (MFN) and most favored nation plus (MFNP) contract terms are closely related to express agreements that restrict sellers from selling to other buyers. MFNs require a producer to give the buyer the advantage of the lowest price any customer pays. These clauses effectively forbid a producer from assisting a new entrant or a firm seeking to expand its market position by providing that buyer with special terms. An MFN thus assures the dominant buyer that no competitor will have lower costs for that input. However, some of the scholarship on these contracts suggests that they can result in higher prices to all buyers.[70] Even so, the gain to the dominant buyer may well offset the higher price. Indeed, such a price might be the premium that buyer pays for the exclusionary and stabilizing benefits of the contract.

Under an MFNP clause, a seller, in return for a significant purchase, agrees to charge any other buyer a price in excess of what the favored buyer is paying. When a buyer is dominant in the market, there may be little choice for a producer that needs the buyer's business to survive. As a result, the MFNP creates an even greater barrier to entry or expansion by smaller competitors of the dominant buyer. The US Department of Justice sued the dominant health insurer in Michigan alleging that the insurer, as a buyer of hospital services, imposed either MFNs or MFNPs on most of the hospitals with which it contracted.[71] The government also alleged that the contracts provided for insurance payments that were at a higher price than the hospitals had previously received. This premium, like the profit sharing in *Mylan*, provided an inducement for the hospitals to adhere to the scheme. But the longer term effect would be to drive competing insurers from the market, giving the hospitals even less capacity to bargain with the dominant insurer. More broadly, an MFNP may also create a waterbed

---

with the ability of buyers to make decisions, even decisions that were arguably irrational from a conventional business perspective.

[70] Jonathan B Baker and Judith A Chevalier, 'The Competitive Consequences of Most-Favored-Nation Provisions' (2013) 27 *Antitrust* 20, 23–5 (arguing that such agreements often result in higher prices and reduced competition).

[71] *United States v Blue Cross Blue Shield of Mich.*, 809 F. Supp. 2d 665 (2011) (dismissed after the state of Michigan adopted legislation prohibiting such contracts).

effect, even when a producer does not wish to impose the price burden on competitors of the dominant buyer.

D. Predatory Buying (Overbidding)

This strategy involves bidding up the price of an input to a level that makes it uneconomic for smaller competitors of the dominant buyer to continue to buy. When the competing buyers exit the market, the dominant buyer can then lower the prices it pays because there is no longer any competition. This is the buying side analog to predatory pricing, which excludes small rivals of a dominant firm on the selling side. For example, competitors of Weyerhaeuser Co., a large lumber company, claimed that it had bid up the price of alder logs making it impossible for competing sawmills to stay in business.[72] In their analysis, the courts assumed that alder lumber produced in the Pacific Northwest where Weyerhaeuser operated competed in a downstream market with similar lumber from many other regions. The only gain would be in the upstream buying market if other buyers were excluded, allowing Weyerhaeuser subsequently to reduce the price it paid for this key input.

Successful predatory buying requires that barriers to entry are sufficiently high to prevent new buyers from easily re-entering the market. Entry was plausible in lumber milling because the opening of a small mill that can process a variety of logs does not require major expense. Moreover, it is possible that the wholesale lumber market is such that entrants can find a ready market for their products without having to develop an expensive distribution system. Therefore, some of the market characteristics in alder lumber would argue against the use of predatory bidding.

Although accepting the plausibility of predatory buying, the Supreme Court analogized it to predatory selling and imposed strict standards of proof.[73] In particular the Court was concerned that disappointed buyers could use antitrust law to challenge successful bidding for scarce resources or use the threat of litigation to deter vigorous buyer competition. These concerns are legitimate and illustrate the difficulty of letting courts make judgments about prices. However, as discussed in Chapter 5, the standard

---

[72] *Weyerhaeuser Co. v Ross-Simmons Hardwood Lumber Co.*, 549 U.S. 312 (2007) (while upholding the applicability of antitrust law to predatory buying, the Court imposed stringent requirements to prove such conduct unlawful and so reversed the jury verdict for the plaintiffs).

[73] *Ibid* at 321–2.

the Court imposed is more draconian than is necessary or desirable to advance the goal of protecting a workable competitive process.[74]

E. Indirect Exclusion

Beyond any overt commitment to exclusive dealing or other express exclusionary conduct, there is a more general pressure on input suppliers in markets where a single buyer or small group of buyers is dominant to engage in 'voluntary' exclusionary conduct. Although it is in the collective interest of suppliers to sell to a new entrant, doing so is likely to antagonize dominant incumbent firms. As a result, the supplier may have a very difficult time renewing its sales to existing firms if the new entrant fails. This economic logic means that a new entrant is likely to have a hard time gaining supplies in such a market, even in the absence of any overtly exclusive agreements.

Producers will find it rational to refuse to deal with new entrants or even competitors of a primary customer if it believes the dominant buyer does not want the producer to supply its competition. For example, Clorox found it rational to limit the sale of the largest containers of its products to its largest buyers, refusing to sell them to smaller regional grocery chains.[75] In the case of cattle feedlots, a study found that there was a very marked pattern of operators selling to only one of the major buyers.[76] The buyers had established a tacit market allocation scheme, and the feedlots complied. A non-complying feedlot would risk having no buyer for its cattle.

A dominant incumbent that buys in multiple input markets can selectively raise the price of inputs in a market where a new entrant seeks to establish itself, often focusing on those suppliers with whom the entrant proposes to deal. The prices need not violate any predatory buying standard, but the entrant or firm seeking to expand will incur a cost squeeze in

---

[74] The Court has also upheld the use of price squeezes, under which a vertically integrated firm sets the price of an intermediate product so high that unintegrated downstream competitors cannot profitably buy the input, process it, and resell in competition with the vertically integrated firm. *Pac. Bell Tel. v linkLine Commc'ns*, 555 U.S. 438 (2009).

[75] *Woodman's Food Mkt. v Clorox Co.*, 2015 WL 420296 (W.D. Wis. 2015), rev'd, 2016 WL 4254935 (7th Cir. 2016).

[76] Lynn Hunnicutt, Michelle Crook and DeeVon Bailey, 'Rigidity in Packer-Feedlot Relationships' (2004) 36 *Journal of Agricultural and Applied Economics* 627 (identifying pattern of buyer consistency in purchases from cattle feedlots and implied reluctance by feeders to look for alternative buyers given highly concentrated buying market).

meeting those prices.[77] Its margins will be depressed or even eliminated. The threat of a cost squeeze may deter entry altogether at the most efficient location; the entrant may decide to enter in a less-efficient region where it can develop its own supply chain.

Selective bidding practices have also been observed when a large buyer acquires a substantial buyer as a means of entering a different geographic market. If the second market has one or more other buyers that operate there exclusively, the multimarket buyer can bid up the prices it pays in that market to establish its dominance. This will either drive the other firms from the market or compel them to follow the pricing lead of the dominant firm.[78] These practices of course may provide some potential gains to the followers if prices for inputs are later depressed and so may not necessarily be resisted too vigorously. But they also create barriers to entry and reinforce the ability of the buyers to coerce producers.

F. The Competitive Policy Analysis of Exclusion

The extent to which competition policy should be concerned about exclusionary practices depends, in part, on which fundamental goal of competition policy is used for the analysis. Legal condemnation of exclusionary buyer conduct lacking legitimate business justification is consistent with all the possible policy goals of antitrust: aggregate welfare, fairness, the competitive process and consumer welfare. To be sure, each of these policy goals requires some analysis of the specific conduct to determine whether it has a legitimate justification. An aggregate welfare approach would be most tolerant because it would require proof of an adverse effect on the total welfare of the economy. Under either a fairness or a competitive process goal, the focus would be more narrowly on the legitimacy of any justification for the exclusionary action.

If a narrow consumer welfare interest is the goal, then only those exclusionary practices that adversely affect downstream markets are of concern. Specifically, when, as in *Weyerhaeuser*, the effects relate only to competitors of the buyer and input suppliers, but create no measurable effect on a downstream market that receives supply from many sources, then a narrow consumer welfare goal would find no competitive harm. Of course, if competition policy concerns itself with both the immediate and

---

[77] The US Supreme Court rejected the argument that such squeezes are a violation of antitrust law in *linkLine*, 555 U.S. 438.

[78] *Cf Cargill, Inc. v Monfort of Colo., Inc.*, 479 U.S. 104 (1986) (no violation of merger law when multimarket buyer enters market by major acquisition creating risk of exclusionary buying strategies).

longer term effects on competition, one might conclude that the exclusion has at least a marginal effect on the downstream market. Lande and Kirkwood illustrate the difficulty of incorporating harm to producers into a consumer welfare goal.[79] While arguing for a consumer welfare, rather than an aggregate welfare, approach, the authors make an exception for harm to 'small' producers and assert that competition law should also protect them.[80] This bifurcated policy analysis suggests that the authors are striving to stay within the conventional debate about goals that emphasize economic abstractions.

III. ABUSE OF MONOPSONY IS WORSE THAN ABUSE OF MONOPOLY

This section contends that monopsonistic conduct that unjustifiably harms the competitive process overall does more damage to competition than does monopoly. There are no recognized metrics for making such a comparison. Ultimately, this is a judgement based on an assessment of the relative harms as well as the capacity of the market to respond to those harms. The seriousness of the harm from monopsony rests on a combination of its aggregate effects and the inherently limited ability of market processes to respond effectively to such exploitation.

A. Monopsony Imposes Relatively Greater Harm than Monopoly on Aggregate Consumption and Undermines the Overall Integrity of the Market

The initial difference between monopoly and monopsony is how each affects the economic process. Conventionally, a monopolist exploits its customers by raising prices, while a monopsonist exploits the market by depressing prices paid for inputs to its goods or services. The monopolist's conduct is immediately visible to buyers in the form of high prices. In contrast, the standard model of the monopsonist does not assume that it will share its gain with its customers. Hence, consumers will not necessarily be aware of the exploitation even if that were a concern. The effect in the downstream market would be a reduction in output causing a resulting

---

[79] John B Kirkwood and Robert H Lande, 'The Fundamental Goal of Antitrust: Protecting Consumers, Not Increasing Efficiency' (2008) 84 *Notre Dame Law Review* 191.

[80] *Ibid* at 233–6.

price increase. However, in many situations, there will be no output effect.[81] A monopsonist may share some of the gain with its customers, especially if its downstream market is competitive.[82] Indeed, the monopsonistic competitors of the monopsonist in the downstream markets may feel compelled to exploit further their upstream suppliers in order to reduce 'costs' and remain competitive. The result is a cyclical downward pressure on suppliers in which the overt motivation is remaining competitive with other buyers.

The cyclical downward pressure of monopsony stands in strong contrast to the potentially more self-correcting nature of monopoly. Prices that exceed costs can induce new entry and tougher bargaining by large customers. In exploiting its monopoly, the monopolist creates the seeds of its own destruction in any market in which entry barriers are not insurmountable. Hence, the law of monopoly focuses today on conduct that imposes entry barriers or otherwise deters competition.

In contrast, successful monopsonistic market exploitation drives down the revenue of the suppliers of the monopsonist, who in turn must lower wages and reduce employment and other investments. This both harms the producer and creates a negative macroeconomic effect. Reduced revenue for suppliers reduces their ongoing capacity to buy, further slowing the economy. Falling demand further affects the economy. Fewer firms are able to compete in the markets to supply the producers because of reduced revenue and demand for inputs. Thus, monopsony creates a dispersed pressure on the economy that defeats the growth and dynamics of the market process.

There are three classic counterarguments to the claim that exploitation of monopsony power leads to greater aggregate economic harm than occurs with monopoly. Each is premised on an analysis that does not fully account for the harms monopsony can cause. They are laid out below with an explanation of their weaknesses.

First is the claim that both monopolists and monopsonists exploit the market resulting in wealth transfers that have adverse effects on the competitive process. Hence, the aggregate harm is presumed to be the same. But, absent significant barriers to entry, monopoly exploitation is likely to be defeated because the enhanced prices invite competitive entry. Monopsony, in contrast, may be more difficult to overcome. To compete

---

81 See Chapter 3, text accompanying notes 6, 7, 12–16.

82 *Cf* John B Kirkwood, 'Buyer Power and Healthcare Prices' (2016) 91 *Washington Law Review* 253, 286 (theorizing that a powerful buyer of healthcare services might share its gains if it faced equally powerful buyer competitors).

with a monopsonist, an entrant must pay more for inputs, incurring costs higher than those of the incumbent. If there is any lag between the time of initial entry and production, the incumbent may be able to bid up input prices in the entrant's input market and make entry even more costly. Worse, if the incumbent has shared some of its monopsonistic underpayment with the downstream customers, the new entrant will face prices even further below the costs it will incur. Thus, market correcting entry is much more problematic on the monopsony side of the market than the monopoly one.[83]

A second counterargument is that the monopsonist gets the economic benefit, in the form of a wealth transfer, of its underpayment to its suppliers. In theory, its monopsony profits will then induce competitive responses by exploited producers, such as forward integration, just as monopoly profits induce competitive entry. Again, this claim is not persuasive in many cases. The monopsonist is often in a chain of production, and the location of any gains is unlikely to be visible to potential entrants. There are, to be sure, examples of gain to a monopsonistic middleman having induced entry. The best historical example is farmer-owned cooperative grain elevators.[84] These cooperatives eliminated the local monopsony, and the owner-members gained from access to a broad market of competing grain buyers. The joint provision of school lunch food is a recent example.[85] But the very scarcity of these responses, as well as the very great coordination and collective action challenges in developing them, tell us that the response to monopsony is weaker and less likely to succeed than the responses to monopoly.

The third counterargument is that the gains of both monopoly and monopsony are wealth transfers, which is not considered a concern of classical competition law. Under monopoly, the wealth transfer represented by monopoly profits is distributed to shareholders and other stakeholders and therefore is not lost to the economy. Under monopsony, it is argued that the monopsonist also obtains and distributes the gains from its exploitation. Hence, the total wealth of the economy is also not reduced. Several rebuttals are in order, however.

---

83 An entrant challenging a monopolist may also face a negative price-cost margin, but it is less likely to face higher input costs unless the monopolist also has significant buyer power in the input markets.

84 See Chapter 3, text accompanying notes 66, 77–80 for a fuller description.

85 See Lihlani Skipper and Alfonso Morales, 'The Right Blend' (2014) 81 *Rural Cooperatives* 12; see also Local Food Hub, http://www.localfoodhub.org/about-us/ (last visited 10 November 2016), a Virginia-based program that links local farmers to school lunch programs.

- The argument assumes that the consumption function is similar for those who gain and those who lose wealth. This is not obviously or necessarily the case. The end result of monopsony is often lower wages and payments to businesses, such as farmers, who spend most of their income on consumption. It is likely that loss of income will lead to a net loss to the economy from this source.[86]
- Even if the gains are dispersed among the customers of the monopsonist, their minor gains are unlikely to offset the losses suffered by the upstream victims. This poses an enormous empirical inquiry that is beyond the scope of this chapter; but, in various sectors, such as wage labor and farming, long-term reductions in relative income are in some significant degree attributable to monopsony. For example, in counties dominated by Tyson's chicken operations, average income is lower than in comparable counties not so dominated.[87] Thus, these harms play out in the broader economy in the form of reduced economic growth and stagnation.
- Global exploitation of buyer power means that the victims are concentrated in the developing world and the gains are distributed among buyers and their customers in the developed world. Hence, there is a potentially significant transfer of wealth away from those most in need of basic income. The longer run, dynamic implications of such exploitation for the market process are strongly negative.
- Reduced compensation for goods or services is likely to affect the quality of the product or the work. For the same reasons, incentives to innovate are impaired when the exploitive buyer is the likely beneficiary. These effects indirectly harm downstream customers who receive lower quality, less choice and a reduction in innovation that can produce new and improved products. Moreover, as quality and

---

[86] The assumption here is that economic growth is demand-driven. Recent scholarship has shown how loss of wealth has retarded economic growth even when income is restored. See 'Wealth Inequality is Slowing Economic Growth, S&P Study Finds' *Christian Science Monitor* (6 August 2014), available at http://www.csmonitor.com/Business/Latest-News-Wires/2014/0806/Wealth-inequality-is-slowing-economic-growth-S-P-study-finds (reporting a study by Standard & Poor's that wealth inequality is retarding American economic growth).

[87] Leonard, *supra* note 4, at 314–18 (setting forth a comparison of average income). See also, Council of Economic Advisers (October 2016), 'Labor Market Monopsony: Trends, Consequences, and Policy Responses', available at https://www.whitehouse.gov/sites/default/files/page/files/20161025_monopsony_labor_mrkt_cea.pdf (explaining how employer power results in lower wages and reduced opportunities for employees and suggesting policies that can alleviate some of these harms).

innovation decline, the downstream buyer has to incur increased expenses to specify and ensure necessary quality. This increases the buyer's costs, ironically, because the reason for the expense is the reduced quality of the upstream components resulting from the earlier exploitation of buyer power.

In sum, unlike most monopolies that impose higher prices on consumers, monopsony directly affects the wealth of producers and their consequent ability to buy goods and services. A successful monopsonist can drive down prices below the competitive level, which affects the income and incentives of the producer. As producer's income declines, it buys less, pays less, looks to cut corners on its products, reduces or eliminates any innovation or product improvement, and again the aggregate economy suffers a net loss. Even if we assume that the buyer uses an all-or-nothing approach so that the quantity obtained is consistent with that which a competitive market would have produced, the seller is receiving suboptimal compensation for that quantity of product. As Chapter 3 demonstrated, such buying distorts the competitive process by transferring the efficiency gains of the producer to the buyer. The other exploitive strategies identified in this Chapter 4 all impose unjustified costs on producers, and they have the same or similar destructive effects. These harms directly injure the competitive process and producers as well as their employees. They do not produce the kinds of gains that can be dispersed among other stakeholders. This stands in strong contrast to the ways in which a monopolist both exploits and then distributes the results of its exploitation to relevant stakeholders.

B. Traditional Measures of Monopsonistic Impact Can Understate its Effects

The general belief that monopsony is unlikely to cause significant harm rests on the assumptions underlying the standard economic model. That model posits that individual producers can sell in discrete quantities and only those facing upward sloping cost curves can be exploited. Therefore, if price declines, the producer will reduce output. Moreover, if demand from other buyers is price elastic, they will increase their purchases, which will limit both the price and output effects. The model assumes that a producer with a flat cost curve is not vulnerable to exploitation. The conclusions of the conventional model, as the critique in Chapter 3 demonstrated, rely on a series of important assumptions. The producer's ability to reduce its output in response to lower prices is essential, as is the assumption that the producer has a significant degree of flexibility in its income needs over any period of time. The model also assumes that a producer with a long-run flat cost curve will be not be vulnerable to exploitive actions even if it has only one or a few buyers. If these assumptions are inconsistent with the economic facts of productive activity, the observed lack of or limited negative output effect does not provide a basis for the conclusion that the buyer has not adversely affected the competitive process.

A producer with fixed revenue needs, to pay debt service, for example, will have an incentive to increase, not decrease, production to offset the reduced income that results from a reduction in unit price. This, of course, adds to total output even as the producer either consumes its capital (such as by deferring maintenance) or accepts unreasonably low returns. The most obvious cases occur in agriculture and employment. In both instances, lower prices or wages result in producing more product (such as milk) or working more hours or jobs. The exploitation does not lead to lower output. Commodity export markets in developing countries demonstrate this same phenomenon. Buyers drive down the price they will pay and are rewarded with increased production from farmers or workers desperate to maintain a minimally acceptable standard of living.[88]

A buyer that can employ an all-or-nothing contract, as explained in Chapter 3, appropriates some or all of the seller's Ricardian rents.[89] Many economists regard this as only a 'wealth transfer'. Moreover, the output result would suggest that no exploitation has occurred. But producers are left with a reduced reward for their risk taking and investment. The more efficient a firm is the more it loses. Over time, this reduces the incentive to enter the production market or improve the product.

Even when a seller has declining or constant costs, a buyer can exploit the relationship, as the analysis in Chapter 3 demonstrated.[90] Under those circumstances, a buyer needs incremental sales to realize greater cost savings; an exploitive buyer can condition those additional purchases on receiving a price reduction greater than that which flows directly from the increased sales volume. This is again a transfer of the producer's surplus to the buyer. Moreover, once a buyer has positioned itself as the buyer

---

[88] The assumption here is that the producer and his or her family need a certain level of income to survive. When the per-unit profit declines, these producers are forced to increase output somehow to restore that basic level of income. The analysis of demand for 'inferior goods' is analogous. See Richard H Leftwich, *The Price System and Resource Allocation* (Rinehart, New York rev edn 1965) 67 ('The quantity taken of an inferior good will decrease as the consumer's income increases, or vice versa').

[89] See Chapter 3, text accompanying note 7.

[90] See Chapter 3, text accompanying notes 10–16.

of a substantial part of the producer's output, the buyer has even more leverage. It can demand special prices or services, and any seller that lacks alternative outlets with comparable volume is going to be hard pressed to refuse to make the demanded concessions.

Exploitation of buyer power can also result in the 'waterbed' effect, in which the producer raises prices to its other customers to make up for the unjustified discount given to a powerful buyer.[91] This survival strategy can lead to pricing actions that are irrational over the long term. The producer strengthens the market position of the dominant buyer by raising the costs of its smaller competitors. The long-run goal of facilitating a workably competitive buying market is vulnerable to the strategy of the large buyer demanding excessively low prices that both enrich it directly and raise its rivals' costs.[92]

The implications of this analysis are that the effects of monopsony are likely to be less visible in the short to intermediate term because the output effects may be muted. In contrast, a monopolist exploits its market position by reducing output and raising prices. These are visible market signals that permit a critical examination of the conduct that facilitated the creation and retention of that market power.

C. Buyer Decisional Control—Retaliation and Discrimination

Another factor, also examined in Chapter 3, that exacerbates monopsony's threat to the competitive process is that, in general, the buyer decides what to buy and, except on a commodity exchange, from whom.[93] Whenever transactions are negotiated one-on-one, any buyer with significant buying capacity can affect a supplier with significant switching

---

[91] See Chapter 3, text accompanying notes 15–16.

[92] Standard Oil's purchases of rail services in the 1880s and 1890s illustrate this. Standard Oil, the dominant shipper of crude and refined petroleum, not only demanded and received rebates from railroads for its shipments, but also received additional payments based on the quantity of petroleum products shipped by its competitors. See Benjamin Klein, 'The "Hub-and-Spoke" Conspiracy that Created the Standard Oil Monopoly' (2012) 85 *Southern California Law Review* 459; Elizabeth Granitz and Benjamin Klein, 'Monopolization by "Raising Rivals' Costs": The Standard Oil Case' (1986) 39 *Journal of Law and Economics* 1; Daniel Crane, 'Were Standard Oil's Rebates and Drawback Cost Justified?' (2012) 85 *Southern California Law Review* 559.

[93] See Chapter 3, section II.A (when there are multiple potential suppliers, the buyer decides from whom to buy, which facilitates discrimination among suppliers).

costs. Indeed, even buyers with only a modest degree of market power can extract concessions.

The capacity of monopsonist buyers to retaliate and to discriminate among their suppliers is a major factor in differentiating buyer power and monopsony from monopoly power. Producers can be intimidated. The greater the buyer power, the greater the ability of buyers to inflict economic harm, making producers increasingly less likely to complain. In 2014, the European Union published a Green Paper on exploitive practices in distribution based on a survey of Member States' experiences and observations related to 'unfair competition'.[94] One strong and consistent finding was that producers are unwilling to complain about buyer power because of the risks of retaliation. In contrast, a monopolist has less discretion. Refusals to sell directly reduce the monopolist's profits. Discriminatory pricing risks arbitrage by favored buyers. Attempting to coerce customers to refuse to deal with alternative sources can result in the total loss of their business if the alternative is at all attractive. Therefore, although monopolists have similar incentives to exploit and exclude, their capacity to do so overall is more constrained by the market itself.

D. Institutional Limits Facilitate Exploitation

When a monopolist exploits without employing exclusion, it faces the risk of competitive entry. Reducing prices to deter entry moves prices and output closer to what would exist in a competitive market.[95] Customers, especially large ones, have a strong incentive to look for alternative sources or to induce entry.[96] Entrepreneurs, viewing the profitability of the industry, have an incentive to enter. Hence, there are market-driven corrections for monopoly. Because a monopolist is frequently subject to the

---

[94] European Commission, *Green Paper on Unfair Trading Practices in the Business-to-Business Food and Non-Food Supply Chain in Europe*, COM(2013) 37 final, available at http://eur-lex.europa.eu/legal-content/EN/TXT/PDF/?uri=CELEX:52013DC0037&from=EN.

[95] The monopolist limits its price increase so that the margin does not induce entry. See Kalman J Cohen and Richard M Cyert, *Theory of the Firm: Resource Allocation in a Market Economy* (Prentice Hall, New Jersey, NJ 1965) 197–8; FM Scherer and David Ross, *Industrial Market Structure and Economic Performance* (Houghton Mifflin, Boston, MA 3rd edn 1990) 356–77.

[96] This point is stressed in a broader analysis of collusion. See William E Kovacic, Robert C Marshall, Leslie M Marx and Halbert L White, 'Plus Factors and Agreement in Antitrust Law' (2011) 110 *Michigan Law Review* 393.

risk of an increasingly competitive market, it is possible to focus competition law primarily on unjustified exclusionary practices.[97]

And in many circumstances customers of a monopoly have the option of buying some other product or service. The elasticity of the demand curve shows this substitution effect, as well as reduced consumption, as price goes up. Only locked-in customers are unavoidably subject to the monopoly price, but they are also the ones who have the most incentive to seek alternative suppliers and whose demand is most likely to attract new entrants. Moreover, the monopoly overcharge harms both aggregate and consumer welfare, as well as the competitive process. As Richard Posner has argued, the monopolist may, in fact, spend most of its monopoly profit to protect its monopoly position,[98] and the wealth transfer may be spent on lawyers, advertising, or other costly monopoly protections. This is economically inefficient. But while the monopoly results in a reduction of the sales of goods and services, the resulting profits are dispersed as income or compensation to large number of stakeholders, which ensures that the gains are not entirely lost to the overall economy.[99]

Moreover, the legal system has successfully responded to problems of strong monopoly when there is a need for the goods or services and monopoly is the unavoidable incident of their provision (often called natural monopoly markets). Historically, either public ownership or direct command and control regulation were the responses. The granting of exclusive franchises by government secured the monopoly but subjected its possessor to rate and service regulation.[100] Consequently, society protected consumers from the risk of exploitation.

In the last 50 years, the necessity for monopoly regulation has been

---

[97] Baker has argued that even in network situations there are strong incentives to create competing networks. Hence, open access requirements can deter the development of competition. Donald I Baker, 'Compulsory Access to Network Joint Venture under the Sherman Act: Rules or Roulette?' (1993) *Utah Law Review* 999.

[98] Richard Posner, 'The Social Costs of Monopoly and Regulation' (1975) *Journal of Political Economy* 83.

[99] If the monopoly is global and transfers wealth from poor countries to richer ones, the distortions to aggregate welfare are more serious and ought to be considered an anticompetitive consequence.

[100] See J Gregory Sidak and Daniel F Spulber, *Deregulatory Takings and the Regulatory Contract* (Cambridge University Press, Cambridge 1997); see also Jim Rossi, 'The Irony of Deregulatory Takings' (1998) 77 *Texas Law Review* 297; Oliver Williamson, 'Response: Deregulatory Takings and the Breach of the Regulatory Contract: Some Precautions' (1996) 71 *New York University Law Review* 1007.

questioned but only when, in context, there were means at hand to reorganize the market to achieve workable competition. Thus, the telecommunications sector was radically altered with the development of wireless communication and the internet, both of which distributed communication through new means.[101] Similarly, both natural gas and electricity have moved from conventional regulated monopolies to partial competition as technological and regulatory understandings have changed.[102] But in those industries there is a residual regulatory control that continues to monitor and limit monopolistic prices and output restrictions. Some experiences, such as Enron's manipulation of the electricity market, suggest that this control has been less effective than it ought to have been in protecting consumers, but that has only sharpened the argument for better oversight.[103]

Responses to buyer power have been much weaker institutionally. Producer efforts at collective action raise serious concerns under competition law unless there is an express exemption.[104] The difficulties of book publishers in resisting deeply discounted resale of the electronic versions of their books are illustrative. Some publishers believed that Amazon's buyer power threatened their long-run viability. The publishers' solution was to join with Apple to adopt a collective policy of dealing with all buyers on similar terms. But from a competition policy perspective, an unregulated cartel is not an acceptable solution to the problem of buyer dominance, and the Department of Justice successfully challenged the legality of this arrangement.[105] That major book publishers, looking at the erosion of their distribution system, felt compelled to create a cartel illustrates the

---

[101] The ongoing debate about net neutrality and the application of the essential facilities doctrine to the internet suggest the complexity of formulating an appropriate legal regime for the governance of this new form of communication and delivery of a variety of services. See generally Bret Frischmann, *Infrastructure: The Social Value of Shared Resources* (Oxford University Press, Oxford 2012).

[102] In both natural gas and electricity, the core regulatory insight was that only some elements of the process of production and distribution are monopolistic. Hence, public policy has focused on limiting the scope of regulation and facilitating the use of market processes to the extent possible.

[103] See Darren Bush and Carrie Mayne, 'In (Reluctant) Defense of Enron: Why Bad Regulation is to Blame for California's Power Woes (or Why Antitrust Law Fails to Protect Against Market Power when the Market Rules Encourage its Use)' (2004) 83 *Oregon Law Review* 207.

[104] The question of producer cartel exemptions is evaluated further in Chapter 6.

[105] *United States v Apple Inc.*, 952 F. Supp. 2d 638 (S.D.N.Y. 2013), aff'd, 791 F.3d 290 (2d Cir. 2015) (rejecting the scheme of the major book publishers and Apple to create an 'agency' distribution plan for e-books as a hub and spoke cartel intended to raise retail prices).

institutional challenges of dealing with buyer power. Indeed, subsequent to the *Apple* case, Amazon cut off the distribution of a major publisher in the United States.[106] Essentially, it foreclosed sales in an effort to compel the publisher to give it more favorable terms. Amazon engaged in similar practices in Germany eliciting access complaints.[107] But so far publishers have failed to find any market solution to Amazon's dominance.

This is not to say that producers are incapable of responding to the dominance of buyers. The development of cooperative grain elevators is an example of forward integration by producers through the level of monopsony to create a more competitive market in which they could sell.[108] The school-food cooperative example, however, highlights the complexity of forward integration and the importance of government assistance to achieve the market-expanding result.[109]

An important institutional factor that made entry feasible for cooperative grain elevators was the ease and practicality of using rail lines to reach buyers in the downstream market. Entry or expansion into the downstream market requires a set of skills, investments and distribution capacity significantly different from those likely to be possessed by the upstream producer. For example, manufacturers of branded consumer goods need diversified retail outlets for their products.[110] But they are unlikely to operate retail outlets themselves. Component part makers sell to buyers that assemble the components, but each provides only a part of the total input required for the ultimate product. These factors also contribute greatly to limiting the capacity of the market's inherent incentive structure to induce the necessary entry or expansion to overcome existing buyer power.

---

[106] See David Streitfeld, 'Amazon Angles to Attract Hachette's Authors to Its Side' *New York Times* (9 July 2014) at B3 (alleging that Amazon offered Hachette authors all the revenue it derives from sales of their books); David Streitfeld, 'Publishing War Is Over, but Fear of Amazon Isn't' *New York Times* (14 November 2014) at A1 (Hachette and Amazon ended their dispute with an agreement after 11 months of conflict).

[107] Melissa Eddy, 'German Publishers Seek Amazon Inquiry' *New York Times* (24 June 2014), available at http://www.nytimes.com/2014/06/25/business/international/amazon-accused-in-Germany-of-antitrust-violation.html?_r=1.

[108] For a fuller discussion of this example, see Chapter 3, text accompanying notes 66, 77–9. The unique characteristics of local wheat markets made such forward integration feasible. Such economic facts are likely to be rare.

[109] See Skipper and Morales, *supra* note 85.

[110] For some producers of branded consumer goods, the internet may provide an alternative way to sell directly to final consumers. The characteristics of the product and consumer demand will affect how significant an alternative this will be for specific firms.

As discussed in Chapter 1, developing countries sought to protect widely dispersed small producers from the exploitation by buyers by creating state marketing agencies. These efforts largely failed because in the markets for bananas and cocoa, for example, the major buyers are so dominant that there is no competitive public market in which to sell.

E. The Monopoly–Monopsony Balance

On balance, the comparison of monopoly and monopsony shows that there is a plausible argument that monopsony markets are likely to be more durable, to exist at lower levels of overall concentration, and to impose more static and dynamic harms on the competitive process than monopoly markets. Hence there is greater need for competition law and policy to control abuse. This is a strong conclusion and one that some readers will feel requires more empirical and theoretic proof than this book can provide or is currently available in the economics literature. However, the analysis demonstrates that, at the very least, monopsony is as harmful to the competitive process as monopoly. The differences between monopoly and monopsony therefore require carefully considered policies that address the unique and pervasive nature of monopsony.

IV. CONCLUSION

Buyer power causes harm both by exploitation and exclusion. What may be most significant about this review is the many ways in which buyers can exploit and harm producers. These harms go to the core of the competitive process and so should be a major source of concern. As the next several chapters will demonstrate, competition law has largely ignored buyer exploitation of producers and has adopted relatively weak standards for dealing with exclusionary practices.

5. Competition policy for unilateral conduct by buyers

This chapter describes and evaluates existing and potential competition policies to govern abusive unilateral conduct by dominant buyers. Both the definition of standards for judging such conduct and the prescription of remedies are problematic. Deciding that such conduct is unreasonable and applying a remedy often involves direct intervention in the core of the competitive process. As a result, any effective response to such conduct poses a serious challenge to the conceptual framework and institutional capacity of competition law and policy.

The focus is on the question whether competition law can frame useful standards for judging the merits of and remedying apparently harmful unilateral buyer conduct. Both elements have been major challenges for every legal system globally. The contrast between the responses of the European Union countries, Australia and Japan, among others, and the United States highlight this fact.[1] The analysis has both descriptive and prescriptive dimensions. It is important to define and critique the current rules that govern buyer conduct as well as propose standards that can better address the competitive risks that abusive conduct creates.

The analysis assumes that a buyer has significant power over its suppliers. There is an empirical question as to the pervasiveness of undue buyer power.[2] But as shown in Chapter 1 and again in Chapter 3, buyer power is more pervasive than conventional competition policy analysts believe.

---

[1] Moreover, as Chapter 6 demonstrates, many legal systems use rules outside conventional competition law to control some aspects of abusive buyer conduct. The need for alternative controls underscores the limits that competition law and policy face in dealing effectively with these abuses.

[2] Some commentators, such as Jonathan Jacobson, contend that there is little or no risk of abusive buyer power because, they argue, supply expands and contracts without changes in cost, that is, the supply curve 'at prevailing levels of production . . . [is] typically flat.' Jonathan M Jacobson, 'Monopsony 2013: Still Not Truly Symmetric' (December 2013) *Antitrust Source* 1, 4, 11, available at http://www.americanbar.org/content/dam/aba/publishing/antitrust_source/dec13_jacobson_12_18f.authcheckdam.pdf. The problems with this contention are examined in Chapter 3, text accompanying notes 32–5.

Moreover, for the reasons explained in Chapter 3, the capacity of the market to self-correct (a primary expectation with respect to seller power) is significantly weaker than in the case of seller power. The irony is that abusive buyer behavior is more in need of remedy than is seller abuse, but remedies are harder to frame.

The discussion begins with an analysis of conduct-oriented theories of liability. The analysis separates the limited set of doctrines, largely developed outside the United States, that focus on controlling exploitive behavior against producers from the doctrines and standards that focus primarily on conduct designed to exclude competition with other buyers. Because it is difficult to fashion conduct-oriented remedies to address the harm of exploiting producers, the analysis also examines how much buyer power and what kinds of abuse would justify a structural remedy and whether structural remedies should receive more emphasis.[3]

I. DOCTRINES TO REGULATE UNILATERAL CONDUCT ARE DIFFICULT TO DESIGN AND ENFORCE

A. Rules Governing Unjustified Exploitation of Buyer Power

The difficulties of controlling abusive buyer power used to exploit producers are substantial and often intractable. On the one hand, freedom to set price and other elements of buying are central to the competitive process. But on the other hand, unreasonable and unjustified exploitation of buyer power is contrary to the long-run public interest in workably competitive markets. It also has a significant adverse effect on the long-run, dynamic efficiency of the economy. Even when the fact of abusive exploitation is indisputable, there remains the very difficult task of identifying a remedy that will protect the supplier without unnecessarily distorting the market. Rigid rules on buying can create an umbrella effect in which inefficient and rigid supply chains are insulated from change.

When the anticompetitive acts that exploit the producer are embedded in the core of the transaction, it is hard for competition agencies or courts to intervene effectively. For example, the waterbed effect, other exploitive price terms, and forcing extra expenses on suppliers have adverse effects on the competitive process, but these are the consequences of decisions that

[3] The use of structural remedies is, however, unlikely under current enforcement policies globally.

are fundamental to the market process—what price to pay, what quantity to buy and other terms of the transaction. Thus, when a firm with buyer power exploits its upstream suppliers to enrich itself to the detriment of those suppliers, competition policy faces the challenge of identifying specific rules of conduct that can constrain the monopsonist's discretion without substituting the direct regulation of specific buying decisions.

If the bargaining process results in an agreement under which a seller is obligated to charge 'too low' a price to the large buyer and has to make up the difference elsewhere, the dominant buyer has caused a waterbed effect. But forcing the dominant buyer to concern itself with the details of the costs its supplier faces and how the supplier will conduct its business would directly interfere with a robust buying process in which buyers negotiate for lower prices. Because there is no necessarily 'correct' price for any product, inhibiting bargaining because of its potential effects on third parties can significantly impair the competitive process. Again, the waterbed effect is a serious competitive problem, and some buyers are fully aware of the consequences that flow from their demands. But intent in such circumstances is unlikely to provide a useful criterion for competitive policy given the myriad ways in which actors can plausibly deny intent to harm.

The mantra from American monopoly law is that monopolists can charge monopoly prices with impunity.[4] Control over exploitive conduct requires, first, that competition law reject that position. This appears to be a less radical step in the European and other legal systems because of the broader mandate against abuse of a dominant position, which speaks to both exploitation and exclusion.[5] Some might question whether American law historically has been so willing to tolerate exploitation of monopoly power,[6] but certainly contemporary American policy on monopoly has been focused almost exclusively on the merits or harms of

---

[4] See *Verizon Commc'ns v Law Offices of Curtis V. Trinko, LLP*, 540 U.S. 398 (2004); *Rambus, Inc. v FTC*, 522 F.3d 456 (D.C. Cir. 2008).

[5] Compare *Rambus*, 522 F.3d 457, with Case COMP/38.636–RAMBUS, at 10–11 (12 September 2009), available at http://ec.europa.eu/competition/antitrust/cases/dec_docs/38636/38636_1203_1.pdf (European Commission settlement that imposed price limits on Rambus).

[6] See *United States v Aluminum Co. of Am. (Alcoa)*, 148 F.2d 416 (2d Cir. 1945); *United States v Reading Co.*, 253 U.S. 26 (1920). Both decisions imposed dissolution based on exploitation of monopoly power. See generally Peter C Carstensen, 'Remedies for Monopolization from *Standard Oil* to *Microsoft* and *Intel*: The Changing Nature of Monopoly Law from Elimination of Market Power to Regulation of Its Use' (2012) 85 *Southern California Law Review* 815 (historically American monopoly law sought to dismantle monopoly rather than merely regulate its use).

specific exclusionary conduct.[7] Hence, to challenge exploitive conduct that has no direct impact on competitors of the buyer would push American law beyond its conventional criteria for reviewing such conduct. There are cases, as discussed in Chapter 7, in which buyer cartels or even buying groups have been condemned because of their exploitive character. In addition, a handful of cases such as *Reading Railroad*[8] in 1920 and the network programming cases[9] in the 1970s have focused almost exclusively on condemning unilateral exploitation of suppliers. Indeed, *Weyerhaeuser* indirectly confirms that exploitation of suppliers without any prospect of effect in the downstream market is objectionable, at least, if unlawful means are employed to achieve the exploitation.[10]

There are, however, two American decisions that appear to authorize exploitation by buyers. In the *Kartel* decision, then-judge, now Justice, Breyer wrote that the exploitation of doctors by the health insurer that purchased their services was acceptable because the insurer allegedly passed on the lower costs to its customers.[11] This is an extreme example of consumer welfare being used as the criterion for determining the merits of restraints of trade. The other decision involved a buyers' cartel that had allocated motion picture films among its members.[12] The Sixth Circuit held that this naked restraint could be judged under the rule of reason on the grounds of its purported service to consumer welfare.[13]

---

[7] See *Trinko*, 540 U.S. 398 at 407 ('[T]he possession of monopoly power will not be found unlawful unless it is accompanied by an element of anticompetitive conduct.'); *Rambus*, 522 F.3d 456 (rejecting a finding of monopolization when excessive prices resulted from inclusion of patented elements within a standard).

[8] *Reading*, 253 U.S. 26.

[9] *United States v CBS, Inc.*, 459 F. Supp. 832 (C.D. Cal. 1978) (forbidding network practices that unreasonably exploited independent program providers); *United States v Nat'l Broad. Co.*, 449 F. Supp. 1127 (C.D. Cal. 1978) (same); *United States v Am. Broad. Co.*, 1980 WL 2013 (C.D. Cal. 1980) (similar consent decree to those imposed on the other networks). See also *Mandeville Island Farms, Inc. v Am. Crystal Sugar Co.*, 334 U.S. 219 (1948) (collusion to exploit producers violates section 1 of the Sherman Act).

[10] See *Weyerhaeuser Co. v Ross-Simmons Hardwood Lumber Co.*, 549 U.S. 312 (2007).

[11] *Kartell v Blue Shield of Mass.*, 749 F.2d 922, 931 (1st Cir. 1984) ('courts at least should be cautious—reluctant to condemn too speedily—an arrangement that, on its face, appears to bring low price benefits to the consumer.').

[12] *Balmoral Cinema Inc. v Allied Artists Pictures Corp.*, 885 F.2d 313 (6th Cir. 1989). But see *United States v Capital Serv. Inc.*, 756 F.2d 502 (7th Cir. 1984) (finding that cartelistic agreements to allocate motion picture exhibitions are per se illegal).

[13] *Balmoral Cinema*, 885 F.2d at 316–17 ('The practice at issue does not facially appear always or almost always to restrict competition, decrease output and raise

The EU traditionally has articulated a strong consumer welfare criterion for its actions. One decision declined to condemn exploitive conduct that harmed only upstream producers.[14] However, a later case suggested in dicta that imposing unduly low prices on suppliers could violate Article 102 of the Treaty on the Functioning of the European Union (TFEU).[15] That case, which involved claims of predatorily low prices for motion picture films, posed particularly difficult questions of valuation on which the determination of unduly low price would depend. A broader definition of consumer harm that incorporates a concern for the long-run dynamics of markets would provide a rationale for action.[16]

The European Commission's Green Paper on abusive trade practices issued in 2014 describes a second dimension of the EU policy.[17] It concluded that there is, in fact, significant concern for harm to producers, but for ideological or conceptual reasons this concern is located in unfair competition law rather than competition law. This formal distinction has little functional utility if the two areas of law work in harmony to ensure that the overall competitive process prospers. Many of the EU member countries have adopted modified regulatory regimes that provide some

prices. Rather it may simply lower prices paid by exhibitors to distributors and hence indirectly to producers in a market where the distributors and the producers have historically wielded great market power over film products at the expense of exhibitors. Exhibitors, as purchasers of films, may be justified in combating the market power of film suppliers by group action. Such action may lower prices to moviegoers at the box office and may serve rather than undermine consumer welfare.')

[14] Case IV.F.1./36.834, *Fenin/SNS+Spain* (Comm'n 1999) (rejecting claim of abuse of dominance by unreasonably delaying payments for medical supplies based on the conclusion that the buyer was not engaged in commerce and was rather a social organization); see also Case C-205/03, *Fenin v Comm'n*, at 66 (Opinion of the Advocate General [same case on appeal]) ('The existence of a monopsony does not pose a serious threat to competition . . . [A]n undertaking in a monopsonistic position has no interest in bringing such pressure to bear on its suppliers that they . . . leave the upstream market.').

[15] Case 298/83, *Comité des Industries Cinématographiques des Communautés Européennes v Comm'n* [1985] ECR 1105.

[16] A study by the staff of the Finnish competition authority identified this point as the basis for its concerns about buyer power in retail grocery markets. See Tom Bjorkroth et al (2012), 'Study on Trade in Groceries', available at http://www.kkv.fi/globalassets/kkv-suomi/julkaisut/selvitykset/2012/en/fca-reports-1-2012-study-on-trade-in-groceries.pdf.

[17] See European Commission, *Green Paper on Unfair Trading Practices in the Business-to-Business Food and Non-Food Supply Chain in Europe*, COM(2013) 37 final, available at http://eur-lex.europa.eu/legal-content/EN/TXT/PDF/?uri=CELEX:52013DC0037&from=EN.

ground rules governing abusive purchasing practices by large buyers. These rules are examined in Chapter 6.

In 2014, Australia's competition authority initiated a case in which it charged a major grocery retailer with violations of the competition law through 'unconscionable' conduct.[18] The retailer demanded rebates from its suppliers based on allegedly misleading claims about the value of services it provided to the suppliers. Subsequently, the retailer consented to an order to cease the conduct and was ordered to pay a substantial fine.[19]

Assuming that competition law can and should concern itself with unjustified exploitation of buyer power by a single firm,[20] one encounters the even more troubling issues of how to frame workable and transparent rules. The difficulty is that, in general, it is hard to separate with coherent criteria the kind of market-based bargaining that is the fundamental objective of a competitive market process from unreasonable and unjustified demands. This would be as true for all-or-nothing contracts as it would be for simple downward price pressures. The size of a purchase is directly related to the needs of the buyer. Requirements contracts and exclusive dealing contracts can also have significant economic efficiency justifications. Moreover, it is likely to be very difficult to separate the permissible contract terms from the impermissible because the difference is not in the contracts themselves but in the impact of those contracts on the producers.[21]

The calculus is further complicated when the wrongful act is simply the price offered for a purchase. The only measure of unreasonableness is the relationship of the contract price to the cost of producing the product. But such price decisions are at the core of a market process, and the seller

---

18 See Press Release, Australian Competition and Consumer Commission, 'ACCC Takes Action Against Coles for Alleged Unconscionable Conduct Towards its Suppliers' (5 May 2014), available at http://www.accc.gov.au/media-release/accc-takes-action-against-coles-for-alleged-unconscionable-conduct-towards-its-suppliers.

19 Press Release, Australian Competition and Consumer Commission, 'Court Finds Coles Engaged in Unconscionable Conduct and Orders Coles to Pay $10 Million Penalties' (22 December 2014), available at https://www.accc.gov.au/media-release/court-finds-coles-engaged-in-unconscionable-conduct-and-orders-coles-pay-10-million-penalties.

20 Interestingly, in cases of conspiracy and merger, this is exactly the focus of concern.

21 Note that the focus of analysis is on the exploitive effect of such agreements; the earlier analysis showed that the use of such terms can have exclusionary effects on competitors of the buyer. When there is an exclusionary effect, competition law is more willing to evaluate the merits of the conduct.

will have 'voluntarily' agreed. In specific circumstances—with extrinsic economic evidence as well as internal documentation—it may be possible to identify specific purchases as having unjustified, adverse effects on producers. From this alone, however, one cannot distill the kinds of predictable standards that business requires, nor does it identify administrable remedies. The challenge of identifying effective and enforceable remedies that avoid undue market distortion is perhaps an even greater challenge than finding that specific conduct is abusive.

Equally intractable are rules that seek to address discrimination and refusals to buy. American law has attempted to regulate differential pricing that results in an adverse effect on competition or a competitor through the Robinson-Patman Act.[22] As discussed in more detail in the next chapter, this law has become largely toothless. First, its focus is on the seller and not the buyer, so that its sanctions do not address the source of the problem in situations in which buyer power is abused. Second, it effectively discourages sales to minor buyers exactly because of the risk of a legal challenge to the prices. Third, in order to be consistent with economic reality, the statute protects prices set in response to competition for a particular sale and allows a cost justification defense. Although some have argued that the statute was a reasonable response to irrational price discounts historically,[23] without a major revision it provides little or no protection to small buyers today.[24] It is therefore unlikely that Robinson-Patman can be used to help disfavored buyers.

Buyers should be subject to standards that prohibit or provide control over abusive conduct that exploits their suppliers. It should be unlawful for a buyer to manipulate commodity market prices to drive down its own input costs.[25] Similarly, a coherent and defined rule of illegality should apply to overpaying for inputs by a monopsonist to drive competing buyers from the market, as discussed in more detail in the next subsection. In addition, also as examined in the next subsection, exclusionary conduct that seeks to exclude downstream competitors of a buyer also entrenches a buyer's power. The lack of legitimate justification for these activities provides the basis for a consistent and coherent basis for condemnation.

---

[22] 15 U.S.C. § 13 (2016).

[23] See Gerald Van Cise, 'Religion and Antitrust' (1978) 23 *Antitrust Bulletin* 455, 475–7.

[24] See, eg, John Kirkwood, 'Reforming the Robinson-Patman Act to Serve Consumers and Control Powerful Buyers' (2015) 60 *Antitrust Bulletin* 358.

[25] See, eg, *Knevelbaard Dairies v Kraft Foods, Inc.*, 232 F.3d 979 (9th Cir. 2000) (cheese buyer manipulated the public commodity market price down in order to negotiate contracts using that price as the basis).

B. Rules Governing Unjustified Exclusionary Use of Buyer Power

The primary policy remedy for abusive monopoly is the prohibition of unjustified barriers to new competition. This approach assumes, implicitly, that buyers have purchasing discretion; if barriers to entry are as low as practicable, the market process (driven by buyer demand and power) will limit and often eliminate monopoly over time.[26] In the case of monopsony, however, producers are less able than buyers to sponsor or support entry into a monopsonistic downstream market. And as discussed earlier, entrepreneurs are substantially less likely to see potential gains from entry. Nonetheless, it is possible to fashion policies that deter powerful buyers from overtly undertaking or inducing exclusionary conduct. The greatest weakness in contemporary competition law is a lack of strict standards for judging the merits of such conduct.

Exclusionary abuses of monopsony power that focus on eliminating rival buyers and entrenching the monopsony are amendable to competition rules. Buyer conduct that directly compels a supplier to refuse to deal with the buyer's competitors or requires that the competitors receive less favorable terms should be prohibited in the absence of a legitimate business justification. The American decisions in *Toys 'R' Us v FTC*[27] and *Klor's v Broadway-Hale*[28] illustrate this response. In each case, buyers compelled their suppliers to collude with each other to refuse to deal with the buyers' competitors. At least two early American decisions involving collusion also condemned this use of buyer power.[29] In 2015, an American trial court again affirmed that antitrust law forbids dominant firms from using their buyer power to exclude or disadvantage their competitors.[30]

The Australian court system reached a similar decision, involving much more explicitly unilateral conduct, when buyer-defendants sought agreements with their suppliers to refuse to deal with competitors of the

---

[26] The durability of many monopolies that are subject only to conduct controls makes this assumption at least questionable and would justify a policy aimed at dismantling the monopoly itself. See, eg, Carstensen, *supra* note 6.

[27] *Toys 'R' Us v FTC*, 221 F.3d 928 (7th Cir. 2000).

[28] *Klor's, Inc. v Broadway-Hale Stores, Inc.*, 359 U.S. 207 (1959).

[29] *Montague v Lowry*, 193 U.S. 38 (1904) (fireplace and mantle retailers coerced suppliers to refuse to deal with competitors of the buyer cartel and enforce resale prices); *United States v E. States Retail Lumber Dealers Ass'n*, 234 U.S. 600 (1914) (retail lumber dealers organized to boycott any wholesaler of lumber who sold directly to retail customers).

[30] *Cobb Theatres III, LLC v AMC Entm't Holdings, Inc.*, 101 F. Supp. 3d 1319 (N.D. Ga. 2015) (holding that larger theater operator had used threats to coerce distributors to refuse licenses to smaller competitor).

buyer.[31] The EU has done little with respect to unilateral exclusionary practices by buyers, but its one decision is consistent with the general proposition that unjustifiable exclusionary practices are unlawful.[32] Cases involving overtly exclusionary buying practices are most likely to occur in markets that have significant potential for competition among buyers in the absence of the exclusionary practices. Two other American cases also involved explicit use of monopsony power in one market to induce sellers to refuse to deal with buyers in adjacent competitive markets.[33] This conduct expanded the multimarket company's monopsony.

Requirements contracts and exclusive supply contracts can also have exclusionary effects with respect to other buyers. A requirements contract, that is, a contract under which a producer provides all of a buyer's requirements of an input, will have such an effect if: (1) the contract commits the supplier to sell a substantial portion of its then-current production capacity to the contracting buyer; (2) the supplier cannot expand production; and (3) other sources of the commodity are not readily available. An exclusive supply contract, in contrast, under which a supplier agrees to sell its entire output to a single buyer, explicitly forecloses competitive buyers from access to the producer.[34] These contracts will have an adverse effect on competition and potential entrants unless sufficient competing supply capacity exists or can readily enter the market.[35] Both types of agreement function as all-or-nothing contracts, which, over time, can harm and deter

---

[31] *TPC v Carlton United Breweries Ltd.* (1990) 24 FCR 532 (Austl.) (dominant brewer coerced one of its can suppliers to refuse to supply a discounting brewer); see also *Austl. Competition & Consumer Comm'n v Austl. Safeway Stores* (2003) 129 FCR 339 (Austl.) (Safeway used its buyer power to refuse to deal with bakeries that sold bread to its competitors at prices lower than those paid by Safeway).

[32] See Case IV/d-2/34,780, *Virgin/British Airways* (Comm'n decision, 1999), aff'd, *British Airways v Comm'n*, [2003] ECR II-5917 (General Court, 2003), aff'd, [2007] ECR I-2331 (Court of Justice) (holding that use of an exclusionary compensation system for travel agents by an airline holding 39 percent of the market had an unlawful effect with respect to a competing airline).

[33] *United States v Griffith*, 334 U.S. 100 (1948); *Schine Chain Theaters v United States*, 334 U.S. 110 (1948).

[34] See, eg, *FTC v Mylan*, 62 F. Supp. 2d 25 (D.D.C. 1999) (drug maker entered into exclusive supply contracts with key ingredient producers; because entry into the supply market was very difficult, the manufacturer was able to raise prices substantially to its customers).

[35] See *In re South African Raisins v SAD Holdings Ltd.*, 16/IR/DEC99 (Competition Tribunal, S. Afr.) (condemning restrictive agreement requiring sale of entire crop as condition of membership in the cooperative); *Competition Comm'n v Patensie Sitrus Behrend Beperk*, 37/CR/Jun01 (Competition Tribunal, S. Afr.) (condemning restrictive buying practices affecting citrus producers).

producers. As the number of producers declines, especially those not subject to either exclusive dealing or high volume requirements, the barriers to entry at both the buying and producing levels will increase.

Because legitimate business justifications exist for some restraints on suppliers' ability to deal with third parties, it is impossible to fashion simple, absolute rules. The challenge for competition law is to distinguish between agreements that unnecessarily restrict supplier access to third parties and those that are necessary for the efficient operation of the market. It is not easy to differentiate between the legitimate and illegitimate uses of such contracts. In addition, if a less harmful restraint serves the legitimate goal, the chosen restraint should be deemed unreasonable. In a market already subject to buyer power, the risks of retaliation or discrimination are very real. Hence, producers may be very reluctant to complain—especially if there are significant risks that they will not prevail.[36]

Tolerant standards for these agreements can very much limit the effectiveness of any effort to protect the competitive process from buyer power. The better policy is to impose a structured rule of reason. The challenger should have the burden of proving that the buyer has monopsony or significant buyer power and that the agreement implementing the refusal to deal has an adverse competitive effect. If the challenger establishes these elements, the burden would shift to the buyer to justify its conduct. It should first prove that the restraint has a legitimate business purpose that a rational non-monopsonist would embrace. Second, the buyer should prove that its conduct is not more anticompetitive than reasonably necessary to achieve the permissible objective. It is feasible for courts or agencies to review and evaluate the merits of buyer-supplied justifications. Putting the persuasion burden on the buyer means that it has to convince the decision maker that its justification is valid; if the issue remains uncertain, the buyer would lose.

The structured approach to exclusionary conduct draws on the analytic model employed in both the *Microsoft* and *Visa* cases.[37] Those decisions employed a four-step process. In the first step, the complainant must establish that the defendant has sufficient market power to warrant review of the complained-of conduct.[38] The complainant then must show that the conduct at issue can harm the competitive process and has caused some

[36] See European Commission, *supra* note 17, at 7.

[37] *United States v Microsoft*, 253 F.3d 34 (D.C. Cir. 2001); *United States v Visa USA*, 344 F.3d 229 (2d Cir. 2003).

[38] *Microsoft*, 253 F.3d at 51; *Visa* 344 F.3d at 238.

harm either to competition itself or to the competitor.[39] The complainant has the burden of persuasion on those steps.[40]

If those two steps are satisfied, the defendant must then advance a legitimate business justification for its conduct.[41] If it does not have a valid justification, its conduct is condemned. But the defendant must both allege the justification *and* offer some proof to support it.[42] If it can, the burden shifts back to the challenger. The challenger must then prove that the proffered justification is pretextual or identify alternatives that would serve the legitimate interest but with less harm to competition. The challenger can prevail if it establishes either.

In seller conduct cases, the American courts put the burden of persuasion on the plaintiff to convince the court that the defendant's justifications are not valid.[43] Only if the challenger bears that burden can it prevail.[44] In the case of buyer power, this review process would be more effective if the defendant carried the burden of persuasion that the proffered justification is not pretextual and that there is no less-anticompetitive course of conduct. The challenger would still have to allege, with some evidentiary support, that the explanation for the restraint is pretextual or identify a potentially less-anticompetitive option. The defendant would then have to persuade the decision maker that the harm had a legitimate justification and that there was no less harmful way to achieve the legitimate goal. This approach does not require the defendant to prove a negative, even if

---

[39] *Microsoft*, 253 F.3d at 59; *Visa*, 344 F.3d at 238.

[40] Proof of monopoly or monopsony power is the least easily defined element of the claim; however, the imposition of unusual or exploitive terms in an agreement should suffice to establish this fact. Indeed, American courts have recognized that proof of market (or monopsony) power can come from proof of specific competitively unjustifiable conduct even if the market remains essentially undefined. See, eg, *Re/Max Int'l v Realty One, Inc.*, 173 F.3d 995, 1018 (6th Cir. 1999).

[41] *Microsoft*, 253 F.3d at 59; *Visa*, 344 F.3d at 238.

[42] This step includes rebuttal of any contention that the restraint lacks a legitimate function. Because the proposed approach for buyer power cases would impose the burden of proof of business justification on the proponent of the restraint, this issue would be separate from and prior to any inquiry into less restrictive alternatives.

[43] *Microsoft*, 253 F.3d at 59; *Visa*, 344 F.3d at 238.

[44] Those decisions also postulate (but never employ) a final step in which the decision maker balances the costs and benefits of the harmful conduct. See *Microsoft*, 253 F.3d at 59; *Visa*, 344 F.3d at 238. An open-ended weighing is not a valid methodology for implementing policies of promoting and protecting the competitive process. It would confer on the decision maker, whether court or agency, too much discretion to condemn conduct which in fact serves a legitimate economic interest.

it bears the burden of showing that it had a legitimate goal that justified the harmful restraint. The rationale for proposing this stricter standard is that exclusionary conduct by buyers is more likely to be durable if not remedied. Hence, the risk of error should rest on the monopsonist and not the producer.

This proposed structure would focus the review process on the merits (or lack thereof) of exclusionary conduct by buyers, but it would still involve extensive and costly efforts to sustain the claim. Hence, policing any but the most exclusionary practices is likely to be difficult and relatively infrequent, especially given the predictable reluctance of producers to complain. Moreover, in the absence of an increase in the number of buyers, the prohibition of specific, unjustified and overt exclusionary agreements is unlikely to keep producers from tacit refusals to deal with, or impose unfavorable terms on, smaller buyers in order to retain the loyalty of a major buyer.

Another means of creating and entrenching buyer power is the use of overbidding (sometimes called overbuying)—paying a price for an input that is higher than competitors of the buyer can afford, thus foreclosing them from its use. By raising its rivals' costs, the dominant buyer creates a price squeeze that drives the competing buyers from the market and confers on the dominant buyer even more power to reduce prices in the future.[45] The primary focus of this conduct is to exclude competing buyers in order to increase the capacity to exploit producers. Competition rules, in contrast to direct regulation that mandates input prices or controls buying relationships, must provide a consistent way to differentiate between unduly high prices and the ordinary results of demand.

The Supreme Court in *Weyerhaeuser* excused conduct that was consistent with a long-run exclusionary strategy of overpaying for logs that the buyer converted into lumber.[46] The resulting lumber was sold in a competitive market. Raising the price of this key input might make it difficult for competing buyers to survive, but a buyer facing increased demand and

---

[45] For the general model of raising rivals' costs, see Thomas Krattenmaker and Steven C Salop, 'Anticompetitive Exclusion: Raising Rivals' Cost by Gaining Power Over Price' (1986) 96 *Yale Law Journal* 209. Salop has focused expressly on overbuying and argues that a violation of antitrust law should be found if the only goal is increased monopsony power, if the price paid is above the expected resale value of the product, and if there is a downstream effect on consumer prices as a result of raising the costs of the rivals. Steven C Salop, 'Anticompetitive Overbuying by Power Buyers' (2005) 72 *Antitrust Law Journal* 669, 670.

[46] *Weyerhaeuser Co. v Ross-Simmons Hardwood Lumber Co.*, 549 U.S. 312 (2007).

a shortage of logs might well bid up the price in order to fulfill its contracts. Although not acknowledged in the Court's decision, Weyerhaeuser had a significant log supply available under long-term, fixed-price contracts.[47] By increasing only the price it paid for incremental supplies, it was able to maintain an average cost below its marginal cost. If, in fact, the prices paid for the incremental logs made the processing of those logs uneconomic at prevailing lumber prices, then the conduct lacked a prima facie legitimate business justification. The proper focus, from a competitive process perspective, should have been on the marginal price paid for logs, not the average costs of logs.[48] But even then, a buyer might argue that it had mistakenly overestimated the future market price of logs. Such a mistake is harmful to the competitive process even if there is no provable intent to harm competition. Certainly the buyer would know that its price decision would raise the price of the input, potentially making it impossible for its competitors to survive. Regardless of the long-run goals of the buyer, there is a recognized harm to the competitive process.

But even if those facts are accepted, the effect of a stricter rule condemning such buying practices would be to impose an inhibition on the large buyer and open the door to strategic challenges by competing buyers who objected to the higher prices. Hence such a standard can result in lower input prices than a more robustly competitive market might produce. After all, errors in buying prices can and do happen regardless of the size of the buyer.

Thus, the hard problem is what rule to impose on a dominant buyer with respect to either the price or quantity of inputs it buys. The Supreme Court's answer was to require proof: (1) that the price paid for the input made the cost of the resulting product exceed the price received for that product; and (2) that the buyer could recoup the excessive expenditure by lowering the price it paid for the input in the future.[49] Most commentators agree that the effect of this ruling is to make it all but impossible to sustain an overbuying claim despite the plausibility of harm to producers over time as the competitive process is undermined.[50] In protecting the freedom of buyers to make mistakes, the Court has imposed a standard

---

[47] Michael E Haglund, '*Weyerhaeuser*'s Aftermath: Increased Vulnerability of Resource-Based Input Markets to Monopsony' (2008) 53 *Antitrust Bulletin* 413, 424–5.

[48] Keith Hylton, '*Weyerhaeuser*, Predatory Bidding, and Error Costs' (2008) 53 *Antitrust Bulletin* 51, 58.

[49] *Weyerhaeuser*, 549 U.S. at 312–13.

[50] See Hylton, *supra* note 48; see also John Lopatka and Roger Blair, 'Predatory Buying and the Antitrust Laws' (2008) *Utah Law Review* 415.

that denies to input markets any control over short-term overbidding that can, in fact, result in substantial long-term harm to the competitive process. The result in *Weyerhaeuser* serves to highlight the challenges of developing workable standards for exclusionary practices that directly affect the market process.

A dominant buyer that buys input in several markets while its competitor buys in only one can also create a price squeeze by bidding up input prices in the competitor's market. The multimarket firm can thus raise the costs of all of its competitor's purchases while adversely affecting only a part of its own. The Supreme Court confronted this exact scenario in a case in which the challenged merger would create a multimarket buyer able to impose a cost squeeze on its rival.[51] The Court ignored the cost increase element of the plaintiff's case and rejected the challenge based on its view that the plaintiff had not suffered a cognizable injury. The Court has similarly rejected any contention that a price squeeze created by a vertically integrated firm selling to downstream buyers raises an antitrust concern.[52]

As with exclusionary agreements, the challenge in developing a predatory buying standard is the need to balance the goal of facilitating the market process by allowing buyers and sellers to have as much freedom of action as possible with the goal of disallowing unjustified high prices for inputs that harm the longer run competitive process. The failure to focus on raising rivals' costs, together with the requirement of proof of recoupment, adds further barriers to effective doctrine. The recoupment criterion, taken from classic predatory pricing doctrine,[53] seeks to distinguish between irrational or misguided overpaying for inputs and those intended to cause harm to the competitive process. The criterion is not well adapted to buyer side abuse because it focuses on the gains to the buyer and not the harm to the competitive process. Irrational exclusionary conduct, that is, overpaying for inputs with neither a reasonable prospect of recoupment nor any other legitimate justification (such as a need to fulfill contractual commitments immediately), can still change the market structure and the future willingness of potential competitors to enter. Therefore, although proof of expected recoupment would identify unambiguous anticompetitive bidding, the absence of proof of recoupment does not disprove the harmfulness of excessive bidding.

---

[51] *Cargill, Inc. v Monfort of Colo., Inc.*, 479 U.S. 104 (1986). This is one of the few private actions seeking to enforce merger law.

[52] *Pac. Bell Tel. Co. v linkLine Commc'ns, Inc.*, 555 U.S. 438 (2009).

[53] The Supreme Court first articulated this doctrine in *Brooke Group Ltd. v Brown and Williamson Corp.*, 509 U.S. 209 (1993), and then adopted it as part of its restrictive ruling in *Weyerhaeuser*.

The Court's failure to focus on the anticompetitive harm of rising rivals' costs is hard to justify. The central evaluative criterion should be the reason for the higher input price. When the challenged action is inconsistent with rational, legitimate business decision making, it makes 'no business sense' and should give rise to liability. Again, the burden-shifting model proposed for other exclusionary conduct would provide a stricter doctrinal constraint on dominant buyers. But when the issue is strictly higher prices that affect competing buyers, the challenger should ultimately have the burden of persuasion with respect to its claim that the dominant buyer's practices lacked economic rationality.[54]

The central observation is that exclusionary conduct—unless unrelated to the transaction, such as express naked restraints on selling to other buyers—is hard to control. There is a significant challenge in articulating a consistent and enforceable standard to govern such issues. The unwillingness of experienced competition law systems like the American system to recognize the damage imposed on the competitive process through the exercise of monopsony power makes this task even more daunting. In addition, there are very practical problems in proving that prices are 'too high' or that other contract terms are 'unreasonable'. When exclusionary practices directly affect downstream markets, competition law doctrine acknowledges their relevance, but it is harder to get recognition of the competitive concerns when only the upstream producers are harmed in the longer run by the exclusion of alternative buyers.

C. Remedying Unreasonable Exploitive and Exclusionary Conduct

For the reasons elaborated in the prior subsection, the development of a workable remedy for exploitation that is consistent with market freedom is extremely problematic except when the exploitation results from the use of unlawful means. Otherwise, the challenge is to define a rule or rules by which the monopsonist is to operate in the future. Any effort to define prices or select the firm's trading partners would create major market distortions. To be sure, in some situations it might be possible to require that a firm make its purchases using a Dutch auction, in which producers offer a price and a quantity and buyers purchase the quantity they require at the highest price bid necessary to acquire that volume. This remedy would be

[54] Some contexts will lend themselves to such proof. For example, when a dominant buyer pays more in one market for inputs than it pays in other markets, the inference is strong that it is acting to raise the prices its competitors pay in that market; presumably it could have obtained the larger quantity in the other supply markets at lower cost.

workable, however, only for relatively standardized commodities. In most instances the buyer would have to define its need and then negotiate and inspect the results.

Remedies for specific exclusionary conduct are more feasible, but necessarily they would focus on prohibiting specific harmful acts. While this could eliminate such conduct, powerful buyers would retain the capacity to use their power overtly or tacitly in other harmful ways. A broader remedy that sought to control overall conduct by a firm that had engaged in specific exclusionary acts would once again put the regulatory system in charge of business decisions and strategy. This is inconsistent with the concept of a competitive market system.

Even when a remedy is feasible, the institutional problem of continued oversight remains. Competition agencies are not well adapted to continued review of marketplace actions and decisions. In effect, the agencies would become part of the buyers' administration. To be sure, regulatory agencies dealing with electricity, natural gas and transportation services have engaged in active price regulation as well as overseeing the rights of purchasers to have access to the relevant good or service. But such systems are anathema to the concept of a workably competitive market. It would require a good deal of ingenuity for an agency to develop a remedy that is largely self-enforcing.

D. The Goals of Competition Policy Applied to Monopsonistic Conduct

As discussed in Chapter 4, the goals of competition policy will strongly affect elements of the policies adopted to deal with unilateral conduct. Exploitive buyer conduct presents a particularly interesting example. A purely consumer-oriented policy would largely ignore such conduct unless it had some demonstrable adverse effect on consumer prices. If maximizing total welfare is the goal, then there should be more concern, but even here the concern would require a complex weighing of gains and losses before any exploitation could be condemned. Moreover, the enforcement costs as well as a concern for error would likely lead to a rejection of any intervention beyond that which a consumer concern would justify. Indeed, even the goal of preserving and protecting the competitive process, while more explicitly recognizing the importance of the abuse of buyer power, does not lead to any general rules that would condemn such conduct because any such rules are likely to interfere with the competitive process itself. Only a fairness goal provides a basis for a stronger set of standards that would allow decision makers to condemn specific exploitive conduct as 'unfair'. But as shown in Chapter 2, this approach does not yield the kind of rules or standards that would provide workable and coherent guidance to economic actors.

In the case of exclusionary conduct directed at competitors of the dominant buyer, using any of the goals as a guide to policy will result in condemnation of conduct that lacks justification. A concern for competition as a process should, however, lead to stricter rules on exclusion. Because exclusionary conduct is particularly harmful to the overall competitive process, that goal will support the stricter standards suggested here.

E. Conclusion—Conduct-oriented Standards and Remedies for Unilateral Abuse have Limited Effect

Remedies focused only on conduct-based remedies assume that such interventions will restore the competitive workings of the market. Explicitly exclusionary elements of buying agreements are amendable to such standards. However, contemporary standards are, overall, too tolerant of exclusionary effects and enable the creation of increased barriers to entry rather than the preserving of workably competitive buying markets.

It is far more difficult to construct meaningful rules that address abusive exploitive conduct of suppliers by buyers. Globally, there has been little or no effort to do this until very recently. Although competition law with the goal of protecting and advancing the competitive process ought to and in theory does condemn such conduct, developing standards and conventional competition-based remedies that are transparent, effective and enforceable is both difficult and likely to have only limited effect. The result, as described in Chapter 6, is that direct regulation has become the favored method of control over exploitive conduct.

II. STRUCTURAL REMEDIES TO AVOID MONOPSONY RISK

Given the extreme difficulty of fashioning specific conduct rules to control the abuse of monopsony, an indirect strategy for dealing with such situations is to restructure monopsonists so that they no longer have sufficient buyer power to distort markets. Although proof of specific abusive conduct would be necessary to establish liability,[55] the remedy would not regulate conduct, and so should not distort efficient production, but

---

[55] From time to time, there have been suggestions for a no-fault regime to control monopoly. Such a regime would apply when a durable but remediable monopoly exists that could be overcome by a restructuring. See Peter C Carstensen, 'False Positives in Identifying Liability for Exclusionary Conduct: Conceptual Error, Business Reality, and *Aspen*' 2008 *Wisconsin Law Review* 295.

would, by reorganizing the buying side of the market, eliminate or significantly reduce the risk of abuse. The goal of such a remedy would be to increase the number of buyers.

A structural remedy would be particularly relevant when the evidence shows supplier exploitation by a buyer rather than the use of buyer power to exclude competitors of the buyer. As discussed earlier, directly remedying exploitation is a challenge for competition policy because a conduct remedy would regulate in some degree the transactional relationships of the buyer. Exploitive conduct by a buyer over a period of time, however, would be powerful evidence of market failure and provide the predicate for restructuring the buying side of the market when feasible.[56]

In many American industries where buyer power is prominent, such as meat packing, poultry production and grocery retailing, firms are many times larger than necessary to achieve reasonable economies of scale.[57] Moreover, these entities operate multiple facilities, each of which produces at or above the minimum efficient scale. In particular, grocery retailing involves firms that are larger than any scale economy would explain. Thus, at a purely structural level, a reduction of concentration is feasible in these industries and would be unlikely to cause any significant or durable inefficiencies.[58] The appropriate standard would require competition authorities to look for persistent exploitation of buyer power and then determine whether dissolution of the enterprise would produce viable, efficient successor firms able to compete on both the buying and selling side of the market.

The structural approach could work in large economies such as the United States, India, the Russian Federation, China or the EU. For small economies, there would probably be more tension between the gains from achieving minimum efficient scale and the unavoidable risks to producers

---

The same approach could be applied to the buying side. However, such a standard is unlikely to appeal to policy makers in the contemporary world.

[56] The elements of a structural case against either monopoly or monopsony are (1) substantial market power; (2) the durability of that power (that is, market processes will not ameliorate it in the foreseeable future); and (3) remediability (the existence of a plausible way to restructure it).

[57] See Peter C Carstensen, 'Concentration and the Destruction of Competition in Agricultural Markets: The Case for Change in Public Policy' 2000 *Wisconsin Law Review* 531, 537.

[58] The restructuring of an enterprise might result in a mismatch in scale among its components, such as the distribution centers needed to support small grocery chains. This is a real challenge for those developing a dissolution plan. But these obstacles are not insurmountable and will diminish over time as the enterprise adjusts its components to its revised scale.

that arise from the substantial buyer power that can result from market restructuring. It is striking that in Australia, for example, there was apparently no consideration of buyer power as its grocery industry consolidated into a nationwide duopoly.[59] Similarly, in Finland, competition authorities have permitted mergers that significantly increased the buying side of the market even as they also recognized in other ways the problem of abusive buying practices.[60] Because there was no inherent correlation between buyer power and scale economies on the buying side, it is at least questionable whether the mergers were the only means of achieving whatever economies might have been claimed. Certainly, however, in smaller economies, there may well be difficult tradeoffs between efficiency and undue buyer power if changing production and distribution methods require greater scale. In such cases, the only feasible option to control exploitation of buyer power may be the use of one or more of the regulatory options examined in Chapter 6.

If a monopsonistic market structure exists, there must be legal authority to impose the remedy of dissolution. It does not appear that the EU Charter has conferred that right on its competition authority. But some jurisdictions other than the United States have granted such authority to their enforcement agencies.[61] But for many countries, a major statutory change would be necessary to empower agencies to seek the restructuring of markets.

The US Supreme Court early interpreted antitrust law to favor structural remedies for monopoly over conduct regulation.[62] However, contemporary

---

59 See Barbora Jedlickovva and Julie Clarke, 'Australia' in Pierre Kobel, Pranvera Këllezi and Bruce Kilpatrick (eds), *Antitrust in the Groceries Sector & Liability Issues in Relation to Corporate Social Responsibility* (Springer, Heidelberg 2015), available at http://www.ligue.org/uploads/documents/cycle%202015/Cycle%202015/Kiev%202013/2013rapportAaustralienaout.pdf.

60 See Bjorkroth et al, *supra* note 16, at 11–12.

61 See Barry J Rodger and Angus MacCulloch, *Competition Law in the EC and UK* (Routledge-Cavendish, London 2nd edn 2001) 120 (structural remedies are available but rarely used in the United Kingdom); and Derek Morris, 'Dominant Firm Behavior Under UK Competition Law' in Barry Hawk (ed), *International Antitrust Law & Policy: Fordham Corporate Law* (Juris Publishing, Huntington, NY 2003) 175, 180. See also Competition Act 89 of 1998 § 60(1)(b) (authorizing divestiture as a remedy for violations of § 8, which prohibits abuse of dominance in South Africa), and Competition Act, No. 12 of 2003, India Code (2014) (§ 4 prohibits abuse of dominance in India and § 28 authorizes 'division' of an enterprise that has violated § 4).

62 *Standard Oil Co. v United States*, 212 U.S. 1, 77–8 (1911) (holding that structural remedies to eliminate monopoly are an essential part of any judicial remedy); accord *United States v American Tobacco Co.*, 212 U.S. 106 (1912). See also Carstensen, *supra* note 6.

American doctrine disfavors such remedies.[63] The basis for this change in policy is the perception, for which there is some empirical support, that structural remedies have proven of limited utility in remedying monopoly.[64] (But, of course, the same is true for conduct remedies.) Furthermore, structural remedies, even if restored to favor, would involve costly and complex litigation. The courts would have to accept the change in strategy, and agencies would face the difficult task of differentiating between undue buyer exploitation and hard bargaining. If a violation was found, the next step would be developing appropriate structural relief. This would certainly be as challenging as defining conduct rules to limit abusive practices.

Another concern is that the risk of the imposition of structural remedies might discourage buyers from seeking efficiency gains. The trigger for liability under this hypothetical structural rule would be evidence of conduct that demonstrates 'market failure' and therefore warrants a structural response. But would any failure to buy or to buy on terms demanded by the producer be treated as evidence of exploitation? Any time a producer sells at prices below some measure of its costs might also be treated as an example of abuse. The risks of such characterization could inhibit buyers from bargaining effectively or discourage them from switching to better or lower-cost suppliers. Moreover, because the market share necessary for a firm to have buyer power is lower than that for monopoly, the number of firms that might see themselves as at risk, and so inhibited, could be substantially greater than the number inhibited by a threat of structural remedies for monopoly exploitation.

Some of these very concerns affect larger firms in Europe, where the standard of 'abuse of a dominant position' covers both buying and selling practices. Moreover, the European Commission has on occasion imposed price controls. Under the TFEU, however, the European Commission apparently lacks the authority to order the dissolution of a firm with dominance. Hence, it can only regulate future conduct.

A more realistic world view might discount these concerns and regard the broad deterrent effect of a potential structural remedy as providing a better means of controlling undue and abusive use of monopsony power.

---

[63] See, eg, *United States v Microsoft*, 253 F.3d 34, 107 (D.C. Cir. 2001) (rejecting structural remedy for a proven monopoly and declaring that 'more extensive equitable relief, particularly remedies such as divestiture designed to eliminate the monopoly altogether, . . . require a clearer indication of significant causal connection between the conduct and creation or maintenance of the market power').

[64] See, eg, William Kovacic, 'Failed Expectations: The Troubled Past and Uncertain Future of the Sherman Act as a Tool for Deconcentration' (1989) 74 *Iowa Law Review* 1105.

But, again, policy realism suggests that it is extremely unlikely that courts and agencies—already unwilling to use structural relief in seller side monopoly cases—would be willing to impose structural remedies on the buying side.

III. POLICY IMPLICATIONS OF THE LIMITS ON DIRECT REMEDY FOR MONOPSONY

Three implications follow from the fact that direct-conduct-oriented standards and remedies are not well suited to relieving the exploitive competitive problems that monopsony creates. First, in the face of a substantial and durable monopsony, feasible structural remedies, despite the general hostility to them, may be an appropriate option. The fact that independent entry is unlikely after a firm establishes its monopsonistic position, even if barriers are reduced, means that structural change to restore or create a more workably competitive buying market may be the only option for the intermediate to long run. But, as discussed in the prior subsection, this would require defining the scope or nature of the buying power that would trigger liability. Moreover, it would require a significant rethinking of American doctrine and a major revision to the competition laws of some other countries.

The second implication (explored in Chapter 6) is that markets in which buyer power is a likely source of anticompetitive harm should be governed by market-facilitating rules. This is the route that many competition policy systems have pursued. Like structural or conduct remedies, the potential for negative results may make it at most a second-best response.

Finally, stricter rules with respect to mergers and joint ventures that demonstrably affect buyer power might provide the best means of avoiding the creation of excessive buyer power in the first place. Chapters 7 and 8 explore these questions, but changes to these policies would be at best an incomplete response because they would not address those situations in which a firm, by internal growth and expansion, created monopsonistic power for itself.

IV. CONCLUSION

Substantial unilateral buyer power can generate more serious and durable harms to the competitive process than current policy recognizes. In fact, there is a credible argument that monopsony is more harmful to the long-run competitive process than is monopoly. Certainly, it is at least as harmful. But the same reasons that support the argument that monopsony is a more serious problem also explain why potential policy remedies are more problematic. Competition policy analysis should more fully and extensively evaluate the potential for direct remedies. The goal of these remedies should be both to increase the potential for entry into the buying side of the market and protect producers from undue exploitation. But the limited effectiveness of remedies once buyer power exists is the strongest argument for a stricter policy to protect against the creation of such power in the first place.

6. Market regulation and other strategies to remedy abuse of buyer power

As shown in Chapters 1 and 3, monopsony is a pervasive and significant feature of every national economy. As Chapter 5 has shown, when the primary impact of abusive buyer conduct is unilateral exploitation of producers, competition law has little capacity directly to limit or avoid these problems. However, a variety of laws and regulations, some of which stand outside conventional competition law, can address such exploitation. The focus of this chapter is the role of these laws in regulating the use of buyer power to assure producers of fair and reasonable treatment. Significant parts of this body of law were not born out of concern with buyer exploitation. Hence, there is often a less than perfect relationship between these laws and the problems that result from the abuse of buyer power.

The use of market conduct regulation to control monopsony highlights the centrality of law to the functioning of the economy. Legal regimes, including contract, business organization, tax, labor, patent, copyright, trademark and bankruptcy law, form the context within which enterprises operate. Without a coherent legal environment, most businesses, especially complex business organizations, could not reliably exist. The legal rules that define basic market organization and transactions can also have a substantial impact on how well or badly the market process functions. Moreover, specific legal regimes will favor particular types of economic organization and transactions. This analysis focuses on how general and specific laws and public policies can affect the durability and exploitation of buyer power. Hence, competition authorities and legislatures should give serious consideration to the likely competitive implications of such rules for both buyers and sellers.

There are three general strategies that can affect buyer power. Section I examines and evaluates regulation of buyer conduct. Section II addresses the strategies that involve the creation and protection of offsetting producer power. Section III evaluates the capacity of public sponsorship or the facilitation of alternative outlets for producers to constrain buyer power. Although in some important instances these may be the only available tools, they are generally inferior to a less-regulated, but workably competitive, buying market. Section IV concludes the chapter.

I. REGULATION OF BUYER CONDUCT

Market regulation policies seek to constrain buyer power to obtain reasonable prices and fair treatment for producers. This section focuses on how these general and specific laws and public policies work and affect the durability and exploitation of such power. Such policies can (1) regulate the behavior of buyers; (2) regulate the market process itself; or (3) impose floors or other transactional requirements. The analysis describes and evaluates these three regulatory approaches to market conduct by buyers.

A. Regulation of Strategic Buyer Conduct

A buyer with power over a supplier may be able to engage in a wide range of exploitive, strategic actions. The buyer may pay different prices to favored and disfavored producers even though there is no legitimate cost basis for the differentiation. Alternatively, monopsonists may force sellers to accept greater risks or costs without increased compensation by, for example, requiring them to provide special services or accept unilateral changes in price or other elements of long-term contracts. The UK Competition Commission has identified a large number of such unfair practices.[1] The Japan Fair Trade Commission has also challenged a number of exploitive practices by dominant buyers.[2]

Regulating specific actions by powerful buyers imposes on them distinct requirements beyond those that generally apply in the market. The underlying theory is that restricting the discretion of large buyers to engage in 'unfair' conduct will result in reasonable buying relationships. Implicit in

---

[1] Competition Commission (UK) (2000), 'Supermarkets: A Report on the Study of Groceries from Multiple Stores in the United Kingdom', available at http://webarchive.nationalarchives.gov.uk/20140402141250/http://www.competition-commission.org.uk/rep_pub/reports/2000/446super.htm. See also Paul W Dobson, 'Exploiting Buyer Power: Lessons from the British Grocery Trade' (2005) 72 *Antitrust Law Journal* 529, 558–9 (summarizing the results of UK Competition Commission report on British supermarkets).

[2] See Masako Wakui and Thomas K Cheng, 'Regulating Abuse of Superior Bargaining Position under the Japanese Competition Law: An Anomaly or a Necessity?' (2015) 3 *Journal of Antitrust Enforcement* 302, 304–07 (detailing recent cases).

such regulation is an acknowledgement of the existence and durability of the underlying buyer power. This type of regulation, therefore, focuses on reducing the abuse of power rather than seeking to eliminate the power itself. The expectation is that the powerful buyer whose buying power is constrained will operate in a reasonable fashion.

A number of countries have adopted limits on strategic conduct by dominant buyers, especially in connection with retailing and farming. In the United States, the Packers and Stockyards Act (PSA), adopted in 1921, prohibited discriminatory and unfair conduct by buyers of livestock.[3] The legislation was a response to a long history of exploitation of farmers by meat packers that culminated in a major Federal Trade Commission (FTC) study of the industry.[4] The Department of Justice relied on the report to file an antitrust case that was settled with a decree that required a fundamental restructuring of the buyers and imposed a number of limits on their conduct.[5] However, Congress determined that the settlement was inadequate to protect beef and pork producers, and it enacted the PSA. Subsequent legislation expanded the PSA's coverage to include contracts with poultry handlers and swine contractors, as contracts came to control all commercial poultry and most hog production.[6] Additional American

---

[3] Packers and Stockyards Act of 1921, 7 U.S.C. §§ 181–229b (2016). The original statute also covered the dairy sector. Later amendments eliminated coverage of the dairy sector and established separate provisions for poultry.

[4] Federal Trade Commission, Report of the Federal Trade Commission on the Meat-Packing Industry (1919–20), available at https://catalog.hathitrust.org/Record/008002972.

[5] The Department filed the suit along with a consent decree in 1920, but the meat packers sought to void the settlement, which was not fully enforced until the 1930s. See *United States v Swift*, 286 U.S. 106 (1932) (upholding and enforcing the decree). The decree was terminated in the 1980s in light of radical changes in the industry, resulting in the rise of a new set of dominant packers. See Peter C Carstensen, 'How to Assess the Impact of Antitrust on the American Economy: Examining History or Theorizing' (1989) 74 *Iowa Law Review* 1175, 1198–210 (the decree, combined with changes in transportation and processing, led to a restructuring and period of deconcentration; but mergers in the 1980s recreated and then exceeded the concentration levels of the pre-1920s industry).

[6] See 7 U.S.C. § 192 (poultry) and § 197A (production contracts). Unfortunately, the statutory language appears to preclude the US Department of Agriculture (USDA) from directly enforcing the PSA rules with respect to poultry producers through administrative proceedings. See 7 U.S.C. §§ 209, 210 (§ 209 authorizes either litigation or administrative proceedings pursuant to § 210, but the latter section does not list poultry producer regulations as included in the group the USDA can enforce). Because swine are included in the provisions of section 182, which forbids discrimination and authorizes the Secretary of Agriculture

legislation provides statutory protection for individuals and groups that seek to organize farmers and represent them in their dealings with buyers.[7]

Several countries have adopted regulations intended to control the behavior of large retailers. In 2010, the United Kingdom adopted rules that require major grocery buyers (defined as firms with a turnover of £1 billion or more) to adhere to specific standards with respect to their buying practices.[8] The regulation provides due process protection for producers against unilateral actions of powerful grocery chains. In addition, the rules focus on internal accountability within each such buyer's organization. In 2013, the government created the position of an adjudicator to interpret and enforce these regulations.[9]

Japan's antitrust law prohibits abuse of a 'superior bargaining position'.[10] Enforcement has been active since 2011, when the Japan Fair Trade Commission established a task force on this topic. One enforcement action condemned a buyer for both returning goods and imposing discounts on the moneys owed to the suppliers, which were deemed to be 'unjust[] in light of normal business practices'.[11] The Republic of Korea, Australia, Finland and Norway have similar regimes that require review of specific actions by dominant buyers in the retail trades.[12]

---

to enforce the law, abuses in swine contracting are potentially subject to public enforcement action, but to date no such action has been brought.

[7] Agricultural Fair Practices Act, as amended, codified at 7 U.S.C. § 2303 (2016).

[8] See Competition Commission (UK), 'Groceries (Supply Chain Practices) Market Investigation Order 2009', available at http://biicl.org/files/5921_uk_-_gscop_order_%28with_code%29.pdf.

[9] Press Release, Groceries Code Adjudicator, 'Groceries Code Adjudicator Formally Established' (14 June 2013), available at https://www.gov.uk/government/news/groceries-code-adjudicator-formally-established. See also Groceries Code Adjudicator, https://www.gov.uk/government/organisations/groceries-code-adjudicator (last visited 23 November 2016).

[10] Act on the Prohibition of Private Monopolization and Maintenance of Fair Trade, arts 19 ('No enterprise shall employ unfair trade practices'), and 2(9)(v) (defining acts by buyers that constitute 'unfair trade practices' by buyers). The General Designations implement these commands and describe the kinds of conduct that are considered unfair trade practices. See Etsuko Kameoka, *Competition Law and Policy in Japan and the EU* (Edward Elgar, Cheltenham, UK and Northampton, MA 2014) 86–91.

[11] Act on the Prohibition of Private Monopolization, art. 2(9)(v). See also Press Release, Japan Fair Trade Comm'n, 'JFTC Issued Cease and Desist Order and Surcharge Payment Order against Toys "R" Us–Japan, Ltd.' (13 December 2011), available at http://www.jftc.go.jp/en/pressreleases/yearly-2011/dec/individual-000456.html.

[12] See OECD, 'Policy Roundtables, Monopsony and Buyer Power', DAF/COMP(2008)38, available at http://www.oecd.org/daf/competition/44445750.pdf.

In 2007, the International Competition Network prepared a report on abuse of superior bargaining position as a competition policy issue.[13] Based on data collected from 32 countries, the report found that seven had specific laws governing such conduct and two more countries were planning to adopt them.[14] Some jurisdictions—in particular the United Kingdom and the United States—were very critical of these laws.[15] The United Kingdom, however, reversed course shortly thereafter and adopted legislation to police these abuses.[16] Interestingly, the United States denied that it had any such laws[17] despite the fact that both the PSA and the Robinson-Patman Act are directed at aspects of the problem of abuse of dominance.[18]

The fundamental challenge for any statute or regulation that seeks to prohibit unfair conduct by buyers is to provide a consistent and defined set of regulations that do not unreasonably constrain market dynamics. The Japan Fair Trade Commission's sanction of Toys 'R' Us for imposing 'unjust' return policies is illustrative.[19] The ruling does not provide a clear definition of acceptable limits to buyer bargaining. To the extent that it enshrines historic practices, the rule adversely affects the ability of market participants to develop new trading practices. The challenge is to develop standards or criteria that are transparent, can be applied with consistency and do not stifle innovation or the freedom to select trading partners—all of which are central to the market process. The Japan Fair Trade Commission has developed some guidelines and has explained its reasoning in specific cases, but to date, most of its cases appear to involve patterns of exploitive conduct that are relatively distinct from ordinary business practices.[20]

The PSA in the United States illustrates the challenge that less-than-transparent standards create. Congress sought to create an oversight process in the Department of Agriculture (USDA), itself not a competition enforcement agency, that would ensure fair, open, efficient and equitable markets for livestock and poultry. But the primary statutory standard is

---

13 ICN Task Force for Abuse of Superior Bargaining Position (2008), 'Report on Abuse of Superior Bargaining Position', available at http://www.internationalcompetitionnetwork.org/uploads/library/doc386.pdf.

14 *Ibid* at 5.

15 *Ibid* at 17.

16 Competition Commission (UK), *supra* note 8.

17 ICN Task Force, *supra* note 13, at 17.

18 See *infra* text accompanying notes 21–32 and 33–6.

19 See Press Release, *supra* note 11.

20 See Wakui and Cheng, *supra* note 2, at 304–07 (describing cases).

one of 'unfair' or 'discriminatory' conduct. The USDA has been unable to adopt regulations to govern a number of situations that arise because of the increasing reliance on contracts in the production of livestock and poultry.[21] It has also failed to bring any significant enforcement actions on its own.

Instead, individual suits, also authorized by the PSA, have been the primary basis for the interpretation of the statute. In a series of decisions, the courts have substantially obstructed the statutory goals and effectively authorized discriminatory buying practices.[22] The courts analogized the PSA to the antitrust laws, but ruled that unfair or discriminatory conduct in pursuit of legitimate goals is lawful even in the face of less harmful alternatives.[23] The plaintiff must also establish that the unfair practice has had an adverse effect on consumers.[24] The usual question is whether the conduct has affected prices in the consumer market, a requirement that individual plaintiffs are extremely unlikely to meet.[25] This interpretation is inconsistent with the legislative intent of the PSA, which was to protect producers as well as consumers from harm.[26] It is also at odds with American antitrust law, which holds that harm to sellers is sufficient to trigger antitrust liability.[27] Even marginal effects

---

21 In 2010, the Department attempted to adopt regulations that would have defined certain conduct as 'unfair' or 'discriminatory', but even those proposed rules had significant ambiguities. Ultimately, Congress blocked the adoption of most of those rules leaving the legal situation unsettled at best. See *infra* text accompanying notes 31–2.

22 See *Pickett v Tyson Fresh Meats Inc.*, 420 F.3d 1272 (11th Cir. 2005); *Terry v Tyson Farms*, 604 F.3d 272 (8th Cir. 2010); *Wheeler v Pilgrim's Pride*, 591 F.3d 455 (5th Cir. 2009) (en banc).

23 See *Pickett*, 420 F.3d at 1282–3 (plaintiffs' expert conceded that contracting might have some value, which excused the arguably discriminatory contracting used by the defendant); *In re Pilgrim's Pride*, 728 F.3d 457, 462–3 (5th Cir. 2013) (per curiam) (closing plants and refusing to sell them to willing buyers, which caused farmers and workers economic loss, not a violation because company had the right to adjust output).

24 See, eg, *Pilgrim's Pride*, 591 F.3d 355, 362–3; *Terry*, 604 F.3d at 279.

25 *Terry*, 604 F.3d at 279 (holding no PSA violation because no harm to competition even though the alleged conduct involved violation of existing USDA regulations governing the conduct of poultry processors).

26 See *Stafford v Wallace*, 258 U.S. 375 (1922) (upholding the constitutionality of the statute and recognizing that it applied to harm to both producers and consumers).

27 See, eg, *Weyerhaeuser Co. v Ross-Simmons Hardwood Lumber Co.*, 549 U.S. 312 (2007); *Mandeville Island Farms, Inc. v Am. Crystal Sugar Co.*, 334 U.S. 219 (1948); *United States v Swift & Co.*, 196 U.S. 375 (1905). See also William K Jones, 'Concerted Refusal to Deal and the Producer Interest in Antitrust' (1989) 50 *Ohio State Law Journal* 73.

on consumer prices can suffice to establish a right to challenge specific conduct.[28]

These judicial interpretations of PSA standards are not incoherent. They reflect the fact that a claim of discrimination or unfair conduct goes to the core of business transactions in which buyers purchase from several suppliers using different buying practices. Prototypical litigation in this area alleges open-ended claims of discrimination and unfair conduct. In the absence of a better definition of these terms, courts can plausibly argue that they needed to impose strict standards for the proof of such restraints.

These laissez-faire interpretations of the PSA, however, encourage and insulate from liability unjustified discrimination and exploitation. For example, in *Terry*, the plaintiff chicken grower alleged that the buyer had violated specific USDA regulations issued pursuant to its authority under the PSA. Such violations are analogous to a per se illegal act in competition law—the conduct is conclusively presumed to harm the competitive process and ultimately harm consumers as well as producers. Under standard antitrust law, these violations are absolutely unlawful, and the victim need not show that there is any specific 'harm to consumers'. Nevertheless, the court ignored the basis for the claim and found no liability because the plaintiff, who operated only one chicken farm, had failed to prove that harm to his operation had any effect on consumer prices.[29] The implication of this result is the inability of individual farmers to obtain a remedy for even direct violations of the regulations intended to govern marketing practices.[30]

Starting in 2010, in response to these judicial interpretations, the USDA sought to adopt a series of regulations explicitly defining and prohibiting various kinds of discrimination by buyers. The proposed rules would also have eliminated the requirement of proof of effect on consumers.[31] But Congress largely rejected the USDA's regulations in response to extensive

---

[28] See *Been v O.K. Indus.*, 398 Fed. App'x. 382, 2010 WL 3995981 (10th Cir. 2010, unpublished). Because the case involved a group of poultry farmers the court found that there was sufficient basis to believe some marginal effect on consumers had occurred.

[29] *Terry*, 604 F.3d at 279.

[30] There are some exceptions for certain types of arbitration. See, eg, 7 U.S.C § 197c (grower may elect to opt out of any contract term mandating arbitration). In addition, it may be possible for the USDA itself to enforce these regulations by direct action; however, its authority to do so in the context of poultry is questionable. See *supra* note 6.

[31] See Implementation of Regulations Required Under Title XI of the Food, Conservation and Energy Act of 2008; Conduct in Violation of the Act, 75 Fed. Reg. 3533863 (proposed 22 June 2010).

and intensive lobbying by buyers and by some livestock producers.[32] These events highlight the limits of regulation. Economically powerful buyers are also politically powerful and can frequently block or limit the adoption of relevant regulations.

For retail markets, the Robinson-Patman Act's prohibition on unjustified differences in prices paid by buyers addresses only indirectly the problem of buyer power. If a major buyer is able to command low prices that are not cost-justified, other buyers, who pay higher prices, are harmed. Unfortunately, the Act targets sellers by forbidding them from charging different prices, revealing a questionable conception of the causal forces that lead to price differences. Its implicit assumption is that the manufacturer is voluntarily charging different prices. In fact, such conduct would often be irrational but for the power of large buyers to compel discounts or other favorable treatment that the supplier cannot refuse.[33] Only in its provision prohibiting inducing price discrimination does the Act address the problem of buyer power. (The Act also has other well-known weaknesses and complexities.[34])

Kirkwood, among others, has written about the problem of interpreting Robinson-Patman to address appropriately the problem of buyer power.[35] As his discussion emphasizes, the problem is to differentiate between situations in which the overall competitive process is not harmed, and may

---

[32] The result was a very limited revision of the rules. See Implementation of Regulations Required Under Title XI of the Food, Conservation and Energy Act of 2008; Suspension of Delivery of Birds, Additional Capital Investment Criteria, Breach of Contract, and Arbitration, 76 Fed. Reg. 76874 (9 December 2011) (codified in various sections of 9 C.F.R. Part 201).

[33] In one case, Clorox refused to sell its largest size containers to a regional grocery retailer. The retailer asserted that the manufacturer was reserving those containers for its largest customers to allow them to differentiate their product offerings. The trial court held that the claim, if proven, would show a violation of Robinson-Patman. *Woodman's Food Mkt., Inc. v Clorox Co.*, 2015 WL 420296 (W.D. Wis. 2015). On appeal, the FTC filed an amicus brief in support of Clorox. See Brief of Amicus Curiae the Federal Trade Commission in Support of Defendants-Appellants and Reversal, *Woodman's Food*, 2015 WL 420296 (No. 15-3001). Ultimately, the lower court was reversed. *Woodman's Food*, 2016 WL 4254935 (7th Cir. 2016).

[34] See Antitrust Modernization Commission, 'Report and Recommendations', 313–32 (2007), available at http://govinfo.library.unt.edu/amc/report_recommendation/toc.htm (arguing that the cost justification defense as well as the 'meeting competition' defense are both extremely complex and ambiguous and that the entire Act may be an unjustified intervention in the freedom of sellers to set prices).

[35] John B Kirkwood, 'Reforming the Robinson-Patman Act to Serve Consumers and Control Powerful Buyers' (2015) 60 *Antitrust Bulletin* 358.

well be advanced, from those in which the buyer has caused a distortion of the process in order to exploit its power. It may be within the power of the FTC to interpret Robinson-Patman in a way that focuses more clearly on the identification of unjustified discounts. This could provide a better structure for analyzing retail market transactions, but to date the FTC has made little effort to refine the interpretation of the Act and has largely abandoned its enforcement. Moreover, the Supreme Court has limited the Act's impact—even on proven price differences—by strictly interpreting the requirements for any attempt to invoke it.[36] In part, the Court's decision reflects an understandable concern that regulation of specific buyer-seller interactions goes to the core of the market process and judicial intervention can result in significant negative unintended consequences.

The United Kingdom has adopted specific regulations governing the conduct of large grocery chains in their dealings with their suppliers.[37] The regulations apply only to a limited number of very large grocery retailers[38] and are more explicit than either the PSA or Robinson-Patman Act standards. Certain practices are prohibited, but the regulations allow a buyer to terminate any producer for 'genuine commercial reasons'.[39] The primary thrust of the termination rules is that a buyer must conduct a full and careful review of decisions affecting its suppliers. But there is also the more explicit entitlement for a supplier to retain its ability to sell to a buyer despite the buyer's desire to terminate the relationship.[40] This is similar to the Japanese regime that also, to some degree, confers rights on producers to continue to make sales.[41]

The UK regime also provides for an ombudsperson, who renders opinions on what is acceptable conduct in response to specific queries.[42] These

---

[36] See, eg, *Volvo Trucks N. Am., Inc. v Reeder-Simco GMC, Inc.*, 546 U.S. 164 (2006) (plaintiff truck dealer showed that it faced higher prices for trucks than other similar dealers because, it claimed, the manufacturer had targeted it for elimination, but the Court rejected the claim because the plaintiff could not show that another dealer for the same manufacturer got a more favorable price when that dealer was competing with the plaintiff for a specific sale).

[37] See Competition Commission (UK), *supra* note 8, at 11–17.

[38] *Ibid* at 18 (listing ten retail chains to which the rules apply).

[39] *Ibid* at 16.

[40] *Ibid* ('[E]xercise by the Supplier of its rights . . . under the Code or this Order will not be a genuine commercial reason to de-list a supplier.')

[41] See Wakui and Cheng, *supra* note 2, for a description of the operation of the Japanese system.

[42] 'Christine Tacon Named as Supermarket Ombudsman', *BBC News Service* (21 January 2013), available at http://www.bbc.com/news/business-21117701. See also sources cited *supra* note 9. See generally Madeline Taylor, 'Wrestling with

responses, like the guidelines in Japan, frame a set of standards that govern these transactions, which could provide greater protection for sellers from arbitrary conduct. It is unlikely, however, that these standards will alter the basic power relationship between buyers and sellers or reduce the related 'fear factor'. They may instead lead to rigidity in the buying system and, ultimately, to longer term inefficiency and diminished innovation.

Rules aimed at regulating abusive conduct by dominant buyers suffer from inherent problems of ambiguity. If regulation prohibits a powerful buyer from employing one way of exploiting suppliers, it may search out other ways to do so. Moreover, given the fear factor, dependent suppliers are likely to acquiesce 'voluntarily' to the demands placed on them by such a buyer even if the demands are otherwise objectionable. Suppliers will accept these demands because they value the continued relationship more than any short-term victory in an individual transaction.[43] In addition, these rules often intrude into suppliers' operations and might rigidify the buying process. Buyers and sellers might find themselves required to adhere to long-standing or conventional practices even if other ways of doing business, especially in an age of global communications, might be more efficient and, over time, no less adverse to their interests.

Therefore, competition policy should focus on the reasonableness of the rules designed to control abusive conduct by dominant buyers. These rules directly affect the ways in which markets operate and will therefore affect both producers and consumers. When the buying market is unavoidably concentrated, such rules are among the few policy tools available to control abuses of buying power; but they must be explicitly defined so that the commands are reasonably clear.

It is also important that a public agency enforce these rules to limit the effect of the fear factor. The agency should focus on the market facilitation goal of these rules and not become a captive protector of either producers or buyers. This is a challenging assignment. Moreover, the agency needs to have the power to revise the rules in light of changing market contexts.

Overall, strategic conduct controls are less desirable than an open and robust market with a substantial number of competing buyers. The larger the number of buyers the more easily suppliers will be able to avoid abusive exploitation. Unfortunately, in many smaller economies, this is not practical because of the need for economies of scope and scale at

---

Giants—A Critical Account of Supermarket Power and Competition Law in Australia and the United Kingdom' (2013) 41 *Australian Business Law Review* 270.

[43] See Stewart Macaulay, 'Non-Contractual Relations in Business: A Preliminary Study' (1963) 28 *American Sociological Review* 1 (formal contracts are not central to many business relationships).

some stages of the market process. Hence, careful delineation of the rules governing abusive buying practices in small markets is necessary to the maintenance of a workably competitive environment.

B. General Market Conduct Regulation

Closely related to the first class of regulations are those that apply to all market participants regardless of their size. These regulations seek to facilitate the market process overall by defining the scope and terms of transactions. Basic contract law provides the starting point. These regulations are unlikely to have an explicit buyer power focus and are more likely to reflect a general public policy that transactional markets require rules to define and constrain the market process.

In addition to establishing the basic terms for business transactions, these rules can limit specific buying practices such as risk- or cost-shifting conduct. Other regulations forbid 'unfair' conduct in general. Such rules can reduce discrimination by buyers toward their suppliers. If the non-discrimination requirement is effective and some producers have bargaining power, prices for all producers should move toward the competitive level. However, such results are difficult to achieve in practice.[44]

The underlying theory is that there is a norm that all buyers should adhere to; non-conforming conduct can then be isolated and forbidden, leaving the seller in a position to get a reasonable price and fair non-price terms for its product or service. These regulations have goals beyond addressing buyer power. They seek more generally to facilitate a workable market by restricting or prohibiting strategic conduct that would undermine the market process. A central premise of this kind of regulation is that the law plays a positive role in constituting and regulating the market process.

General conduct market regulation establishes general rules that govern all participants in specific markets. For example, part of the PSA gives livestock and poultry producers priority over other creditors to ensure that they are paid for what they deliver to a buyer.[45] This duty applies to most buyers and so serves to limit opportunistic conduct that would

---

[44] For example, a primary goal of the Robinson-Patman Act, 15 U.S.C. §13 (2016), was to eliminate discrimination against small businesses that competed with large buyers. Although the Act has had some positive effects, it is generally regarded as unsuccessful in achieving its goals and as creating a great deal of confusion. This criticism is long-standing. See, eg, Joel B Dirlam and Alfred E Kahn, *Fair Competition: The Law and Economics of Antitrust Policy* (Cornell University Press, Ithaca, NY 1956) 119–24.

[45] 7 U.S.C. §§ 206, 207 (2016).

frustrate the market process.[46] In addition to protections for livestock and poultry producers, Congress also adopted the Grain Inspection Act, which provides for a system of federal inspection and grading of grain.[47] This prohibits buyers from undergrading grain, which would allow them to pay less than full market value. The statute was reenacted in 1921 and expressly authorized cooperatives to join commodity exchanges, including the Chicago Board of Trade.[48] Producers were thereafter allowed to use their cooperatives as agents for transactions and share in the overcharges imposed on rural grain elevators through fixed commission rates.[49] Only in the 1970s did antitrust law object to the fixing of commission rates, which were a way of exploiting buyers and sellers of commodities and securities.[50]

When the Clayton Act was originally adopted in 1914, it imposed a general prohibition on price discrimination in the sale of commodities.[51] During the Great Depression, Congress repealed this provision and substituted the Robinson-Patman Act.[52] Robinson-Patman focused explicitly on the distribution process by forbidding sellers from charging different prices to competing buyers unless the seller could prove either a cost justification or that it was responding to competition.[53] The underlying motivation was the protection of small retailers from discriminatory discounts given by manufacturers of consumer goods to large volume buyers. But these discounts were the result of the exercise of buyer power by the large retailers themselves. Thus, the statute's focus on upstream

---

[46] Meat packers with less than $500,000 in purchases and poultry buyers with less than $100,000 in purchases are exempt. 7 U.S.C. § 206(b) (meat) and § 207(b) (poultry).

[47] Grain Standards Act, Pub. L. No. 64-190, 39 Stat. 482 (codified as amended in scattered sections of 7 U.S.C.).

[48] The Chicago Board of Trade had adopted a method of enforcing its fixed commissions even for 'off-exchange' transactions, that is, transactions in which the buyer bought directly from the rural grain elevator. See Peter C Carstensen, 'The Content of the Hollow Core of Antitrust: The Chicago Board of Trade Case and the Meaning of the "Rule of Reason" in Restraint of Trade Analysis' (1992) 15 *Research in Law and Economics* 1, 32–3.

[49] *Ibid* at 70. See also *Bd. of Trade v Olsen*, 262 U.S. 1 (1923) (upholding the revised statute against challenges focused on cooperative access to membership).

[50] See *United States v Bd. of Trade*, 1973 WL 892 (N.D. Ill. 1973); see generally William Baxter, 'NYSE Fixed Commission Rates: A Private Cartel Goes Public' (1970) 22 *Stanford Law Review* 675.

[51] Pub. L. No. 63-312, 38 Stat. 730, repealed Pub. L. No. 113-100, 49 Stat. 1526.

[52] Pub. L. 113-100, 49 Stat. 1526, codified as amended at 15 U.S.C. § 13 (2016).

[53] *Ibid* § 13(a) (cost justification) and § 13(b) (meeting competition).

suppliers was misdirected, although it also makes it unlawful 'to knowingly induce or receive a discrimination in price which is prohibited . . .'[54] As with the protection of farmers, the effects of this statute are disputed and controversial.[55]

Some rules are more focused. For example, many American states forbid general construction contractors from requiring subcontractors to provide insurance that protects the general contractor from liability for its own negligence.[56] Only buyer power would enable general contractors to transfer the risk of negligence to their subcontractors. General contractors are not likely to have substantial market share, but they can still have significant power over subcontractors that have few other buyers for their services and the need to maintain their businesses.

There have also been unsuccessful proposals that would have created more opportunity for open access to buying markets. A major buying problem in American cattle markets is the significant difference in the prices paid to producers under contract and those that sell in the open market. The contracts usually provide a premium over the contemporaneous cash market price.[57] Some buyers set their contract prices based on the current prices they are paying in the cash market. The use of an 'own' price gives such buyers a strong incentive to keep that price low because of its effect on the price for the large volume of contract cattle. The Western Organization of Research Councils (WORC) proposed that all forward cattle contracts be offered on a basis that allowed any feeder to respond and required that buyers using contracts offer either a firm price or a price calculated on a basis other than the price contemporaneously paid by the buyer in the cash market.[58] WORC wanted the USDA to use its

---

54 *Ibid* § 13(f).

55 See, eg, Antitrust Modernization Commission *supra* note 34 at 311–32; Dirlam and Kahn, *supra* note 44, at 202–53.

56 Sandra K Pearson, '2013 Revisions to ISO's Commercial General Liability Coverage Forms' (August 2013) *For the Defense* 20, 23–24, available at http:// www.bassford.com/InsuranceCoverage/DRI_ISO_Pearson_2013.pdf.

57 See *Pickett v Tyson Fresh Meats, Inc.*, 420 F.3d 1272 (11th Cir. 2005) (jury finding of significant price differences between contracts and open market sales held not to violate PSA because there were legitimate business reasons to use contracts). See also David Domina and C Robert Taylor, 'The Debilitating Effects of Concentration in Markets Affecting Agriculture' (2010) 15 *Drake Journal of Agricultural Law* 61.

58 Western Organization of Research Councils, 'Petition for Rule-making on Captive Supply Procurement Practices under the Packers and Stockyards Act (1996)', available at http://www.gipsa.usda.gov/psp/publication/worc_petition/petition.pdf.

rule-making authority under the PSA to adopt this rule. If adopted, buyers would not have had the ability to select arbitrarily among producers or use easily manipulated prices. The rule, as proposed, would have applied to all forward-looking purchases of cattle although the pricing strategy was used primarily by large packers.

Despite substantial support from many cattle feeders, the USDA did not adopt the proposal. The primary reason was the strong opposition of the major beef packers and some large cattle feeders who were concerned that the rule would restrict their freedom to act in economically rational and desirable ways. There were several very contentious public hearings. Indeed, some of the buying practices of the large packers were generally condemned,[59] but ultimately the USDA made no changes to the rules governing cattle purchases.

The WORC proposal rests in part on the insight that anonymous markets in which sellers can tender products for purchase by any buyer provide a means of avoiding discrimination among sellers and are somewhat more likely to generate competitive prices because of the buyer's uncertainty about achieving its desired volume of inputs. Commodity markets can also provide this protection—*if run fairly*. Indeed, it was the ability to sell grain on the Chicago Board of Trade that made it possible for grain cooperatives to break a boycott organized by vertically integrated grain merchants.[60] As long as there is a significant number of potential buyers, other marketing systems can operate effectively because the gain from discrimination is minimal or even negative. But the potential for abusive contracts has increased further with the movement in American production of swine and poultry to a vertical contract system in which the processor owns the animals and the farmer provides the care and feeding.[61] Once a farmer has made a major and specialized capital investment, there are few alternative outlets for the service that the farmer provides.

The Wisconsin rules governing contracts for vegetables raised for canning or freezing provide a useful contrast and demonstrate how contracting can be fair and reasonable. In the 1990s, the state's agricultural agency participated with both growers and processors to revise and update rules governing contracts for these crops. Contracts were essential to

[59] Observers from all perspectives believed that the practice of basing contract prices on the contemporaneous market price being paid for cattle was inherently suspect because of its potential for abuse.

[60] Carstensen, *supra* note 48, at 28–9.

[61] See Christopher Leonard, *The Meat Racket* (Simon and Schuster, New York 2014) (describing Tyson's practices with respect to poultry and hogs).

insulate farmers and processors from the risks of the lag between planting and harvesting. Because no individual buyer was powerful, and because contracting was essential to the market process, it was possible for buyers and sellers to agree on rules to govern the contracting process that preserved significant buyer discretion, but also protected producers from abuse. The resulting rules were then adopted as state regulations ensuring public enforcement of any breach.[62]

Covenants not to compete are a common element of many employment relationships in the United States. Employers often use their buyer power when hiring to insist that the new employee agree to such a covenant as a condition of employment. These covenants bar an employee from opening a competing business or going to work for a competitor of his or her employer. Some American states, including California, prohibit such post-employment restraints. Gilson has argued that this prohibition explains in part the relative success of new technological industries in California compared to those in Massachusetts, where substantial amounts of technology originated but where such covenants are enforced.[63] The theory is that the greater freedom of workers to use their skills in related employment contributed importantly to the dynamics of the industry.

In 2016, the United States Treasury issued a report summarizing various studies that suggest these covenants adversely affect worker wages and mobility.[64] The clauses create risk and uncertainty for workers and deter them from job hunting in fields where they have relevant skills, even in California, where, although invalid, such covenants are frequently used.[65]

---

[62] See Wisconsin Admin. Code ATCP § 101 (2011). The farmers needed assurance that their investment would not be wasted—including both the need to have a buyer with a negotiated price and an assurance that if for some reason (such as wet land) the buyer would not or could not harvest the crop when it was ready, the farmer would still be paid. The buyers needed assurance that they would get the benefit of their bargain—produce that meets their specifications and the flexibility to harvest in the most efficient manner. The author was an observer at these negotiations and was impressed with the willingness of each side to understand the interests and concerns of the other. Neither side seemed to see the contracts as a means of achieving any significant strategic advantage.

[63] Ronald J Gilson, 'The Legal Infrastructure of High Technology in Industrial Districts: Silicon Valley, Route 128, and Covenants Not to Compete' (1999) 74 *New York University Law Review* 575.

[64] US Department of Treasury (March 2016), 'Non-Compete Contracts: Economic Effects and Policy Implications', available at https://www.treasury.gov/resource-center/economic-policy/Documents/UST%20Non-competes%20Report.pdf.

[65] See *ibid* at 4 (19 percent of workers reporting being subject to such covenants).

This in turn adversely affects wages.[66] Since about 2005, various American states have banned or restricted the use of such clauses in employment contracts.[67] Restricting the use of such covenants in markets where employees have the skills for a variety of job opportunities is a potentially important strategy to overcome some of the buyer power of employers.

Also in 2016, the US Council of Economic Advisors issued a report that highlighted the ways in which monopsony affects labor markets.[68] The report stressed the increasing inequity among workers as well as between employees and other economic stakeholders.[69] In addition to reforming the law governing covenants not to compete and enhanced antitrust enforcement, the report stressed the importance of providing information to workers about job opportunities and wages, laws to require equal pay for men and women, revision of exclusionary occupational licensing, and other even more general reforms that facilitate worker mobility.[70]

Another type of market-improving regulation consists of rules that require the collection and public disclosure of certain information about market transactions. In theory, buyers and sellers in competitive markets possess perfect information, including information on the supply and demand characteristics of the market. Government agencies collect and publish a wide variety of information about the production of commodities, especially agricultural commodities. This can help overcome the informational imbalance between large buyers and small producers. However, information disclosure may also facilitate coordination of prices in markets with few buyers. In many concentrated buying markets, major buyers probably already have reliable ways of keeping track of each other's prices. And absent significant supply shortages, there is little

---

66 See *ibid* at 18–21 (discussing evidence of adverse wage effects).

67 See, eg, Oregon Revised Statute § 653.295 (2015) (restricting use of covenants); Idaho Code § 44-2701 (2016) (limiting the classes of employees subject to such covenants); Hawaii Revised Statute § 480-4 (undated), available at https://portal.ehawaii.gov/government/hawaii-legislature/hawaii-revised-statutes/ (prohibiting such contracts in technology industries) (last visited 30 November 2016).

68 Council of Economic Advisers (October 2016), 'Labor Market Monopsony: Trends, Consequences, and Policy Responses', available at https://www.whitehouse.gov/sites/default/files/page/files/20161025_monopsony_labor_mrkt_cea.pdf.

69 *Ibid* at 2–3.

70 *Ibid* at 13–16. Among the more general recommendations were revisions of zoning laws to allow workers to find housing in areas where employment is available and modifying health care insurance access to reduce dependency on employers as providers. Currently, the majority of Americans get their health insurance through their employers as a benefit. This can tie them to their current employer over a prospective employer or business that lacks this benefit.

incentive to bid up the price of inputs. Therefore, although there is the risk of enhanced price coordination, the reality is that limiting the public disclosure of prices is more likely to harm sellers than to significantly enhance coordination among buyers.

The American experience, even when there is a purportedly strong commitment to providing information, however, is quite discouraging. For example, with respect to livestock prices, the USDA does not provide information about the most concentrated markets.[71] And courts have refused to impose liability on buyers who take knowing advantage of erroneous, publicly available USDA pricing information.[72] Nevertheless, government can play a major role in facilitating better market operation by requirements controlling the type and timing of information disclosed to the market.

Although information disclosure does not, in and of itself, deter or limit the exploitation of buyer power, over time the existence of negative information may discourage entry into such markets absent reliable guarantees about price and other terms.[73] Both poultry and hog buyers imposed confidentiality requirements on farmers. Ultimately, Congress stepped in and required that farmers be allowed to discuss proposed contracts with key advisers regardless of any confidentiality provision.[74] Fuller disclosure of information to poultry growers, combined with limits on loan guarantees, might have discouraged excessive entry and induced major buyers to improve their contracts to attract investment.[75] Under a settlement of litigation with Smithfield, a major hog processor and contractor, the Iowa attorney general established a website that provided hog contract information. The initiative was successful, while it operated, in ensuring that

---

[71] See Livestock Mandatory Reporting, 7 C.F.R. § 59.10(c) (2016) ('The Secretary shall make information obtained under this part available to the public only in a manner that: . . . (2) Ensures that the identity of a reporting person or the entity which they represent is not disclosed; and (3) Market information . . . shall be aggregated in such a manner that the market reports issued will not disclose the identity of persons, packers and importers, including parties to a contract and packer's and importer's proprietary information.') Effectively, this precludes disclosure of regional price data in any region with a limited numbers of buyers.

[72] See *Schumacher v Cargill Meat Solutions Corp.*, 515 F.3d 867 (8th Cir. 2008) (judgment against meat packers for knowing use of erroneous price data in setting prices reversed for lack of specific intent to defraud producers).

[73] In the case of poultry, both the price to be paid as well as the number and size of flocks per year are essential elements of the contract.

[74] Packers and Stockyards Act, 7 U.S.C. § 229b (2016) (authorizes any party to a production contract of one year or more to discuss its terms with various advisers regardless of any confidentiality asserted by the packer or integrator).

[75] See generally Leonard, *supra* note 61.

farmers could compare contract terms and seek the better agreements.[76] But the value of disclosure is dependent on the buying market being workably competitive.

Despite their practical limits, information disclosure regulations in agricultural markets provide an illustrative framework for dealing with a variety of issues involving buyer power through market facilitation. The goal of such regulation is to create legal rules that assist in creating an informed, accessible and efficient market. Such rules can require disclosure of information about prices and other relevant contract terms in a timely fashion, limit or forbid inclusion of specific elements in transactions such as compulsory arbitration under unreasonable terms,[77] prohibit confidentiality with respect to contract terms,[78] and require market access for all producers.[79] As a result some, if not all, of the incentives for buyers to discriminate among competing producers can be eliminated.

Market-facilitating regulations, while providing enough flexibility to allow innovation by suppliers, can constrain the discretion of buyers and alter their ability to exploit producers through various kinds of unjustified discrimination. Through the mandated provision of information, producers can develop alternative outlets for their products. Competition policy concerns are relevant to developing and modifying general market regulation; explicit consideration of their effect on the competitive process is essential.[80]

---

76 That website was closed in 2015 after the expiration of the consent decree entered into as a result of the litigation. See *ibid* at 255–8 (description of the overall settlement that included other important rights for contract producers). In 1999, Congress amended the PSA to require the USDA to establish a similar reporting system and after a long delay the site was created. See 75 Fed. Reg. 16641 (2 April 2010) (final rules reestablishing the contract reporting library although the library itself was not available online until 2016). See generally, Packers and Stockyards Act 7 U.S.C. § 198b (authorizing the USDA to collect and report different types of swine contracts by packer) and 9 C.F.R. § 206 (rules implementing the reporting and publication process).

77 7 U.S.C. § 197c (farmers can opt out of compulsory arbitration when entering into a contract).

78 *Ibid* § 229c.

79 See *supra* text accompanying notes 57–9. In the fluid milk market, control over access to higher prices usually requires membership in a cooperative that sells at least some percentage of its milk for fluid use. If all farmers producing Grade A milk were allowed to avail themselves of the advantageous price, the buyer power of some cooperatives would be substantially limited. See Peter C Carstensen, 'Agricultural Cooperatives and the Law: Obsolete Statutes in a Dynamic Economy' (2013) 58 *South Dakota Law Review* 462.

80 These controls conflict with the economic interests of buyers by restricting their freedom to engage in a variety of practices that transfer wealth to them from

When there is less buyer-side dominance, regulators may be able to get buyers and producers to agree on a set of guidelines or regulations for transactions, whether contractual or market, in the specific commodity. If there are a reasonable number of buyers and sellers, strategic gain will not be a high priority for either group, and the result can be a set of rules that facilitate efficient market operation.[81] Such regulations in turn may retard or discourage efforts to further concentrate either side of the market because neither side can expect to achieve an exploitive gain.

It may be difficult to draft commodity-specific market-facilitating regulations for input markets. Generalist competition enforcement agencies are unlikely to have sufficient expertise, even if they have the legal authority, to promulgate and enforce such regulations. Exceptions exist, but mostly on the selling side of the market where there are industry-specific regulations of selling practices for products such as eyeglasses and funeral services.[82] An analogous regime exists to regulate the sale of franchises to investors and other business opportunities.[83] That regulatory system focuses on information disclosure so that buyers have access to relevant information *before* they have entered into a contract. This illustrates that, at some points in the development of a business, there may be opportunities to make choices free from the power that will arise in the counterparty once the commitment is made.

In sum, general market regulations—including requirements for information collection and disclosure—are important to establishing some limits on the abuse of buyer power. The likely impact on competition and the exploitation of buyer power should be considered when formulating such policies. These regulations neither change buyer power generally nor provide direct means to limit or reduce that power, except when the information disclosed reveals alternative outlets to producers. Although helpful, therefore, these regulations cannot provide a significant check on the capacity of powerful buyers to exploit producers.

---

producers. One would expect that buyers would employ as much political muscle as they have to lobby against such regulations.

[81] See *supra* note 62 and accompanying text for a discussion of Wisconsin's vegetable contract regulation.

[82] See FTC, Funeral Industry Practices, 16 C.F.R § 453 (2016); Ophthalmic Practice Rules, 16 C.F.R. § 456 (2016).

[83] See FTC, Disclosure Requirements and Prohibitions Concerning Franchising, 16 C.F.R. § 436 (2016); and FTC, Disclosure Requirements and Prohibitions Concerning Business Opportunities, 16 C.F.R. § 437 (2016).

C. Imposing Floors or Other Transactional Constraints

The final type of market regulation creates a general constraint on the right of any buyer to impose terms of its choosing with respect to prices or other transactional conditions. The theory is that some sellers lack the bargaining power, knowledge or market alternatives to enable them to avoid exploitation by buyers. These regulations impose floors, but rarely ceilings, on what can be paid or provided to the seller. Such regulations assume that only some market participants need protection. The floor provides a starting point for the negotiation. Those producers who offer more desirable goods or services are likely to receive prices or conditions above the floor. Unlike utility rate regulation,[84] the base line does not reflect a determination of the value of the good or service provided. It does not constrain price increases if the market generates them. With respect to buyer power, the concern is with the low price paid, but there is no process for determining what a reasonable price might be.

In the United States, for example, most employers must provide health care and provide a minimum level of income for workers that suffer injury on the job through the workers' compensation system.[85] Minimum wage rules, workplace safety standards and other limits on the treatment of employees provide other examples of legal 'floors'. These regulations reflect a policy determination that many workers are unable to bargain effectively for wages, working conditions or income protection. Setting safety and other standards serves additional social goals, but the underlying rationale for imposing these requirements is that the market process will not consistently achieve the optimal result absent the floor.

In agriculture, many of the countries that produce export commodities established minimum payment schedules, which provided a guaranteed level of income for producers.[86] Starting in the 1990s, however, most of these guarantees, along with the state agencies that acted as monopsonistic buyers, were eliminated. The EU has also moved away

---

[84] In utility rate regulation, the regulator determines the cost of producing the good or service and requires the seller to charge no more and no less than that price. This constrains monopoly power exploitation in essential services.

[85] See generally Lex K Larson and Thomas A Robinson, *Larson's Workers' Compensation Law* (LexisNexis, New York 2015). General health care is often a benefit provided by employers at their discretion or as a result of a union contract.

[86] See generally Food and Agriculture Organization, 'Agricultural and Food Marketing Management' (1997) ch. 1, available at http://www.fao.org/docrep/004/w3240e/W3240E01.htm.

from some of its agricultural quota controls, including those restricting milk production.[87]

In the United States, some agricultural commodities are subject to producers' rights to establish minimum prices through the use of marketing orders.[88] The most durable example is milk.[89] There are both (1) a minimum price that must be paid for milk in any region in which dairy farmers directly or through their cooperative have approved the creation of a milk order, and (2) a complex system intended to ensure that all participating dairy farmers receive a reasonable share of the resulting payments.[90] Other crops are also subject to orders that limit the quantity of the crop that can be sold.[91] The Secretary of Agriculture must approve both direct price setting and rules limiting the quantity to be marketed, and secretaries have occasionally refused to approve proposals.[92] Overall, the American order system has moved away from either price or output restrictions in most crops, leaving milk as the most important exception.

Oligopoly markets respond to price controls by increasing supply to satisfy the increased demand that results from lower prices. In contrast,

---

87 See European Commission, 'The Common Agricultural Policy after 2013', available at http://ec.europa.eu/agriculture/cap-post-2013/. See also Tyler R Smith, 'Note: No Time to Cry Over Spilt Milk: The Effect of the European Milk Quota Repeal on American Dairy Farmers' (2016) 21 *Drake Journal of Agricultural Law* 217.

88 The Agricultural Marketing Agreement Act, as amended, 7 U.S.C. §§ 671–4 (2016), authorizes growers of certain types of crops, under the supervision of the Secretary of Agriculture, to set prices and output. This legislation, an artifact of the Great Depression, was intended to provide an alternative means of obtaining higher prices for crops not subject to direct government subsidy. Few price-fixing orders remain, and a recent Supreme Court decision raised a significant question as to the continued viability of the entire system. See *Horne v USDA*, 135 S. Ct. 2419 (2015) (output restrictions imposed by an order constituted a 'taking', which requires the government to compensate the farmer for the lost value of the production denied access to the market).

89 See David L Baumer, Robert T Masson and Robin Abrahamson Masson, 'Curdling the Competition: An Economic and Legal Analysis of the Antitrust Exemption for Agriculture' (1986) 31 *Villanova Law Review* 183.

90 For a fuller discussion of the milk order system, see ABA Antitrust Section, Federal Statutory Exemptions from Antitrust Law, Monograph 24, ch. 4 (2007), and sources cited therein.

91 See, eg, Tart Cherry Order, 7 C.F.R. § 930 (2014).

92 Compare Wisconsin Ag Connection (21 August 2014), 'USDA Turns Down Request to Limit Cranberry Production', available at http://www.wisconsinagconnection.com/story-state.php?Id=989&yr=2014 (denial of cranberry output limit), with Tart Cherry Order, 7 C.F.R. § 930 (acceptance of limits on sales of tart cherries).

competitive markets reduce output in such situations, and the lower price results in rationing as demand exceeds the capacity of those markets to supply goods or services in the quantity demanded.[93] The same logic applies on the buying side. By setting minimum wage or other minimum requirements and providing for effective public enforcement, the legal system can modify more directly a firm's capacity to exploit buyer power. If a monopsonist is forced to raise the prices it pays for labor or other inputs, it may then find it rational to expand output and increase its purchases.[94] But floors apply across the board. Therefore, a buyer in both a competitive buying market and a competitive resale market may need to reduce output to bring its costs in line with its revenue.

The tradeoff in competitive buying markets is between a social policy that requires some minimum level of safety or income and the willingness of producers to accept less than that minimum. One might argue that, in many circumstances, the choice is essentially involuntary.[95] The producer or worker has, for a variety of reasons, little real choice, and so the buyer is able to exercise its buyer power in that specific transaction. Applying conventional economic theory, the producer's goods or services are worth as much as or more than the buyer pays for them. Given information asymmetry and the other limits on producers who take below market prices, it is not unreasonable to infer that the buyer's gain exceeds the level required by such floors as minimum wage and other working conditions. Put somewhat differently, society might conclude that any business that does not generate sufficient wealth to afford the minimum wage and other working conditions is not socially desirable.

Because floors are general regulations,[96] they affect market participants with and without buyer power. Moreover, some buyers, especially larger ones, may be able to limit or avoid the impact of the floor by, for example,

---

[93] See Peter C Carstensen, 'Antitrust Law, Competition, and the Macroeconomy' (1981) 14 *University of Michigan Journal of Law Reform* 173.

[94] The assumption is that, given the higher required price, the monopsonist can increase its quantity purchased without any change in the marginal price of the input. Hence, a monopsonist will have an incentive to expand production if it sells in a workably competitive downstream market.

[95] Some commentators reject this perspective and assert that all individuals are rational actors making rational and reasonable choices. From that perspective, floors interfere with the freedom of contract for such individuals to accept the low wages or other risks in return for whatever compensation they may desire. See Richard Epstein (11 May 2015), 'The Political Economy of Nail Salons', available at http://www.hoover.org/research/political-economy-nail-salons. This perspective does not reflect real-world economic choices.

[96] Some contain exceptions for small enterprises or classes of enterprise.

transferring productive activities to locations where there are no or less onerous floors. This explains in part why major firms move production to low-wage countries. If a buyer uses independent contractors instead of employees, it does not have to pay many of the labor costs incident to the more regulated employment relationship, such as paying into the Social Security or workers' compensation systems.[97]

Floors set only a minimum and do not provide any means of calibrating the value that might be added to the price paid. Thus, they are not effective in controlling buyer exploitation in the range of prices above the floor. On the other hand, minimum wage laws, workplace safety requirements and workers' compensation laws all provide basic protections for workers that constrain the capacity of employers to exploit workers beyond the established minimums. To be effective, such laws must be rigorously enforced.

Regulation of contract terms through competition policy could ensure compliance with minimum standards and substitute for the imposition of a floor. Certainly, in the context of poultry and swine contracts in the United States, a good case could be made for imposing some requirements as to compensation and the duty of a buyer to compensate a seller for the risks of various externalities, such as pollution. But such policies cannot quickly adapt to the changing realities of production. Hence, these rules can be either irrelevant or impose unnecessary burdens and costs that do not serve any important social or economic goal. The better option is for producers to have more options for contracting and workers to have sufficient disclosure of relevant information to allow them to make reasonable choices.

II. CREATING AND PROTECTING OFFSETTING PRODUCER POWER

The basis for the use of these strategies is that individual producers lack both the capacity to bargain effectively with dominant buyers and ready access to alternative outlets for their products. John Kenneth

---

[97] A few courts have rejected the independent contractor classification in some circumstances. See, eg, *Vizcaino v Microsoft Corp.*, 97 F.3d 1187 (9th Cir. 1995), aff'd, 120 F.3d 1006 (9th Cir. 1997) (en banc) (holding full-time 'contractors' working at Microsoft to be employees and entitled to benefits). But, in general, independent contractor status provides a means of avoiding most obligations. This is partly why swine and poultry buyers use independent contractors rather than directly employing the laborers to raise the animals.

Galbraith gave the concept of countervailing power its leading statement.[98] The broad theory is that effective markets require a balance of power. Powerless parties should combine to create offsetting bargaining power. The strategies proposed to remedy this imbalance, however, take divergent paths. One strand emphasizes cartelistic organizations that can withhold production to enable effective bargaining with buyers. A second strand focuses on creating more efficient and effective markets for the commodities involved either through horizontal combination or vertical integration through enough stages of production to reach more workably competitive buying markets.

A. Producer Cartels

The creation of a producer cartel is a recurring strategy to address potential abuses of buyer power. Producers may be subject to exploitation by buyers that are able to compel lower prices for the producers' products. Every producer seeks a 'reasonable' price. The central problem is that individual producers, if at all numerous, cannot effectively withhold their production when facing prices they do not find acceptable, precisely because they do not have the market power to negotiate effectively. But by creating a cartel, agreeing on the prices or other conditions that they will collectively demand, and then adhering to those demands, producers can solve their collective action problem. If successful, a cartel can achieve higher prices for its participants' products or services even from a powerful buyer.

If the powerful buyer resells into a competitive market, the only immediate effect is on the price for the input.[99] The result becomes a bargaining process over the allocation of any rents that accrue from overall production. The cartel gives producers countervailing power that should enable them to obtain a reasonable price for their contribution.[100]

If the buyer has downstream market power, then the results are more likely to conform to a version of the bilateral monopoly problem. When

---

[98] John Kenneth Galbraith, *American Capitalism: The Concept of Countervailing Power* (Houghton Mifflin, Boston, MA rev edn 1956).

[99] See, eg, *Mandeville Island Farms, Inc. v Am. Crystal Sugar Co.*, 334 U.S. 219 (1948); *Treasure Valley Potato Bargaining Ass'n v Ore-Ida Foods*, 497 F.2d 203 (9th Cir. 1974).

[100] Under these assumptions, producer output may increase if all producers are part of the cartel or can exclude non-members from the market and the buyers face downstream competition that prevents the producers' cartel from affecting the downstream price.

the upstream firm has a monopoly and the downstream firm is both monopsony buyer and downstream monopolist, the model suggests that they will bargain over the distribution of the monopoly profit that comes from the ultimate consumers. Assuming the input is used in fixed proportions, the only real question is the allocation of the ultimate consumer overcharge.[101] The monopoly producers are likely to raise the input price above the competitive level, which will increase the 'costs' to the buyer, which in turn will raise its price to seek its own monopoly profit. If producers bargain effectively, consumers will pay a price that approximates what a vertically integrated monopolist would have charged, and the bilateral monopolists will divide that overcharge.[102] If the producers lack bargaining power, consumers will still face increased prices and lower output but all the profits would go to the buyer. The argument for creating a producer cartel is that the producers with power share in the overcharge while those without power do not.

A cartel must have some effective way to limit output in order to increase prices. Individual producers will have an incentive to increase their production.[103] This requires either limiting access to production of the commodity or restricting the output of the participants or both. When a cartel must accept and market all that its members produce, its ability to control price is likely to be very limited. Its power is even more constrained if it is obliged to admit any producer that wants to join. Any real capacity to control price will be eliminated.[104]

To achieve countervailing power through a cartel, producers must overcome potentially serious challenges to collective action. They must be willing to act together to fend off a buyer's attempts to disrupt their efforts. Buyers may offer premiums to individual producers to

---

[101] The assumption of fixed proportions means that the buyer has no capacity to reduce the quantity of the input it takes relative to its output.

[102] Many years ago, three economists and a law professor observed that a rational 'deal' between the two levels would be one that maximizes the monopoly profit. See Roger D Blair, David L Kaserman and Richard E Romano, 'A Pedagogical Treatment of Bilateral Monopoly' (1989) 55 *Southern Economic Journal* 831; Richard D Friedman, 'Antitrust Analysis and Bilateral Monopoly' 1986 *Wisconsin Law Review* 873. Remedying monopsonistic exploitation in this way, however, might result in lower output and higher prices than prevailed under the prior monopsony.

[103] 'Cheating' by cartel members is a major cause for failure of such efforts. An effective cartel must have a way of detecting and policing deviance.

[104] See Willard Fritz Mueller, Peter G Helmberger and Thomas W Paterson, *The Sunkist Case: A Study in Legal-Economic Analysis* (Lexington Books, Lexington, MA 1987).

withdraw from the collective or selectively refuse to deal with the organizers of the effort before it is firmly established.[105] In addition, as with any cartel, when a group seeks to limit production and raises prices, members can defect and expand production to capture greater profits.

There are a variety of ways that such cartelistic countervailing power can be created. In agriculture, many countries that export commodities have used state-sponsored or state-run agencies, such as marketing boards, to buy and resell their crops. One of the primary goals of this process was to protect small landholders from exploitation by large, global buyers. The agency's commitment usually included a guarantee of payment, thus removing, in theory at least, the risk of default. In addition, the regulating agency could impose quality controls to protect the reputation of the commodity. The agencies acted as monopsonists with the capacity to exploit their position between the downstream buyers and the upstream producers. Many agencies were terminated in the 1980s and 1990s with the move toward greater reliance on markets. Some agencies remain; the most notable perhaps is the Canadian Wheat Board that dominates the market for some types of wheat.[106]

In Europe, many agricultural commodities producers are represented by extensive organizations with public authority to regulate aspects of commodity marketing.[107] Many of these organizations provide initial processing of the commodity as well as regulate various aspects of its marketing. In some cases, this has produced significant bargaining power for sellers.[108] But in other instances, and despite the inclusion of producers, the combined entity still faces significant buyer power.

The experience of the American agricultural markets subject to market

---

[105] For example, in the 1960s, chicken processors succeeded in rebuffing various efforts to create growers associations. See Leonard, *supra* note 61, at 84.

[106] See G3 Can. Ltd., http://www.g3.ca/ (last visited 15 November 2016).

[107] See European Commission, 'Economic Impact of Modern Retail on Choices and Innovation in the EU Food Sector' (2014) 54, 82, 108 and 134, available at ec.europa.eu/competition/sectors/agriculture/retail_study_presentation_en.pdf (describing organizations of farmers producing commodities in various countries). In 2016, a European Union task force recommended further exemption for agricultural cartels. See Agricultural Markets Task Force, 'Improving Market Outcomes' ¶¶ 155–7, available at https://ec.europa.eu/agriculture/sites/agriculture/files/agri-markets-task-force/improving-markets-outcomes_en.pdf (urging a clearer exemption for agricultural cartels).

[108] EU Commission, *ibid* at 14 (Finnish milk producers' cooperative controls 70 percent of production and appears to have significant leverage in negotiating prices with retailers).

orders (an analogous approach) suggests that producers may gain little even if consumers pay a premium for the commodities in question.

An alternative to the state-sponsored cartel is state authorization of private associations of sellers to create countervailing power in the market. Efforts at collective action are almost always illegal because they are essentially cartelistic and therefore require some form of state authorization to avoid running afoul of competition law's prohibitions. Most private associations of sellers are state-authorized. In the United States, the Capper-Volstead Act provides farm cooperatives with a limited exemption from the prohibitions of antitrust law.[109] The exemption is most relevant to cooperatives whose members agree on the prices they will accept for their crops in direct sales. These agreements would be per se illegal cartels absent the statutory exemption. Many agricultural cooperatives act as marketing agents or as processors of their members' produce and would not be deemed inherently illegal organizations under contemporary American competition law.[110] Although these ventures are usually lawful, farm groups concerned about the risks of antitrust liability seem strongly wedded to their exemptions, despite the exemptions' adverse effects on their ability to raise investment capital.[111]

In some cases the authorization can require even unwilling participants to join. This can confer significant power on such entities. An American agricultural marketing order[112] combined with a strong cooperative, such as in cranberries, can create private, buyer-side control over an industry's output.[113] Indeed, even without a cooperative, members of an industry can overcome their collective action problems and reduce output if the gains are sufficiently well communicated. The Tart Cherry Order in the United States provides an example. Its implementation has required the removal

---

109 Associations of Agricultural Products Producers, 7 U.S.C. §§ 291, 292 (2016).

110 See Carstensen, *supra* note 79, at 473–4.

111 See *ibid* at 496 (recounting how the Antitrust Division leadership backed away from any suggestion of amending the act).

112 See *supra* text accompanying notes 88–92.

113 The cranberry cooperative has been the target of a number of public and private antitrust lawsuits focused on its exclusionary and exploitive conduct. See, eg, *Cape Cod Food Prod. v Nat'l Cranberry Ass'n*, 119 F. Supp. 900 (D. Mass. 1954) (instructions in monopoly case against cranberry cooperative; jury awarded damages), *April v Nat'l Cranberry Ass'n*, 168 F. Supp. 919 (D. Mass. 1958) (opinion refusing summary judgment in a suit against cranberry cooperative charged with using 'predatory' acts to monopolize business); but see *Northland Cranberries v Ocean Spray Cranberries, Inc.*, 382 F. Supp. 2d 221 (D. Mass. 2004) (suggesting that exclusionary conduct and collusion by cranberry cooperative may be exempt from antitrust law).

of up to one-third of all cherries from the market in order to sustain prices.[114] To increase their relative share of the premium, each grower had an incentive to increase production. Thus, the cartel's goal of increasing prices beyond those which supply and demand would have produced led to an over-investment in productive capacity and wasteful production.

Moreover, in the United States, several agricultural groups have sought to use ostensible cooperatives as a means of reducing output.[115] By agreeing to limit output, the participants can raise prices without having to engage in direct price fixing. This conduct seems somewhat less vulnerable to opportunistic conduct and defection, most likely because commitment to the common scheme is more obvious than is adherence to a pricing restraint. The narrow definition of the exemption from antitrust law has frustrated these cartels. But, historically, some cooperative cartels resorted to coercion or destruction of the business or property of those who do not participate.[116] Recent examples include allegations in a case involving cranberries.[117]

Affirmative legislative authorization often contains significant limitations. In the United States, labor unions and farm cooperatives may act collectively, but collaboration with third parties is impermissible.[118]

---

[114] Tart Cherry Order, 7 C.F.R. § 930 (2011). Some further modification of these output controls was proposed in 2016, but there is no indication that the basic focus on this order on controlling the quantity of the crop available for consumption has changed. See Tart Cherries Grown in the States of Michigan, et al.; Revision of Optimum Supply Requirements and Establishment of Inventory Release Procedures, 81 Fed. Reg. 63,676 (Sept. 16, 2016).

[115] See, eg, *In re Mushroom Direct Purchaser Antitrust Litig.*, 641 F. Supp. 2d 274 (E.D. Pa. 2009) (cooperative bought caves that grew mushrooms and resold them with covenants forbidding such use); *In re Fresh and Process Potatoes Antitrust Litig.*, 834 F. Supp. 2d 1141 (D. Idaho 2011) (through cooperatives, potato growers restricted the quantity of land devoted to production).

[116] See Victoria Saker Woeste, *The Farmer's Benevolent Trust: Law and Agricultural Cooperation in Industrial America*, 1865–1945 (The University of North Carolina Press, Chapel Hill, NC 1989) 129–34 (raisin cooperative or its members engaged in predatory acts against independent growers); *United States v King*, 229 F. 275 (D. Mass. 1915); *United States v King*, 250 F. 908 (D. Mass. 1916) (potato growers cooperative engaged in unlawful conduct to suppress independent production).

[117] *Growers 1–7 v Ocean Spray Cranberries, Inc.*, 2014 WL 1764533 (D. Mass. 2014) (rejecting in part motion to dismiss claims of anticompetitive and exclusionary conduct by cranberry cooperative).

[118] See, eg, *Nat'l Broiler Marketing Ass'n v United States*, 436 U.S. 816 (1978); *United States v Borden Co.*, 308 U.S. 188, 205 (1939) (the Capper-Volstead Act does not exempt collusion between cooperatives and their customers to set prices). See also Carstensen, *supra* note 79, at 485; *Allen Bradley Co. v Int'l Brotherhood*

In addition, these exemptions are narrowly construed. For example, an American court enjoined efforts by loggers to create an entity to bargain with the monopsony buyer.[119] The loggers argued, unsuccessfully, either that they were similar to farmers and should be afforded the same rights under Capper-Volstead or that their organization was similar to a labor union exempt under section 6 of the Clayton Act.[120]

Because employment is a common arena in which buyer power can be exploited, many countries have authorized labor unions and given workers the right to strike as means of balancing the power of large employers. Industry-wide bargaining is a common feature of contracts in some industries. Such agreements ensure that all covered employers provide the same basic pay and benefit plans for their workers. They are also essentially cartelistic arrangements between a worker cartel (the seller of labor) and a buyer cartel (the combined unionized employers in that industry). The resulting wage bargains still reflect the relative power of the contending parties as well as the force of the state in supporting or opposing one side or the other.[121]

An example of a very broad exemption for producer cartels is found in Australia. The law authorizes the Competition and Consumer Commission to license producer cartels subject to specific conditions and a limited period of operation with the possibility of renewal.[122] Such a strategy can ensure ongoing public interest-based oversight. Even so, there may be

---

of Elec. Workers Local 3, 325 U.S. 797 (1945) (labor union cannot collude with employers to exclude competitors of the employers from the market).

119 *Boise Cascade Int'l, Inc. v N. Minn. Pulpwood Producers Ass'n*, 294 F. Supp. 1015 (D. Minn. 1968) (finding against an association of independent contractors that engaged in a collective refusal to deal).

120 *Ibid* at 1022–5.

121 When bargaining is done employer-by-employer, there is a greater potential that firms will 'play off' their employees against employees of other employers, especially if other employers are nonunion and have lower wages.

122 See Australian Competition and Consumer Commission (ACCC) (2013), 'Authorisation Guidelines 12', available at http://www.accc.gov.au/system/files/Authorisation%20guidelines.pdf ('Examples of the types of conduct or arrangements where authorisation has been sought include . . . alliances, and collective bargaining.'). The ACCC will authorize groups of small businesses to negotiate terms and conditions for sales to customers. See ACCC (2011), 'Streamlined Collective Bargaining for Small Business', available at http://www.accc.gov.au/system/files/Streamlined%20Collective%20Bargaining.pdf. The ACCC will also set time limits for the authorization. See ACCC, 'Authorisation Guidelines', *supra*, at 68 ('The ACCC may grant authorisation for a limited period of time and, in practice, will only grant authorisations without a time limit in exceptional circumstances.').

issues of overinclusion, agency capture and the creation of vested interests that could exclude competition and retard evolution of the market.

Some scholars, such as John Kirkwood, have advocated that competition law recognize a general defense for a producers' cartel that faces a powerful buyer.[123] The assumption is that buying power is durable and that, by enhancing the countervailing power through cartelization of the input market, competitive balance will be restored. Although not discussed in Kirkwood's proposal, suppliers could seek a 'business review clearance' from the Department of Justice prior to launching their cartel.[124] Although some competition authorities (such as the Australian Competition and Consumer Commission) have the statutory entitlement to grant such authorization, it is doubtful that American competition authorities can do so without additional statutory authority because a cartel without statutory authorization is per se illegal.

In any event, cartelization as a solution to the problem of buyer power is questionable for a number of reasons. In the absence of government authorization, the cartelizing parties expose themselves to potentially significant liability. Kirkwood has proposed allowing a cartelization defense subject to a number of stringent conditions that would leave it with only limited application in practice.[125] Even so, cartel enforcement could be weakened, especially if the limiting conditions were interpreted less stringently than Kirkwood advocates. Many cartels in intermediate industries could potentially advance such a defense. Indeed, such a defense would create a significant potential for false negatives, immunizing competitively harmful cartelization. Even if American enforcement authorities could provide advance clearance, those agencies lack the capacity to engage in ongoing oversight of such cartels. Agencies in other countries may have greater legal capacity, but any such effort would entail a significant investment of resources.

The creation of countervailing cartel power can have additional adverse effects on individual producers. The entity that exercises the cartelized power may exploit its power over its participants. For example, insurance brokers who acted on behalf of large blocks of customers seeking major

---

[123] John B Kirkwood, 'Collusion to Control a Powerful Customer: Amazon, E-Books, and Antitrust Policy' (2014) 69 *Miami Law Review* 1, 51–63.

[124] The Antitrust Division will provide a statement of its enforcement intent in response to requests from parties prior to the commencement of their activity. See Antitrust Division Business Review Procedure, 28 C.F.R. § 50.6 (2015).

[125] Kirkwood, *supra* note 123, at 53–6 (the monopsony power must be legally acquired, substantial, persistent, and durable before a producer's cartel can be lawful).

insurance policies induced the insurers to inflate their charges and then shared the overcharges with the agents.[126] Similar situations have occurred in the milk cooperatives.[127]

Finally, effective countervailing power can be pernicious if it is linked to downstream market power.[128] In that case, the 'monopoly' input supplier that can limit output will bargain with the downstream monopolist over output and price. Both will have an interest in barring new entry at either level of production.[129] The result is likely to be a higher price and reduced output. Because many farm cooperatives must accept all of their members' production, they have little incentive to monopolize the input by reducing sales.[130] These cooperatives will seek ways to maximize downstream uses of their commodity.

Naked countervailing power is generally an unattractive solution to the problem of buyer power outside the unique case of industrial labor. It is, at best, a problematic means of protecting the interests of producers of goods from buyer exploitation. Collective action is difficult and may create incentives to further monopolize the input market by excluding entry. As the entity acting for the producers becomes distinct from the producers, classic agency problems arise, and the entity can become a monopsonist in its own right. Chapter 7 returns to a discussion of harms to the competitive process that arise from buyer cartels. Because buyer power is pervasive, and all alternatives are imperfect to some degree, there may be rare circumstances in which effectively regulated seller cartels are the least imperfect option. As discussed in the next subsection, productive joint ventures that provide marketing services and perhaps some basic

---

[126] In re *Ins. Brokers Antitrust Litig.*, 618 F.3d 300 (3rd Cir. 2010) (upholding the validity of antitrust claims involving broker bid rigging despite potential exemption).

[127] In re *Se. Milk Antitrust Litig.*, 555 F. Supp. 2d 934 (E.D. Tenn. 2008). Dairy farmers both in and outside the cooperative claimed that they had suffered significant losses as a result of the cooperative's sweetheart deals with milk processors. The case ultimately settled with substantial payments to farmers and some reforms in the operation of the cooperative. See Se. Milk Antitrust Litig., website http://www.southeastdairyclass.com/CourtDocuments.htm.

[128] Kirkwood, *supra* note 123, at 60–3 (proposing to deny access to the countervailing power defense in the event of downstream market power).

[129] *Cf* Thomas K McCraw, 'Competition and "Fair Trade": History and Theory' (2001) 16 *Research in Economic History* 185 (concluding that General Electric used resale price maintenance to create a symbiotic relationship between itself and large retailers, causing barriers to entry at both levels of business).

[130] See Mueller, Helmberger and Paterson, *supra* note 104 (analysis showing that an orange and lemon cooperative with a monopoly market share did not exploit the market because it had to market all of its members' production).

processing of inputs would be better alternatives for producers seeking an enhanced bargaining position.

B. Producer Integration

Individual producers may lack the market power, the bargaining skills and sufficient market information to bargain effectively with powerful buyers. But if these producers integrate their marketing efforts, they may achieve a stronger market position because consolidated control of volume supports more effective marketing. This is a primary motivation for mergers among suppliers as their customer base consolidates. Horizontal consolidation is more likely in input industries because a buyer, whether an automobile manufacturer or a retailer, combines a large number of inputs in its product or service.

Input producers in many industries give as a reason for merger that they face few buyers and those buyers want to make their purchases from a single supplier. In 2015, two large global computer chip makers sought to merge. The primary reason given by the parties for their proposed merger was improved bargaining power in a consolidated buyer market.[131] They implied that downstream mergers gave their customers enhanced buyer power that could only be offset by upstream consolidation. This is a recurring pattern in consumer goods markets and component markets for many industrial products, from computers to automobiles. Vertical integration is nearly impossible in these situations as the downstream products or services (in the case of retailing) involve a combination of many inputs.

For horizontal integration to be feasible, the businesses must either have no significant diseconomies of scale or comprise a number of producing units that can be consolidated under a single owner. These conditions may be true for the producers of manufactured components, but not for labor, agriculture or input producers that are subject to other strong barriers to integration.

Horizontal integration of upstream production into a single entity able

---

[131] See Takashi Amano and Brian Womack, 'Applied Materials to Buy Tokyo Electron for $9.39 Billion' *Bloomberg News* (25 September 2013), http://www.bloomberg.com/news/articles/2013-09-24/applied-materials-shares-slip-as-sales-miss-estimates. The parties abandoned the merger, however, because of antitrust objections from the US Department of Justice. See Jane Onyanga-Omara and Kevin McCoy, 'Applied Materials–Tokyo Electron Merger Scrapped' *USA Today* (27 April 2015), available at http://www.usatoday.com/story/money/business/2015/04/27/applied-materials-tokyo-electron/26438619/.

to bargain with its downstream customers would be better for overall efficiency than cartelization. An integrated producer has an incentive to operate efficiently. As its scale increases, it may be able to seek a wider range of outlets for its output and produce a greater range of products. But the American merger guidelines, for example, recognize buyer power as a factor that may excuse increased concentration of producers. The rationale is that powerful buyers will prevent a significant price increase,[132] suggesting that major buyers are likely to dominate the merged producers even if the merger creates an otherwise questionable level of market concentration. Therefore, consolidating producers—within an acceptable range of concentration—may not reduce buyer power significantly.

In addition, producer combinations provide an excuse for buyers to combine, which sets up a process of bilateral consolidation in which each level uses the increased concentration of the other as an argument for another round of mergers. If allowed to continue, this feedback loop of consolidation will transform the markets involved from workably competitive to oligopolistic and create a mutual interest in limiting competition and excluding new entry. The implication is that substantial horizontal mergers cannot be justified as a response to buyer power. This is the topic of Chapter 8.

When full ownership integration is not feasible, a joint venture to perform specific functions can provide partial integration and enhance the bargaining position of the producers. For example, producers can create a marketing entity that takes title to the upstream output and resells it. This entity is responsible for ensuring the uniformity of the product, consolidating individual output to ensure a marketable quantity, and may provide some basic preparation for marketing. Indeed, the boundary between a legitimate marketing joint venture and a producer cartel may be ambiguous, as will be discussed in more detail in Chapter 7. That chapter addresses the other side of the continuum that extends from buyer cartels to buying groups, but the analytic issues are similar.

Although productive joint ventures are usually prima facie lawful under competition law,[133] some protection from the risk of claims that the entity violates competition law may be necessary. These ventures take the form of a horizontal collaboration among competing producers and often employ exclusive dealing or other restraints on members to ensure

---

[132] US Department of Justice and FTC (2010), 'Horizontal Merger Guidelines' § 8.2 ('powerful buyers may constrain the ability of the merging parties to raise prices').

[133] As discussed in section III of this chapter, they may require assistance in organization to overcome collective action problems.

their commitment to the enterprise.[134] The potential for costly litigation and fears of potential liability can deter economically rational collaboration.[135] Agricultural cooperatives that act as marketing agents or as processors of their members' produce are not illegal under contemporary American competition law.[136] But powerful buyers will have an incentive to promote concern about the risks of costly litigation and potential liability as a way of discouraging producers from forming or joining joint ventures. Moreover, the line between unlawful cartels and lawful selling ventures is ambiguous, and buyers can readily manufacture antitrust concerns. Therefore some insulation from the risk of liability is often critical.[137]

Competition law enforcement needs to be supportive of joint venture efforts and avoid formalistic objections. For example, agricultural cooperatives generally impose either a requirement of exclusive dealing or a penalty for selling outside the cooperative to prevent selective poaching by major buyers. Either strategy creates some risk of an antitrust challenge because of its exclusionary impact. Enforcement agencies should assist courts by providing justification for the restraints imposed by a legitimate joint venture facing significant sunk costs

---

134 For example, grain elevator cooperatives have substantial sunk investments in the elevator and are vulnerable to opportunistic 'overbidding' by deep pocket competitors. Some elevator cooperatives required members to sign exclusive delivery commitments while others imposed a penalty if the member sold grain elsewhere. Dairy cooperatives make commitments to deliver specific quantities of milk to various buyers and need contractual commitments that their members will provide the necessary milk.

135 Another example comes from international trade, which offers an important means of increasing sales. Smaller producers, however, are unable to market effectively individually in a global market, but are concerned that collaboration would subject them to antitrust liability. Congress has responded with a statutory antitrust exemption, but it requires certification by the Antitrust Division of the Department of Justice that the venture will not violate antitrust law. See Export Trading Companies and Trade Associations, 15 U.S.C. §§ 4001–20 (2016). The exemption is granted only if the agreement will not result in 'a substantial lessening of competition or restraint of trade . . .' *Ibid* § 4013(a)(1).

136 See Carstensen, *supra* note 79, at 473–4.

137 A plausible explanation for the survival of some statutory exemptions in the transportation industry is that the gains to participants in legitimate joint ventures are modest even though these ventures may produce significant economies; hence the participants require greater assurance of protection from the costs and risks of antitrust litigation. See Peter C Carstensen, 'Replacing Antitrust Exemptions for Transportation Industries: The Potential for a "Robust Business Review Clearance"' (2011) 89 *Oregon Law Review* 1059.

and buyer resistance, as well as criteria for judging the reasonableness of particular restraints.[138] Restraints that unjustifiably exclude competing buyers and entrench the dominant venture should not be accepted.

Vertical forward integration is not feasible for most suppliers. It can occur when the upstream input is a major element of the downstream product. The historical example of farmer integration into cooperative ownership of grain elevators is an example of both horizontal and vertical consolidation. A grain elevator with access to rail service could sell to many buyers—unlike the individual farmer who had access only to local elevators. Other examples include farm cooperatives that produce branded products such as Ocean Spray cranberry products[139] and Valio, the Finnish milk cooperative that has its own brands.[140]

Vertical integration can be a more effective way to defeat buyer power, especially if forward integration does not require the extensive development of new capacity. A grain elevator is a relatively straightforward business for grain farmers, while automobile assembly and distribution would be daunting for even a large manufacturer of motor vehicle components. Also, producers are likely to lack the depth of resources necessary to sustain significant forward integration into any line of business that has the inherent capacity to exercise buyer power.

Vertical forward integration does not require affirmative legal protection. But, like horizontal combinations, it can create longer term issues for market conduct. Powerful buyers might partially integrate backward in order to create even more pressure on independent producers. Contract integration in American cattle markets provides an illustration of this. Independent producers became residual suppliers subject to greater risks and price fluctuation, while contract producers were assured of prices at or above those prevailing in the market at any given time.[141]

---

[138] See, eg, Case Comp/M.5046, *Friesland Foods/Campina*, C(2008) 8459 final, available at http://ec.europa.eu/competition/mergers/cases/decisions/m5046_20081217_20600_en.pdf (allowing the merger of two major dairy processors despite risk of exclusion); Case IV/M.1313, *Danish Crown/Vestjyske Slagterier*, available at http://ec.europa.eu/competition/mergers/cases/decisions/m1313_en.pdf (two largest hog slaughter cooperatives allowed to merger with undertakings not to discriminate against non-members).

[139] See Ocean Spray Cranberries, Inc., http://www.oceanspray.com/ (last visited 15 November 2016).

[140] See European Commission, *supra* note 107, at 19.

[141] See, eg, Domina and Taylor, *supra* note 57 (describing losses to cattle feeders who did not benefit from contracts).

III. PUBLIC SPONSORSHIP OF ALTERNATIVE MARKETS FOR PRODUCERS

Finding new markets and uses for products is another way to circumvent the power of existing buyers. Expanding the market options for producers both provides support for economic development and is key to overcoming buyer power, but collective action, complexity and investment challenges present significant barriers.

Public authorities can facilitate the development of alternative markets for producers. These efforts include addressing the collective action problems inherent in any joint venture through education and support. The first challenge is to identify potential new outlets for production, which requires sophisticated, focused market evaluation and business planning. A public agency can provide or finance such efforts. A new venture may require a capital investment beyond the financial capacity of the producers themselves and may therefore appear to be unduly risky for private underwriters. State sponsorship can help to overcome these obstacles. Thus, public authorities can identify alternative markets for producers and facilitate the development of the entities necessary to serve them. Public support for local vegetable producers that develop products for use in public schools is an illustration.[142]

Equally important are public subsidies, either directly or in the form of tax relief, which can help lower the startup costs for such enterprises. Other examples include subsidies for the development of commodity processing facilities, especially in developing countries. Public support may also include tariff protection, tax benefits and direct investment. These investments may improve the relationship between upstream producers and a workably competitive downstream market.

Another major problem is the lack of information about opportunities and options. Public agencies can provide important information about such opportunities, organize initial producer meetings and provide information about best practices. In some cases, as discussed earlier, providing information will overcome some of the greatest barriers, such as enabling grain farmers to create cooperative elevators that reached competitive downstream buying markets. In the case of labor markets, reducing the

---

[142] See Lihlani Skipper and Alfonso Morales, 'The Right Blend' (May/June 2014) 81 *Rural Cooperatives* 12, 16–17 (describing program to provide fresh local produce for school lunches from small farms through a cooperative organization that had key support from a USDA grant). See generally USDA Agricultural Marketing Service, 'Specialty Crop Block Grant Program', available at https://www.ams.usda.gov/services/grants/scbgp.

adverse impact of restrictive employment covenants should be linked with improved information about job opportunities.[143]

The challenges of attracting new buyers into a concentrated buying market can be substantial. Because entry takes time and investment—as well as a commitment by producers to supply the entrant—incumbent buyers will have significant opportunities to frustrate it. Chapter 3 examined these institutional constraints in more general terms. For present purposes, it suffices to state that facilitated entry is a potentially useful way to limit buyer power, but is inherently difficult to achieve whenever buyer power is substantial. Moreover, even if a producer is successful in finding new outlets, the results may be inadequate to counterbalance existing buyer power.

Creating new markets for output is outside the scope of authority of most competition authorities. Government support for these projects generally comes from other agencies, which are unlikely to pursue a conscious and consistent policy of promoting deconcentration of buying markets. Thus the same agency may in one project seek to create new outlets for producers but in another facilitate excessive participation in the supply market that further weakens the bargaining power of the producers. An illustration of this practice in the United States is the USDA's guaranteeing of loans for the building of poultry facilities.[144] Because the government guaranteed the loans, the lending banks made no effort to ascertain whether a borrower had a realistic prospect of surviving as a producer for the loan's duration. Between the resale of the facilities when the original producer went into bankruptcy and the guarantee, the banks bore no risk. Absent the guarantee, banks would have insisted that a borrower have a sufficiently long-term contract to provide a reasonable prospect of enough income to ensure repayment of the loan. Thus, had there been no guarantee or had the banks had sufficient risk in the loans to act as reasonable lenders, excessive entry would have been unprofitable and producer bargaining power would have been enhanced.

But competition authorities can advocate for appropriate investments that will enable producers to access new buyers. They should also identify programs that undermine the capacity of producers to have workably competitive markets. The institutional divide and consequent lack of coordination between the agencies able to provide support for the creation of alternative outlet markets and those most likely to be able to identify the need to respond to buyer power means that public investment is

---

143 See Council of Economic Advisers, *supra* note 68.

144 Leonard, *supra* note 61, at 67–8, 139–45.

likely to have only limited utility in many circumstances. In developing economies, agricultural and business agencies ought to take an interest in developing effective alternatives for the production and distribution of goods. Implicit in such efforts should be a concern for buyer power and its circumvention. Limiting buyer power is important for economic development. Better coordination between competition authorities and public agencies providing support for new business development is particularly relevant in these economies.

All of these efforts are likely to encounter major political problems. Those in possession of buyer power are likely to resist efforts to undermine their hegemony. Political opportunism may influence the choice of industries and participants to be supported. Those with strong political connections are likely to be favored over those whose case may be better on the merits but who lack the same level of political clout. Therefore, although the development of alternative production outlets seems to be a useful addition to the regulatory toolkit for controlling buyer power, its actual use and effectiveness are limited.

IV. CONCLUSION

This chapter has surveyed three ways that public policy has responded to buyer power: regulation of buyer conduct; offsetting producer power; and public support for alternative markets. Each has significant weaknesses.[145]

Market regulation—whether focused on specific exploitation by dominant buyers or on the more general market process—has a limited capacity to ameliorate the harmful effects of abuses of buyer power. A review of these limits serves to underscore and reinforce the thesis of Chapter 5 that controlling buyer exploitation through market regulation is extremely difficult. Except for forward integration, none of these options directly affects the power that a buyer possesses. At best, they limit how a buyer can

---

[145] In some contexts, specific conduct regulation may reduce some of the barriers to entry for competing buyers. For example, recent reports in the United States have identified a number of other ways in which the general legal context of employment can be reformed to reduce the buyer power of employers. See US Department of Treasury, *supra* note 64 (identifying the adverse effects of restrictive employment covenants); Council of Economic Advisors, *supra* note 68 (listing a variety of policies that can improve the economic conditions of workers). In addition, mandatory disclosure of risks and returns as well as comparative data on contract options can provide sufficient information to potential entrants into the supply market to enable them to bargain more effectively with dominant buyers.

exploit that power. And these limits are rarely self-enforcing. Producers must stand ready to complain to public enforcement agencies or initiate litigation. Either of these responses risks overt as well as subtle retaliation by a powerful buyer. The European Commission's Green Paper on unfair trade practices points up the pervasive impact of this 'fear factor' in limiting the effectiveness of any regulation of unfair buying practices.[146]

Dominant buyers are also likely to find ways around market regulations to continue to exercise their power. Regulations prohibiting 'unfair' or 'discriminatory' conduct are unlikely to provide the kind of clarity that is essential to efficient markets. Setting floors, or minimum standards, limits the maximum amount of exploitation, provided enforcement is effective. But floors leave a buyer the opportunity to undercompensate or otherwise exploit suppliers that provide goods or services valued in excess of whatever the floor mandates.

Focused market conduct regulations also create the risk of market rigidification. These regulations can potentially 'freeze' market relationships into patterns that reflect contemporary supply, demand and technology, but which may be inapposite as these factors naturally evolve. Any system that regulates market relationships is likely to create winners and losers. When changes in underlying market conditions make regulatory changes appropriate, those who benefit from the existing rules are likely to resist change and can, if they are politically effective, delay or even totally frustrate it. Given the immense benefits of open, dynamic markets, the risks of rigidification are a serious cause for concern in evaluating the merits of particular regulatory schemes.

The primary utility of stimulating countervailing market power is to offset incumbent buyer power. The least desirable method is the creation of a sellers' cartel. In the United States, cartel-like organizations have been allowed in the agriculture and labor markets. Agricultural cartels have not generally produced significant gains for producers and have often resulted in harm to the intended beneficiaries. The case for labor unions may be stronger, in part, perhaps because workers in most industrial occupations have no other practical way to address the superior bargaining power of their employer.

Countervailing seller power can directly reduce buyer power only through the creation of alternative sales outlets, and such efforts may well

---

[146] European Commission, *Green Paper on Unfair Trading Practices in the Business-to-Business Food and Non-Food Supply Chain in Europe*, COM(2013) 37 final, available at http://eur-lex.europa.eu/legal-content/EN/ALL/?uri=CELEX:52013DC0037.

require significant public support. Horizontal integration through either joint ventures or ownership can provide countervailing power and perhaps afford some opportunity to find or develop additional outlets. Forward integration into downstream markets can actually change the power of buyers by opening new outlets. But these strategies are largely outside the scope of competition agencies' authority.

Public support for the development of alternative outlets for producers requires the engagement of more elements of government beyond the competition authorities. It can provide the kinds of knowledge, training, coordination and financial support necessary to overcome the inherent challenges that entrenched buyer power creates. However, to achieve such market transformation requires both a political commitment that may be difficult to achieve and a coordination among elements of government that frequently are unfamiliar with each other.

Despite this pessimistic summary, it is important to remember that all alternatives are imperfect.[147] Even a robustly competitive buying market may still be flawed. And because buyer power is pervasive, market regulation and countervailing power are the only tools that can modify and constrain the abuse of power in many circumstances. Properly constituted market regulations are essential elements in the overall competitive process. Competition authorities should increase the time and attention they devote to such regulations because of their inherent impact on the overall competitive process, including abuses of buyer power.

---

147 Neil Komesar, *Imperfect Alternatives* (University of Chicago Press, Chicago 1994).

7. Competition policy for buyer cartels, buying groups and other contractual restraints involving buyer power

Buyers employ both vertical and horizontal arrangements that may restrain competition. Inherent in every vertical agreement with a supplier, whatever its duration, is some limit on the freedom of action of both parties. In addition, buyers act horizontally by participating in buying groups or cartels. This chapter first, and primarily, examines the law and policy governing horizontal agreements among buyers. It stresses the distinction between buying groups and buyer cartels. The former can be lawful if reasonable, but the latter *should be* absolutely illegal unless expressly authorized and regulated. Some scholars have argued that pure buyer cartels should be lawful just as some have argued for the legality of seller cartels facing buyer power.[1] Second, the chapter briefly examines vertical agreements between buyers and sellers.[2]

The central thesis of this chapter is that both buyer cartels and buying groups can pose potentially serious risks to the market process. Unregulated buyer cartels should be unlawful under all circumstances despite the potential negative effects of seller power on buyers. Enforcement agencies should also carefully review any proposed buying group that will account for the purchase of appreciable amount of any input. Such groups can create unnecessary harm to the competitive process.

---

[1] See Chapter 6, text accompanying notes 123–30.

[2] Chapter 5 provides the primary analysis of these restraints. That discussion is briefly reiterated here because many jurisdictions treat such restraints as unreasonable contracts rather than unilateral conduct.

I. HORIZONTAL AGREEMENTS AMONG BUYERS—BUYER CARTELS AND BUYING GROUPS

Many competition laws expressly prohibit cartel agreements among buyers. The oldest known cartel case involved a grain buying conspiracy in ancient Athens.[3] It appears that the conspirators were put to death—a stricter penalty than is currently available even among countries that use criminal sanctions.[4] In the United States it is unlawful, as well as a basis for treble damage liability, for buyers to agree (1) on what they individually will pay for goods or services; (2) that they will not bid against each other for particular items at an auction; or (3) that they will restrict wage or employment competition.[5] Thailand's competition law expressly prohibits horizontal restraints on buying,[6] although the law appears generally to be

---

[3] See Lamabros E Kotsiris, 'An Antitrust Case in Ancient Greek Law' (1988) 22 *The International Lawyer* 451.

[4] *Ibid* at 457.

[5] See, eg, *United States v Crescent Amusement Co.*, 323 U.S. 173 (1944) (conspiracy to allocate distribution rights to motion pictures); *Swift & Co. v United States*, 196 U.S. 375 (1905) (conspiracy to limit the price paid for cattle); *Knevelbaard Dairies v Kraft Foods, Inc.*, 232 F.3d 979 (9th Cir. 2000) (conspiracy and unilateral conduct to reduce price of milk); *United States v Romer*, 148 F.3d 359 (4th Cir. 1998) (conspiracy to limit prices of real estate); *Reid Bros. Logging Co. v Ketchikan Pulp Co.*, 699 F.2d 1292 (9th Cir. 1983) (conspiracy to allocate timber purchases). See John Asker, 'A Study of the Internal Organization of a Bidding Cartel' (2010) 100 *American Economic Review* 724 (describing the operation of a postage stamp cartel). For cases dealing with employment issues, see, for example, *Todd v Exxon Corp.*, 275 F.3d 191 (2d Cir. 2001) (upholding treble damages in class action complaint charging a conspiracy to stabilize wage rates for various classes of technical workers at major oil and gas companies); *Fleischman v Albany Med. Ctr.*, No. 1:06-CV-165, 2008 WL 2945993, at *7 (N.D.N.Y. July 28, 2008) (conspiracy to restrain wage competition for nurses); *Del. Health Care, Inc. v MCD Holding Co.*, 893 F. Supp. 1279 (D. Del. 1995) (hospital collusion on hiring and salaries of nurses); *cf All Care Nursing Serv., Inc. v High Tech Staffing Servs., Inc.*, 135 F.3d 740 (11th Cir. 1998) (rejecting per se treatment of agreement among hospitals to restrict competition for nurses). In 2011 a number of high tech companies agreed to abandon understandings not to compete for each other's employees. See Final Judgment, *United States v Adobe Sys. Inc.*, No. 1:10-cv-01629 (D.D.C. Mar. 18, 2011), available at https://www.justice.gov/atr/case/us-v-adobe-systems-inc-et-al. (computer hardware and software companies consented to decree prohibiting restraints in competition for employees).

[6] Trade Competition Act B.E. 2542 §§ 25(1) and 27(2) (1999) (Thailand), available at http://www.apeccp.org.tw/doc/Thailand/Competition/thcom2.htm.

unenforced.[7] South Africa similarly forbids buyer-side restraints.[8] Despite its reliance on consumer welfare as the basis for its competition policy, the European Union (EU) has also held such conduct to be absolutely illegal.[9] This is consistent with the express terms of Article 101(1) of the Treaty on the Functioning of the European Union.[10] Indeed globally, there is general recognition that buyer cartels are anticompetitive and should be prohibited.

At the same time, American enforcement agencies, the EU and other competition authorities rarely object to the creation of 'buying groups'.[11] A buying group is a set of potentially competing buyers that pool their purchases and negotiate prices for the inputs they seek even if the products obtained will be shipped directly to each buyer and billed separately.[12] Indeed, based on its enforcement policy statement for health care, the only place where any guidance on buying agreements is found, the United States apparently presumes that such groups are lawful if they buy no more than 35 percent of the total volume of purchases in a particular market.[13] Some EU decisions suggest that adverse competitive effects will

---

7 See Chitanong Poomipark, Manuswi Intaranont and Sivinee Thanapase, 'Thailand to Overhaul Trade Competition Law' (25 February 2010), available at http://www.martindale.com/matter/asr-929360.Thailand.pdf ('The Trade Competition Law is widely seen as playing no role and having no impact on the trade practices of business operators'). See generally Nisit Intamano, 'Implementing Competition Law and Policies in Thailand and Enhancing its Efficacy' (unpublished S.J.D. dissertation, University of Wisconsin, 2013) (on file at the University of Wisconsin Law School Library).

8 Competition Act 98 of 1999, as amended, § 4(1)(b)(i) (S. Afr.) (an agreement among firms is prohibited 'if it involves any of the following restrictive horizontal practices: (i) directly or indirectly fixing a *purchase* or selling price or any other trading condition . . .') (emphasis added).

9 See, eg, Case C-209/07, *Competition Authority v Beef Industry Dev. Soc'y Ltd.*, [2008] ECR I08637; Case COMP/C.38.238/B.2, *Raw Tobacco Spain* (Comm'n, 2004).

10 Consolidated Version of the Treaty on the Functioning of the European Union, art. 101, 9 May, 2008, 2008 O.J. (C 115) 47 ('The following shall be prohibited . . . all agreements [that] directly or indirectly fix purchase . . . prices or any other trading conditions. . .').

11 See, eg, US Department of Justice and Federal Trade Commission, 'Statements of Antitrust Enforcement Policy in Health Care' 54–5 (1996) (hereinafter 'Enforcement Policy in Health Care').

12 See Thomas A Piraino, Jr., 'A Proposed Antitrust Approach to High Technology Competition' (2002) 44 *William and Mary Law Review* 65, 92–93 (hereinafter Piraino, 'High Technology Competition'); Thomas A Piraino, Jr., 'A Proposed Antitrust Approach to Buyers' Competitive Conduct' (2005) 56 *Hastings Law Journal* 1121, 1151 n.139 (hereinafter Piraino, 'Buyers' Competitive Conduct').

13 See 'Enforcement Policy in Health Care', *supra* note 11, at 54–5 ('The Agencies will not challenge, absent extraordinary circumstances, any joint

arise only if a buyer takes more than 22 percent of the volume in a market, but its guidelines require review if a buying group takes more than 15 percent of any commodity.[14]

As an initial matter, it may seem difficult to distinguish between the buyers at an auction who act collectively to decide who will buy and what they will pay for items and a group of hospitals that pool their purchases and demand lower prices in return for the volume they offer.[15] In the United States, the auction-buying ring (which is a cartel) is generally held to be illegal per se and its members to be committing a felony,[16] while the hospital buying group is subject to a rule of reason with a strong presumption of legality.[17]

What differentiates these situations is both the functional and legal characterization of the buyer-entity. However, neither courts nor commentators have done a satisfactory job of explaining the reasons and justifications for the dichotomous characterization and divergent standards of review.[18] Moreover, the distinction is not always easily made. Indeed,

---

purchasing arrangement among health care providers where two conditions are present: (1) the purchases account for less than 35 percent of the total sales of the purchased product or service in the relevant market; and (2) the cost of the products and services purchased jointly accounts for less than 20 percent of the total revenues from all products or services sold by each competing participant in the joint purchasing arrangement.'); see also Mark J Botti, 'Observations on and from the Antitrust Division's Buyer-Side Cases: How Can "Lower" Prices Violate the Antitrust Laws?' (paper presented at the 2007 meeting of the ABA Antitrust Section meeting, 19 April 2007), available at http://www.abanet.org /antitrust/at-committees/at-hcic/pdt7program-papers/Botti-Paper.pdf.

[14] See European Union, 'Guidelines on the Applicability of Article 101 of the Treaty on the Functioning of the European Union to Horizontal Co-operation Agreements', 2011 O.J. (C 11) 1, ¶ 204; see also Case 1V/M.1221, *Rewe/Meinl*, C (1999) 228 final, at 99 (survey of sellers showed that on average a buyer taking 22 percent or more of a commodity had substantial power over the seller); see also Chloe Binet, 'Buyer Power in EU Competition Law: A Boon or Impediment to Consumer Welfare?' (2015) 167–85 (unpublished Ph.D. dissertation, Catholic University of Louvain), available at http://dial.uclouvain.be/pr/boreal/fr/object/boreal%3A156352.

[15] See Barry Meier and Mary Williams Walsh, 'Senate Panel Criticizes Hospital Buying Groups' *New York Times* (1 May 2002) at C1.

[16] See, eg, *United States v Taubman*, 297 F.3d 161 (2d Cir. 2002).

[17] See, eg, *Nw. Wholesale Stationers v Pac. Stationery and Printing*, 472 U.S. 284, 297–8 (1985); see also Jonathan M Jacobson and Gary J Dorman, 'Joint Purchasing, Monopsony and Antitrust' (1991) 36 *Antitrust Bulletin* 1, 4 (arguing that joint purchasing should be treated more leniently than joint ventures among sellers).

[18] But see, eg, William K Jones, 'Concerted Refusals to Deal and the Producer Interest in Antitrust' (1989) 50 *Ohio State Law Journal* 73 (clear and strong statement of the law and policy justifying enforcement of producer claims).

a nominally lawful buying group can *become* a cartel akin to the auction conspiracy.[19] Conversely, a group of bidders at an auction might lawfully collaborate to make a better (that is, higher) bid for an item than any one individual bidder could offer.[20] In some circumstances, commentators and an occasional court have argued that buyers should be allowed to collude simply to fix prices or allocate inputs.[21] Many courts and commentators seem unaware of the potential risks that apparently legitimate buying groups can pose to the competitive process.

This section will explicate, evaluate and critique the differences between buyer cartels and buying groups and the competition rules that apply to each characterization. It is important to appreciate the continuum of functions that a buying group can pursue and the implications of those functions for the competitive process. Therefore, effective policy must identify the factors internal to such a group, as well as those external market conditions that justify alternative characterization of the entity. Because buyer power, as shown in Chapter 3, can arise from much smaller market shares than is usually associated with seller power, there are important policy

---

[19] See *In re Brand Name Prescription Drugs Antitrust Litig.*, 123 F.3d 599, 606 (7th Cir. 1997).

[20] In construction and highway contracting, buyers often allow sellers to collaborate using joint bidding. See Antonio Estache and Atsushi Iimi, *Joint Bidding in Infrastructure Procurement* (World Bank, Policy Research Working Paper No. 4664, 2008), available at http://ssrn.com/abstract=1232760. On the buying side, when items are sold in a bundle, there is a plausible basis for a joint buying agreement in order to facilitate the most efficient use of the goods by combining the highest value a set of buyers would give for each component of the bundle. See George J Stigler, 'A Note on Block Booking' (1963) *Supreme Court Review* 152 (movie bundling explained in terms of maximizing value to distributor). This can make the seller better off than selling the bundle to a buyer who values only part of it and must then resell the remainder. Such agreements can, however, create antitrust issues. See, eg, *United States v Seminole Fertilizer Corp.*, No. 97-1507-CIV-T-17E, 1997 WL 692953 (M.D. Fla. Sept. 19, 1997) (two potential bidders for assets to be sold in a bankruptcy auction agreed not to bid against each other and split the assets after the sale; the defendants ultimately entered into a consent decree).

[21] See, eg, *Balmoral Cinema, Inc. v Allied Artists Pictures Corp.*, 885 F.2d 313, 316–17 (6th Cir. 1989) (holding that an agreement allocating the rights to movies among theaters is not per se illegal); Alan Devlin, 'Questioning the Per Se Standard in Cases of Concerted Monopsony' (2007) 3 *Hastings Business Law Journal* 223, 241–3 (arguing that reduced costs resulting from monopsony should be considered in assessing the reasonableness of such collusion); Christopher Leslie, 'Achieving Efficiency Through Collusion: A Market Failure Defense to Horizontal Price-Fixing' (1993) 81 *California Law Review* 243; Roger D Blair and D Daniel Sokol, 'The Rule of Reason and the Goals of Antitrust: An Economic Approach' (2012) 78 *Antitrust Law Journal* 471, 487–90.

implications for both the identification of buyer cartels and for the assessment of the competitive risks that legitimate buying groups can present.

Standard predictions adopted by antitrust law to infer agreement need to be modified in light of the economic incentives of buyer cartels. Buyer cartels can include more participants and face lower risks of defection because of the strong incentives to remain. Such agreements can be more informal, even tacit, for the same reason. Thus, the explication of buyer cartel issues requires a fuller recognition of the incentives that motivate and facilitate such conduct.

Finally, although legitimate buying groups efficiently respond to the needs of their participants, they can pose real threats to the long-term competitiveness of both the supply and demand sides of the market. The prevailing assumption that even very large buying groups are competitively benign[22] ignores the differences between buyer and seller power that result in competitive risks from buyer power at levels that arguably do not create serious antitrust concerns on the selling side. Competition policy needs to recognize and articulate, much more clearly than it does at present, the risks that powerful buying groups can pose and, in light of those risks, adopt better standards for judging the reasonableness of the conduct of any buying group.

Section A of this part focuses on the differences between buyer cartels and buying groups. It first examines the different functional goals of these alternative buyer entities and discusses how to categorize entities whose categorizations are not clear-cut.

Section B evaluates the policy arguments that have so far condemned all unauthorized buyer cartels as per se illegal, while imposing a reasonableness standard for buying groups. Subsection B.1 summarizes the arguments advanced by some scholars for allowing such cartels in some circumstances but argues that proven cartels should continue to be per se illegal despite arguments for excusing buyer collusion in some contexts with a very limited exception for expressly authorized and regulated cartels in a few industrial circumstances. With respect to buying groups, subsection B.2 argues that the current standards for judging the merits of such entities can be too tolerant of conduct that, in reality, is likely to have long-run adverse effects on the competitive process. Hence, stricter standards are needed to limit those risks—either by imposing lower thresholds for any safe harbor or by developing a stronger set of standards to govern buyer conduct so that the concerted activities do not adversely affect the competitive process.

---

[22] See, eg, Jacobson and Dorman, *supra* note 17.

Section C reviews how competition law has responded to both kinds of buyer combinations. Globally, buyer cartels are generally held to be absolute violations of law unless there is an express or implied public authorization for a specific cartel arrangement. The standards for examining buying groups remain vague and very tolerant. Many competition authorities assume that buying groups generally enhance efficiency and provide countervailing market power against powerful sellers. This tolerance has longer run adverse implications for the competitive process. Thus, the analysis here points toward the retention of the current per se rule for buyer cartels and stricter standards for buying groups.

The central policy conclusions that emerge from this analysis are set forth in section D. First, although it can sometimes be difficult to distinguish buyer cartels from legitimate buying groups, cartels not expressly authorized by public authority should remain per se illegal. Second, buyer cartels can involve larger and less-well-organized groups than standard cartel theory postulates. Third, buyer power, whether in the form of a cartel or a buying group, can exist at lower levels of market concentration than is customarily assumed. Fourth, even legitimate buying groups can create significant competitive risks—meriting stricter scrutiny of such organizations than they have traditionally received.

A. Defining Buyer Cartels and Buying Groups

Distinguishing between a buyer cartel and a buying group is easy at an abstract, conceptual level.[23] But in application, the two activities exist on a continuum ranging from a pure cartel[24] to a buying group through which the participants agree to fully integrate their purchases of all inputs.[25] The central problems in characterization are that form and function are not congruent, and buyers do not necessarily differentiate the bases on which they obtain lower input prices. Hence, a group that is functionally a buying group can appear to be little more than a cartel, while it is equally possible to 'dress up' a cartel to look like a buying group.

---

[23] See Piraino, 'Buyers' Competitive Conduct', *supra* note 12, at 1131–2.

[24] An agreement that controls how each participant will conduct its own buying.

[25] See Joseph F Brodley, 'Joint Ventures and Antitrust Policy' (1982) 95 *Harvard Law Review* 1521, 1569–70.

1. Buyer cartels

A cartel is a group of competitors who have agreed to limit or eliminate their competition in some economically relevant dimension.[26] The sole objective of such a combination is to create, allocate and exploit power in the market. Thus defined, this concept is more inclusive than the prototypical price fixing cartel of standard legal analysis. In addition to fixing prices, cartels can (1) allocate customers or suppliers; (2) agree on the composition of the output or input ratios; or (3) share competitively significant information. Sharing of such information facilitates the standardization of operations to ensure uniformity of costs and prices.[27] Indeed, buyer cartels sometimes use their collective power to exclude or restrain their competitors in the markets in which they buy goods or otherwise regulate the non-price dimensions of the supply market.[28]

A buyer cartel focuses on the input side of the market rather than the output side. The objective of such a group is to eliminate competition for input purchases to reduce prices or otherwise control supplier conduct. Because downstream prices are a function of the market or markets in which such sales are made, buyers may collude to drive down input prices even though they sell in highly competitive markets where cartelization is unlikely.[29] Such buyer collusion may eventually reduce the total output in the market. (The likelihood of this effect and its substantiality are functions of the elasticity of supply, as discussed in Chapter 3.) A significant

---

[26] See Natalie Rosenfelt, 'The Verdict on Monopsony' (2008) 20 *Loyola Consumer Law Review* 402, 405–06.

[27] See Robert Lande and Howard Marvel, 'The Three Types of Collusion: Fixing Prices, Rivals, and Rules' 2000 *Wisconsin Law Review* 941, 951–3 (describing various ways in which naked restraints can achieve anticompetitive results).

[28] See, eg, *Klor's, Inc. v Broadway-Hale Stores, Inc.*, 359 U.S. 207, 212–13 (1959) (buyer induced or coerced suppliers to engage in a collective refusal to deal); *Montague v Lowry*, 193 U.S. 38, 45 (1904) (buyer organization induced sellers to refuse to deal with nonmembers and to enforce resale price maintenance); *Toys 'R' Us, Inc. v Fed. Trade Comm'n*, 221 F.3d 928, 936–8 (7th Cir. 2000) (major toy buyer induced sellers of toys to agree to refuse to sell selected toys to competitors of the buyer).

[29] A good example is the timber buyer's cartel in Alaska that drove down the price of trees in the regions where those companies operated, but which had no effect on the overall price of the lumber produced from those trees because that lumber competed in a much broader geographic market. *Reid Bros. Logging Co. v Ketchikan Pulp Co.*, 699 F.2d 1292, 1303 (9th Cir. 1983); *cf Weyerhaeuser Co. v Ross-Simmons Hardwood Lumber Co.*, 549 U.S. 312 (2007) (buyer of timber drove competitors from the market by bidding up the price of logs while reselling the resulting lumber in a market where it presumably had no market power; proof did not satisfy the narrow requirements for antitrust monopolization claim).

reduction in output can affect the downstream market by reducing the volume of the output product, resulting in higher prices for the remaining production.[30]

Examples of buyer cartels abound. One of the earliest was *Montague v Lowry*, an American Supreme Court case involving a private-party challenge to a buyer cartel of retailers of mantels and fireplace tiles.[31] The cartel insisted that manufacturers deal only with its members, thereby boycotting the cartel's competitors, and adopt and enforce resale price maintenance. Requiring a supplier to enforce the cartel's commands is often a more effective way for retailers to police their cartel than doing so directly.[32] Another early case involved the Eastern States Retail Lumber Dealers' Association, which used its buying power to compel lumber companies to refuse to deal with integrated wholesaler-retailers.[33] As in *Montague*, the cartel used its buyer power to eliminate potentially more efficient competition.

Other buyer cartels have focused on labor or agricultural inputs. Several cases have challenged the practices of hospitals and other employers of nurses, alleging that employers engaged in collective wage-setting outside a union contract.[34] In another case, a court of appeals decision upheld a complaint challenging as a buyer cartel a scheme to coordinate job classifications and consequent wage rates for various types of professional

---

30 This effect is discussed in Roger D Blair and Jeffrey L Harrison, *Monopsony: Antitrust Law and Economics* (Princeton University Press, Princeton, NJ 1993) 36–42. See also Richard Sexton and Mingxia Zhang, 'An Assessment of the Impact of Food Industry Market Power on U.S. Consumers' (2001) 17 *Agribusiness* 59; Chris Doyle and Martijn A Han, 'Expropriating Monopoly Rents through Stable Buyer Groups' (Amsterdam Centre for Law and Economics, Working Paper No. 2009-03); see also Martijn A Han, 'How Buyer Groups Can Effectively Operate as Stable Cartels' (2009) 62 *Aenorm* 14.

31 *Montague v Lowry*, 193 U.S. 38 (1904).

32 See Joseph C Palamountain, Jr., *The Politics of Distribution* (Harvard University Press, Harvard, MA 1955) 99–100 (in late 1800s and early 1900s wholesale drug suppliers pressured manufacturers to protect the suppliers' cartel by use of resale price maintenance); Ward Bowman, 'The Prerequisites and Effects of Resale Price Maintenance' (1955) 22 *University of Chicago Law Review* 825, 834–5 (cartel explanation for resale price maintenance); Lester Telser, 'Why Should Manufacturers Want Fair Trade?' (1960) 3 *Journal of Law and Economics* 86 (explaining that cartels are a plausible explanation for resale price maintenance). See also Doyle and Han, *supra* note 30 (model of buyer cartel using suppliers to increase buyer revenue).

33 *E. States Retail Lumber Dealers' Ass'n v United States*, 234 U.S. 600 (1914).

34 See, eg, *Fleischman v Albany Med. Ctr.*, 728 F. Supp. 2d 130 (N.D.N.Y. 2010).

workers in the energy industry.[35] Similar cartels have been documented in agriculture with respect to blueberries in Maine[36] and tobacco in the Southeast.[37] Another classic case involved an agreement to set the percentage of durum wheat in macaroni and spaghetti at a time when durum wheat was in short supply.[38] Finally, there are auction cartels, such as those involving postage stamps.[39]

The EU has condemned similar buyer cartels,[40] and EU state competition authorities have been aggressive in challenging them.[41] There is a tension between the policy goal of consumer welfare and challenges to buyer cartels that present no evidence of direct harm to consumers. European case law reflects a consistent policy that such cartels are unlawful. This is more consistent with the goal of facilitating the competitive process than with the narrow focus on consumer welfare only.[42] Other examples include cases from Canada.[43]

As these examples suggest, buyer cartels can use their power directly, to lower prices paid by participants, or indirectly, to regulate aspects of competition in downstream markets. The extent to which cartel power is used varies depending on the goals and interests of the participants, but also, importantly, on the nature of the supply market. If supply is relatively price inelastic, then colluding buyers have a strong incentive to drive

---

35 *Todd v Exxon Corp.*, 275 F.3d 191, 191 (2nd Cir. 2001).

36 See 'Judge OK's Award in Blueberry Lawsuit' *Boston Globe* (4 January 2004), available at http://www.boston.com/news/local/articles/2004/01/04/judge_oks_award_in_blueberry_lawsuit/.

37 *DeLoach v Lorillard Tobacco Co.*, 391 F.3d 551, 554 (4th Cir. 2004).

38 *Nat'l Macaroni Mfrs. Ass'n v Fed. Trade Comm'n*, 45 F.2d 421, 426–7 (7th Cir. 1965) (holding that an agreement of macaroni producers to reduce the amount of durum wheat purchased as an input for pasta production was per se unlawful).

39 See Asker, *supra* note 5; Robert C Marshall and Michael J Meurer, 'Bidder Collusion and Antitrust Law: Refining the Analysis of Price Fixing to Account for the Special Features of Auction Markets' (2004) 72 *Antitrust Law Journal* 83.

40 See *supra* notes 9, 10 and 14 and accompanying text.

41 See European Competition Network (ECN) (2012), 'ECN Activities in the Food Sector', available at http://ec.europa.eu/competition/ecn/food_report_en.pdf.

42 Victoria Daskalova, *Consumer Welfare in EU Competition Law: What Is It (Not) About?* 20–22 (TILEC Discussion Paper 2015-011, 2015), available at http://papers.ssrn.com/sol3/papers.cfm?abstract_id=2605777&rec=1&srcabs=2586584&alg=1&pos=10 (pointing out that despite a nominal goal of 'consumer welfare', EU competition law provided protections against exploitation and exclusion of producers even in the absence of an immediate gain to consumers).

43 See, eg, *R. v Abitibi Power & Paper Co.*, 36 C.P.R. 1888 (Que. Q.B.) (17 pulp wood buyers unlawfully conspired to avoid competition in buying); *321665 Alberta Ltd. v Mobil Oil Can. Ltd.*, 2011 ABQB 292 (Can.) (unlawful conspiracy to boycott a supplier).

down price because it will not significantly reduce the supply of the input. In other cases, supply may be more price elastic and reducing price would result in an inadequate supply;[44] but buyers can still use their collective power to compel their suppliers to discriminate in price or refuse to deal with new entrants or marginal buyers.[45] Thus, supply elasticity will affect the methods used by a cartel but not its goals.[46]

In another type of buyer cartel, an agent acts as the buyer of goods or services for an economically significant group of clients. The consolidation of demand enables the agent to wield substantial buyer power in bargaining on behalf of its principals. If the agent exploits that collective power by forcing down input prices, it functions as a cartel coordinator. The agent may also use its power to demand that sellers provide the agent with extra benefits. This is most likely to occur when the principals are not fully aware that the agent has created buyer power by demand-pooling.[47]

The hallmark of a buyer cartel is that the buyers have coordinated their individual buying only to exercise power over sellers. The clearest cases involve situations in which each buyer undertakes the buying activity that is necessary to obtain its needed supply, but even when agents are used the result can still be a cartel. The key characteristic is that the buyers have not integrated their buying activity to any degree.

---

[44] If, however, buyers can obtain additional inputs from another, more competitive market, they may be able to exploit one set of suppliers while still filling their residual supply needs. They will then be somewhat less concerned about supplier reaction.

[45] The collective volume of purchases gives a cartel significant leverage over any individual seller, as discussed in Chapter 3, text accompanying note 39, because that seller must engage in a costly and time consuming search for other buyers. See Peter C Carstensen, 'Buyer Power, Competition Policy, and Antitrust: The Competitive Effects of Discrimination among Suppliers' (2008) 53 *Antitrust Bulletin* 271, 281, 284.

[46] Doyle and Han, *supra* note 30, posit a buyer cartel that requires suppliers to raise their prices, thus causing some reduction in sales but generating significant profits for the sellers, which the sellers then rebate to the buyers in the form of slotting fees or other kickbacks. See *Discon v NYNEX*, 525 U.S. 128 (1998) (supplier got contract with higher price by agreeing to pay parent company a large sum thus evading rate regulation); *NicSand v 3M*, 507 F.3d 442 (6th Cir. 2007) (large firm drove small supplier from market by offering large payments to buyers who raised prices once supply competition was eliminated).

[47] See *In re Ins. Brokerage Antitrust Litig.*, 618 F.3d 300 (3rd Cir. 2010) (agents for insureds coordinated price fixing by insurers and shared in the resulting overcharges).

2. Legitimate buying groups

The fundamental distinction between a legitimate buying group and a cartel is that a buying group acts to gain the efficiencies of a joint enterprise. Efficiencies (passed on through lower prices) can result from longer production runs, reductions in transaction costs or lower costs per unit of quality control, and can include protection against defective or dangerous products, preferred status with shipping services based on high volume and improved ability to develop new products.[48] The buyer-participants have integrated some or all of their input acquisition function by creating or participating in the buying group.

Overt buying groups are consciously organized. They occur in a number of retail activities. Two prominent American examples are Topco, which provides a joint buying program and house brands for its mid-sized grocery store chains,[49] and Northwest Wholesale Stationers, which provides buying, warehousing and delivery services to retail stationery stores in the Pacific Northwest.[50] Other American examples include cooperative buying groups in auto parts and hardware. In the EU, Euronics is a buying group for independent electrical appliance retailers, representing 11,000 stores.[51] The ten largest European grocery buying groups had between 30 and 100 billion euros in annual turnover as of 2011.[52]

Other buying groups originate with an entrepreneurial actor that sponsors the group and acts as its agent. Sometimes these arrangements

---

48 See Piraino, 'High Technology Competition', *supra* note 12, at 835–6 (discussing buying group efficiencies in reselling markets).

49 See *United States v Topco Assocs. Inc.*, 405 U.S. 596, 598 (1972) (Topco's downstream market allocation among its members was the subject of the challenge; the opinion acknowledges the legitimacy of the buying group itself); see also Peter C Carstensen and Harry First, 'Rambling Through Economic Theory: Topco's Closer Look' in Eleanor Fox and Dan Crane (eds), *Antitrust Stories* (West Academic Publishing, Eagan, MN 2007) 171 (examining the record in the case and extrinsic information to show that the Court correctly condemned the restraints).

50 See *Nw. Wholesale Stationers, Inc. v Pac. Stationery & Printing Co.*, 472 U.S. 284, 286–7 (1985) (recognizing the value of a buying group and holding that the exclusion of a potential participant was not a per se violation). See also Ed Brunet and David J Sweeney, 'Integrating Antitrust Procedure and Substance After *Northwest Wholesale Stationers*: Evolving Approaches to Pleadings, Burden of Proof, and Boycotts' (1986) 72 *Virginia Law Review* 1015.

51 Euronics, http://www.euronics.com/ (last visited 18 November 2016).

52 Institute of Grocery Distribution, 'Grocery Buying Groups', available at http://www.igd.com/our-expertise/Retail/retail-outlook/3395/Grocery-Buying-Groups/ (last visited 18 November 2016).

follow a franchise model.[53] The participants in the downstream market benefit from the efforts of an upstream coordinator, a third party with more efficient skills, in this case for the provision of inputs. This is a form of partial vertical integration. The economic logic is that some functions (here supplying important categories of inputs, including branding and advertising) are subject to significant economies of scale and scope that will generate gains for the participants. But other aspects of the same business may be subject to diseconomies of scale. If those functions are separated, the resulting partially integrated enterprises are more efficient at both levels than a fully integrated enterprise of the same size. The evidence from the American grocery market is that in the 1950s and 1960s, at least, national chains were less efficient than regional chains,[54] in part because the regional chains used buying groups to mimic the buying efficiency of the national chains but avoided the inefficiencies of the national chains' central management systems.[55]

There are no fixed parameters for a buying group. A legitimate buying group involves some integration of activities, but the integration is limited to facilitating the functioning of the particular enterprise.[56] One way to distinguish a buying group from a buyer cartel is to focus on its functional goals. If the participants make an investment in, and share some productive activities to consolidate, coordinate and administer their buying activity, then they belong to a prima facie buying group. Conversely, if the group exists only to agree on how the parties will conduct their own purchases, it is prima facie a cartel.[57]

3. Distinguishing buying groups from cartels

Because of the flexibility inherent in the organization of legitimate buying groups, there can be significant difficulty in distinguishing them from

---

[53] In the United States, examples include the IGA and Piggly Wiggly grocery chains. IGA claims to be the largest grocery provider with over 4,000 participating stores in 41 countries. See IGA, 'About IGA', available at http://www.iga.com/about.aspx (last visited 18 November 2016); Piggly Wiggly, 'About Us', available at http://www.pigglywiggly.com (last visited 18 November 2016).

[54] Carstensen and First, *supra* note 49, at 178–9.

[55] Central management must coordinate retailing operations in a large number and variety of diverse and dispersed local markets.

[56] See Paul W Dobson, 'Exploiting Buyer Power: Lessons from the British Grocery Trade' (2005) 72 *Antitrust Law Journal* 529, 543–4 (discussing integrated buying groups in the British grocery industry).

[57] See, eg, *Mandeville Island Farms, Inc. v Am. Crystal Sugar Co.*, 334 U.S. 219, 223–4 (1948) (holding that buying agreement among sugar refiners constituted a cartel).

cartels. Once a buying group has been organized, it may be able to impose other restraints on its suppliers, such as requiring them to refuse to deal with non-members or requiring more favorable terms than non-group buyers would enjoy. In addition, the group may coordinate downstream competition through various restraints, including resale price controls or territorial allocation.[58] There are plausible theoretical arguments in support of many of these restraints as necessary to facilitate the legitimate interests of the group. Therefore, groups of competitors that want to coordinate their buying activities can, with only modest planning, create an entity that has the appearance of a buying group, but which is, in fact, a naked cartel.

Nevertheless, it is possible to characterize some agreements among buyers as nothing but cartels. The central preliminary factual question is whether the group has integrated any of its buying activity. In situations where there is no integration, but only an agreement about how each independent participant will behave as a buyer, then the resulting entity is a cartel. This is true if the group has agreed to coordinate job and wage classifications,[59] has engaged in refusals to deal to enforce regulations on downstream competition,[60] has set input proportions to reduce the price of a scarce input,[61] or has allocated bidding or other options among the participants.[62] Indeed, a group that is primarily focused on using its buyer power to regulate competition in the downstream market is more easily characterized as a cartel than is a group that focuses more directly on input prices.

In contrast, a buying group can be readily distinguished when its purchases involve a modest share of the total market, particularly when sellers are likely to experience economies of scale resulting from larger orders and would generally welcome volume buyers. Buying groups are also more likely legitimate when input production is price elastic, because attempts by a buying group to depress input prices will be met with reduced output

---

58 See, eg, *United States v Topco Assocs. Inc.*, 405 U.S. 596, 601–04 (1972) (describing the territorial assignment system).

59 *Todd v Exxon Corp.*, 275 F.3d 191, 195–7 (2nd Cir. 2001) (information exchange to eliminate variation in employment categories).

60 See, eg, *E. States Retail Lumber Dealers' Ass'n v United States*, 234 U.S. 600 (1914) (retailer boycott of suppliers to enforce restrictions on who could sell at retail); *Klor's, Inc. v Broadway-Hale Stores, Inc.*, 359 U.S. 207, 209 (1959) (large buyer induced competing suppliers to agree to boycott its small competitor).

61 *Nat'l Macaroni Mfrs. Ass'n v Fed. Trade Comm'n*, 345 F.2d 421, 422–3 (7th Cir. 1965) (agreement among pasta makers to reduce use of scarce input).

62 *United States v Taubman*, 297 F.3d 161, 165–6 (2nd Cir. 2002) (affirming guilty verdict in art auction conspiracy).

levels. In these situations, a buying group is likely seeking economies and efficiencies of input acquisition. This creates higher net profits (and increased output) for producers while at the same time holding the total cost (price plus transactional expenses) down for buyers. Again, a focus on the specific activities and functions of the buying group is important because, even when supply markets are elastic, a group with a sufficient share of the buying side might well impose its will on producers with respect to non-price aspects of competition.

Legitimate buying groups can also provide cover for cartelistic behavior, however. Indeed, given their underlying goal of reducing the cost of inputs, a buying group with any appreciable buying power has an incentive to use that power to reduce input prices further. Of course, if suppliers respond by reducing output, then the buying group must ration supply among its members or find a way to induce increased output despite lower prices, such as using all-or-nothing contracts. Moreover, if the producer achieves economies of scale or scope through a large volume contract, an all-or-nothing offer provides a contractual means for the buying group to capture some or all of the efficiency gain that results from their joint purchase.[63] Hence, the elasticity of supply and the consequences for efficiency of increased output are important characteristics in differentiating the competitive implications of apparently similar actions.

Competition authorities in many countries employ safe harbor standards as a short-hand method of insulating certain buyer groups from close antitrust scrutiny while more carefully examining those buyer groups more likely to create competitive concerns. Safe harbors create a presumption of legitimacy for entities that buy no more than some fraction of the total supply purchased in the market.[64] Such a system assumes that buyers that collectively take no more than the safe harbor percentage will lack the power to impose conditions that unduly restrict competition in input markets. As long as the safe harbor does no more than create a presumption of legality for the venture, it is probably a useful enforcement screen. But the screen needs to be set at a level that reflects the actual risk of abuse of buyer power, whether the group has a legitimate function or not. Moreover, this screen should be understood as creating no more than a *presumption* of lawfulness for the group.

---

63 Carstensen, *supra* note 45, at 301–02.

64 See 'Enforcement Policy in Health Care', *supra* note 11, at 53–4; Thomas A Piraino, Jr., 'Beyond Per Se, Rule of Reason or Merger Analysis: A New Antitrust Standard for Joint Ventures' (1991) 76 *Minnesota Law Review* 1, 41 n.184 (noting that the European Economic Community and Japan have safe harbor provisions for 'firms that lack significant market power').

B. The Merits and Demerits of Buyer Cartels and Buying Groups

Conventional analysis says that buyer cartels cause economic harm similar to that caused by seller cartels. But as with seller cartels, some scholars defend buyer cartels as enhancing efficiency in some circumstances.[65] The credibility of these arguments depends in large part on the goals of competition policy against which those arguments are measured. Although the conventional explanation of why buyer cartels are undesirable has serious limitations, as discussed below, there remain serious and substantial reasons to object to such cartels and the justifications appear to overestimate substantially the potential gains to the competitive process.

1. Buyer cartels—competitive harms, market justifications

(a) Theories of competitive harm The conventional economic welfare argument against buyer cartels rests on the assumptions that buyers purchase in discrete units and resell in a market in which they are the only sellers and that producers face increasing unit costs as volume increases. Under these assumptions, when the price paid for inputs is reduced, output of that commodity declines. As a result, the static comparison of a world with and without a buyer cartel shows that the cartel causes a reduction in production and a consequent increase in prices to consumers. The conclusion, therefore, is that buyer cartels harm consumers as well as aggregate welfare by causing lower output and higher prices.

The force of the economic welfare argument is contingent on the validity of its factual assumptions. The argument loses force if the cartel uses all-or-nothing contracts to compel producers to deliver approximately the same output at a lower price or if the cartel members compete with many other producers in a competitive resale market and have no incentive or capacity to raise the prices of their output.[66] In either case, there would be no adverse effect on the static price-output parameters on which the conventional economic models are based.

A second weakness in the standard story is its assumption that the buying market and the markets into which the buyers resell are congruent—that all buyers compete in the same buying and selling markets without any

---

[65] See Devlin, *supra* note 21; Leslie, *supra* note 21; Blair and Sokol, *supra* note 21.

[66] See, eg, *Reid Bros. Logging Co. v Ketchikan Pulp Co.*, 699 F.2d 1292 (9th Cir. 1983) (saw mills had no capacity to increase downstream lumber prices but could collude on timber purchases).

other competitors. This is often an inaccurate description. A buying market can be quite narrow in both geographic and product terms, but the market for the product being sold can be large and subject to more competition from other sources and substitutes.[67] In such a situation, the cartel's output will be lower than it would have been, but prices will not be noticeably affected. There is a wealth transfer from sellers to buyers, and a dynamic harm to aggregate efficiency as the afflicted producers reduce output that would have been economically rational had there been workable competition in the market for the input. But consumers are unaffected in the static short run.

As shown above, a focus on static measures of economic welfare as the goal of competition law weakens the argument that buyer cartels are necessarily undesirable. But if the primary goal of competition law is the protection and advancement of economic competition as a process, two related policy arguments support a broader condemnation of buyer cartels. First, buyer cartels, like seller cartels, directly distort the market process through private agreement.[68] By preempting the market, any cartel undermines the fundamental goal of ensuring that goods and services clear markets at competitively determined prices.

Second, a buyer cartel distorts incentives and causes a misallocation of economic rewards over time, undermining the core goals of a competitive market system. Competition policy should focus on the dynamic interest of providing incentives to invest and develop new, innovative solutions to problems. Buyer cartels, however they operate, diminish the rewards to a producer below the level that a competitive market would have provided,[69] which sends the wrong signal to investors and innovators. Indeed, the strategic responses to cartels, such as vertical integration, although rational, can, in dynamic terms, result in further distortions of the market process away from better structural options.[70]

---

[67] Many agricultural products fit this model, as do perishables and other low-value, bulky inputs.

[68] See, eg, *Fed. Trade Comm'n v Super. Ct. Trial Lawyers Ass'n*, 493 U.S. 411 (1990) (lawyers agreed to boycott buyers unless paid more); *Fashion Originators Guild of Am. Inc. v Fed. Trade Comm'n*, 312 U.S. 457 (1941) (makers of original dresses agreed to boycott retailers who sold copies of their designs).

[69] See Blair and Harrison, *supra* note 30, at 156–63.

[70] See *Omega Envtl. Inc. v Gibarco, Inc.*, 127 F.3d 1157 (9th Cir. 1997) (upholding a vertical exclusive dealing scheme foreclosing an alternative distribution plan even though serious questions existed as to whether exclusivity served efficiency interests of consumers).

(b) The market justification for buyer cartels The primary argument for buyer cartels rests on a notion of countervailing power.[71] Small buyers facing a monopoly or oligopoly-seller market are individually powerless to bargain for lower prices;[72] they are compelled to accept the monopoly or oligopoly price. However, if these buyers together can make a credible threat that they will withhold their purchases unless they receive lower prices, they might succeed.[73] Independent pharmacies sought an antitrust exemption that would enable them to bargain collectively over prices with wholesalers.[74] Their argument was that their upstream supplier markets were oligopolistic and their suppliers both engaged in price discrimination and imposed excessively low reimbursement prices on independent retailers.[75] The pharmacies' belief was that if they were allowed to band together, they could obtain lower prices and higher reimbursement rates for the prescription drugs they resell.[76] Lower prices would allow them to increase sales volume as well as obtain a higher margin on sales. (Because many drugs are unique, the merits of this claim may be questionable, but the concept is clear enough.)

This analysis is based on a competition policy goal of static comparative welfare. The theory is that the successful buyer cartel will induce the seller to reduce prices and increase output, moving the market toward competitive price and output levels,[77] and the model assumes that the buyer cartel has sufficient power to do so. But this outcome is contingent on the relative options of each side, as well as the bargaining skill and sophistication of the parties. A group held together only by a cartelistic objective is often

---

[71] John Kenneth Galbraith, *American Capitalism: The Concept of Countervailing Power* (Houghton Mifflin, Boston, MA 1952) 109–12; see also Blair and Sokol, *supra* note 21, at 487–90.

[72] See generally Thomas Campbell, 'Bilateral Monopoly in Mergers' (2007) 74 *Antitrust Law Journal* 521 (small sellers should be allowed to merge to monopoly). This article produced some strong disagreement. See Jonathan B Baker, Joseph Farrell and Carl Shapiro, 'Merger to Monopoly to Serve a Single Buyer: Comment' (2008) 75 *Antitrust Law Journal* 637, 637–46 (contesting the claim that bilateral monopoly is economically more efficient than competitive markets on at least one side of the marketplace).

[73] Baker, Farrell and Shapiro, *supra* note 72, at 638–46.

[74] See *Impact of Our Antitrust Laws on Community Pharmacies and Their Patients: Hearing Before the Task Force on Antitrust and Competition Policy of the H. Comm. on the Judiciary*, 110th Congress (2007), available at https://archive.org/details/gov.gpo.fdsys.CHRG-110hhrg38336.

[75] *Ibid* at 82–3 (statement of David A Balto, representing the National Community Pharmacists Association).

[76] *Ibid* at 11 (statement of Rep. Weiner).

[77] See Devlin, *supra* note 21 at 241–3; Blair and Sokol, *supra* note 21, at 487–90.

thought to be fragile and easily disrupted.[78] Powerful sellers can disrupt the group by offering some participants secret discounts to defect. In the short run, the defector would gain a head start in competing with the other members of the group in processing the input and producing saleable output. Under these circumstances, cartels might prove ineffective, as farmer cooperatives on the selling side have been when they are not supported by express government regulation that restricts competition.[79]

The case for buyer cartels is plausible in the short run only if no other reasonable alternative exists.[80] Monopoly profits at the producer level ought, over time, to induce other responses, such as creating an entity to produce the input, sponsoring entry, or finding substitute inputs. Entry or innovation would reduce or avoid the need for the monopolized product. Therefore, unless there is a strong argument that the seller's power is not likely to dissipate even in the long run, the justification for a buyer cartel is weak.[81] Buyers that pay the monopoly price have both the resources and the incentive to seek alternatives. Those incentives are stronger than those of producers facing buyer power.

Even if a market would benefit from cartelistic buyer behavior, engaging in such activities without ongoing public supervision creates further risks to competition. Historically, when public policy deemed monopoly or cartel organization necessary for the selling side of markets, prices and services were also regulated. This is the history of railroads, airlines, natural gas, electricity, insurance and telecommunications. To be sure, in all the foregoing industries, more recent experience is that more competi-

---

78 See John S McGee, 'Ocean Freight Rate Conferences and the American Merchant Marine' (1960) 27 *University of Chicago Law Review* 191, 201 (setting forth conditions for successful cartelization).

79 See, eg, Willard E Mueller, Peter G Helmberger and Thomas W Paterson, *The Sunkist Case: A Study in Legal-Economic Analysis* (Lexington Books, Lexington, MA 1987) 198–9 (discussing Sunkist cooperative's difficulties dealing with increased member production); Victoria Saker Woeste, *The Farmer's Benevolent Trust: Law and Agricultural Cooperation in Industrial America 1865–1945* (The University of North Carolina Press, Chapel Hill, NC 1998) at 175–9 (discussing Sun-Maid cooperative's difficulties dealing with increased member production).

80 Donald Baker has argued for limiting the rules that require access to networks, which he believes reduce the incentives for the creation of competing networks. Donald I Baker, 'Compulsory Access to Network Joint Ventures Under the Sherman Act: Rules or Roulette?' (1993) *Utah Law Review* 999, 1127–8. The same argument applies to other issues in buyer power contexts.

81 In addition, a buyer cartel can result in coordination on the downstream side of the market if the buyers constitute a substantial part of the resale market. If that occurs, the buyer cartel would morph into a seller cartel whose function would be to raise price and reduce output to the customers of its participants.

tion provides a better set of incentives than command and control regulation.[82] But in these transforming industries, the central insight is that there is and ought to be direct oversight of how those markets operate, often to the exclusion of antitrust.[83] Indeed, in some highly competitive markets, the courts have decided that the regulatory regime necessary to assure the integrity of those markets preempts antitrust law.[84] If the inherent obstacles to moving a producer market toward a more competitive structure and conduct make a buyer cartel the least worst option for establishing equitable prices and services, then an appropriate public regulatory body should oversee the cartel process—the interests of private parties will not necessarily be congruent with the public interest.

2. Buying groups—efficiency gains and competitive risks

A number of efficiency arguments justify the organization of buying groups, but their competitive risks frequently go unrecognized or are unduly minimized.

(a) Efficiency gain from buying groups A buying group can reduce transaction costs by acting as a single buyer for a given input. If the group participants require similar inputs, the result can be a more efficient system. There are coordination issues, however. A centralized buying system must have the authority to enforce compliance by its members and have a coordinated way to distribute the inputs among participants as well as assure payment for them. The scale of purchases and the range or variety of inputs required will determine whether the participants find a buying group to be useful. Indeed, if the only advantage of the group is savings in the transactional and distributional dimensions, the market will provide a good test for participants. For example, Northwest Wholesale Stationers, a cooperative located in the Pacific Northwest, bought and warehoused a variety of stationery store supplies and provided prompt

---

[82] See generally Peter C Carstensen, 'Reflections on Mergers and Competition in Formerly Regulated Industries' in Peter C Carstensen and Susan Beth Farmer (eds), *Competition Policy and Merger Analysis in Deregulated and Newly Competitive Industries* (Edward Elgar Publishing, Cheltenham, UK and Northampton, MA 2008) 225, 226.

[83] See, eg, *Verizon Commc'ns Inc. v Law Offices of Curtis V. Trinko*, LLP, 540 U.S. 398, 412 (2004) (rejecting antitrust liability for exclusionary conduct that was subject to direct state and federal regulation).

[84] See, eg, *Credit Suisse Sec. (USA), LLC v Billing*, 551 U.S. 264, 273–7 (2007) (holding that securities law precludes antitrust claims where investment banks formed syndicates to help execute initial public offerings for hundreds of technology companies).

delivery from its warehouse to individual stores, giving the stores access to a full line of products from one source.[85] Thus, membership would be desirable if the efficiency gains in the buying, transportation, warehousing and distribution of these products exceeded the costs of membership, including any limitations on the variety of products available through the cooperative, or any restraints on buying outside the group.

A buying cooperative can also bargain for price. In the abstract model of competitive prices, all prices arise from a market process that results in a single price known to all buyers and sellers. But in a real-world, workably competitive market, sellers almost always have some latitude in pricing. In particular, a seller may find it attractive to lower prices slightly to gain a large order that will ensure more efficient volume in the production facility. A buyer seeking a large volume may make a more extensive search of the market for suppliers and generate a more active bidding process as a result. Therefore, in a market where competition is imperfect but workable, buyers can gain a price advantage by employing more sophisticated and effective searches for the inputs they need. At the same time, sellers can profit from making larger sales at lower prices when the transaction reduces selling costs or when the resulting volume takes advantage of scale economies.

Because 'perfect' competition is an unachievable abstraction, the use of collective buying can enhance efficiency with respect to the pricing of goods. Indeed, any system that moves the market process closer to the abstract ideal is likely to have much the same effect. The advent of internet business-to-business venues—where buyers can post their needs and sellers can respond—illustrates another mechanism that can achieve comparable results without any buyer collaboration.[86]

(b) The competitive risks from buying groups By marshaling a significant share of the market demand for an input, a buying group can also create a variety of competitive risks in both upstream supply markets and the downstream markets in which the participants compete. As the volume

[85] *Nw. Wholesale Stationers, Inc. v Pac. Stationery and Printing Co.*, 472 U.S. 284, 286–7 (1985).

[86] Of course, such sites also provide potential means of coordinating input prices and potentially stabilizing output prices. The Federal Trade Commission (FTC) has discussed some of these risks in its report on these operations. FTC (2000), 'Entering the 21st Century: Competition Policy in the World of Electronic Marketplaces', available at https://www.ftc.gov/sites/default/files/documents/reports/entering-21st-century-competition-policy-world-b2b-electronic-marketplaces/b2breport_0.pdf.

of sales taken by a single buyer increases, the power of that buyer over the suppliers also increases. With increased power, the buyer can impose onerous conditions on sellers that directly affect the price paid, require restrictions on access to the inputs that foreclose competitors in the buying market, or use control of significant inputs to achieve coordination of competition in the downstream market. Chapter 4 examined these competitive risks in some detail.

The most obvious risk is that the buying group will exploit its power to drive prices below a competitive level. The buying group gains economically whether the reason for the lower prices is transactional efficiency, productive efficiency or market power exploitation. For example, buyers can achieve lower total costs by requiring a producer to bundle products in a way that mixes products for which the producer might have some advantage with more competitive goods, resulting in lower total revenue to the producer.[87]

A second, related risk, illustrated in a number of cases, is the use of buyer power to exclude competing producers from access to inputs. Such practices are of long standing, as illustrated by two prominent Supreme Court cases.[88] Other countries have similar cases.[89] In the context of a legitimate buying group, some restraints on the freedom of suppliers might be reasonable and even essential to the efficient operation of the agreement. For example, if a buying group contracts for a differentiated good—especially if it has invested in its development—it should be entitled to retain the rights to that product to avoid the risks of free-riding or other strategic conduct by either the producer or competing buyers.[90] This analysis parallels that in Chapter 5, which treated the same strategies as

---

[87] This type of bundling (discussed in Chapter 5) has an adverse effect on producers in the market for the competitive product lines. Buyers that are able to bundle also have less incentive to find ways to diminish the power of the dominant sellers of the noncompetitive products.

[88] *E. States Retail Lumber Dealers' Ass'n v United States*, 234 U.S. 600, 606 (1914); *Montague v Lowry*, 193 U.S. 38, 38 (1904).

[89] See, eg, *Competition Comm'n v Patensie Sitrus Behrend Beperk*, 37/CR/Jun01 (Competition Tribunal, S. Afr.) (denial of right to sell fruit to third parties violated competition law); *In re S. Afr. Raisins (Pty) Ltd. v SAD Holdings Ltd.*, 16/IR/Dec99 (Competition Tribunal, S. Afr.) (interlocutory order requiring access to necessary facilities to allow producer to compete in downstream markets).

[90] A group that invested in research and development to create an improved input could rationally insist that the contract producer provide that input only to the group that had made the investment and taken the risks.

unilateral conduct.[91] The potentially relevant difference is that a buying group's restraints are the product of concerted action and more easily examined. The factual-functional question is whether the restraint is reasonably necessary for the legitimate needs of the venture. This is a more tractable issue when the inquiry is directed at a joint venture.[92] But at its core it is the same analysis that the appellate court used to reject Microsoft's justifications for its monopolizing actions.[93]

The third risk, illustrated by *Topco*, is the use of the buying group to allocate downstream markets or set resale prices.[94] Topco's members used their annual meeting to allocate and reallocate territory to minimize intra-group competition.[95] There was no justification for allocating territory to promote the legitimate activities of Topco, which served its members by developing and buying housebrand groceries.[96] It is unlikely the resulting territorial assignments created a significant amount of market power because other grocery chains were present in those markets. But an efficient group of retailers meeting for other legitimate reasons could allocate territory at a low administrative cost. The allocation was rational as long as the expected gain of limiting or eliminating head-to-head competition was greater than the costs associated with reaching and enforcing these agreements.[97]

A buying group also provides a means of potentially coordinating input prices and creates a culture of price stability and minimal competition, all of which carry the risk of other anticompetitive outcomes. Buying groups can contribute to tacit price collusion by reducing the number of independent actors in the market. The buying group coordinates the input purchases for its members, yielding cost savings for them. If input costs are a substantial part of the total cost of the products being sold, the participants proceed with relatively uniform costs. If there are relatively few competitors outside the group serving the downstream market, or if other competitors are also in buying groups, there is a greater risk of tacit price coordination than if all competitors bought their inputs independently.

---

[91] See Chapter 5, notes 32–9 and accompanying text.

[92] See, eg, *United States v Visa*, 344 F.3d 229 (2nd Cir. 2003) (rejecting specific restraints by a joint venture that issued credit cards for lack of justification).

[93] *United States v Microsoft*, 253 F.3d 34 (D.C. Cir. 2001) (en banc) (per curiam).

[94] See *United States v Topco Assocs. Inc.*, 405 U.S. 596 (1972).

[95] *Ibid* at 601–03.

[96] Carstensen and First, *supra* note 49, at 182–5.

[97] See *ibid.* Topco still operates and is larger than ever, but its members freely compete with each other. Topco now creates retailer-specific house brands to avoid any concerns about strategic exploitation of prior promotional investments.

Similarly, buying groups might use their power to discourage innovation in the input markets. New inputs might require buyer investment in a new plant or equipment and might alter the barriers to entry. Moreover, innovations might induce more competition among buyers in their downstream markets. Using their buyer power to insist on limits to the kinds of innovation that suppliers engage in would reduce the risk of disruptive innovation. (Even if attempted, this use of buyer power might have no effect in many markets.) Nevertheless, even a legitimate buying group with buyer power has an incentive to consider the full range of ways in which its power can be used to protect its participants, raising sufficient competitive risks to warrant strict review.

A small number of buyer groups active in an input market can collectively, but not necessarily collusively, foreclose competition in the input market by selecting the same supplier. This will foreclose entry and indeed eliminate existing competition. The resulting monopoly price from the supplier will raise downstream prices, but the buyers may be able to use their buyer power to bargain for a substantial share of the profit. An illustrative example occurred in the automotive sandpaper market.[98] A supplier with deep pockets made attractive long-term offers to buyers, forcing out the more poorly financed incumbent, and ultimately resulting in the entrant's capture of nearly 100 percent of the sales.[99] The excluded competitor claimed that the entrant then shared a substantial part of its projected monopoly profits with the buyers, who collectively dominated the downstream retail market.[100] This community of interest eliminated the buyers' incentive to seek competitive supplies.[101]

The size of a buying group becomes competitively problematic when its purchase volume exceeds the quantity necessary for minimum efficient scale. For example, the EU expressly requires that buying groups be no

---

98 *NicSand Inc. v 3M Co.*, 507 F.3d 442 (6th Cir. 2007) (rejecting a claim by the excluded competitor despite evidence of adverse effects).

99 *Ibid* at 447–9.

100 *Ibid.* Nevertheless, the court held that there was no antitrust violation on these facts.

101 This conclusion assumes that the downstream market is not subject to easy entry. See Julie C Klish, 'Serving Economic Efficiencies or Anticompetitive Purposes? The Future of Group Purchasing Organizations and the Antitrust Safety Zone' (2005) 2 *Indiana Health Law Review* 173. In the sandpaper case, as in the case of hospital supplies discussed by Klish, it was not feasible to enter the downstream market only to market the specific product. Hence, the buyer-resellers can gain significant monopoly profits from these sales. A more general model of this conduct is found in Doyle and Han, *supra* note 30.

more restrictive than necessary to achieve their legitimate objectives.[102] But it may be inappropriate to condemn a group that provides significant efficiency savings to its participants, unless it is possible to fashion two or more efficient entities from the participants and unaffiliated members. The EU has a safe harbor for buying groups that take no more than 15 percent of the input and sell no more than 15 percent of the relevant output.[103] Larger groups must seek advance approval although, as illustrated in the examples in the guidelines, larger groups are allowed in some contexts.[104] The EU policies frame a set of basic criteria that recognize and seek to address the potential exclusionary and exploitive risks that buying groups present.

In sum, buying groups can contribute to efficiency, but can also be used to exploit producers, retard innovation, facilitate tacit or express downstream collusion as well as exclude the group's competitors from access to essential inputs. Risks to competition exist whenever a buying group acquires a substantial share of the inputs on which it is focused. Substantial should mean a share of 20 percent or more of general inputs or 15 percent or more of a class of goods resold by retail members of the buying group. The EU policies, the UK studies and the American cases show that significant risks of buyer power exist at these levels.

C. Current Competition Policy on Buyer Combinations

1. Buyer cartels

Contemporary American competition policy treats buyer cartels as per se illegal and provides the potential for criminal penalties.[105] The case law is largely consistent with this.[106] The illegality cannot be rebutted even

---

[102] See Consolidated Version of the Treaty on the Functioning of the European Union, art 1013(a), 9 May, 2008, 2008 O.J. (C 115) 47 (no agreement having a lawful objective can 'impose on the undertakings concerned restrictions which are not indispensable to the attainment of these objectives'). See also European Union, *supra* note 14, ¶¶ 189–224 (policy on buying groups).

[103] European Union, *supra* note 14, ¶ 208. By way of comparison, American antitrust authorities use a 35 percent share of inputs. See 'Enforcement Policy in Health Care', *supra* note 11, at 53–4.

[104] European Union, *supra* note 14, ¶¶ 221–4.

[105] See, eg, Department of Justice and Federal Trade Commission (2016), 'Antitrust Guidance for Human Resource Professionals 5', available at https://www.ftc.gov/system/files/documents/public_statements/992623/ftc-doj_hr_guidance_final_10-20-16.pdf.

[106] See *Vogel v Am. Soc'y of Appraisers*, 744 F.2d 598, 601 (7th Cir. 1984) ('[B]uyer cartels, the object of which is to force the prices that suppliers charge

by a plausible showing that the buyers are acting to counteract seller monopoly or oligopoly power. The rationale for this absolute prohibition is the impossibility of differentiating between legitimate efforts to create countervailing buyer power and collusive efforts to exploit buyer power.

Legislatures have been willing to grant limited exemptions for cartels when buyer power is a major source of concern, as in the case of American agriculture and unions. This can offset some of the potential unfairness of this absolutist policy. Chapter 6 examined the use of these exemptions as one means of responding to buyer power. Globally, there are few examples of authorized buyer cartels. This suggests that, in general, buyer cartels are not necessary to achieve workable competition and desirable economic policy goals. In any event, it is unlikely that a buyer cartel can successfully resist a powerful seller.[107]

The incentives to create and adhere to a buyer cartel are significantly different from those for a seller cartel. Defection by a seller from a price fixing or market allocating cartel results in a direct and immediate increase in sales and revenue to the defecting enterprise. Defection is economically rational if the seller projects that its profits in the short run will exceed whatever costs subsequent reaction will produce. In contrast, a defecting buyer faces higher prices as it bids up input costs to achieve a larger volume of production. Increased production, however, usually means an increase in volume in the market into which the product is sold. Hence, the product faces higher input prices and constant or lower resale prices. Even so, it is possible that the marginal increase in costs will be more than offset by the opportunity to make more sales at slightly lower prices. But the unlikely chance of gaining from defection increases the incentive to remain loyal to a buyer cartel.[108]

Some American courts have recognized the implications of this analysis and allowed cases to proceed against alleged buyer cartels when the number of participants and their arguably different interests would make a seller cartel less plausible. One illustrative case is *Todd v Exxon Corp.*,[109]

---

the members of the cartel below the competitive level, are illegal per se.'). See also cases cited *supra* note 5. But see *Balmoral Theaters v United Artists*, 885 F.2d 313 (6th Cir. 1989) (motion picture allocation cartel upheld as reasonable).

107 The argument for a buyer cartel as a source of countervailing power is most powerful when a group of buyers faces a single dominant seller. But the seller can break up a buyer cartel by offering discounts to selected participants. Defection by a sufficient number of buyers will destroy the cartel because the only link among them is their individual interest in lower prices.

108 See Marshall and Meurer, *supra* note 39, at 85.

109 275 F.3d 191, 195 (2nd Cir. 2001).

in which the plaintiffs alleged that the defendant oil and gas companies shared detailed information about job descriptions and wage scales in order to stabilize and restrain competition for engineers and other skilled workers. The Second Circuit, in reversing summary judgment against the plaintiffs, focused on the common incentive of the defendant-employers to control wages and limit competition for workers.[110] The supply of potential employees may have been moderately inelastic, and the gain to an employer from hiring any particular employee relatively minor. Hence, the incentive to defect from the agreement would be limited, and the common interest in reducing wage costs would encourage even firms with disparate interests to cooperate and share an expectation of loyalty to the scheme. Similar cartelistic labor supply agreements have affected competition for employees in both nursing and technology.[111] In 2016, the American enforcement agencies issued guidance about the illegality of agreements among competitors with respect to wages or other terms of employment as well as of exchanging excessive information.[112] The guidance included the warning that 'the [Department of Justice] intends to proceed criminally against naked wage-fixing or no-poaching agreements.'[113]

Recognizing that tacit and secret collusion may be more rational and less vulnerable to opportunistic behavior by the participants has significant implications for competition policy. First, it would suggest that courts should hesitate to reject buyer-side conspiracy theories based solely on the argument that large numbers and diverse economic goals make collusion implausible.[114] Second, it means that public antitrust enforcement officials should look critically at buyer-side information exchanges,[115] which are more likely to facilitate the creation and enforcement of naked

---

[110] *Ibid* at 208–09.

[111] See, eg, *Fleischman v Albany Med. Ctr.*, 728 F. Supp. 2d 130 (N.D.N.Y. 2010) (upholding validity of claim against a group of hospitals for coordinating wages for nurses); *In re High-Tech Employee Antitrust Litig.*, 856 F. Supp. 2d 1103 (N.D. Cal. 2012) (upholding complaint demanding damages resulting from agreement among technology firms not to compete for each other's employees).

[112] Department of Justice and Federal Trade Commission, *supra* note 105.

[113] *Ibid* at 5.

[114] Thus, applying the stricter pleading standards of *Bell Atl. Corp. v Twombly*, 550 U.S. 544, 556–7 (2007), should not result in dismissal of complaints charging collusion merely because a selling-side conspiracy involving many parties or a wide range of economic interests would be implausible.

[115] See Amitai Aviram and Avishalom Tor, 'Overcoming Impediments to Information Sharing' (2004) 55 *Alabama Law Review* 231, 231–4. See also Department of Justice and Federal Trade Commission, *supra* note 105, at 4–6 (warning that excessive information sharing can result in an antitrust violation).

restraints on competition than information sharing agreements among competing sellers.[116] These questions are explored further in the next part.

In some cases, all or most firms in an industry are engaged in what could be considered rational unilateral conduct.[117] Consciously parallel conduct does not create an inference of collusion unless there is a basis for concluding that the conduct makes sense only if engaged in collectively.[118] The parallel behavior of a set of leading high-tech firms in Silicon Valley in refusing to solicit the employees of other such firms to switch employers serves as an example.[119] Despite plausible unilateral reasons for such conduct, it discourages competition on salary and benefits for a set of workers with similar skills. Competition likely would raise the average wage level, but the distribution of employees among the companies would probably be roughly the same. Hence, there is a clear incentive not to engage in vigorous competition for their services.

However, the Silicon Valley firms colluded to restrict competition for employees. The record showed that there was a conscious, intentional and clearly articulated understanding.[120] Significantly, the collusion made sense to the parties even though other competing employers were not

---

[116] Gregory J Werden, 'Economic Evidence on the Existence of Collusion: Reconciling Antitrust Law With Oligopoly Theory' (2004) 71 *Antitrust Law Journal* 719, 779.

[117] See John E Lopatka and William H Page, 'Economic Authority and the Limits of Expertise in Antitrust Cases' (2005) 90 *Cornell Law Review* 617, 677–9 (discussing courts' unwillingness to infer tacit collusion without evidence of certain 'plus factors', thus excluding the possibility that defendants 'engaged in lawful conscious parallelism').

[118] See William E Kovacic, Robert C Marshall, Leslie M Marx and Halbert L White, 'Plus Factors and Agreement in Antitrust Law' (2011) 110 *Michigan Law Review* 393 (evaluating the strength of various plus factors as evidence of collusion); see also Brian Thomas Fitzsimons, 'The Injustice of Notice and Heightened Pleading Standards for Antitrust Conspiracy Claims: It Is Time to Balance the Scale for Plaintiffs, Defendants, and Society' (2007) 39 *Rutgers Law Journal* 199, 209 n.39 (listing common plus factors).

[119] See, eg, Complaint, *United States v Adobe Sys., Inc.*, No. 1:10-cv-01629 (D.D.C. 24 September 2010); Cecilia Kang, 'Federal Antitrust Probe Targets Tech Giants, Sources Say' *Washington Post* (3 June 2009), available at http://www.washingtonpost.com/wp-dyn/content/article/2009/06/02/AR2009060203412.html.

[120] Not only did the parties agree to a settlement with the United States that enjoined these agreements, Final Judgment, *Adobe* (D.D.C. Mar. 18, 2011), available at https://www.justice.gov/atr/case-document/final-judgment-0, they also settled a private class action by paying more than $415 million to be shared among the employees denied the benefit of competition. See Order Granting Plaintiffs' Motion for Final Approval of Class Action Settlement, *In re High-Tech Employee Antitrust Litig.*, No. 11-CV-02509-LHK (N.D. Cal. Sept. 2, 2015).

parties. Major motion picture chains have also exercised their buyer power to exclude or regulate competition either by facilitating a supply cartel to regulate prices[121] or by excluding or limiting new entry.[122] In such cases, courts have expressed the standard view that such agreements—if proven—are unlawful. The most conspicuous exception in American case law involved an agreement among motion picture theaters to allocate first run movies among the participants without competitive bidding.[123]

Other countries have similar records of condemning buyer cartels. Two South African cases involved exclusionary practices by agricultural groups.[124] Australia condemned a conspiracy among a group of brewers to deny cans to a competing brewer.[125] The EU has condemned conspiracies that had no effect on consumers.[126] Russian antitrust authorities have condemned a grocer cartel that exploited both retailers and suppliers.[127] A global database of cartels identifies nearly 30 buyer cartels for which econometric or other data document actual harm.[128]

Most competition authorities consistently condemn buyer cartels. The

---

121 See, eg, *Interstate Circuit v United States*, 306 U.S. 208 (1939) (dominant buyer coordinated a cartel among its suppliers to raise prices and limit access to competitors).

122 See, eg, *Cobb Theatres III, LLC v AMC Entm't. Holdings, Inc.*, 101 F. Supp. 3d 1319 (N.D. Ga. 2015) (upholding complaint charging conspiracy to exclude new entrant from market); Order for Temporary Injunction, *iPic-Gold Class Entm't., LLC v Regal Entm't. Group*, No. 2015-68745 (234th D. Tex. Jan. 25, 2016) (new entrant obtained preliminary injunction barring exclusionary conduct by incumbent movie theater owner group). Such exclusionary practices were historically common in this industry. See, eg, *United States v Crescent Amusement Co.*, 323 U.S. 173 (1944) (upholding finding of conspiracy to use buyer power to exclude competition).

123 *Balmoral Cinema, Inc. v Allied Artists Pictures Corp.*, 885 F.2d 313 (6th Cir. 1989).

124 See *supra* note 89.

125 See *TPC v Carlton United Breweries Ltd.* (1990) 24 FCR 532 (Austl.) (dominant brewer coerced one of its can suppliers to refuse to supply a discounting brewer).

126 See, eg, Case C-8/08, *T-Mobile Netherlands BV v Raad van Bestuur van de Nederlandse Mededingingsautoriteit*, [2009] ECR 1-4529 (condemning conspiracy to fix commissions of resellers).

127 See International Competition Network (2008), 'Report on Abuse of Superior Bargaining Position 67', available at http://www.internationalcompetitionnetwork.org/uploads/library/doc386.pdf.

128 See John M Connor, 'The Private International Cartels (PIC) Data Set' (2016) (on file with author); see also John M Connor (2014), 'The Private International Cartels (PIC) Data Set: Guide and Summary Statistics, 1990–2013', available at http://papers.ssrn.com/sol3/papers.cfm?abstract_id=247827.

primary open question is what constitutes a factual showing that permits the inference of conspiracy.

2. Buying groups

Although buyer cartels are illegal per se and, as noted above, tacit collusion among buyers is plausible under a wider range of circumstances than is the case with seller conspiracies, current competition law tends to give broad latitude for any enterprise that holds itself out as a buying group, even when the group takes a large share of the input market.[129] The American guidelines for health care provide a safe harbor for any buying group that takes less than 35 percent of the sales in an input market.[130] Such an input market could have as few as three buying groups and still not raise antitrust concerns under those guidelines. The EU, based on its investigations in merger cases involving buyer power, concluded that control in excess of 20 percent of the market for an input might raise concerns.[131]

The case law in both the United States and the EU is inconsistent and not well focused on the issue of the reasonableness of buying groups as such. The American case most on point is *Northwest Wholesale Stationers v Pacific Stationery*.[132] The plaintiff alleged that the defendant buyer group committed a per se violation of antitrust law by arbitrarily excluding the plaintiff from the buying group. The Ninth Circuit accepted that theory,[133] but the Supreme Court reversed on that claim, emphasizing that, as a private economic venture, the buying group was entitled to terminate a member for a legitimate business reason without due process.[134] But the Court also concluded that the case could continue on a rule of reason basis if the plaintiff could allege either that the refusal to deal itself was pretextual (that is, it was in furtherance of an anticompetitive conspiracy of the membership) or that the venture had sufficient market power in the upstream office supply market that participation in the group was essential to the economic survival of the retailers of such goods.[135] There is no report of any decision after remand, suggesting that the plaintiff

---

129 See, eg, Jacobson and Dorman, *supra* note 17.

130 See 'Enforcement Policy in Health Care', *supra* note 11.

131 See *supra* note 14. See also *supra* notes 102–04 (EU policy requiring review of buyer groups that take more than 15 percent of an input).

132 *Nw. Wholesale Stationers, Inc. v Pac. Stationery & Printing Co.*, 472 U.S. 284, 288 (1985).

133 *Pacific Stationery & Printing Co. v Nw. Wholesale Stationers, Inc.*, 715 F.2d 1393 (9th Cir. 1983).

134 *Nw. Wholesale Stationers*, 472 U.S. at 289–93.

135 *Ibid* at 296–7 and n.7.

could not sustain either theory, and the case disappeared. In praising the buying group, the Supreme Court focused on its potential efficiency as a buyer and the potential effect of exclusion on the capacity to compete in the downstream market for office supplies. Thus, as in *Topco*, no attention was paid to the potential competitive implications of the buying group's actions as a buyer.[136]

One might infer from these cases that the only competitive risk of buying groups is their effect on downstream competition. However, as discussed earlier, buying groups can impose a variety of adverse, competitive effects on both upstream suppliers and competing buyers. Yet, there is a strong presumption of legality with respect to conduct and practices that affect upstream suppliers.[137] Given the lack of comprehensive data, it is difficult to discern whether this is a result of a lack of legal challenges or because cases involving such issues have emphasized other concerns, leaving the upstream effects under-discussed. The current inventory of cases comes largely from the standard-setting organizations that are collective buyers of key technology licenses and from amateur and professional athletics.

The creation of standards using patented components can cause competitive harms to suppliers.[138] Standard-setting organizations consist of stakeholders that collectively establish a standard for adoption by all participants in a market. Establishing a workable and uniform standard often requires the integration of patented components.[139] A standard setter with discretion in the formulation of the standard functions like a buyer with a strong bargaining position.[140] A patent holder can be forced to license the patent to the standard setter or find itself excluded from the standard. Two problems arise: (1) prices that are below a reasonable competitive level; and (2) abuse of buying power to favor the technology of insiders.

The first risk is probably modest; a seller that holds preferred technology has a credible bargaining position. Moreover, there is unlikely to be a clearly 'correct' price. Indeed, except in the patent holdup cases, in which the concern is the exploitation of patent rights disclosed only after

---

136 *United States v Topco Assocs., Inc.*, 405 U.S. 596 (1972). Like *Topco*, *Northwest Wholesale Stationers* does not appear to have been a major buyer of office supplies in what was at least a national, and perhaps international, market. See *Nw. Wholesale Stationers*, 472 U.S. at 284.

137 See Jacobson and Dorman, *supra* note 17.

138 See generally J Gregory Sidak, 'Patent Holdup and Oligopsonistic Collusion in Standard-Setting Organizations' (2009) 5 *Journal of Competition Law and Economics* 123.

139 *Ibid* at 124.

140 *Ibid* at 126.

the standard is adopted,[141] there appears to be little concern about this issue. Exclusionary decisions, in contrast, have resulted in some litigation. Standard-setting decisions that favor the technology of insiders inherently exclude other technology. The claim is that the selection process was biased.[142]

In amateur athletics, the dominant organization for American college sports is the National Collegiate Athletic Association (NCAA). It serves more as a regulatory agency with de facto authorization to control some aspects of college sports than as a true joint venture.[143] Nevertheless, many observers regard it as a joint venture that produces college athletics. Its participants are 'buyers' of college-age athletes, and the NCAA's role is to regulate the buyers in that market. But it has also sought to regulate a number of other ways in which colleges might compete on the buying side. These regulations control the overall costs of producing athletic programs and therefore increase the gain (or reduce the loss) to the members.

---

[141] See, eg, *In re Union Oil Co.*, 140 F.T.C. 123 (27 July 2005). The Federal Trade Commission's 2004 opinion reinstating the case is available at https://www.ftc.gov/sites/default/files/documents/cases/2004/07/040706commissionopinion.pdf. See also *Rambus v Fed. Trade Comm'n*, 522 F.3d 456 (D.C. Cir. 2008) (rejecting claim of unlawful monopolization where patent holder concealed patent rights until included in a standard and then asserted them, demanding substantial license fees).

[142] See, eg, *Sony Elecs. v Soundview Tech.*, 157 F. Supp. 2d 180 (D. Conn. 2001) (claim of monopsonistic price fixing and exclusion related to a standard stated a claim and would not be dismissed); *Addamax Corp. v Open Software Found., Inc.*, 888 F. Supp. 274 (D. Mass. 1995) (upholding the validity of a claim of conspiracy to exclude from standard).

[143] In football and many other college sports, the NCAA places naked restraints on colleges, such as the maximum number and level of scholarships, and on college athletes, such as restricting their ability to work outside the program. See generally Joe Nocera and Ben Strauss, *Indentured: The Inside Story of the Rebellion Against the NCAA* (Portfolio Publishing, London 2016). The case of basketball is more complex because all teams adhering to a specific set of constraints are eligible to participate in post-season tournaments and share in the revenue. Hence, in basketball, the NCAA functions as joint venture as well as a regulator. Still, overall, the NCAA's regulation of college sports is more akin to the New York Stock Exchange's regulation of the ethics of its members and their trading partners in *Silver v New York Stock Exch.*, 373 U.S. 341 (1963), than the joint ventures that constitute most of America's professional league sports. For a fuller development of the regulatory exemption from antitrust's condemnation of cartels, see Peter C Carstensen and Bette Roth, 'The Per Se Legality of Some Naked Restraints: A [Re]Conceptualization of the Antitrust Analysis of Cartelistic Organizations' (2000) 45 *Antitrust Bulletin* 349, 402–08. See also *O'Bannon v NCAA*, 802 F. 3d 1049 (9th Cir. 2015) (upholding the NCAA's naked restraints on player compensation because of its de facto authority to regulate college athletics).

However, the NCAA's effort to restrict salaries for assistant coaches in basketball was struck down as an illegal restraint.[144] The prohibition against salaries for college athletes and related restraints on their freedom have been upheld in the past.[145]

In the case of professional football, the courts have on several occasions struck down as unreasonable specific practices affecting the market for player services.[146] Other rules, including some relating to entry and compensation, have been upheld as aspects of labor-management relations shielded from antitrust law by the labor exemption.[147] Still, those cases also illustrate how the buyers have used their power to affect the market for player services, even if the specific conduct was not reviewable under the antitrust laws. Baseball, although exempt from antitrust law,[148] has experienced similar concerns for abuse of buyer power.[149]

Congressional hearings have focused on the potential for abuse of buying power in hospital supplies.[150] The competitive problems identified first involved foreclosure of potential competition in the supply market resulting from bundling and requirements contracts that limited the freedom of hospitals to accept attractive alternatives.

---

144 *Law v NCAA*, 134 F.3d 1010, 1024 (10th Cir. 1998).

145 See, eg, *Smith v NCAA*, 139 F.3d 180, 185 (3rd Cir. 1998) (holding Sherman Act inapplicable to NCAA eligibility requirements). But see *O'Bannon v NCAA*, 802 F.3d 1049 (9th Cir. 2015) (holding unreasonable some limits on scholarship support, but accepting the NCAA's overall right to set 'reasonable' rules, specifically the ban on direct compensation of college athletes).

146 See, eg, *Smith v Pro Football, Inc.*, 593 F.2d 1173, 1188–9 (D.C. Cir. 1978) (holding NFL draft in its 1968 form unreasonably restrained trade); *Mackey v Nat'l Football League*, 543 F.2d 606, 617 (8th Cir. 1976) (citing cases applying Sherman Act to restraints on competition for players' services).

147 See, eg, *Brown v Pro Football, Inc.*, 518 U.S. 231, 234–5 (1996) (holding that despite lapse in collective bargaining agreement, the labor exemption from antitrust still applied).

148 *Flood v Kuhn*, 407 U.S. 258, 282 (1972) (refusing to reverse prior holding that baseball was exempt from antitrust law); *Fed. Baseball Club of Balt., Inc. v Nat'l League of Prof. Baseball Clubs*, 259 U.S. 200, 209 (1922) (holding baseball was not commerce as the term was understood at that time and was therefore exempt from antitrust law).

149 The Curt Flood Act, 15 U.S.C. § 26b (2016), limits this exemption with respect to treatment of players. See also Brad Snyder, *A Well-Paid Slave: Curt Flood's Fight for Free Agency in Professional Sports* (Viking Books, New York 2006) 2–3.

150 See *Hospital Group Purchasing: Lowering Costs at the Expense of Patient Health and Medical Innovation?: Hearing Before the Subcomm. on Antitrust, Business Rights, and Competition of the S. Comm. on the Judiciary*, 107th Congress (2002), available at https://archive.org/details/gov.gpo.fdsys.CHRG-107shrg85986.

Second, the organizers of these buying groups appeared to have made very large profits on the purchase and resale of supplies to the hospitals.

Both the EU and Australia have explicit standards that differentiate between buyer cartels and buying groups.[151] However, the application of these rules to buying groups is rare. In the EU, the leading case recognizes that a buying cooperative for farmers can impose restraints on members buying from other suppliers provided those restraints are reasonably related to the legitimate needs of the buying group and no more restrictive than necessary to accomplish the goal.[152]

Thus, despite the common view that most buying groups are lawful with respect to their upstream activities,[153] courts that have engaged in focused inquiries into the competitive impact of specific conduct have been more critical of buying group restraints. However, these episodic interventions have not led to a more calibrated standard for evaluating buying groups. Scholars of a variety of ideological persuasions seem to share this benign view of buying groups,[154] having focused only on the positive aspects of buying groups and ignoring the potential for the range of harm they might create for competition.

D. Rethinking Competition Policy for Buyer Combinations

Two areas of competition law relating to buyer combinations need thoughtful reappraisal today. First, there is greater potential for tacit or ambiguous conspiracy to create buyer cartels than current law recognizes. Second, buying groups can cause serious competitive problems even when they capture only a modest share of the input market.

Already explored is the need for investigators to distinguish carefully between cartelistic buying arrangements and legitimate buying groups. At the margin, it is going to be very difficult to tell the difference. Some rules of thumb based on market share are plausible, but as previously pointed

---

151 See European Union, *supra* note 14; Competition and Consumer Act 2010 § 44ZZRD (Austl.) (prohibiting unauthorized cartel agreements but allowing legitimate joint ventures).

152 Case C-250/92, *Gottrup-Klim Grovvareforeninger v Dansk Landbrugs Grovvareselskab AmbA*, [1994] ECR I-5641.

153 See, eg, Jacobson and Dorman, *supra* note 17, at 23, 40.

154 See, eg, *ibid*; John B Kirkwood and Robert H Lande, 'The Fundamental Goal of Antitrust: Protecting Consumers, Not Increasing Efficiency' (2008) 84 *Notre Dame Law Review* 191, 192, 196, 234; see also 'Enforcement Policy in Health Care', *supra* note 11.

out, the current levels for such a presumption in the United States are too generous.

1. Addressing the potential for buyer side cartels

The general paucity of buyer cartel cases stands in stark contrast to data from merger analysis, which show that significant savings come from reductions in input prices.[155] This suggests that there is substantial potential for conspiracies among competing buyers to affect prices. Indeed, in the beef-processing market, tacitly collusive conduct among the three or four major buyers resulted in significantly depressed prices.[156]

In addition to looking more critically at interdependent buying practices, it is also important to consider the kinds of remedies that litigation might accomplish. Especially for tacit collusion, industry structure may be such that some interdependence in buying decisions is unavoidable. But it may be possible to decrease the transparency of the buying practices that facilitate such collusion. GE and Westinghouse had developed different pricing formulas for electric generators that resulted in identical prices. Moreover, each committed to retroactive most favored nation

---

[155] C Edward Fee and Shawn Thomas, 'Sources of Gains in Horizontal Mergers: Evidence from Customer, Supplier, and Rival Firms' (2004) 74 *Journal of Financial Economics* 423, 424–7; Sugato Bhattacharyya and Amrita Nain, 'Horizontal Acquisitions and Buying Power: A Product Market Analysis' (2011) 99 *Journal of Financial Economics* 97. Consistent with that observation, other scholars have found substantial losses to sellers resulting from buyer cartels. See John E Kwoka, Jr., 'The Price Effects of Bidding Conspiracies: Evidence from Real Estate Auction "Knockouts"' (1997) 42 *Antitrust Bulletin* 503, 503 (finding that a 32 percent price decrease resulted from bid-rigging in real estate auctions); Jon P Nelson, 'Comparative Antitrust Damages in Bid-Rigging Cases: Some Findings from a Used Vehicle Auction' (1993) 38 *Antitrust Bulletin* 369, 386 tbl.4, 392–4 (finding that a significant price decrease resulted from bid rigging in auctions for used police cars).

[156] Ranchers-Cattlemen Action Legal Fund (known as R-CALF), an advocacy group for farmers raising beef, has provided a detailed analysis of how buyer power works in that industry. Its submission in connection with the JBS-National and Smithfield beef merger contains detailed assertions of how beef buyers manipulated the prices for feed cattle. See *Concentration in Agriculture and an Examination of the JBS/Swift Acquisition: Hearing Before the Subcomm. on Antitrust, Competition Policy and Consumer Rights of the S. Comm. on the Judiciary*, 110th Congress (2008) 131–65, available at https://archive.org/details/gov.gpo.fdsys.CHRG-110shrg45064 (statement of Bill Bullard, CEO, R-CALF, United Stockgrowers of America). See also Xiaowei Cai, Kyle W Stiegert and Stephen Koontz, 'Regime Switching and Oligopsony Power: The Case of U.S. Beef Processing' (2011) 42 *Agricultural Economics* 99 (tacit buyer collusion recurs in beef markets).

treatment—all buyers would receive, through a rebate, the benefit of any price reduction in the six months after their purchase.[157] The government negotiated revisions to a pre-existing consent decree that mandated confidentiality as to pricing formulas and prohibited rebates. Such remedies may be particularly relevant in smaller economies where there are few buyers because of the need for scale economies. Although remedies focused on eliminating overt collusion will not eliminate the potential for tacit collusion (especially because defection is much less likely in buyer-side tacit collusion), they can increase the potential for more competition among buyers.

Market conduct regulation already exists in certain markets as discussed in Chapter 6. In such markets, a successful demonstration of serious tacit collusion ought to lead to market-facilitating regulations that make it more difficult for buyers to collude. The Western Organization of Resource Councils' proposal on cattle buying is illustrative,[158] but its adoption in the United States has been blocked by the political influence of large buyers. But there are proposals that could limit both strategic buying and other practices that frustrate the competitive process.

2. Stricter review of the competitive impact of buying groups

It is essential that there be closer scrutiny of buying groups because of their potential to cause anticompetitive effects in both upstream and downstream markets. The strong presumption of legality for a group that has some formal characteristics of a legitimate joint venture and a market share in the buying market below a generous threshold creates a serious risk of false negatives (allowing ventures that create avoidable competitive harm based on the erroneous determination that no risk exists).[159]

As shown in Chapter 3, buyer power arises at market shares below those currently considered problematic.[160] Indeed, in some American healthcare cases the government has objected to mergers or acquisitions in which the post-merger share of the input market would be below the threshold set

---

[157] See *United States v Gen. Elec. Co.*, No. 28228, 1977 WL 1475, at *3-4 (E.D. Pa. Sept. 19, 1977).

[158] See Chapter 6, text accompanying notes 57–9 (proposed rule that would require meat packers to offer contracts with either firm prices or prices based on some basis other than the packer's own contemporary price as well as allowing all feeders to offer cattle in response to packer requests for such commitments).

[159] See Thomas A Lambert, 'Evaluating Bundled Discounts' (2005) 89 *Minnesota Law Review* 1688, 1698–9.

[160] See Chapter 3, text accompanying notes 40–2.

forth in its healthcare guidelines.[161] Other analyses have revealed exclusionary conduct in hospital supply markets with large buying groups.[162]

The difficulty in evaluating such organizations is that they can and do serve legitimate functions that facilitate the efficient operation of the competitive process. Thus, the challenge is to design screens and filters that more accurately identify the buying groups that are likely to raise competitive concerns.

The first screen should be based upon the proportion of the input market taken by the buying group and the structural concentration of the buying side of the market. In general, a buying group should be prima facie lawful if it takes less than ten percent of a commodity, whether an input or a branded retail product, and regardless of the overall concentration of the market. This should not, however, preclude investigation of cartelizing restraints.[163]

Whether the commodity is a general input or a branded retail product is relevant to the market share that should trigger more focused inquiry. Buying groups for production inputs create a lower risk of harm to producers than buying groups for branded goods. As shown in Chapter 3, a minimum of five buyers is usually necessary to ensure a workably competitive buying market. Input buying groups in the ten to 20 percent range and an overall Herfindahl-Hirschman Index (HHI) below 2000 should still be subject to review for adverse downstream effects.[164] When the HHI exceeds 2000 in the overall buying market, the possibility of competitive harm is sufficiently high to warrant stricter review of buying groups in that size range for their potential adverse effect on producers. But if the group takes 20 percent or more of the input market (HHI for the group at or above 400) and the overall HHI exceeds 2000, there should be a presumption that the group is unnecessarily large and so likely to have an adverse effect on producers and the competitive process. Before permitting such a group to exist or continue, there should be a close evaluation of the justification for and specific conduct of such a dominant group.

---

161 Botti, *supra* note 13, at 11 (discussing Department of Justice challenge to the merger of United Health and PacifiCare).

162 See Klish, *supra* note 101, at 176.

163 See, eg, *United States v Topco*, 405 U.S. 596 (1972) where the downstream territorial restraints had no functional relationship to the purposes of the buying group. See Carstensen and First, *supra* note 49, at 203.

164 When the total HHI is below 2000, it is likely that there are more than five substantial buyers. The most likely competitive risk that a buying group in such market structure could create is some kind of downstream market allocation or coordination among the participants.

For buying groups acting on behalf of retailers, a collective share of between ten and 20 percent of the total input market creates potential risks of exploitation—especially if the remainder of the buying market has an HHI of 2000 or higher. Such a buying group should be carefully examined to ensure that it is in fact legitimate and necessary (that is, that the observed scale is required for transactional efficiency). A retailers' buying group that takes more than 20 percent of a branded commodity in a relevant buying market should be presumptively illegal because it is likely to cause undue harm to the overall competitive process. It is unlikely that a buying group needs to take such a large share of the total market to be efficient, and several smaller buying groups could replace it if the legality of the dominant group is questionable.[165] The presumption should be rebuttable, enabling the buying group to prove its need for a larger market share. But in any case, its methods of buying ought to be carefully reviewed to limit their potential for adverse competitive effects.

The second screen should be a rough estimate of the elasticities of supply and demand in the buying group market. The barriers to exit on the supply side are relevant, as is the capacity and willingness of other buyers to take the commodity if its price declines slightly. If supply is price inelastic (that is, if there are constraints on expanding or contracting output) and overall demand is relatively unresponsive to price changes, the potential for anticompetitive conduct that exploits suppliers increases. In contrast, if there is credible evidence of entry and exit or of significant demand changes in response to price changes, then the need for more focused analysis is limited. Buying groups in these markets—even if they buy a substantial share of the commodity—are unlikely to cause significant competitive harm.

The third screen should be the scope and range of scale economies in the supply market. When such economies exist, there are both incentives for legitimate efficiency-enhancing transactions and for anticompetitive use of control over the volume of business necessary to achieve scale economy. The key competitive risks involve both exclusionary agreements that foreclose competitors of the buying group from gaining access to the output of the larger-scale producers, and the exploitation of producers who need volume sales to achieve efficiency. Here, policy has to balance the gains from efficiency with the harms, actual and potential, to the competitive process.

---

[165] See Baker, *supra* note 80 (arguing that, unless the creation of a competing network is impractical, those seeking the benefits of a network should establish their own rather than compel an existing network to give access).

Efficiency gains provide the primary justification for groups that fall into the presumptively illegal category after focused review using the first two screens. The burden of proving that the scale of the organization is necessary to achieve economies should rest on the buyer group and its members. If other efficient buyers are significantly smaller than the buyer group, then its efficiency claims are likely false. In larger economies at least, buying more than 20 percent of any input or 15 percent of any branded product is unlikely to contribute to any significant efficiency.

Before condemning a group and requiring its dissolution, however, it is essential to determine the minimum efficient size for such a group. It is reasonable to condemn a buying group that purchases quantities in excess of twice the minimum efficient scale. When feasible, dissolution is the preferable remedy because it ensures a more robustly competitive buying market without the need for ongoing regulatory oversight.

If dissolution is impractical due to economies of scale, competition agencies should examine carefully the policies and procedures of the buying group to ensure that it has no greater adverse effect on the competitive process than is absolutely necessary to achieve its legitimate function. Any policy that excludes the participation of smaller buyers, denying them access to an efficient source of supply, results in serious harm to the competitive process. Thus the inquiry should balance the need for smaller buyers to pool their demand to achieve transactional efficiencies with the potential adverse effects of large volume buyers on producers. For general inputs, the use of open tenders (perhaps with volume limits for individual sellers), Dutch auctions or similar systems should be considered. These mechanisms are effective because they mimic natural market pricing methods.[166] The EU's requirement that buying groups allow participants to buy outside the group is particularly relevant here because it allows a producer with scale economies to offer the input directly to buyers; its cost savings may make its price competitive with what the buyer could obtain through the buying group.

---

[166] A Dutch auction involves offers of set quantities at proposed prices. The buyer selects the desired volume and pays all offerees the price of the final offer that satisfies the required quantity. Thus, offers at lower prices are rewarded with the marginal price and earn Ricardian rents. These systems have been used in the purchase of electricity and for stock repurchases. They are vulnerable to manipulation, however; if the number of suppliers is limited, they can behave strategically to manipulate prices. See Darren Bush and Carrie Mayne, 'In (Reluctant) Defense of Enron: Why Bad Regulation Is to Blame for California's Power Woes, or Why Antitrust Law Fails to Protect Against Market Power When the Market Rules Encourage Its Use' (2004) 83 *Oregon Law Review* 204 (discussing California's system for purchasing electric power).

If economies of scale exist and are important, the evaluation should also consider restrictive terms that exclude actual or potential competitors in the buying market or that might facilitate more downstream coordination. Exclusion of competing small buyers can harm producers by reducing the total demand for the input. The size and structure of each downstream market in which the group's members sell their products are relevant to assessing whether the group may affect these markets either by reducing the number of competitors or facilitating coordination among them. Again, assuming that there are significant efficiencies to the buying group and the buying group size approximates the minimum efficient scale, the challenge would be to develop requirements that limit the capacity of the group to affect downstream competition.

Ultimately, the goal of the screening process is to focus inquiry on the kinds of buyer groups that create the greatest risk of anticompetitive conduct. The goal should not be to eliminate an efficiency-enhancing buyer group merely because it creates risks of anticompetitive conduct, but rather, to focus on ways of avoiding or reducing the risks of such conduct. *Topco* is an illustration.[167] The venture was prohibited from engaging in downstream territorial allocations among its members, but continued to survive and prosper because its members found the group's other services valuable.[168]

Indeed, crafting an effective remedy is a significant challenge when the efficiencies of production and distribution require a substantial level of market concentration. As observed earlier, this issue is much more likely to be a serious concern in smaller economies. The central goal of competition policy should be to constrain discretionary conduct by a buying group that can unduly exploit producers, foreclose competitors of the group from access to inputs, or facilitate downstream coordination. This is relatively easy in the abstract, but business realities can make implementation very difficult. Solutions that rely on periodic tenders or some form of open-access market (such as a commodities market), should be considered, as they leave the core of the market process more fully intact.

The structural fact of substantial market share creates the need to look carefully at how a specific group operates, including its buying practices and whether these practices might facilitate coordination among its participants in their downstream market, achieve exclusion of competitors or result in avoidable exploitation of producers. These issues are currently recognized in the American healthcare guidelines.[169] EU policy requires

---

167 *United States v Topco Assocs., Inc.*, 405 U.S. 596 (1972).
168 Carstensen and First, *supra* note 49, at 201–02.
169 'Enforcement Policy in Health Care', *supra* note 11.

buying groups that take more than 15 percent of the input market to establish the economic necessity for the venture and to show that there is no less restrictive alternative.[170] The EU also requires that groups permit their members to purchase a portion of their requirements from outside the group.[171] These EU requirements are consistent with the analysis and recommendations of this part.

The regulation of grocery buying practices in the United Kingdom applies to both integrated enterprises and buying groups. Similarly, the Japanese regulation of abusive contracting would appear to apply to buying groups as well as to single firms, although it is not clear whether it has been applied to buying groups to date. But as discussed in Chapter 6, such regulation can also have negative implications for the competitive process.

E. Summary

Both buyer cartels and legitimate buying groups present serious challenges to maintaining a strong and viable competitive process. Despite some plausible arguments that buyer cartels provide countervailing market power to a concentrated sellers' market the demands of a workable competitive process preclude accepting this justification as a defense. Naked restraints of competition by buyers should be absolutely illegal unless subject to direct public regulation. In addition, the incentives of large groups of buyers are likely to make tacit collusion more feasible and attractive than those ordinarily found in seller side cartels. Enforcement authorities ought to look more broadly at the impact of parallel buying practices—especially in markets with relatively few buyers and many sellers.

In contrast to naked restraints of competition by buyers, legitimate buying groups provide transactional efficiency as well as negotiating capacity that individual small volume buyers lack. As such they can make positive contributions to the overall competitive process. However, the different ways in which such groups are constituted, ranging from substantial integration of buying services to very limited agency, make it hard sometimes to differentiate between legitimate joint buying ventures and naked restraints of buyer competition. For this reason, it is not irrational to implement a screening process, beginning with market share benchmarks, to help identify the kinds of arrangements, whether facially legitimate or not, that merit further review. Thus, the general thrust of the

---

170 European Union, *supra* note 14, §§ 189–224.

171 *Ibid.*

current enforcement policies in the United States and the EU is appropriate, but the market-share screen in the United States, derived from seller side analogies, is too generous given the enhanced ability of buyer groups to impose harm on both upstream and downstream markets. In large economies, limited efficiency gains are likely to accrue to groups beyond a modest market share.

In smaller economies, a somewhat higher threshold could be justified, but any buying practice that discriminates among suppliers, restricts supplier opportunities to make direct sales, affects access to supplies for competing buyers, actual or potential, or creates the potential to coordinate downstream competition should be subject to greater scrutiny. Overall, competition authorities ought to be more focused on the competitive risks that buying groups pose to the market. Employing appropriate screens to identify the groups most likely to create such risks would enable a more systematic and critical review of their buying practices and serve as an important contribution to preserving and advancing the competitive process.

II. VERTICAL RESTRAINTS

Chapter 5 dealt in some detail with the legal and policy analysis of unilateral exclusionary conduct by buyers. Much of that conduct involves agreements between buyers and their suppliers. Any agreement between a powerful buyer and its upstream supplier that limits the freedom of action of the supplier is a restraint of trade. The imposition on a supplier of an obligation to discriminate among its customers by use of a most favored nation clause or an exclusive supply obligation can harm both upstream and downstream competition. The analytical difficulties are the same as those for unilateral conduct. If sufficient market power exists to justify review on the merits, the same justifications and consideration of less harmful alternatives will be relevant.

In addition, as discussed earlier, buyers and producers can collaborate to entrench their positions in their respective markets. Buyers can insist on resale price maintenance enforced by the seller to ensure against competition and transfer to the buyer a greater share of the value of the commodity being resold. Slotting fees, loyalty rebates and similar restraints can have comparable adverse effects on downstream competition.[172]

---

[172] See, eg, John Asker and Heski Bar-Isaac, 'Raising Retailers' Profits: On Vertical Practices and the Exclusion of Rivals' (2014) 104 *American Economic Review* 672.

Under conventional American antitrust analysis, courts will not look critically at contracts of this sort, characterized as vertical restraints, unless there is evidence of market power on the part of the party benefitting from the restraint.[173] Similar standards appear to apply globally.[174] As in monopsony analysis, the existence of sufficient power should be inferred from market shares substantially lower than those used in seller power cases.

If a correct analysis of buyer power was applied, many more agreements restraining sellers' freedom of action or imposing discriminatory terms on sellers would be subject to critical review on their merits. There will be little dispute as to the existence of the agreement and its discriminatory or exclusionary characteristics. Rather, the focus should be on the justification for such restraints. As with unilateral monopsonistic conduct, the challenge is to assess whether particular agreements are reasonably necessary to accomplish the legitimate needs of the business transaction. Because the degree of power necessary to trigger critical review under restraint of trade analysis is less than that necessary for unilateral conduct, it is plausible that courts and agencies might be more comfortable employing restraint of trade analysis as the jurisdictional basis for review combined with the *Microsoft* analytic framework. Indeed, the Second Circuit used a similar approach in deciding the *Visa* case,[175] which was a Sherman Act section 1 claim.

Contemporary American case law and policy statements from the EU suggest that, in many circumstances, these risks are largely ignored. An illustrative decision is that in *Kartell v Blue Shield of Massachusetts.*[176] Judge (now Justice) Breyer upheld a contractual requirement imposed by the dominant healthcare insurer in the state that precluded doctors from charging patients more than the amount reimbursed by the insurer

---

[173] See, eg, *Leegin Creative Leather Prods., Inc v PSKS, Inc.*, 551 U.S. 877 (2007) (resale price maintenance lawful absent proof of market power and harm to competition); *Bus. Elecs. Corp. v Sharp Elecs. Corp.*, 485 U.S. 717 (1988) (refusal to deal with a customer based on price not illegal if no specific price involved); *Cont'l T.V., Inc. v GTE Sylvania, Inc.*, 433 U.S. 36 (1977) (territorial restraints imposed by manufacturers are lawful unless unreasonable).

[174] See European Commission (2010), 'Guidelines on Vertical Restraints', available at http://ec.europa.eu/competition/antitrust/legislation/guidelines_vertical_en.pdf (revising policies toward many vertical restraints to more tolerant standards). See generally Sandra Marco Colino, *Vertical Agreements and Competition Law: A Comparative Study of the EU and US Regimes* (Bloomsbury Professional, London 2010).

[175] *United States v Visa*, 344 F.3d 229 (2nd Cir. 2003).

[176] *Kartell v Blue Shield of Mass.*, 749 F.2d 922 (1st Cir. 1984).

(known as 'balance billing'). While recognizing that an agreement among insurers to impose such a restraint would be unlawful,[177] the opinion declares that a monopsonist buyer can impose any price or other terms it demands as long as those terms are not 'predatory'.[178] In healthcare markets, where the patient relies on the insurer to pay for medical services, a prohibition on the use of balance billing is credible, but the sweep of the decision in asserting an almost absolute right of a dominant buyer to set terms illustrates the difficulty of challenging unreasonable restrictive contracts imposed unilaterally by buyers.[179]

The plaintiffs contended that the competitive harm included a waterbed effect (patients not insured by the defendant were forced to pay higher prices), harm to innovation (doctors would not employ newer or better techniques for fear of uneconomic reimbursement rates), and an incentive for patients to refuse to deal with other insurers thus reinforcing the defendant's dominance.[180] At the same time, the reluctance of the Court to dictate prices or other contract terms, because of the consequent need for ongoing judicial oversight, provides a plausible explanation for the result.[181] From a competitive policy perspective, the failure of the decision to recognize or address the risks to the competitive process of the power of a dominant buyer's contractual demands is very regrettable. But it does highlight the significant challenges for competition policy in attempting to regulate abuses of buyer power. The EU seems to take a similarly benign view of buyer power—focusing largely on concentrated supply-side markets.[182]

Restraint of trade analysis could provide a useful tool for evaluating the discriminatory, exploitive,[183] and exclusionary agreements that individual buyers employ. First, however, there needs to be a clear recognition of the risks to the competitive process. The analysis is the same as that advanced in Chapter 5 for monopsony: when are the consequences likely to harm

---

177 *Ibid* at 930.

178 *Ibid* at 930–1.

179 See *ibid* at 927–9.

180 *Ibid* at 929–30.

181 *Ibid* at 934. While the case was pending, the state legislature adopted a statute that prohibited balance billing. *Ibid* at 925.

182 See, eg, Case No. IV/M.1225, *Enso/Stora* (Comm'n, 1998); Case No. IV/M.4057, *Korsnas/AssiDoman Cartonboard* (Comm'n, 2006); see also Binet, *supra* note 14, at 161–8.

183 Exploitive conduct of the sort at issue in *Kartell* provides the greatest challenge because the remedy involves direct control over the terms of the transactions. In contrast, discriminatory and exclusionary terms can be excised from purchase contracts with less need for detailed ongoing oversight.

the competitive process and when are they likely to serve legitimate needs of the parties with no more harm than is necessary to achieve those goals? Second, and again as in the monopsony analysis, what conduct-oriented remedies are both likely to result in significant positive changes and be administrable? These are major challenges because the conduct at issue often involves the core of the transactional process.

III. CONCLUSION

Current competition policy does not adequately address competitive issues arising from agreements among buyers and between powerful buyers and their suppliers. In order to limit the creation of serious and intractable problems that come from trying to police conduct in monopsonized markets or ones infected with significant buyer power and the concomitant abuses that come from that power, it is important that competition authorities carefully police the dangers to competition that come from both excessively large buying groups and buyer cartels. Constraining the size of buying groups and having a rigorous policy of prohibition against buyer cartels are important steps in limiting the risks that undue and avoidable buyer power raise. It is also important for competition law authorities to develop criteria that limit vertical restraints to prevent avoidable exclusion or undue exploitation. These steps are central to maintaining a workable competitive process.

8. Controlling the creation of buyer power through merger policy

I. INTRODUCTION

Chapters 3 and 4 argue that buyer power is a pervasive problem in market economies. Chapters 5 and 6 show that seeking to remedy directly the abuse of such power, especially its durable exploitation of producers, is difficult and often unlikely to produce meaningful change in the market. Hence, and consistent with Chapter 7, the basic argument of this chapter is that competition policy, through strict enforcement of merger regulations, should seek to limit the creation of excessive buyer power. Moreover, because buyer power can arise at lower market shares than seller power,[1] merger policy must have buyer-side-specific metrics for measuring the risks of anticompetitive harm. This policy perspective—with its strong structural emphasis—reflects the institutional differences between buyer power and seller power. This chapter also compares the ways in which the United States, the European Union (EU) and other countries have responded to mergers that create buyer power.

In 2010, the US Department of Justice and the Federal Trade Commission (FTC) promulgated a new set of Horizontal Merger Guidelines ('the 2010 Guidelines').[2] For the first time, there was an explicit analysis of mergers that affected the buying side of the market.[3] The 2010 Guidelines are a substantial step forward from the 1992 and 1997 guidelines (which referenced buyer-side issues in a single paragraph narrowly focused on monopsonistic conduct),[4] but the discussion remains brief and the

---

1 See Chapter 3.

2 US Department of Justice and FTC, 'Horizontal Merger Guidelines' (2010) (hereinafter '2010 Guidelines').

3 *Ibid* § 12.

4 US Department of Justice and FTC, 'Horizontal Merger Guidelines' § 0.1 (1992, modified 1997). ('Market power also encompasses the ability of a single buyer (a "monopsonist"), a coordinating group of buyers, or a single buyer, not a monopsonist, to depress the price paid for a product to a level that is below the competitive price and thereby depress output. The exercise of market power by buyers ("monopsony power") has adverse effects comparable to those associated

guidance limited. Other jurisdictions have similarly acknowledged that buyer-side issues are relevant in merger analysis.[5] Overall, the analysis of the buyer-side of mergers has not received extensive scholarly or agency attention.[6] Strikingly, many jurisdictions, including those with smaller national markets, have largely or completely ignored buyer power issues in reviewing mergers only to subsequently detect market failures caused by excessive buyer power.[7]

The starting point of merger policy should be a recognition that any substantial merger may have an impact on market competition on the buying side as well as the selling side of the combination. Currently few enforcement agencies consistently review both dimensions. The more common practice is a primary focus on the selling side with buying side analysis limited to a few industries. The thesis of this chapter is that this approach is myopic and should be replaced with a consistent focus on *both* sides of any major combination. Competing firms are very likely to be competing buyers of inputs, even if they are not substantial competitors in selling markets. The effects of a merger on the geographic and product dimensions of the buying side bear no consistent relationship to those on the selling side; therefore, merger review must engage in two distinct analyses—one for upstream market effects and the other for downstream market effects of the businesses involved.[8]

---

with the exercise of market power by sellers. In order to assess potential monopsony concerns, the [a]gency will apply an analytical framework analogous to the framework of these Guidelines').

5 See, eg, European Commission, 'Guidelines on the Assessment of Horizontal Mergers under the Council Regulation on the Control of Concentrations between Undertakings', 2004 O.J. (C 31) 16, ¶¶ 61–4. The EU guidelines emphasize buyer power as an offset to the risks created by a merger between sellers. *Ibid* at ¶¶ 64–7. The American position is that buyer power is a less convincing excuse to justify the conclusion that a seller merger will not create undue market power. See 2010 Guidelines, *supra* note 2, § 8.

6 Some studies focus on the United States. See Peter C Carstensen, 'Buyer Power and the Horizontal Merger Guidelines: Minor Progress on an Important Issue' (2012) 14 *University of Pennsylvania Journal of Business Law* 775; John B Kirkwood, 'Powerful Buyers and Merger Enforcement' (2012) 92 *Boston University Law Review* 1485; Dennis W Carlton, Mary Coleman and Mark Israel, 'Buyer Power in Merger Review' in Roger D Blair and D Daniel Sokol (eds), *Oxford Handbook of International Antitrust Economics* (Oxford University Press, Oxford 2015) 569.

7 For example, Norway, Finland and Australia each allowed the merger of two of their very few grocery chains and subsequently had to develop conduct regulation to control abuse of buyer power.

8 The American review process for major mergers does not require the parties to provide information on the buying side. See Hart-Scott-Rodino Notification

Section II discusses how the harms that can arise from the abuse of buyer power are similar to those associated with seller-side merger power. Section III identifies the factors that make the potential competitive effects of buyer-side mergers distinctive and require explicit enforcement policies that focus on buyer-side competitive risks. Section IV then sets forth an analysis of buyer-side mergers that recognizes the distinctive elements of buyer power to avoid undue concentration and competitive risks. Section V provides a survey of enforcement actions with respect to buyer power. Those actions fall far short of the comprehensive policy that ought to guide merger analysis when buyer power is at issue. Section VI concludes.

II. MERGERS CREATING UNJUSTIFIED BUYER POWER CREATE CONVENTIONAL MERGER HARM

Conventional merger analysis is concerned with whether a merger will increase the potential for either exploitive conduct or exclusionary conduct by the resulting enterprise. Such conduct threatens both short-term static harm as well as longer run dynamic injury to the competitive process. These harms can arise from either collective or unilateral post-merger conduct. This section briefly reviews the analysis in Chapter 4 to show that buyer-side harm falls into a similar pattern.

A. Exploitive Harms

Increased buyer power can lead to market exploitation, which causes immediate anticompetitive consequences.[9] Buyers with market power can compel unreasonably low prices for inputs. Upstream suppliers (and the marketplace in general) can also be exploited on non-price dimensions.[10] Dominant buyers are often able to dictate terms and conditions that transfer financial risks to a producer without commensurate

---

and Report Form, available at https://www.ftc.gov/enforcement/premerger-notification-program/form-instructions. Only if regulators are independently aware of a buying-side issue will they seek such information.

[9] See Chapter 4, section I.

[10] See Stephanie Storm, 'Giant Food Companies Pay Later, Squeezing Their Suppliers' *New York Times* (7 April 2015) at B 1 (reporting that large buyers were unilaterally extending the time period for paying their suppliers). See generally Peter C Carstensen, 'Buyer Power, Competition Policy, and Antitrust: The Competitive Effects of Discrimination among Suppliers' (2008) 53 *Antitrust Bulletin* 271.

compensation.[11] Buyers in moderately oligopsonistic markets often have the incentive and capacity to engage in price discrimination among their suppliers, especially if modest scale or the geographic constraints inherent in the market for the upstream product limit a producer's ability to seek other buyers. Dominant buyers can also limit the options available to sellers by allocating their purchases among producers in a way that minimizes or eliminates competition among the buyers.[12]

Mergers that result in entities that buy in several markets create the incentive and capacity to engage in geographic price discrimination among suppliers. Traditional seller-side merger analysis recognizes the capacity of firms to separate groups of buyers and engage in downstream price discrimination.[13] Merger analysis must consider whether the same capacity to discriminate among classes of sellers exists on the buying side of the market either within or among geographic markets.[14] Indeed, multimarket buyers can create anticompetitive, linked oligopolies that respect each other's primary buying territories.[15] Because of the shared interest in obtaining and maintaining the lowest input prices possible, buyers will find it attractive to avoid competition for inputs as much as possible.

From a dynamic perspective, market exploitation diminishes the long-run incentives of producers to engage in innovative and efficiency-enhancing activities, because the dominant buyer simply appropriates the Ricardian rents that would otherwise accrue to the producer.[16] Traditional competition policy treats this appropriation as a wealth transfer and therefore not of competitive concern; such conduct, however, has profound negative consequences for the longer run dynamics of the market.

---

11 See generally Joseph Miller, 'Contracting in Agriculture: Potential Problems' (2003) 8 *Drake Journal of Agricultural Law* 57.

12 See Lynn Hunnicutt, DeeVon Bailey and Michelle Crook, 'Rigidity in Packer-Feedlot Relationships' (2004) 36 *Journal of Agricultural and Applied Economics* 627 (cattle feed lots show pattern of dealing exclusively with a single buyer).

13 See '2010 Merger Guidelines', *supra* note 2, §§ 6–7.

14 Multimarket buying is particularly important in buyer power analysis. If alternative markets are available, the exploitation of the disfavored market is rational even if it causes a substantial reduction in output.

15 See Elinor Solomon, 'Bank Merger Policies and Problems: A Linkage Theory of Oligopoly' (1970) 2 *Journal of Money, Credit and Banking* 323. See also *Cargill, Inc. v Monfort of Colo., Inc.*, 479 U.S. 104 (1986) (denying standing to a single-plant company challenging a multiplant operator's purchase of a directly competing slaughter house).

16 See Chapter 3, text accompanying note 6.

B. Exclusionary Harms

Firms with buyer power can impose constraints on an upstream supplier that causes competing buyers to pay higher prices for the same supply or even blocks such competitors from access to that supply. In one case, a buyer entered into exclusive dealing contracts with all the major suppliers of a key input. As a result, the buyer's competitors were fenced out of the market.[17] Other examples have arisen in the toy and appliance markets.[18] Closely related is the use of buyer power to create cartels to the advantage of the buyer itself or its agents.[19] All of these risks increase as buyers consolidate.[20] Static and dynamic harms flow from these actions that are likely to lead to artificially higher prices in the short term and deter entry and innovation in upstream markets.

C. Collusive Harms

As shown in Chapters 3 and 7, the incentives for powerful buyers to engage in tacit collusion to restrict price or allocate suppliers are different from those for powerful sellers. The immediate effect of a buyer's 'cheating' is to raise input costs or even create a trade war if one buyer 'poaches' a source of supply tacitly assigned to another buyer. Moreover, the gains to the cheater accrue only after the input is converted to an output, which may require increased purchases of other costly inputs. Hence, retaliation is more effective on the buyer-side because of the inherent lag in the financial benefit. And because most inputs are purchased directly, rather than

---

17 *FTC v Mylan Labs., Inc.*, 62 F. Supp. 2d 25 (D.D.C. 1999), on reconsideration in part, 99 F. Supp. 2d 1 (D.D.C. 1999).

18 *Toys 'R' Us v FTC*, 221 F.3d 928 (7th Cir. 2000) (toys); *Klor's, Inc. v Broadway-Hale Stores, Inc.*, 359 U.S. 207 (1959) (appliances).

19 See, eg, *Interstate Circuit v United States*, 306 U.S. 208 (1939) (buyer used its power to induce suppliers to engage in horizontal price fixing agreement that harmed other buyers and protected the dominant buyer from price competition); *Toys 'R' Us*, 221 F.3d at 932 (toy buyer induced toy producers to enter into horizontal agreement to refuse to deal with buyer's key competitors). The best example of an agent's use of buyer power is in the insurance industry. Major brokers used their ability to control the buying decisions of major insureds to induce insurers to engage in a cartel to raise prices and split the resulting cartel profits with the agents. See *In re Ins. Brokerage Antitrust Litig.*, 618 F.3d 300 (3rd Cir. 2010). See generally Peter C Carstensen, 'Buyer Cartels versus Buying Groups: Legal Distinctions, Competitive Realities, and Antitrust Policy' (2010) 1 *William and Mary Business Law Review* 1.

20 Buyer consolidation includes combinations across buying markets that facilitate either linked oligopoly or multiple spheres of influence.

through anonymous open markets, those buyers wishing to enforce a tacit understanding can target the specific suppliers of the cheater and offer them higher prices, forcing the cheater to match those prices in order to retain the input. This is akin to the involuntary base-point pricing system used to enforce delivered-pricing schemes.[21]

Various scholarly studies provide further support for this conclusion. Marshall and Meurer have generated a model of bidding auctions in which the conspiracy cannot be disrupted.[22] Asker's study of a stamp buyers' cartel found that it was possible to sustain the cartel even with turnover among the participants.[23] Finally, Hunnicutt and others found that the identity of buyers from cattle feedlots is stable,[24] which is consistent with tacit upstream allocation.[25]

In buying markets, the probability of tacit collusion is significant whenever there are relatively few buyers and even more likely when there are numerous producers. Suppliers can more feasibly be allocated among buyers and made highly dependent on their continued relationship with the buyers to whom they sell. Therefore, allocation (and its coordinated effects) is a prelude to the use of unilateral power to further exploit the upstream supplier. Collusion can also take the form of standardizing input elements or contract terms in ways that increase the relative gain to the coordinating buyers. And because such collusive arrangements are durable (because of the costs of deviating from them), the risks of harm to competition are greater than they would be on the seller side and can occur even if the number of buyers is larger than standard theory predicts for seller-side power.

The fundamental implication is that if a merger of buyers reduces the number of competing buyers in any relevant input market to a modest

---

[21] See, eg, *FTC v Cement Inst.*, 333 U.S. 683 (1948) (cement was sold on a base-point pricing system of a free-on-board price plus the shipping rate from a base point, making price to the buyer transparent and facilitating tacit price collusion; by making a deviant competitor's plant a base-point and driving down the net price to buyers, which the deviant had to meet to make any sales, other cement producers could enforce the cartel arrangement at modest cost to themselves).

[22] Michael Meurer and Robert Marshall, 'Bidder Collusion and Antitrust Law: Refining the Analysis of Price Fixing to Account for the Special Features of Auction Markets' (2004) 72 *Antitrust Law Journal* 83.

[23] John Asker, 'A Study of the Internal Organization of a Bidding Cartel' (2010) 100 *American Economic Review* 724.

[24] Hunnicutt, Bailey and Crook, *supra* note 12.

[25] See Xiaowei Cai, Kyle W Stiegert and Stephen Koontz, 'Regime Switching and Oligopsony Power: The Case of U.S. Beef Processing' (2011) 42 *Agricultural Economics* 99.

number (even one substantially larger than currently deemed of concern in seller-side merger analysis), there is a cognizable risk of coordinated conduct. If producers can shift to making other goods or there is high demand elasticity, buyers' incentives to coordinate their buying actions can be constrained.

D. Unilateral Harm

A central element of efficient product markets is the change in the price of an input as the demand for the input increases or decreases. When inputs are purchased sequentially, the price can vary over time. This smooths out demand and encourages the marginal purchase.[26] However, the capacity to pay different prices creates the risks of unilateral harm that merged buyers present to the competitive process. For this reason, the analysis of potential unilateral effects is complex and contingent on the options available to both buyers and sellers. The greater the price elasticity of supply, the less likely the adverse effects. Therefore, the focus is on the ability of producers to adjust output or find other buyers in the face of lower prices.

A producer that sells much or all of its output to a single buyer will be vulnerable to pressure to sign an all-or-nothing contract.[27] All-or-nothing contracts allow buyers to appropriate the efficiency gains of a producer without any reduction in immediate output, ultimately reducing producers' incentives to invest in innovation. Under an all-or-nothing contract, a producer will be discouraged by significant switching costs from moving to another buyer, creating a barrier to competition in the buying market.[28] Mergers in markets in which producers routinely sell their output to a single buyer require careful assessment of the risk of such conduct, post-merger.

The potential for exploitation also exists if the merging firms are major buyers of different inputs that, from the supplier's perspective, would serve as the closest alternative product lines in the event that one line is subject to monopsony or oligopsony. This risk is analogous to the seller-side concern for the unilateral effect of a merger involving two

---

[26] The alternative, in the context of rising prices, is that all prior input commitments must be repriced to the new, higher price. Hence, the increased price of the incremental unit drives up the cost of all units. This is a particularly challenging issue in labor markets where uniform pay levels are more common. This may explain why price fixing and other coordination is a recurring issue. See *Todd v Exxon Corp.*, 275 F.3d 191 (2nd Cir. 2001).

[27] See Chapter 3, text accompanying note 6.

[28] Examples include employment contracts and sales from cattle feed lots.

differentiated products that are next-best alternatives.[29] A merged firm that is a major buyer of both input lines would be more able to impose its will on its suppliers.

Increased buyer power resulting from a merger can have a significant upstream effect. The consolidated firm is likely to reduce the number of its suppliers, generating substantial competition among them and enabling the merged buyer to use its power to drive down input prices. But the surviving suppliers will also have increased buyer power with respect to their suppliers upstream.[30] Hence, the effect of a merger that enhances buyer power may be felt one or two stages upstream from the merger itself. This is an indirect unilateral effect.

A merger may also create sufficient buyer power for the merged firm to use its power, as *Broadway-Hale* and *Toys 'R' Us* did, to demand exclusionary favors from its suppliers.[31] Price may be less important to some merged buyers than protection from competition in the downstream market. In return for its continued patronage, the merged buyer may demand of its suppliers either coordinated or unilateral refusals to deal with the buyer's competitors. The rational producer faces a trade-off between the gains from a continued course of dealing with the large volume buyer and its capacity to develop other markets. The producer is more likely to support the incumbent buyer's demands and exclude its new or smaller competitors.[32]

Finally, a merger that leads to increased buying power can cause the waterbed effect,[33] which results in an economically inefficient allocation of costs—the exploiting buyer receives a de facto subsidy from the exploited buyers. This distortion harms the competitive process by giving

---

29 The 2010 Guidelines address the competitive risk of seller-side unilateral effects, but ignore the buyer side analogy. '2010 Guidelines', *supra* note 2, § 6.

30 See C Edward Fee and Thomas Shawn, 'Sources of Gains in Horizontal Mergers: Evidence from Customer, Supplier, and Rival Firms' (2004) 74 *Journal of Financial Economics* 423. The manipulation of cheese prices illustrates this secondary effect. The price paid to cheese makers fell, but dairy farmers bore the ultimate burden when cheese makers reduced the price they paid for milk. See *Knevelbaard Dairies v Kraft Foods, Inc.*, 232 F.3d 979 (9th Cir. 2000).

31 *Klor's, Inc. v Broadway-Hale Stores, Inc.*, 359 U.S. 207 (1959); *Toys 'R' Us v FTC*, 221 F.3d 928 (7th Cir. 2000).

32 Clorox's actions are illustrative. It refused to provide a midsize retailer with the largest sizes of its products, reserving those for high volume, big-box retail chains such as Costco and Sam's Club. *Woodman's Food Mkt. v Clorox Co.*, 2015 WL 420296 (W.D. Wis. 2015), rev'd, 2016 WL 4254935 (7th Cir. 2016) (unilateral refusal to sell specific container sizes not a violation of the Robinson-Patman Act).

33 See Chapter 3, text accompanying note 15.

one buyer an unjustified market advantage. Moreover, when the other buyers are also downstream competitors of the favored buyer, the result is an even more dramatic distortion of the market process. The disfavored competitor-buyers are effectively subsidizing the favored competitor-buyer in the downstream market.

Cases of the waterbed effect are distinguishable from cases in which a powerful supplier reduces its prices from a supracompetitive level to a price that is more competitive, but still above average total cost. Such a supplier can recoup its reduced profits from sales to the now-powerful buyer by continuing to charge supracompetitive prices, or even increasing prices, to its other customers. The implications of a merger that causes this response are ambiguous. The merger increases the relative exploitation of the supplier's other customers, but the merged entity pays something closer to an approximation of the competitive price. If the downstream market is workably competitive and all the buyers compete in that market, the higher prices might not hold; the upstream supplier will lose sales volume if the competitors of the dominant buyer either substitute away from the input sold by the supplier or go out of business. But, if the competitors of the dominant buyer lack viable alternative sources of supply, if the collective supply volume taken by the competitors of the dominant buyer is not sufficient to induce the seller to respond by reducing prices, or if the powerful buyer has imposed most favored nation plus terms,[34] the merger will have indirectly raised rivals' costs. If the competitors of the dominant buyer resell in other markets, the effect is, as noted earlier, a distortion of the relative input costs as between the dominant buyer's market and the other market in which the input is used.

E. Summary

The foregoing discussion demonstrates that undue buyer power can cause the same kinds of adverse consequences that are associated with seller-side harms from mergers. Buyer-side exclusionary conduct carries with it the potential for a direct impact on consumers. But exploitive harms directly affect only a buyer's upstream suppliers and not its downstream customers. Seller-side mergers are condemned because they are likely to enhance exploitation of consumers; when buyer-side mergers threaten exploitation of producers (who are also consumers ultimately), many competition

---

[34] A most favored nation plus contract imposes on the seller the obligation to sell the same commodity to all other buyers at a price above that charged to the favored buyer. See Chapter 4, text accompanying notes 70–71.

agencies are at best agnostic about whether such harms should be of concern. The preceding analysis establishes that they should be.

III. THE DISTINCTIVE ELEMENTS OF BUYER POWER ANALYSIS IN MERGERS

A central thesis of this book is that the analysis of the competitive implications of buyer power requires metrics and standards specific to the competitive harms that result from its exercise. This section identifies the factors that differentiate buyer-side from seller-side merger analysis. The differences between these two sets of factors justify different standards and measures for evaluating mergers.

A. Harm Can Arise from Modest Increases in Concentration

A merger between two significant buyers necessarily results in a firm with increased buyer power. The empirical and theoretical work of economists who have evaluated the issues associated with buyer power and observable patterns in the reported cases demonstrate that relatively modest increases in buyer power can significantly increase the exploitive capacity of the merged buyer over vulnerable suppliers.[35] That power derives from several economic facts that distinguish buyers from sellers. First, the buyer is the 'decider' with respect to whether, when and how much to purchase. Moreover, in one-to-one transactions, the buyer also decides from whom to make the purchase. This decisional power differentiates the buyer from the seller and is a major reason why buyers can have significant power even if they do not structurally dominate the buying side of the market to the same extent as sellers.[36]

Second, it is more difficult for a producer to engage in arbitrage the way a buyer can. Buyers can price discriminate among producers in direct (one-to-one) buying or resell excess inputs purchased to gain a volume discount. Producers, however, may be required by their sales contracts to supply the inputs rather than deliver goods from another producer. In addition, a producer with a favorable selling price and available production capacity has little incentive to supplement its production by buying

---

[35] See Chapter 3, section II.B for the evidence for this conclusion.

[36] Indeed, implicit in the usual assumption that a seller must have a large market share in order to have market power is the recognition that buyers may be able to switch to other reasonable alternatives.

from a disfavored producer. The same considerations make price discrimination (both within a single buying market and among distinct buying markets) more likely at levels of buyer concentration lower than those that would create seller power. Because arbitrage among producers is unlikely, there will be less inhibition on buyer conduct. Hence robust competition among buyers is the best control of this incentive.

Third, buyer power also increases as a supplier's switching costs increase. The greater a supplier's buyer- or product-specific investment, the more difficult it is for the supplier to move into another line of production and thus free itself from the exploitive power of a dominant buyer. Such problems are evident in poultry, livestock and dairy production. Doctors and hospitals are in a similar situation, owing to large, specialized investments in medical equipment and expertise.[37] The costs of switching increase further when the current buyer takes all or most of a supplier's output. A switch would then involve not a marginal shift in sales, but a massive change.

Fourth, informational issues may exacerbate the problems that result from buyer- or product-specific supplier investment. If producers lack reliable information about and access to alternative buyers for their production, they will face significant uncertainty about the probable success of any switch and therefore will be less able to resist the demands of their current buyer.[38]

Fifth, a producer of branded consumer goods usually needs access to a large number of buyers for its product, and one buyer may not be a good substitute for another. If two major customers merge, the merging companies will take the equivalent of the combined share of the producer's output. Indeed, it has often been observed that high volume retailers have

---

[37] See, eg, Complaint, *United States v Blue Cross Blue Shield of Mich.*, 2010 WL 4108490 (E.D. Mich. 2010) (as a condition of favorable payment terms, monopoly insurer compelled hospitals to charge competing insurers the same or higher prices); *W. Penn Allegheny Health Sys., Inc. v Univ. Pittsburgh Med. Ctr.*, 627 F.3d 85 (3rd Cir. 2010) (dominant buyer of healthcare services used its buyer power to exclude competition). See also Marius Schwartz, Economics Director of Enforcement, Department of Justice, 'Buyer Power Concerns and the Aetna-Prudential Merger', Speech at the 5th Annual Health Care Antitrust Forum (20 October 1999), available at https://www.justice.gov/atr/speech/buyer-power-concerns-and-aetna-prudential-merger.

[38] See Jeremy Sandford, 'Competition and Endogenous Impatience in Credence-Good Markets' (2013) 169 *Journal of Institutional and Theoretical Economics* 531 (switching in concentrated markets when an actor has limited or imperfect knowledge is inherently risky because of the limited options).

significant leverage over their suppliers.[39] Because of the need to have access to a large number of outlets to maintain a sufficient volume of sales, producers are very dependent upon their large volume customers.[40]

Hence, a retailer with a 15 or 20 percent share of a relevant buying market may be able to exercise substantial power over a branded goods supplier because the loss of the retailer would mean the loss of one-sixth or more of the supplier's outlets. Reducing to that degree the number of a supplier's outlets can create a serious problem for the supplier. Mergers that create or enhance a retailer's market share to more than 15 percent of the overall supply market can create serious risks of adverse competitive effects.

With respect to basic inputs, a merger that produces a firm with a more than 20 percent share of the buying side of a market would raise similar concerns. As discussed in Chapter 7, elasticity of supply and demand are relevant to the degree of risk, as are other structural characteristics—especially the number of sellers in relation to the number of buyers. And although these factors would be relevant to mergers that slightly exceed the levels suggested above, a merger that generates a buying-side market share of more than 20 percent should carry a presumption of significant buyer power.

B. Buyer Power is More Durable than Seller Power

In evaluating the risk of anticompetitive consequences from a merger that increases market power on either the buying or selling side, it is important to consider the incentives of the merged firm to engage in such conduct,

---

39 See, eg, *Toys 'R' Us v FTC*, 221 F.3d 928 (7th Cir. 2000). Additional support comes from Europe. See also Roger Clarke et al, *Buyer Power and Competition in European Food Retailing* (Edward Elgar Publishing, Cheltenham, UK and Northampton, MA 2002); Press Release, United Food and Commercial Workers International Union (21 May 2010), 'Food Workers Union Asks DOJ/USDA Panel To Investigate Walmart', available at http://www.ufcw.org/2010/05/21/food-workers-union-asks-dojusda-panel-to-investigate-walmarts-role-in-driving-agriculture-consolidation-2/; Charles Fishman, *The Wal-Mart Effect* (Penguin, New York 2006).

40 The automobile industry may have long insisted on using independent dealers rather than chains of retailers to avoid the risk of chains acquiring significant buyer power. Palamountain suggests a similar explanation for the historical experience of the gasoline industry, which initially tried ownership integration into retailing, but then moved to individually owned gas stations over which the producers still sought to exercise substantial control. Joseph Palamountain, *The Politics of Distribution* (Harvard University Press, Cambridge, MA 1955).

as well as the potential market forces that might deter such conduct. In selling markets, there is a rational basis to be skeptical about the gain to the seller from trying to raise price either through coordination or unilaterally because of the potential that competitors would undercut that price. Hence, it is often said that there needs to be an alignment of interests and incentives for an oligopoly to engage in coordinated market exploitation. Similarly, the analysis of unilateral conduct must address both the barriers to new entry and the potential for existing competitors to respond.

Although the same considerations are relevant on the buying side, there are important differences with respect to incentives and opportunities. The interest of the firm is served regardless of its position in the downstream markets in which it participates because exploiting buyer power can result in lower input costs. The incentives to exploit these opportunities are greater than those that arise from seller power. Moreover, the potential deterrent effect of competitors is less likely to impose a significant constraint on powerful buyers because all buyers share an interest in keeping input prices down. Only if demand for an input exceeds supply at the prevailing price and input supply is price elastic do buyers generally have an incentive to raise input prices. Even then, there remain strong incentives to resume unilateral or collective exploitation as soon as supply recovers.[41]

As shown in Chapter 7, there is less potential for disruption by a maverick of tacit buyer cartels than of seller cartels.[42] A price cut on the selling side results in an immediate increase in sales; paying more for an input does not immediately increase sales or profits. This lag allows for retaliation by the competing buyers against the cheating member. They can, for example, bid up further the price of the input in direct competition with the maverick buyer.[43] When buyers deal directly with sellers, the colluding buyers can employ selective bidding to drive up the cheater's costs.[44]

---

[41] See Cai, Stiegert and Koontz, *supra* note 25 (cattle buyers' tacit collusion to keep prices down is disrupted in periods of short supply and resumes when supply grows).

[42] See Chapter 7, text accompanying notes 108–16. See generally Jonathan B Baker, 'Mavericks, Mergers, and Exclusion: Proving Coordinated Competitive Effects Under the Antitrust Laws' (2002) 77 *New York University Law Review* 135.

[43] This conduct is akin to the involuntary base-point pricing used to discipline sellers in markets in which such pricing was used to facilitate an underlying price fixing cartel. See *supra* note 21 and accompanying text.

[44] If the cartel can identify the specific suppliers to the cheater, it can bid up the prices paid to them. The cheater must match those prices if it wants to continue its supply. Because the cartel does not have to offer the higher prices to its other suppliers, it can focus on 'raising [its] rival(s') costs' without undue risk of disrupting the price of the bulk of its supplies. See Thomas G Krattenmaker and Steven

Powerful buyers have an incentive to exploit public-market pricing mechanisms to create lower input prices for sales that are made off the exchange through direct transactions. A buyer with a significant enough market share for the gains from manipulation to outweigh the costs can take this step unilaterally.[45] Hence, even where a public market plays a substantial role in the setting of prices, any merger that creates a sufficient level of concentrated buyer power creates a significant risk of such conduct. Moreover, a merger or mergers that lead to a buying oligopsony will also carry the incentive to engage in joint manipulation to depress input market prices, and non-participants are unlikely to disrupt such manipulation. Raising prices is unlikely to be in the interests of any buyer.

Another risk that may be enhanced on the buying side is the potential for linked oligopoly.[46] Buyers purchasing inputs in multiple markets have strong incentives not to compete with each other in any particular market regardless of their relative positions in downstream markets. Buying competition will result in higher input costs. Allocating territory or suppliers, on the other hand, will allow each to engage in whatever upstream exploitive conduct it wishes. In addition, cross-market links provide a common defense against new entry. Incumbent buyers have a shared incentive to deny new buyers access to necessary inputs. Because of the limited capacity of arbitrage on the buying side, selective bidding up of prices can either deny the entrant resources or raise its costs. These same tactics can be used to discipline any buyer-side cartel cheater.

When the downstream market is also oligopolistic, there is a further incentive to keep prices of inputs down to increase the margins between input and output prices and potentially limit the supply of inputs available to competitors at the prevailing, depressed input market price. Reduced input availability in turn provides each oligopolist with a greater opportunity to raise price in the downstream market, confident in the knowledge that its few competitors are unlikely to bid up input prices (thus lowering their own margins) in order to reduce resale prices (which would further lower the

---

C Salop, 'Anticompetitive Exclusion: Raising Rivals' Costs to Achieve Power over Price' (1986) 96 *Yale Law Journal* 209, 214.

45 For example, Kraft allegedly found it profitable to manipulate the wheat futures market in order to drive down the prices it paid for direct purchases at its mill in Ohio. See Complaint, *Commodity Futures Trading Comm'n v Kraft Foods Group, Inc.*, No. 1:15-cv-02881 (N.D. Ill April 1, 2015), available at http://www.cftc.gov/idc/groups/public/@lrenforcementactions/documents/legalpleading/enfkraftcomplaint040115.pdf.

46 See Solomon, *supra* note 15.

total margin).[47] Thus, two aspects of a concentrated buyers' market make anticompetitive conduct especially likely: (1) the general incentive to create and exploit buyer power; and (2) less inherent capacity for self-correction of market distortions. An analysis of auctions provides further support for the conclusion that it is difficult to disrupt tacit buyer collusion.[48]

These observations have two implications for merger analysis. First, coordinated efforts to keep input prices down can encompass a large number of potential participants without serious risk of opportunistic defection. Moreover, price limitation efforts require very little coordination among buyers because each has an interest in the retention of low input prices.[49] Indeed, buyers can resume tacit collusion after any period of disruption.[50] This demonstrates the potential strength of the tit-for-tat strategy found to be the long-run best strategy in the prisoners' dilemma.[51] Therefore, the number of buyers needs to be kept at a level high enough to make tacit collusion less likely.

Second, even in the absence of overt or tacit coordination, a buyer with increased monopsony or oligopsony power will have an incentive to drive down input prices and increase the price spread between the input and output markets. And, in many situations, its downstream competitors will have little incentive to disrupt this unilateral conduct. To be sure, raising rivals' costs is a plausible strategy, but if the target responds in kind, the result will be that both firms have higher input costs than their competitors which could put both of them at a potentially significant competitive disadvantage.[52] Furthermore, new buyer-entrants would generally find it more attractive to enter a market with no currently operating buyer. New input suppliers would be quasi-captive, and the entrant would not risk

---

[47] See Richard J Sexton and Mingxia Zhang, 'An Assessment of the Impact of Food Industry Market Power on U.S. Consumers' (2001) 17 *Agribusiness* 59.

[48] See Meurer and Marshall, *supra* note 22; Asker, *supra* note 23.

[49] The settlements with various Silicon Valley high tech firms that terminated a series of agreements not to raid each other's employees by cold calling is illustrative of the possible limited cartel arrangements. See, eg, Final Judgment, *United States v Adobe Sys., Inc.*, No.1:10-cv-01629 (D.D.C. Mar. 18, 2011), available at https://www.justice.gov/atr/case-document/file/483426/download.

[50] See Cai, Stiegert and Koontz, *supra* note 25.

[51] See Robert Axelrod, *The Evolution of Cooperation* (Basic Books, New York 1984). For an analysis of the relevance of this work to antitrust, see Peter C Carstensen, 'While Antitrust Was Out to Lunch: Lessons from the 1980s for the Next Century of Enforcement' (1995) 48 *SMU Law Review* 1881, 1886–93.

[52] The logic arguing against such conduct may explain, in part, the Supreme Court's skeptical and restrictive standard for finding predatory buying. See *Weyerhaeuser Co. v Ross-Simmons Hardwood Lumber Co.*, 549 U.S. 312 (2007).

a competition with an established buyer. Competition, after all, leads to higher input prices and lower profit margins.

C. Upstream Effects

In standard seller-side merger analysis, the primary focus is on the immediate downstream market; if the merger results in higher output prices, the effects further downstream can be predicted. Although a merger creating buyer power can have an analogous effect (reducing prices to producers), explanations for lower input prices post-merger are more ambiguous. On the one hand, the 'cost savings' that result from lower input prices appear to promise an efficiency gain.[53] On the other hand, however, the capacity of an upstream supplier to provide further price discounts to a dominant buyer may reflect only that the supplier, given its increased volume of purchases resulting from the downstream merger, can now exert its own increased monopsony power against its vulnerable upstream input providers.

Thus, the adverse effects of the consolidation in grocery retailing or the manufacture of food products may be on farmers and ranchers who receive lower prices for their products,[54] even if they result in lower prices in public markets and contracts for supplies. Consolidation among downstream buyers not only creates more leverage over immediate suppliers but, as the downstream buyer consolidates its purchases, it derivatively endows its upstream supplier with greater buyer power.

An example of this phenomenon was the manipulation of cheese prices.[55] The direct goal of the manipulation was to lower the price of

---

[53] See Fee and Shawn, *supra* note 30 (although lowering of input costs was found to be clear evidence of increased efficiency, characterization may be weakened to the extent cost savings are the result of buyer exploitation of upstream suppliers). See *infra* text accompanying notes 95–103 (evaluating efficiency defenses). See also 2010 Guidelines, *supra* note 2, § 12 (excluding wealth transfers as part of an efficiency defense).

[54] See Einer Elhauge, 'Analysis of Proposed Nestlé-Ralston Purina Merger', Report prepared on behalf of the National Grange (2001) (on file with author) (showing how pet food merger would increase buyer power over animal byproducts, causing adverse consequences for livestock producers). Processors, especially meat packers, regularly assert that their buying practices are driven by the demands of powerful downstream customers. See generally Press Release, *supra* note 39 (offering evidence of the ways in which Walmart, the nation's largest food retailer, exploits its buyer power). See also *Knevelbaard Dairies v Kraft Foods, Inc.*, 232 F.3d 979 (9th Cir. 2000) (price manipulation in cheese market resulted in harm to dairy farmers).

[55] Willard F Mueller, Bruce W Marion, Maqbool H Sial and Frederick E Geithman (1996), 'Cheese Pricing: A Study of National Cheese Exchange',

cheese for the benefit of major cheese buyers. But when the price of cheese declined, cheese makers reduced the price paid for milk. The cheese makers may have absorbed a small amount of the price reduction, but the great bulk of this loss was passed on to the dairy farmers.[56] Obviously, further concentration on the cheese buying side of the market would increase the incentive and capacity to engage in such manipulation, further threatening the income of dairy farmers.

The point is that the negative effect of anticompetitive conduct on the buyer side of the market often occurs one or two stages up the supply chain from the party bearing the immediate impact of the lower price. A comprehensive evaluation of the potential competitive harms from a merger that increases buying power must analyze the potential for such effects.[57]

Such pressures also need to be carefully distinguished from transformations in the technology of production or methods of transaction that may both generate real cost savings and result in significant changes in demand for inputs. Only if the productive efficiency gains outweigh the losses from increased buyer power can a merger be said to increase static allocative efficiency. From a dynamic perspective, it is also essential to consider the impact of wealth transfers. Therefore, in most cases the aggregate static and dynamic adverse effects on immediate or more distant components of the supply chain will not be offset unless there is a *very substantial* concomitant gain to productive efficiency. Such gains are extremely implausible, however, in the case of relatively large firms operating at or above minimum efficient scale.

Finally, there is the risk of the waterbed effect examined in Chapter 4.[58] If the supply price is driven below a producer's average cost in one downstream market, the producer may be compelled to raise its prices to customers in other downstream markets. A merger that increases the risk of such buying practices harms both competitors of the merged buyer and buyers serving other markets. The harm to the competitive process

---

available at https://www.researchgate.net/publication/262698134_Cheese_Pricing_A_Study_of_National_Cheese_Exchange.

56 See *Knevelbaard Dairies*, 232 F.3d at 985. Dairy farms are, at least in the intermediate term, very price inelastic. A herd of cows, every day, seven days a week, produces a relatively set and stable quantity of milk, depending on the season. Until the herd is reduced or liquidated, the dairy farmer has to sell that output at whatever price the market provides.

57 The 2010 Horizontal Merger Guidelines indeed declare that, even if there is no expected change in the quantity of good purchased, a merger creating enhanced buyer power may still be objectionable. 2010 Guidelines, *supra* note 2, § 12.

58 See Chapter 3, text accompanying note 15.

is generalized because of the range of buyers that will face higher prices. When the merged entity would be a dominant buyer, merger analysis requires a greater willingness to identify and evaluate the potential harm to the broader competitive environment.

D. Summary

The foregoing factors make the potential risks of harm from buyer power qualitatively different from the risks of harm arising from seller power. It follows that different metrics should guide the analysis of buyer power issues when the result of a merger is an increase in buyer power, regardless of the merger's effect on seller power.

Not all mergers that significantly increase buyer power will necessarily lead to exploitive conduct. Buyers that recognize their long-term interests and the need to retain good input sources are unlikely to exploit their suppliers so much as to drive them from the market. But they still have an incentive to limit input costs, shift risks and expect dependent suppliers to assist in excluding new competitors of the buyer. Overall, as buyer power increases, producers become more dependent on the buyer's decisions and expectations. This dependency, even without excessive price reduction or risk transfer, undermines the overall dynamic of the market. The dependent producer ceases to be an independent economic actor; its interests instead align with those of its primary buyer. The producer becomes a de facto division of its buyer's enterprise. This consolidates the entire market process, making it more centralized and hindering new direct competition at one or both levels, as well as impairing the capacity of the producer to develop new products and serve additional markets.

IV. BASIC MERGER ANALYSIS OF BUYER POWER ISSUES

A. Competition Policy for Mergers Creating Buyer Power

There is no need to repeat here the analysis of Chapter 2 on policy, but it is useful to reiterate the central point that a competition policy whose goal is to preserve, protect and enhance the competitive process must be *as concerned* with the risks of competitive harm on the buying side of the market as on the selling side. This position contrasts with traditional notions of consumer welfare that tolerate increases in buyer power as long as the buyer shares some of the resulting producer exploitation with its downstream customers.

It is significant that American law has from its earliest days reflected a concern with the exploitation of producers.[59] The EU charter is explicit in its identification of harm to producers as a basis for action by the competition authorities.[60] Viewed more generally, all producers are, directly or indirectly, consumers. Therefore, ignoring their exploitation as producers undermines their capacity as consumers in the production chain. Additionally, competitive harms to producers are in general harder for the market process to overcome than exploitation by sellers.

Despite this logic, the history of competition law enforcement shows a strong focus on the seller side of transactions and only modest and intermittent attention to the buyer side. This is so partly because the public is more aware (and supportive) of market interventions that address unduly high prices to consumers than those that address unduly low prices paid to producers. A defendant in a buyer-side case can (and often does) argue that lower input prices help consumers. That argument, derived from the predominant consumer welfare rationale, leads to a bias in enforcement. Competition authorities frequently center their merger cases on the selling-side effects of a merger even if adverse buying-side effects are equally strong. In such cases, it is probably easier and politically more effective—given the overall history of merger case law—to focus on the selling side. But this focus risks reinforcing the short shrift given to buyer-side effects. The omission may also result in inadequate remedies.

Despite the political explanations for a predominant focus on the selling side, even in the presence of buying side issues, separate attention should nonetheless be given to the buying side. Moreover, as Chapters 3 and 4 have demonstrated, competitive effects on the buying side can and do

---

[59] See, eg, *United States v Trans-Missouri Freight Ass'n*, 166 U.S. 290 (1897) (condemning a railroad cartel whose prices affected producers); *Swift & Co. v United States*, 196 U.S. 375 (1905) (condemning a meat packer cartel that depressed prices paid for livestock). See also William K Jones, 'Concerted Refusals to Deal and the Producer Interest in Antitrust' (1989) 50 *Ohio State Law Journal* 73; Renata Hesse, Acting Assistant Attorney General, 'And Never the Twain Shall Meet? Connecting Popular and Professional Visions for Antitrust Enforcement', Remarks at 2016 Global Antitrust Enforcement Symposium (20 September 2016), available at https://www.justice.gov/opa/speech/acting-assistant-attorney-general-renata-hesse-antitrust-division-delivers-opening ('[A] merger that gives a company the power to depress wages or salaries or to reduce the prices it pays for inputs is illegal whether or not it also gives that company the power to increase prices downstream.').

[60] See Consolidated Version of the Treaty on the Functioning of the European Union, art 101(1), 9 May 2008, 2008 O.J. (C 115) 47 ('The following shall be prohibited . . .: concerted practices . . . which have as their object or effect . . . [to] directly or indirectly fix purchase . . . prices or any other trading conditions . . .').

emerge even when there is no cognizable selling-side violation. It follows that if competition policy has as its goal the protection of the competitive process, then it must consider the buying side effects of mergers with the same degree of care and analysis as the selling side.

B. Market Definition

Market definition is the first step in assessing the probability that increased buyer power might result from the merger of two firms that compete in an input market. By identifying the likely product and geographic dimensions of the market, it is possible to estimate the resulting increase in concentration. On the selling side, competing buyers might not compete at all in downstream markets either because they use the inputs in different outputs or because they sell their outputs in different geographic markets. Alternatively, the merged entities' outputs may be sold in workably competitive downstream markets that cause no post-merger concern. Neither possibility, however, affects the interest or potential ability of the combination to exercise buyer power. Rather, the focus of market definition has to be on the role of merging firms as buyers, and the 2010 Guidelines correctly separate the buying side of the merged firm in their analysis of market definition.[61]

Comprehensive merger analysis requires a separate inquiry into the competitive implications for downstream and upstream markets. For example, when two major foods producers combine, as Kraft and Heinz did in 2015, the analysis should focus not only on whether their products overlap (very little, as it turned out), but also on whether the inputs they use to produce those products come from the same or closely related markets. From the public reports about this merger, it is not clear whether any such inquiry was made. Yet Kraft already had been implicated in two cases involving market price manipulation related to inputs that it purchased.[62] Thus, the more important focus should have been on the potential for further buyer-side competitive risks.

---

[61] See 2010 Guidelines, *supra* note 2, § 12 ('In defining relevant markets, the [a]gencies focus on alternatives available to sellers in the face of a decrease in the price paid by a hypothetical monopsonist').

[62] See Complaint, *Commodity Futures Trading Comm'n v Kraft Foods Group, Inc.*, No. 1:15-cv-02881 (N.D. Ill. April 1, 2015), available at http://www.cftc.gov/idc/groups/public/@lrenforcementactions/documents/legalpleading/enfkraftcomplaint040115.pdf (alleged manipulation of wheat market prices); *Knevelbaard Dairies*, 232 F. 3d 979 (cheese market price manipulation).

1. Product market definition

When defining buyer-side product markets, it is important to determine what alternatives are open to the upstream producers of the combining parties. Both the product and geographic dimensions of the buying market must be investigated from the perspective of an upstream seller's search for alternative buyers. In some cases, suppliers may have the flexibility to produce different products that can be used as inputs in other downstream markets. For example, farmers can choose what crops to plant. Even if only one or two firms dominate the buying side for a particular crop, the capacity of any particular buyer to exploit farmers will be substantially constrained if the farmers can switch annually among different crops and sell them to different buyers.[63] Indeed, in this situation, forward contracting can help farmers avoid some of the risks of exploitation. But entry into alternative markets must be relatively easy and the potential buyers different from the merging entities. Logically, markets that can be easily entered should be included in the definition of the product market. Alternatively, lower barriers to 'exit' should be used to discount any inference of buyer power. Market analysis has to be sensitive to the alternative products and outlets available to upstream producers.

In other cases, the nature of the potential output can severely limit its alternate uses. A chicken house cannot easily be converted to the raising of turkeys and would be totally useless for dairy or beef cattle or hogs. In earlier time periods, American farmers often raised hogs and cattle as well as poultry using multipurpose facilities. Thus, the farmer had the capacity to increase or decrease production in any particular line depending upon the expected return. Today, agricultural production specialization in many lines, such as livestock and poultry, has virtually eliminated that switching capacity. Similarly, dairy farms are now specialized because of the need for separate facilities to process the milk. Historically, such farms included other livestock and even row crops in the mix of production. The trees and vines of fruit and nut producers also represent a long term, sunk investment. There is no alternative use for a cranberry bog or an apple orchard.

Milk illustrates the issue of differentiation in product market definition. Milk has a number of uses including cheese, ice cream, butter and fluid (drinking) milk. In the United States, government regulation dictates

---

[63] Michael K Adjemian et al, 'Thinning Markets in US Agriculture: What Are the Implications for Producers and Processors?' (US Department of Agriculture Economic Information Bulletin No. 148, 2016), available at http://www.ers.usda.gov/webdocs/publications/eib148/56926_eib148.pdf.

a higher price for fluid milk than for milk used for other purposes.[64] Naturally, dairy farmers want the higher price.[65] In this context, the relevant product market might be limited to milk that is eligible for inclusion in the fluid market. This differentiation in product market definition is a result of government policy. Institutional or market characteristics can also cause market segmentation in otherwise homogeneous product markets.

2. Geographic market definition

The challenge in geographic market definition is determining where producers can realistically look for alternative outlets for their goods. Some inputs must be produced close to the place of consumption for logistical reasons. For example, live poultry cannot be transported more than a relatively short distance, generally less than 100 miles, to a processing plant. Other types of livestock can travel greater distances before processing.[66] The earlier the stage of the production process, the more feasible it is to ship live animals long distances; they will then have time to recover from any bruising or other minor injuries.

Some high weight-to-value ratio inputs have relatively narrow geographic

---

[64] Grade A milk is suitable for use as fluid milk; Grade B milk is used only for manufactured products. Although almost all American dairy farms have invested in the facilities required for Grade A certification, only about one-third of all Grade A milk is sold as fluid milk. The vast majority of Grade A milk goes for other uses.

[65] The pricing of milk is a complex and convoluted process. See generally Bob Cropp and Ed Jesse, 'Basic Milk Pricing Concepts for Dairy Farmers' (University of Wisconsin-Extension Bulletin A3379, 2008), available at http://future.aae.wisc.edu/publications/a3379.pdf. For present purposes, it suffices that the farmer can share in the premium for fluid milk only if the farmer's milk is pooled in some way that makes it available for use as fluid milk. Hence, control of access to fluid processing plants can confer significant capacity to control milk supplies. See *In re Se. Milk Antitrust Litig.*, 555 F. Supp. 2d 934, 940–44 (E.D. Tenn. 2008) (upholding complaint alleging that large dairy cooperative exploited farmer members and non-members with respect to allocation of premiums paid for fluid milk).

[66] In refusing to challenge a merger between the only two major hog processors in the southeast, the Department of Justice claimed that there was no risk to hog raisers because mature hogs could be shipped to distant slaughter facilities. Those knowledgeable in the business regarded this claim as highly questionable. In the long run, the risks of weight loss and death, as well as the high cost of long distance shipping of live animals, made this an impractical option for a large-scale hog producer in the region. See Press Release, US Department of Justice, 'Statement of the Antitrust Division on its Decision to Close Its Investigation of Smithfield, Inc.'s Acquisition of Premium Standard Farms Inc.' (4 May 2007), available at https://www.justice.gov/archive/atr/public/press_releases/2007/223077.htm.

markets, but other products can be shipped long distances if the cost of shipping is a relatively small component of total cost. Centralized production can provide a cost advantage if there are economies of scale in the production process. Products with a low weight-to-value ratio that are consumed in relatively low volumes can economically be transported and sold into a global market.

In some instances, government inspection and certification requirements complicate geographic market definition. For example, some countries prohibit the sale of genetically modified crops and animals. And even when saleable, they must often be specially approved and certified for sale in the consuming country. The cost, burden and delays inherent in such registration may effectively limit the market in which the input can be sold even in the absence of physical barriers.[67]

3. Assessing the validity of a proposed market

In defining selling markets, merger analysis has often relied on the 'SSNIP' test—whether a firm controlling a set of products in a geographic market could impose a 'small but significant and nontransitory increase in price' without a major loss in volume of sales. Its function is to determine whether a change in the structure of a market as defined creates a risk of competitive harm. A comparable test for the buying side similarly needs to identify actual buyer power. Applying seller-side metrics can result in misleading conclusions. For example, if a buyer can obtain part of its input from an out-of-market source with relatively high price elasticity,[68] then the buyer can exercise power over a set of sellers in the target market even if those sellers would reduce output substantially.[69] On the selling side, such a reduction in sales would demonstrate that some larger market must exist because the seller could not sustain itself with such a limited volume, but on the buying side such a projected response might still indicate buyer power. A buyer in such a situation would compare the cost savings from reducing prices for the input in the target market, even if it results in a much lower volume, with the additional cost of replacing the

---

[67] For example, farmers lost large foreign markets when genetically modified genes were found in American rice. See *In re Genetically Modified Rice Litig.*, 764 F.3d 864 (8th Cir. 2014).

[68] High price elasticity of supply implies that the buyer can obtain any additional supplies from that market if its exploitation of the target market were to result in a substantial decline in production.

[69] This is consistent with the wording of the 2010 Guidelines, *supra* note 2, §12 ('The Agencies do not view a short-run reduction in the quantity purchased as the only, or best, indicator of whether a merger enhances buyer market power').

lost volume from an out-of-market source. Thus, when buyers can procure inputs from several geographically distinct markets, the interaction among these markets must be part of the analysis of the potential for exploitive or exclusionary conduct in each market. In short, the buying side product market must be carefully defined in terms of the economic realities facing producers—including the potential that linking two or more buying markets will result in an increase in a dominant buyer's ability to treat producers in the two markets differently.[70]

In sum, buyer-side market definition is roughly analogous to that on the seller-side. But both the product and geographic dimensions can be and often are quite different from the analogous downstream markets. As a result, the evaluation of a merger must focus on input rather than output markets, but even more importantly must focus on where sellers can sell and not where buyers might buy. Hence, the resulting markets may be larger or smaller geographically than the selling side, but in many instances are likely to have narrower product dimensions.

C. Triggers for Investigation and Potential Liability

1. Post-merger market structure and changes in structure

Every buyer of any size has some power (especially in a one-to-one market context) to bargain over prices and other conditions with its input suppliers. The larger the buyer the greater its capacity and incentive to bargain, both because the high total cost of the input makes bargaining rational and because, as a larger entity, it may have the financial capacity to invest in better information about available sources and prices. A small buyer buying even costly inputs may lack the resources to do a similar search. Therefore we must ask: at what point is increased buyer power likely to substantially lessen competition?

The capacity to choose among potential suppliers can create a great deal of power even when a buyer's market share is modest by seller-side metrics.[71] In the United Kingdom, a single firm's market share of less than ten percent of some classes of groceries has produced significant buyer

---

[70] This analysis is analogous to the seller side market definition that focuses on the potential for price discrimination. See 2010 Guidelines, *supra* note 2, § 4.1.4.

[71] The Blair-Harrison Index of Buyer Power predicts that when the elasticity of supply and fringe demand equal one, a firm buying ten percent of the volume in a product market can impose a five percent decrease in its suppliers' prices. Roger D Blair and Jeffrey L Harrison, *Monopsony: Antitrust Law and Economics* (Princeton University Press, Princeton 1993) 59.

power effects.[72] In *Toys 'R' Us*, approximately 20 percent of the national market for toys allowed the firm to impose anticompetitive restraints on its suppliers.[73] Although its market share is not reported, it is unlikely that Broadway-Hale dominated the retail appliance market in California or nationally, but it still had the power to coerce its suppliers into agreeing to cut off Klors.[74] These cases suggest that unilateral effects are possible from mergers resulting in control of ten to 20 percent of the buying market. The EU surveyed manufacturers of consumer products in an effort to define the market share of a product line that would confer significant buyer power on a retailer. The survey found that if a retailer handled a little over 20 percent of the commodity in any market, it was likely to have significant buyer power.[75] The EU has objected to at least two other major retail mergers based on buyer power concerns.[76]

Economies and diseconomies in production explain why a buyer in the retail grocery business holding as little as a ten percent market share can have significant buyer power.[77] If two of those buyers combine, their combined purchases become significantly more important to the producer, and the producer becomes much more dependent on the merged buyer's continued patronage.[78] The extent of that dependency (and the extent of the combined buyer's market power) will be a function of the diseconomies that might result from a reduction in output as well as the extent to which the producer can find other outlets for its products. This is the converse of the committed and uncommitted entrant analysis in seller-side

---

[72] Paul Dobson, 'Exploiting Buyer Power: Lessons from the British Grocery Trade' (2005) 72 *Antitrust Law Journal* 529, 535. One might also ask whether buyer power exists at even smaller market shares in markets with smaller sales volume. This question ought to be addressed in rethinking the merger guidelines, but to date it has received no noticeable attention.

[73] *Toys 'R' Us v FTC*, 221 F.3d 928 (7th Cir. 2000).

[74] *Klors, Inc. v Broadway-Hale Stores, Inc.*, 359 U.S. 207 (1959).

[75] See Case No IV/M.1221, *Rewe/Meinl*, 1999 O.J. (L 274) 1, ¶ 101 ('on average 22% of turnover is the figure above which a customer can be replaced only at the cost of very heavy financial losses, if at all').

[76] See Case IV/M.748, *Kesko/Tuko*, 1997 O.J. (L 110) 53; Case COMP/M.1684, *Carrefour/Promodes*, 2000 O.J. (C 164) 5.

[77] The lack of alternative outlets either in the market as a whole or in a regional segment important to achieving efficient use of national advertising makes retail buyer power analysis an especially important focal point. See *supra* text accompanying notes 38–9.

[78] This effect is most obvious in contexts such as grocery retailing, where the seller is already selling to other major outlets. The lost sales cannot easily or readily be recouped by adding other outlets. But any specialized input provider may face a similar problem if two of its major customers combine.

merger evaluation,[79] but it is framed in terms of committed and uncommitted buyers. This raises a host of questions specific to the likely impact of the merged firm as a larger volume buyer of an input.

Buyer power may also arise at relatively low market shares when a buyer takes all or most of the output of a seller and the merger eliminates the next-best alternative outlet for the seller's products.[80] Switching to yet another buyer because the original buyer and the next-best alternative have combined would involve tremendous transition costs and risks. If the switch does not work out, the seller may be without any market for its output. A regular customer can impose great damage on a supplier by refusing to deal or imposing lower prices, especially as the number of alternative outlets declines.[81] In these contexts, mergers among such buyers will likely reduce the power of all sellers in the market through the reduction in alternative outlets. Mergers that would result in a buyer that controls more than 15 to 20 percent of an input market merit a focused review with respect to potential unilateral effects. As Blair and Harrison have shown, the relative levels of elasticity of both the supply and demand side very much affect the level of power that will result.[82]

Supply-side market structure may produce countervailing bargaining power, but such power may result in higher consumer prices as the concentrated buyers and concentrated sellers collectively raise input prices and find ways to share the overcharge even if the downstream market appears competitive.[83] Despite the proclivity of both American and EU enforcers to justify merger approvals on the grounds that buyer power will act as

---

[79] See '2010 Guidelines', *supra* note 2, at 15–16 (discussing 'rapid entrants') and 27–9 (discussing entry conditions).

[80] This explains in part why the Antitrust Division of the US Department of Justice challenged mergers among health insurers whose market shares were below the safe harbor levels set by the Division's own guidelines set for health-care buying groups. See Mark J Botti (19 April 2007), 'Observations on and from the Antitrust Division Buyer-Side Cases: How Can "Lower" Prices Violate the Antitrust Laws?', available at http://www.cybermanual.com/observations-on-and-from-the-antitrust-divisions-buyer-side.html.

[81] See Sandford, *supra* note 38.

[82] Blair and Harrison, *supra* note 71, at 36–42. See also Sexton and Zhang, *supra* note 47.

[83] See Chris Doyle and Martijn A Han, 'Expropriating Monopoly Rents through Stable Buyer Groups' (Amsterdam Centre for Law and Economics Working Paper No. 2009-03, 2009). For an example of how this might work, see *NicSand, Inc. v 3M Co.*, 507 F.3d 442 (6th Cir. 2007) (en banc) (producer eliminated competitor in supply market and then retailers raised prices to consumers once competition in supply was eliminated).

a constraint on seller power,[84] the effect is to create increasingly concentrated buyer and seller markets with the resulting risks of direct harm to consumers and upstream producers.

Todd[85] teaches that a dispersed set of buyers is more likely to find it rational to coordinate their buying activities than a dispersed set of sellers would be to coordinate their sales. Therefore, buyer markets are more at risk for coordinated effects at lower levels of concentration than would be necessary in seller markets. In concrete terms, a reduction in the number of substantial buyers from six to five should be a cause for concern. There should be even greater concern if the number of major buyers is fewer than five. Thus, if a market's Herfindahl-Hirschman Index (HHI) approaches 1600, there should be careful review of any merger that increases the HHI by 100 or more.[86]

This is not to say that all mergers that result in the control of 15 percent or more of an input market should be condemned. But any such merger requires a more searching investigation. If the post-merger HHI market exceeds 2000, and the change in HHI exceeds 100, there should be a rebuttable presumption that the merger is illegal.[87] Current seller-side merger analysis requires substantially higher concentration levels.[88] A strong case can be made that mergers below that selling-side range should be presumed illegal with relatively limited defenses.[89] The central point here

---

84 See 2010 Guidelines, *supra* note 2, § 8. EU decisions allowing mergers based, in part, on the existence of powerful buyers include Case IV/M.877, *Boeing/McDonnell Douglas*, 1997 C (97) 2598 final; Case Comp. /M.4300, *Philips/Intermagnetics*, 2007 O.J. (C 123) 1; Case IV/M.1225, *Enso/Stora*, 1999 O.J. (L 254) 9. An Irish decision explicitly overturned the rejection of a merger based on the existence of powerful buyers. *Rye Invs. Ltd. v Competition Auth.* [2009] I.E.H.C. 140. A German decision permitted the merger of Permaswage Holding SAS and Precision Castparts Corp., which created a dominant supplier, in part to counterbalance the power of buyers. See Robert SK Bell et al, 'The Sky's the Limit! German Federal Cartel Office Clears U.S.-French Merger of Component Suppliers to the Aerospace Industry' (9 December 2013) *Lexology*, available at http://www.lexology.com/library/detail.aspx?g=343ae535-3066-43cb-ad29-df9dbe77550e.

85 *Todd v Exxon Corp.*, 275 F.3d 191 (2nd Cir. 2001).

86 The logic is that a merger that generates a 100-point change is very likely to involve firms with a combined market share exceeding 15 percent. If the HHI moves above 1600, a merger is likely to leave six or fewer major buyers in the market.

87 A market with a post-merger HHI of 2000 or more would probably have five or fewer substantial firms.

88 See, eg, 2010 Guidelines, *supra* note 2, § 5.3 (presumptive illegality arises only if the post-merger HHI is above 2500 and the HHI change is above 100).

89 See Peter C Carstensen, 'The *Philadelphia National Bank* Presumption: Merger Analysis in a Dynamic Economy' (2015) 80 *Antitrust Law Journal* 219.

is that review of the merits of a merger having buyer-side impact should occur at lower increases to concentration than are currently tolerated on the selling side.

2. Additional factors

Beyond basic market structure, there are other objective market factors that are relevant to an assessment of the risks that any merger presents. There is, however, a great danger in using these factors to make ad hoc judgements about specific cases rather than incorporating them into a well-conceived and consistent analysis of mergers. Retrospective studies of the effects of mergers demonstrate that American enforcement has failed to identify (or even challenge) a number of mergers with significant adverse price effects on the selling side.[90] An apparently significant source of error was the willingness of regulators to use additional factors to justify approving a merger that probably should not have been allowed.[91] The counterargument is that focus on market structure alone can yield a non-trivial number of false positives, in which a merger would not result in higher prices or other evidence of harm to competition but is nevertheless condemned.[92] However, there is at best little risk of serious harm to competition, efficiency or the dynamics of markets from over-enforcement of merger law. But the consequences of under-enforcement are a long-run distortion of market structure that can harm efficiency, dynamics and basic competition for decades or longer. Hence, merger law enforcement should concern itself primarily with avoiding under-enforcement. Still, to reduce the potential for false positives it is reasonable to look at two additional objective market factors.

---

[90] John E Kwoka, Jr, *Mergers, Merger Control, and Remedies: A Retrospective Analysis of U.S. Policy* (MIT Press, Cambridge, MA 2015).

[91] *Ibid* at 158–9.

[92] John E Kwoka, Jr and Chengyan Gu, 'Predicting Merger Outcomes: The Accuracy of Stock Market Event Studies, Market Structure Characteristics, and Agency Decisions' (2015) 58 *Journal of Law and Economics* 519 (concluding that agency decisions were much less accurate than the market-structure approach at identifying risky mergers, but better than the market-structure approach at identifying mergers that did not increase prices). Some have argued that in the context of seller mergers the risk of false positives is not serious because the efficiency costs are minimal. See Carstensen, *supra* note 89. Indeed, Kwoka has now changed his view and regards structural change as the primary focal point for determining whether a merger should be challenged. See John E Kwoka, Jr, 'The Structural Presumption and the Safe Harbor in Merger Review: False Positives, or Unwarranted Concerns' (Northeastern University, Department of Economics Working Paper, 2016), available at http://ssrn.com/abstract=2782152.

One of the most important factors in assessing the risk whether buyer power can create significant adverse competitive effects is the elasticity of supply. If suppliers are able to exit the market or reduce production easily and with little or no economic loss (that is, with low switching costs), then it is unlikely that even a dominant buyer will be able to exercise much power. Suppliers that find the lower price attractive will respond, while others will turn to their next-best alternative.

It is not always easy to tell, in short time periods, whether supply is price elastic. But investigators can learn a good deal from interviewing producers as well as from looking at production history over time in response to changing prices. When there is strong evidence of significant elasticity, even a merger that leads to substantially concentrated buyer power probably does not create significant risks of harm to the competitive process.

Even if the market definition is relatively clear on the buying side, supply-side exit barriers may be low. If so, it is unlikely that a buyer would be able to exploit its market power either to exploit or exclude. The challenge here is finding convincing proof of the ability to exit. The existence of upstream suppliers with few or no sunk costs constitutes another structural factor that limits the power of a buyer. This suggests that the relevant market for analysis encompasses the full range of potential outputs from the sellers' productive capacity. Hence, ease of entry and exit may affect the determination of the appropriate market definition for buyer power analysis. A buyer with dominance in the downstream market may have more incentive to create barriers to entry for competitors.[93] It may share some of its anticipated gains with its suppliers in return for exclusive dealing, to the detriment of one or more competitors. The changed buying structure might be relevant to an assessment of downstream competitive risks even if there is no significant risk of exploitation of upstream producers.

Another market factor is buying-side elasticity. For example, if slightly lower prices would induce marginal buyers to substantially increase their purchases of an upstream good, a dominant buyer would not be able to force input prices down or impose other upstream burdens without losing substantial volume. This situation might occur if the input is one of several alternatives of equivalent utility. Buyers could switch among the inputs depending on price.[94] The input markets would be distinct but not significantly differentiated from the buying side because buyers could and

[93] The car service Uber, for example, has negotiated statutory protections for its operation that impose significant costs on new entrants. See Wisconsin Statute § 440.48(c)1 (2015) (requiring $1 million in liability insurance).

[94] Fish oil and lysine involve different production processes but are substitutes in consumption for many uses. If a dominant buyer of fish oil forced the price

would quickly substitute between alternative inputs based on their relative price.

However, a buyer may change its purchasing strategy in response to a change in the percentage of the total input it buys. A buyer with a large market share may engage in exploitive or exclusionary practices that were not available when suppliers had more options even if there are alternative buyers available. When the loss of any one customer is of less significance to the producer's total sales, it has more freedom of action. When a single customer takes a great deal, the switching costs are likely to be much larger and so more likely to inhibit the producer from resisting a dominant buyer's demands, especially those that do not go directly to price.

The foregoing discussion of elasticities highlights the relevance of a deeper analysis of initial structural inferences. Basic structural change in the buying market should be the primary focus of analysis. Enforcement authorities should take care to avoid over-emphasizing additional market factors because they may result in a decision to forgo enforcement action when a false negative (under-enforcement) might result in long-term harm to the competitive process. Clear evidence should be required to support any claim based on one or more of these factors. It is also important to consider whether the changed buying structure might open the way to future strategic conduct by the merged buyer that could change the elasticity of either supply or demand.[95]

D. Defenses to Merger Enforcement

1. Efficiency claims

Contemporary merger policy assumes that most mergers yield real efficiency gains to the parties. This premise is empirically questionable and conceptually ambiguous in many cases.[96] But given its significance in actual enforcement decisions involving the seller side, it is important to define carefully the kinds of efficiencies that buying-side mergers might legitimately claim. These efficiencies can arise from transactional cost savings or, in some circumstances, economies of scale or scope that

---

down significantly, lysine buyers would be likely to switch, increasing the demand for fish oil.

[95] For example, a buyer might insist on long-term contracts, thus locking up supply and committing the supplier to provide the supply on a set basis.

[96] FM Scherer, 'Some Principles for Post-Chicago Antitrust Analysis' (2001) 52 *Case Western Reserve Law Review* 5, 11–22. See also Thomas J Horton, 'Efficiencies and Antitrust Reconsidered: An Evolutionary Perspective' (2015) 60 *Antitrust Bulletin* 168.

upstream suppliers might achieve and share given a large assured volume of business.

Merely transferring producer surplus to buyers is not an efficiency gain. The 2010 Guidelines' position suggests that any buyer gains be disaggregated to identify the functional cause for a lower price.[97] A transfer based on enhanced buyer power does not change any of the production or transaction costs involved in producing or supplying the input. However, when the 'transfer' reflects a reduction in a previously supra-competitive price charged by the supplier, the fact that in some sense this is only a wealth transfer should not preclude entirely viewing such an outcome as a positive justification for the merger.[98]

The potential economies resulting from combinations that increase buyer-side concentration must be balanced against the risks of adverse effects. An old saying in merger analysis is that *efficiencies are easy to claim, but hard to prove*. Few efficiencies are unique to a particular firm or specific market structure. For the great majority there are, to paraphrase Mao, 'many roads' to efficiency, especially when each of the combining firms is a multi-plant operation enjoying most or all of the available economies of scale.[99] There is unlikely to be any appreciable production cost savings resulting from the combination of such firms. It is equally doubtful that the combination of such buyers alone would lead to significantly reduced input costs. Absent evidence of seller cartelization or other market power on the selling side, there would be no reason to believe that seller prices had been excessive. Therefore, the most likely explanation for any putative 'efficiency' gains from reduced input prices is the exploitation of buyer power. It bears emphasis that a buyer has no incentive to share any of those gains with a downstream customer unless the downstream

---

97 See 2010 Guidelines, *supra* note 2, § 12 ('Example 24: Merging Firms A and B are the only two buyers in the relevant geographic market for an agricultural product. Their merger will enhance buyer power and depress the price paid to farmers for this product, causing a transfer of wealth from farmers to the merged firm and inefficiently reducing supply. These effects can arise even if the merger will not lead to any increase in the price charged by the merged firm for its output.').

98 These mergers raise complex questions because price reductions to the favored buyer may increase prices to the supplier's other customers. See *supra* text accompanying notes 33–4.

99 In the beef and pork industries, a rough estimate is that eight to ten firms each operating two or three plants could operate at or above minimum efficient scale. Peter C Carstensen, 'Concentration and the Destruction of Competition in Agricultural Markets: The Case for Change in Public Policy' 2000 *Wisconsin Law Review* 531, 537.

customer has its own buyer power that drives the upstream market exploitation.

Another difficulty with contemporary efficiency analysis in competition policy is its focus on cost savings to the parties without consideration of the extent to which those costs are externalized to other participants in the economic process. Sometimes the imputed cost of such 'shadow work'[100] is less than the costs previously incurred by the enterprise that provided those goods or services. But actions such as the closing of a number of outlets by a retailer can impose more costs overall on customers who must then expend more resources getting to remaining locations than the retailer saved in closing those outlets. The cost savings to the retailer measure only the gain accruing to it; they do not measure net cost savings because the newly created costs are ignored.

Undoubtedly some mergers will both generate efficiency gains and increase buyer power. It is important to determine whether such a combination will advance static allocative efficiency and the long-run need for dynamic efficiency. The famous Williamson tradeoff argument suggests that there is a real possibility of gain.[101] Some criticize Williamson's model because it focuses on the downstream markets in which goods are sold. Richard Sexton and Mingxia Zhang have examined the tradeoff between increased monopsony power and increased efficiency in production.[102] They conclude that the balance tips strongly against a net allocative efficiency gain from such combinations if the firm has both buyer and seller power unless the productive efficiency gain is very large. Indeed, from a competitive process perspective, both consumers and producers are at risk of exploitation.[103] The temptation to use combined market power is likely to overwhelm the incentives to reduce price and increase output that arise from any realized

---

[100] See Craig Lambert, *Shadow Work* (Counterpoint, Berkeley, CA 2015) (describing ways in which individuals are obliged to provide services that were once provided to them, but without any coherent economic analysis of the tradeoff between the cost of external production and the imputed cost to the individual providing the same service).

[101] See Oliver Williamson, 'Economies as an Antitrust Defense: The Welfare Trade-Offs' (1968) 58 *American Economic Review* 18. For an application of the Williamson analysis to buyer side mergers, see Roger Blair, 'Merger to Monopsony: An Efficiencies Defense' (2010) 55 *Antitrust Bulletin* 689.

[102] Sexton and Zhang, *supra* note 47. See also Richard T Rogers and Richard J Sexton, 'Assessing the Importance of Oligopsony Power in Agricultural Markets' (1994) 76 *American Journal of Agricultural Economics* 1143.

[103] Sexton and Zhang, *supra* note 47. See also Catherine C de Fontenay and Joshua S Gans, 'Can Vertical Integration by a Monopsonist Harm Consumer Welfare?' (2004) 22 *International Journal of Industrial Organization* 821.

productive efficiencies. This again suggests the need for a more complete analysis of mergers that may increase power in both buying and selling markets. In combination the adverse effects can be much more significant than would appear if the investigation focused only on one side or the other.

If the firm has buyer power but not seller power, the Sexton-Zhang model shows that for static tradeoffs the deadweight loss resulting from increased monopsony power can be offset by relatively modest levels of productive efficiency gain. But the model also shows that there is a substantial wealth transfer from upstream producers to the buyer. In dynamic terms, the transfer would create a strong disincentive for new producers to enter the market or existing producers to innovate within it. If the integrity of the competitive process is the fundamental goal, this exploitation of buyer power is anticompetitive in the long run.

Thus, real efficiency gains need to be carefully distinguished from mere wealth transfers when both result from the exercise of monopsony power. Because monopsony power can force down the price of inputs, which effects a wealth transfer from the upstream producer to the downstream buyer, the gain to the buyer is at best pecuniary. It does not affect the social costs of production. Upon closer examination, much of the gain that merging parties claim will arise from their combination is nothing more than a wealth transfer, which should not be accepted as an efficiency justification for the merger. In fact, such gains provide direct evidence that the merger will result in buyer power that the merged entity intends to exploit.

Smaller national markets face more intractable problems when the combining entities would achieve both buying-side efficiencies and significant buyer power. Scale is important in some kinds of production and distribution. If constrained to deal only with dominant buyers, input suppliers will necessarily face real risks of exploitation. As Chapter 6 has shown, the regulation of such conduct is at best difficult and its effectiveness problematic. Nevertheless, the efficiency gains may warrant substantially greater tolerance for consolidation, but with a thoughtful and creative response to the resulting buyer power. This is a major challenge for competition authorities.

2. Failing firm defense

Any transaction involving a failing firm should be examined from both seller and buyer perspectives. Particularly important is whether the purchase of the firm by an alternative buyer would avoid competitive risks.[104]

---

[104] See generally Max Huffman, 'Worlds in Collision: Antitrust Review of Bankruptcy Asset Sales' (2015) 60 *Villanova Law Review* 839 (providing a general analysis of the role of competition policy considerations in bankruptcy).

For example, Smithfield was allowed to buy Farmland's pork processing operations following Farmland's bankruptcy.[105] In allowing the transaction, the Antitrust Division focused on the downstream effects in pork markets.[106] It failed to consider the upstream implications for regional hog producers, especially lower volume producers with limited geographic mobility. If the adverse impact on those sellers had been considered, a bidder with no hog processing operations would clearly have been more desirable.

3. Seller power

Some argue that a buyer merger might create countervailing power, in the sense that Galbraith used the term, against the power of dominant sellers. As the foregoing analysis has shown, this is a tenuous claim. Buyers, as deciders, have the capacity to induce new entry or otherwise stimulate competition in supply markets. Increased concentration on the buying side is reflected upstream, often increasing concentration further up the input chain. Some empirical data support the contention that increased buyer power can ameliorate the exercise of seller power in concentrated markets,[107] but the better strategy would be for existing buyers to find other means of inducing increased supplier competition. Only if concentration in the input market is driven by some inherent technological factors would an offsetting buyer power defense be plausible.[108] Even then, there would be a dynamic cost in the loss of competition and innovation that comes from having a workably competitive market.[109]

---

[105] See 'Smithfield is Buying Farmland Foods' *Pork Network* (17 January 2011), available at http://www.porknetwork.com/pork-news/smithfield-is-buying-farmland-foods-113895039.html.

[106] Chris Flores, 'Smithfield Foods to Acquire Farmland Industries' Pork Business' *Daily Press* (Newport News) (14 October 2003), available at http://articles.dailypress.com/2003-10-14/business/0310140173_1_smithfield-foods-farmland-foods-pork-processor.

[107] See Sugato Bhattacharyya and Amrita Nain, 'Horizontal Acquisitions and Buying Power: A Product Market Analysis' (2011) 99 *Journal of Financial Economics* 97; Fee and Shawn, *supra* note 30.

[108] Tom Campbell and several economists debated the merits of merger to monopsony as a response to seller monopoly. The responses seem more persuasive. See Tom Campbell, 'Bilateral Monopoly in Mergers' (2007) 74 *Antitrust Law Journal* 521; Tom Campbell, 'Bilateral Monopoly: Further Comment' (2008) 75 *Antitrust Law Journal* 647; Jonathan Baker, Joseph Farrell and Carl Shapiro, 'Merger to Monopoly to Serve a Single Buyer: Comment (on Tom Campbell)' (2008) 75 *Antitrust Law Journal* 637.

[109] In general, only those mergers that marginally increase concentration on the selling side should be permitted to counteract dominant buyers. Similar

E. Remedies

The ideal remedy in merger cases is to block the merger itself. This leaves the market as is, without modification. In the United States, however, the contemporary response is not to block mergers, but only to require divestiture of those elements of the enterprise that raise significant competitive concerns. This type of relief has proven ineffective in controlling adverse downstream effects[110] and is equally unlikely to prove effective in addressing buyer-side issues. Moreover, in selling-side cases, the relief should also take account of the impact on the buying side of the market.

The EU and, to a slightly lesser degree, the United States also employ conduct remedies. As a condition of merger approval, the combining parties must agree to take specific actions to ensure that the conduct of the combined entity does not inflict competitive harm. The outcomes have not been very positive in the United States, where post hoc evaluations demonstrate the ineffectiveness of such remedies.[111] Absent direct regulation of prices and other contract terms, the most likely result of allowing mergers subject only to conduct control is both exploitation and exclusion that competition enforcement agencies will not be able to effectively remedy. This poses a serious dilemma for enforcement agencies. If reorganizing the buying process would produce significant long-run gains, then solutions other than merger or a consolidated buying group will emerge over time. The long-run cost of obtaining an immediate efficiency gain by creating a market structure of monopsony or oligopsony is almost certain to exceed the value of the short-run gain. Hence, even when the immediate gains appear significant, there is a strong case to block any merger that would create substantial, long-term buyer power.

---

restraint should be applied to the use of seller power as a defense to a buyer-side merger. Some modest increase in concentration might produce the incentives and resources to overcome a supply oligopoly.

110 Kwoka, *supra* note 90, at 134–41.

111 *Ibid.* In smaller economies there may be significant efficiency gains from mergers that also create significant buyer power. As shown in Chapter 6, direct regulation of buyer power is very difficult. However, agencies can reduce buyer power by restricting the methods of purchase to minimize exploitation (no long-term contracts, purchases by tender only) and to limit the risks of exclusion (no most favored nation clauses, no exclusive dealing) to keep the barriers to entry as low as possible.

F. A Framework for Analysis

The appropriate framework for analysis of mergers where buyer power is a concern mirrors traditional seller-side merger analysis but must reflect the buyer-side metrics and concerns. The first step is to define the market and measure the share of each input market that the merged buyer will take. Further analysis is required if (1) the merger results in an increase in HHI of 100 or more; (2) the merged firms' share of the input market exceeds 15 percent; and (3) the post-merger HHI for the market exceeds 1600. If the resulting market share exceeds 20 percent and the post-merger HHI is above 2000, a presumption should arise that the merger is likely to have adverse competitive effects in the buying market. The parties can, of course, rebut that presumption by producing credible evidence that such adverse effects are unlikely.[112]

If the range is between 15 and 20 percent, or if the change in the HHI is below 100 points, careful analysis is necessary to determine whether the proposed merger will cause a change in the structure of the buying market that is likely to have adverse effects sufficient to warrant regulatory challenge. The burden is on the agency to demonstrate a cognizable risk to competition.

A close and critical analysis of the expectations of the merged enterprise with respect to buying-side cost savings may shed light on whether the merger will create undue buyer power. If there are no readily apparent transactional gains or economies of scale or scope, then the merged entity may expect to use its post-merger enhanced buyer power to directly force down input prices. The analysis then needs to look critically at ability of sellers to reduce prices in such cases.

Bhattacharyya and Nain report that when input producers are concentrated, buyers are able to force down prices even in the absence of evidence that producers paid less for their own inputs except labor.[113] The implication is that the increased buyer power resulted in countervailing bargaining power that moved prices closer to a competitive

---

[112] Such claims would be analogous to those in *United States v Gen. Dynamics*, 415 U.S. 486 (1974) (arguing that there would be no competitive effect on the selling market because the acquired firm had committed almost all of its capacity to long-term contracts and had no capacity to compete for new sales). See Carstensen, *supra* note 89, at 232–4.

[113] Bhattacharyya and Nain, *supra* note 107, at 108. Moreover, there were statistically significant negative changes in wages for workers in the supply industry; a classic example of upstream input suppliers being forced to accept lower prices as a result of indirect buyer power. *Ibid* at 109.

level without significant upstream effects. But within their sample was a good deal of heterogeneity, reflected in the relatively low power of the equations to explain observed variances.[114] Further transaction-specific inquiries are warranted in such cases to ascertain whether the change in downstream buyer power will increase the buying power of an upstream supplier over its own input suppliers. The indirect competitive effects of a merger should be prominent in the examination of the merits of the transaction. It is conceivable that the expected gains of the downstream buyer could come largely or exclusively from creating more buyer power in its suppliers and compelling them to exploit further their upstream input sources.

V. ENFORCEMENT OF MERGER LAW IN BUYER POWER CASES

A. The United States

Even though the United States has the largest number of challenges to mergers based exclusively or primarily on buyer-side market effects, there are not many. The earliest challenge that directly fits this category involved the production of lubricating oil in Pennsylvania. The two dominant buyers proposed a merger that would have resulted in a market share for the combined entity of 54 percent of crude oil purchases.[115] Their share in the overall selling market for lubricating oil was not substantial, although there was some product differentiation with respect to Pennsylvania oil. Because the merger would have adversely affected producers whose investments were fixed and immobile, the court enjoined the merger.[116]

Another example of a pure buyer-side case was Cargill's acquisition of the grain-marketing division of Continental Grain.[117] The Antitrust Division did not allege downstream effects from the merger, but still negotiated a partial divestiture that it believed was necessary to preserve competition on the buying side in various regions and would enhance the

---

114 *Ibid* at 108–09 (the R^2 was 0.33, which indicates that much of the observed variance was unexplained).

115 *United States v Pennzoil Co.*, 252 F. Supp. 962 (W.D. Pa. 1965).

116 *Ibid* at 983 (granting preliminary injunction).

117 Final Judgment, *United States v Cargill Inc.*, No. 99-1875 (D.D.C. June 29, 2000), available at http://www.justice.gov/atr/case-document/final-judgment-37.

capacity of a smaller global exporter to buy and trade in the American grain market.[118]

When JBS Swift proposed to acquire National Beef, a merger that would have combined the second and fourth largest beef packers in an already concentrated market, the government suit focused on the foreclosure effects on the buying side even though many of the producers operated large feedlots that handled thousands of head of cattle.[119] The complaint also identified a selling market for boxed beef that would potentially also be harmed, but the focus was on the increased buyer power and the harms to competition that could result.[120] The parties abandoned the merger following the filing of the lawsuit.

At least two health insurance mergers were subject to settlements that included some focus on buyer power. Health insurers in the United States minimize their direct costs by entering into agreements with doctors and hospitals that control where insured patients can be treated. Hence, combinations of insurers with substantial market shares result in significant buyer power over both doctor and hospital services. In both the acquisition of Prudential's healthcare operation in Texas[121] and the United Health-Sierra merger in Nevada,[122] the government settled the cases in return for the divestiture of operations that purchased health services to limit the increase in buyer concentration.[123] In 2010, a Department of Justice challenge caused two health insurers to abandon a proposed merger that would have resulted in a high level of concentration and that, among other adverse effects, would allegedly have harmed doctors as a result of increased buyer power.[124]

---

118 Competitive Impact Statement, *United States v Cargill Inc.*, No. 1:99CV01875 (GK) (D.D.C. July 23, 1999), available at http://www.justice.gov/atr/case-document/competitive-impact-statement-57.

119 Amended Complaint, *United States v JBS S.A.*, No. 08-CV-5992 (N.D. Ill. Nov. 7, 2008), available at http://www.justice.gov/atr/case-document/amended-complaint-5.

120 *Ibid* ¶¶ 22–4.

121 Complaint, *United States v Aetna, Inc.*, No. 3-99CV1398-H (N.D. Tex. June 21, 1999), available at http://www.justice.gov/atr/case-document/complaint-1; Revised Final Judgment, *Aetna*, No. 3-99CV1398-H (N.D. Tex. Dec. 9, 1999), available at http://www.justice.gov/atr/case-document/revised-final-judgment.

122 Complaint, *United States v UnitedHealth Group, Inc.*, No.1:08-cv-00322 (D.D.C. Feb. 25, 2008), available at http://www.justice.gov/atr/case-document/complaint-230; Final Judgment, *UnitedHealth*, No.1:08-cv-00322 (D.D.C. Sept. 24, 2008), available at http://www.justice.gov/atr/case-document/final-judgment-186.

123 For an explanation of these settlements by a Justice Department economist, see Schwartz, *supra* note 37.

124 See Press Release, US Department of Justice, 'Blue Cross Blue Shield of Michigan and Physicians Health Plan of Mid-Michigan Abandon Merger Plans'

Several mergers that enhanced buyer power in agriculture have been allowed to proceed without objection. When Smithfield purchased Premium Standard Brands, the number of hog processors in the southeastern United States was reduced from two to one. Despite this apparent monopsony, and in the face of a study done for the Department of Agriculture that found that buyer power already existed in hog markets,[125] the Department of Justice chose not to challenge the merger.[126] It asserted that hog farmers could transport their hogs to the next closest slaughter facility.[127] But the closest of these was in Louisville, Kentucky, more than 400 miles away.[128] Transporting live animals long distances creates significant risks of death and injury as well as loss of saleable weight. The price differential would have to be substantial to justify a movement of that distance. Moreover, most hog raising in the region was done under contract with the slaughterhouses, and so competition took the form of competing contract offers to raise hogs. After the merger, a farmer that did not want to raise hogs under contract would have had to buy hogs and then sell in a distant market, a riskier proposition than contracting with the monopsony buyer.

The Justice Department also gave inadequate attention to buyer power effects when it allowed Cargill, Cenex and ConAgra to combine their flour milling operations in an entity that mills about 30 percent of America's flour.[129] Although grain producers can sell into a global market, some

---

(8 March 2010), available at http://www.justice.gov/opa/pr/blue-cross-blue-shield-michigan-and-physicians-health-plan-mid-michigan-abandon-merger-plans.

[125] See GIPSA, 'Livestock and Meat Marketing Study, Vol. 4: Hog and Pork Industries Final Report', at ES-10 (2007), available at http://www.gipsa.usda.gov/psp/publication/livemarketstudy/LMMS_Vol_1.pdf.

[126] Press Release, *supra* note 66 (concluding that 'farmers who sell hogs or hog-raising services to the merged firm would have competitive alternatives that would deter the merged firm from lowering prices').

[127] *Ibid.*

[128] The nearest company identified in the Department of Justice's Press Release, *supra* note 66, was in Logansport, Indiana; Swift had a plant in Louisville, Kentucky. See Steve Meyer, 'U.S. and Canadian Pork Packing Plants Are Adjusting to Current Production Levels' *National Hog Farmer* tbl.2 (26 May 2011), available at http://nationalhogfarmer.com/marketing/us-canadian-packing-plants-adjusting-0515.

[129] Motion and Memorandum of the United States in Support of Entry of Final Judgment, *United States v ConAgra Foods, Inc.*, No.1:14-cv-00823 (D.D.C. Aug. 14, 2014), available at https://www.justice.gov/atr/case-document/file/492486/download. Although the Antitrust Division gave some attention to buyer-side issues at the investigation stage, those considerations seem to have played no role in the final settlement of the case. One element of concern to the Division,

producers may not have adequate access to this market, which, as the Cargill-Continental merger illustrated, is also facing increased concentration. Moreover, the moisture and weather conditions needed for the production of wheat may not be suitable for other crops, limiting the capacity of many farmers to substitute. Hence, this merger is likely to enhance the buyer power of the resulting firm; and two of its owners, Cargill and ConAgra, are major global grain traders with the potential to manipulate global market prices.[130]

The FTC was even more negligent in considering buyer side effects when, for example, it allowed, without any evidence of review, the dominant wholesaler of swimming pool supplies to expand substantially by merger. But, it later alleged that the merged firm used its buyer power to exclude rivals.[131] Somewhat more surprisingly, the FTC has not discussed buyer power at all in its evaluation of the large number of grocery mergers in the United States. Most recently, the FTC conditioned the merger of two large retailers, Safeway and Albertsons, on their agreeing to divest a substantial number of stores in local retail markets.[132] However, the largest number of those divested stores failed when the buyer went into bankruptcy; the buyer had claimed that Albertsons had acted to drive the buyer out of business.[133] Moreover, Albertsons then reacquired those stores! Occasionally, the FTC has blocked mergers that carried clear buyer-side implications even if it made no reference to them.[134]

---

however, was the capacity of the merged flour producer to coordinate with the grain trading activities of Cargill and ConAgra, which implicated buying markets as much as selling markets. See Competitive Impact Statement at 16–17, *ConAgra Foods*, No.1:14-cv-00823 (D.D.C. May 20, 2014), available at http://www.justice.gov/atr/case-document/file/492501/download.

[130] The settlement of the case required divestiture of several flour mills in regions of the country with preexisting seller concentration. These divestitures may have reduced the buyer power of the consolidation to some degree, even if that was not acknowledged.

[131] Decision and Order, *Pool Corp.*, No. C-4345 (FTC Jan. 10, 2012), available at https://www.ftc.gov/sites/default/files/documents/cases/2012/01/120113poolcorpcmpt.pdf. See also Carstensen, *supra* note 6, at 777–8.

[132] Decision and Order, *Cerberus Institutional Partners*, No. C-4054 (FTC July 2, 2015), available at https://www.ftc.gov/system/files/documents/cases/150702cerberusdo.pdf. If kept as a buying group, the divested stores would have been a substantial force in the buying market for grocery products.

[133] See Press Release, Haggen Food and Pharmacy, 'Haggen Sues Albertsons' (1 September 2015), available at http://www.haggen.com/haggen-sues-albertsons/.

[134] See *FTC v Sysco Corp.*, 113 F. Supp. 3d 1 (D.D.C. 2015) (blocking the merger of the two largest distributors of food and related goods to restaurant chains, hospitals and other institutional buyers).

B. The EU

Three EU decisions reject in whole or in part mergers based on buyer power. Each involved retail chains with large shares of national markets. The first case involved the dominant supermarkets in Finland; the market share of the combined firms would have been 55 percent, three times larger than the next largest firm.[135] The second involved Austrian firms whose combined market shares would have been 40 percent.[136] The European Commission identified seller power risks in both the Austrian and Finnish cases, but also focused on the potential harm to upstream producers resulting from the concentration of buying power. The last case involved the proposed merger of two large French supermarket chains.[137] The French case focused primarily on the buying side. The combined firm would have had a 25 percent market share of the grocery input market, and the top three buyers post-merger would have had an input market share of 60 percent or more.[138] Hence, the Commission recognized the risk of oligopsonistic collusion on the buying side.

The Commission has rarely expressed concerns about buyer power in other mergers.[139] In its analysis of consolidation among farm cooperatives in Denmark and the Netherlands, the Commission did focus on the potential exclusion of other buyers.[140] In the Danish case, the Commission permitted the consolidation of nearly 60 percent of the live cattle purchases in a single enterprise,[141] but found problems with respect to hog buying because the cooperative took 76 percent of production and used exclusive supply agreements, which limited greatly the competitive capacity of the two small domestic cooperatives and foreign buyers.[142] These cases

---

135 Case IV/M.784, *Kesko/Tuko,* 1997 O.J. (L 110) 53. See also John J Curtin, Daniel L Goldberg and Daniel S Savrin, 'The EC's Rejection of the Kesko/Tuko Merger: Leading the Way to the Application of a "Gatekeeper" Analysis of Retailer Market Power Under U.S. Antitrust Laws' (1999) 40 *Boston College Law Review* 537.

136 Case IV/M.1221, *Rewe/Meinl*, C(1999) ¶ 228 final.

137 Case Comp/M.1684, *Carrefour/Promodes*, 2000 O.J. (C 164) 5.

138 *Ibid* ¶ 98.

139 See Chloe Binet, 'Buyer Power in EU Competition Law: A Boon or Impediment to Consumer Welfare?' (unpublished Ph.D. dissertation, Catholic Univ. of Louvain, 2015), 192–5, available at http://dial.uclouvain.be/pr/boreal/fr/object/boreal%3A156352 (summarizing cases).

140 See Case IV/M.1313, *Danish Crown/Vestjyske Slagterier* (European Comm'n 9 March 1999); Case Comp/M.5046, *Friesland Foods/Campina*, C(2008) 8459 final.

141 See *Danish Crown*, ¶ 136.

142 *Ibid* ¶ 121.

indicate a failure of the Commission to appreciate the long-run dangers of concentrated buying, a persistent problem in competition analysis. In assessing the EU's concern for buyer power, Binet concluded:

> In the majority of the decisions in which an increase in buyer power was assessed by the Commission, it . . . concluded that the transaction was not likely to impede effective competition . . . [including] several decisions on mergers . . . [in which] the share of the parties was definitely not insignificant. . .[143]

The EU, like the United States, has recognized that buyer power can be a source of anticompetitive effect in mergers, but it has, again like the United States, failed to adopt strict standards to protect the competitive process from excessive buyer power.

C. Other Countries

The EU preempts national competition authorities from reviewing mergers involving substantial enterprises that operate in more than one Member State, hence those agencies have no jurisdiction over most large intra-EU mergers.[144] The national agencies do retain oversight of mergers where the primary impact is limited to that country. A 2014 survey of European merger cases in which buyer power figured either as a source of concern or as a defense identified only a couple of cases in which national agencies acted to stop or restrict mergers based on buyer power.[145] In 2009, Poland rejected the merger of the only two buyers of used auto batteries on the grounds that it would create a monopsony.[146] A German case involved a joint venture between two large milk processors that eventually merged.[147] The German authorities recognized that dairy farmers faced only a few powerful buyers and a limited ability to switch products, but nevertheless

---

[143] Binet, *supra* note 139, at 192.

[144] Perhaps because of their limited control over major mergers, a number of EU countries have exercised their authority to impose direct regulation over the conduct of large retailers, especially grocery stores operating within their territories

[145] See Ariel Ezrachi and Maria Ioannidou, 'Buyer Power in Merger Control: An Overview of EU and National Case Law' *e-Competitions Bulletin* (May 2015), available at https://www.concurrences.com/bulletin/special-issues/Buying-Power/Buyer-Power-in-Merger-Control-An.

[146] See Porter Elliott, 'Polish Competition Authority Prohibits Monopsony-Creating Merger' in Van Bael and Bellis, (2009) 4 *VBB on Competition Law* 7.

[147] See Bill Bruce, 'Humana Milchindustrie and Nordmilch Merge to Form DMK', *FoodBev Media* (18 May 2011), available at http://www.foodbev.com/news/new-branding-for-germanys-largest-dairy/.

authorized the combination.[148] Beyond these cases, what seems curious in light of the highly concentrated nature of so many European grocery retail markets is the failure of EU Member States to use merger control to seek more competitive structures.

In 2015, the German antitrust authority did issue an order prohibiting the acquisition of 450 grocery stores by the largest grocery retailer in the country.[149] The retail grocery market was already highly concentrated, and the decision focused on both the increased retail concentration in many local markets and the probable adverse effect on suppliers.[150] The competition authority had already imposed a sanction on the buyer for abuse of its dominance.[151] However, the parties appealed to the Ministry of Economic Affairs and Energy. The ministry reversed the decision on the grounds that the overall gains from the merger outweighed its competitive risks.[152] The apparent justification for this reversal was the claim that the merger would preserve 16,000 jobs.[153] This is analogous to the failing firm defense, but the reports are unclear as to whether there was any consideration of alternative buyers.

In South Africa, various unions and elected officials objected to Walmart's acquisition of a large grocery retailer. The competition authority evaluated the merger. Even though Walmart was not a competitor in the grocery market, the objections related to Walmart's past pattern of buying and employment practices. Ultimately, Walmart was allowed to make the acquisition after it committed to expand its local purchases and retain existing employees.[154] Earlier, the competition tribunal reversed a decision of the Competition Commission to prohibit a merger between

---

[148] See Press Release, Bundeskartellamt, 'Humana and Nordmilch Can Pool Sales of their Dairy Products' (6 September 2009), available at http://www.bundeskartellamt.de/SharedDocs/Meldung/EN/Pressemitteilungen/2009/09_06_2009_Humana_Nordmilch.html.

[149] Case Summary, Prohibition of Acquisition of Kaiser's Tengelmann Outlets by Edeka, B2– 96/14 (31 March 2015), available at http://www.bundeskartellamt.de/SharedDocs/Entscheidung/EN/Fallberichte/Fusionskontrolle/2015/B2-96-14.html?nn=3591568.

[150] *Ibid* at 3.

[151] *Ibid* at 4. An appeal of that sanction was pending at the time of the merger decision.

[152] See 'Germany Approves Edeka, Kaiser's Supermarkets Merger' *International Supermarket News* (17 March 2016), available at http://www.internationalsupermarketnews.com/news/23727.

[153] *Ibid.*

[154] See Harry First and Eleanor Fox, '*Philadelphia National Bank*, Globalization, and the Public Interest' (2015) 80 *Antitrust Law Journal* 307, 329–47.

two substantial grocery wholesalers in a regional market where one of the competition concerns was buyer power.[155] However, in 2015, the Commission created a study group to investigate the retail grocery market industry including issues of buyer power.[156]

In 1988, Australia's competition authority sought to block a merger in the meat packing industry.[157] The challenge asserted that the merger would create undue market power in the buying of cattle for slaughter in a regional market. The court upheld the challenge and ordered divestiture.[158] In contrast, Australia allowed its grocery retailing industry to consolidate with no apparent concern for the implications of these mergers for buyer power resulting in the two largest firms having a combined share of 60 to 80 percent of all sales.[159] But it has now adopted provisions to regulate the use of the buyer power resulting from this high level of concentration.[160]

VI. CONCLUSION

The central goal of merger control is workably competitive markets without the need to police specific conduct. Mergers resulting in increased buyer power—like those that result in increased seller power—give rise to the kinds of risks to competition that warrant an active and informed competition policy. For the reasons discussed in this chapter and earlier, the risks of abusive buyer power arise from lower market shares than are customarily associated with the risks of abusive seller power. Other

---

155 Competition Tribunal, *Masscash Holdings & Finro Enter.*, 04/LM/Jan09 (Competition Tribunal Sept. 22, 2009) (S. Afr.), available at http://www.comptrib.co.za/assets/Uploads/Case-Documents/04LMJan09.pdf.

156 See Competition Commission, 'Grocery Retail Sector Market Inquiry Draft Statement of Issues' (May 2016) (S. Afr.), available at http://www.compcom.co.za/wp-content/uploads/2015/06/Statement-of-Issues.pdf. See also Thabelo Ravhugoni and Mfundo Ngobese (2010), 'Disappearance of Small Independent Retailers in South Africa: The Waterbed and Spiral Effects of Bargaining Power', available at http://www.compcom.co.za/wp-content/uploads/2014/09/Disappearance-of-Small-Independent-Retailers-in-South-Africafinal.pdf.

157 *Trade Practices Comm'n v Australia Meat Holdings Pty Ltd.* [1988] 83 ALR 299.

158 *Ibid* ¶¶ 240, 241.

159 See Barbora Jedličková, 'Vertical Issues Arising from Conduct Between Large Supermarkets and Small Suppliers in the Grocery Market: Law and Industry Codes of Conduct 2015 *European Competition Law Review* 19, 20 (identifying different ways that market shares had been measured).

160 See *ibid* at 21–4 (describing Australian code and comparing it with the code in force in the United Kingdom).

considerations can inform the analysis of specific risks of undue buyer power. But competition enforcement authorities need to examine every substantial merger to see what impact it will have on the buying side of the market.

Contemporary policy is far too tolerant of combinations that create significant buyer power without legitimate justification. The standing caveat is that it may be necessary, in smaller economies, to allow combinations that create significant buyer power to achieve the benefits of economies of scale and scope. In such cases, it is incumbent on regulators to implement appropriate conduct remedies that will limit the risks of abuse. The failure to be aggressive in merger enforcement will enable the development of noncompetitive market structures, which will eventually need to be controlled by detailed conduct regulation and its attendant economic costs.

9. Conclusion: the centrality of market structure and the limits of national authority

This chapter summarizes the arguments and analysis advanced in this book. First, abuse of buyer power constitutes as serious a threat, or perhaps a more serious threat, to the competitive process as abuse of seller power. Second, interventions that address the abuse of buyer power directly are difficult to implement, unlikely to be effective in many situations, and may be more limited than the options available for confronting seller power. Third, competition policy can more effectively avoid the creation of undue buyer power than it can regulate to restrict abuse; consequently, public policy toward buyer power should focus explicitly on preserving and retaining market structures conducive to robust buying markets. Fourth, the competitive risks that buyer power creates require that public policy address all instances in which such power is enhanced regardless of the relative size of producers. Finally, this chapter concludes with a brief discussion of an important enforcement problem—buyer power and its abuse often reach across countries in the global market so that harms occurring in one nation have their origin in another. This jurisdictional problem is one that competition policy generally, and policy aimed at buyer power in particular, must confront.

I. BUYER POWER—A SIGNIFICANT THREAT TO THE COMPETITIVE PROCESS

In 1989, William K Jones, the Milton Handler Professor of Trade Regulation at Columbia, declared: 'The antitrust laws were intended to protect producers as well as consumers and may properly be invoked by producers in cases in which consumer interests are not implicated.'[1] The abuse of buyer power is the competitive concern of producers; abuses arise

[1] William K Jones, 'Concerted Refusals to Deal and the Producer Interest in Antitrust' (1989) 50 *Ohio State Law Journal* 73, 73.

in many contexts and create significant risks to the long-run viability of the competitive process.

The received tradition that competition law and policy should focus primarily on consumer welfare (or alternatively aggregate welfare) has obstructed the recognition of these issues and the development of effective enforcement. Although impact on consumers is a very important consideration, it should not be the *sine qua non* for policy. Consumer welfare and aggregate welfare become highly ambiguous concepts when employed as dynamic, long-term goals. Neither is a useful basis for formulating policy. Competition is an economic process that requires rules and standards to avoid an unhealthy transformation into economic warfare. Over time, a healthy and competitive market system should produce great benefits for all participants in the economy—producers and consumers alike. The system must be understood holistically so that the regulations that govern it promote the competitive process, not just the single dimension of consumer welfare.

Competition policymakers and advocates have employed the consumer welfare mantra as part of an argument for competition as a socially desirable objective. In doing so, however, they have lost sight of the limitation of that slogan—it blinds policy to the harms that occur on the production side of the market. The emergence of specialized regulations to govern abusive buying practices generally or in specific categories of business (such as grocery retailing) confirm that competition policy needs to incorporate a robust concern and focus on buyer power and how to control its exploitation.

The greatest harm that arises from abuse of buyer power is the exploitation of producers. In contrast to seller-side competition policy, which often accepts unilateral exploitation of market power as part of the competitive process, buying-side policy must look critically at harmful consequences that can be dispersed over a wide range of upstream stakeholders. A buyer that exploits its position to extract wealth from a producer leaves the producer with fewer resources with which to avoid buyer-imposed harm. The market process is distorted. Thus, buyer exploitation presents a serious problem for competition policy intended to promote and protect the competitive process.

Buyers have a collective interest in controlling their costs and externalizing risks. Moreover, powerful buyers can often exploit their power with little or no adverse effect on the output of the supply market. The lack of immediate impact on supply may explain why many observers and enforcement agencies have been slow to respond to the threats that abuse of buyer power creates for the competitive process. Buyers can also directly or tacitly induce dependent producers to perform exclusionary acts on their behalf. Such conduct may be irrational from a longer term perspective, but effective response requires collective action by producers. These actions are likely to be cartelistic and result in serious legal challenges. In addition, they face the usual problems that come from creating and maintaining a collective response.

To be sure, a supplier's alternatives affect its vulnerability. There may be costs to switching to other buyers (assuming they exist), but if buyer demand is relatively price elastic, a producer may be able to reject the unreasonable demands of any one buyer. Similarly, when faced with unacceptable demands, a producer can avoid undue exploitation if it can switch its capacity to other reasonably profitable lines of work. Bargaining may well be vigorous in such contexts. These basic issues of market structure allow the degree of risk of the abuse of buyer power to be predicted.

If a buyer purchases a substantial share of the total volume in any relevant product market, it is likely to have leverage over its suppliers and the capacity to use that power to serve its anticompetitive interests. The empirical data show that buyer-market shares well below those associated with seller monopoly produce competitive concerns. The reasons, as set forth in Chapters 3 and 4, are both institutional and inherent in the nature of the buying process. A buyer that takes 20 percent or more of the output in a relevant product market is very likely to have significant buyer power over producers in that market. Indeed, there is evidence that even with much smaller market shares—less than ten percent in some instances—buyers can exercise significant control over suppliers that have few alternative outlets.

Buyers that share an incentive to obtain lower input costs and deter new entry at their own level are less likely to engage in disruptive buying practices, such as competing for suppliers. When these incentives are combined with the inherent limits on producer arbitrage, the buying side of the market is more amendable to stable tacit collusion even if there are a moderate number of buyers. Indeed, as auction theory teaches, exploitive conduct is likely to be the dominant force in any buying market with fewer than five or six buyers. Although not all buying markets are vulnerable to buyer power, many more are vulnerable than contemporary enforcement has recognized. Moreover, powerful buyers and sellers have a collective interest in limiting sales competition at their respective levels. This community of interest creates a further impediment to the robust and innovative competition that is central to the market process. Even buyers that take a long-term perspective and are willing to pay reasonable prices have an interest in deterring entry into their own markets. Powerful buyers can overtly and tacitly cause suppliers to support and protect the buyers' own market position.

II. THE LIMITED EFFECTIVENESS OF DIRECTLY REMEDYING UNILATERAL ABUSE OF BUYER POWER

The core problems of market exploitation and exclusion that buyer power poses are at the center of the transactional process. Using competition rules to directly control these abuses, especially exploitive conduct, may intrude profoundly into the operation of the market. Workable rules to deal with unjustified exploitation are difficult to formulate and enforce. At the same time, limits on the capacity of the victims to respond make it significantly less likely that the self-correcting nature of the market will remedy anticompetitive buying practices. The central conclusion of Chapter 5, therefore, was that conduct-oriented rules based on conventional competition policy precepts would have limited utility in ameliorating exploitive harms arising from buyer power.

Rules prohibiting particular exclusionary practices are more feasible, but they would have to be substantially stricter than they are currently to have any effect. Even then, it is unlikely that limiting those practices will bring about significant changes in buyer power (and therefore the potential for abuse) in most contexts.

Although legitimate in some circumstances, vertical contracts that restrict the freedom of sellers to deal with other buyers can create serious foreclosure concerns if they affect a significant share of the output supply in the market. A rebuttable presumption of illegality should arise when a specified threshold is crossed. The presumption should put the burden on the parties to both justify the use of any exclusionary terms in a purchase agreement or supply contract and prove that it is no more restrictive than reasonably necessary to accomplish its legitimate functions. A simple rule of this sort creates the incentive to solve any transactional cost or other efficiency need within the scope of a buying position that allows the long-run dynamics of the market to operate effectively.

Implicitly recognizing the limited capacity of competition policy, narrowly defined, to address the harms of buyer power, there is a global movement to develop specific regulations to control the abuse of buyer power by dominant buyers. This movement is strong in some parts of the world, while other countries, including the United States, lag behind. The goal of this expanded competition policy should still be to facilitate a dynamic competitive process. But there are serious problems, as explored in Chapter 6, with the use of these regulations to control the abuse of buyer power. Such regulation can constrain, to some degree, arbitrary conduct by buyers, but it is impossible to substitute direct control over price and output decisions by buyers for the competitive marketplace without eliminating or significantly impairing the market process itself.

Economic activity evolves and changes over time. Detailed regulation of buyer conduct can itself become a threat to the critical dynamics of the competitive process. Therefore, any regulatory process must have the capacity to revisit and revise regulation. This is a politically challenging task because stakeholders who gain from regulatory control will seek to frustrate change. Moreover, the capacity of even the most dedicated regulatory regime to identify relevant conduct and impose the appropriate control is limited. Regulation often attacks the symptoms, but not the disease. Market dynamics make comprehensive regulatory wisdom rare. Still, despite its many flaws, buyer-oriented regulation is, in some cases, the least-bad public policy because of the existing structural characteristics of the affected buying markets. The regulations imposed by Japan, the United Kingdom and some other countries on the conduct of large buyers can limit gratuitous exploitation, but are, for the reasons discussed in Chapter 6, largely ineffective in addressing the core problems of balance in the fundamental transactions.

General market regulation can also ameliorate some of the problems created by buyer power. A major challenge is to convince competition authorities of the role these regulations can play in preventing or ameliorating the use of buyer power. The facilitation of more open market practices in agricultural markets is one example.[2] In addition, imposing floors on some contractual provisions, such as minimum wages and other worker protections, can provide a further constraint on the abuse of buyer power, especially when the buyer's power is not obvious.

When general market regulation is the better option, it is vital to ensure it is no more intrusive than necessary, focuses on market facilitation rather than direct regulation, and has as much capacity as possible for flexibility and responsiveness to changing market conditions and relationships. This is an extraordinary challenge in part because of the inevitable political pressures that will emerge from winners and losers in any regulatory regime. The impact of market regulation on the competitive process also means that competition agencies ought to take an active role in

---

[2] It might be possible to compel the use of public markets for the sale of certain commodities by producers to buyers. Historically, such markets have shown the capacity to shield producers from exploitation as long as there are enough buyers, probably six or more, to ensure a workably competitive buying market. But ordering the creation of such a market is beyond the scope of what competition agencies can or should do; it requires a broader governmental commitment to the process of market transformation. It is a very unlikely response.

commenting on proposals from other more specialized agencies, as well as challenging legislative proposals that do not advance the fundamental public interest in fair, open and efficient markets.

Chapter 6 also identified other ways that buyer power might be constrained or even reduced. First is by the use of countervailing power. The use of a producer cartel to accomplish this goal raises serious competitive concerns. If, however, there is no other long-term, viable solution to the abusive power of a dominant buyer, then a government might consider the creation of such a cartel. It should be expressly authorized, include a sunset provision and be subject to some form of public oversight. Australia has used this strategy to deal with concentration in some buying markets. Indeed, although legislation has sometimes authorized producer cartels in fields such as agriculture and labor, it appears that only Australia has authorized general producer cartels.

More promising are efforts by producers to achieve horizontal integration, either through consolidated ownership or joint ventures, which will provide the depth of resources to support better bargaining and ideally locate more buyers. Forward vertical integration by such ventures provides an even more promising route to limiting the impact of existing buyer power. These efforts require that the enterprises themselves undertake the primary efforts. Competition law can and should be supportive. Indeed, as discussed at the end of Chapter 6, more direct public support for such efforts is possible, although it too is fraught with challenges.

In sum, there are real and pervasive concerns that ought to embolden competition policy enforcers to control the abuse of buyer power. On balance, however, conduct-oriented responses have limited potential to reduce or eliminate that power and restore a workably competitive buying market once strong buyer power has emerged. The more promising routes to countervailing power are unlikely to be used or useful in any but a limited number of circumstances. This leads to the conclusion that the better policy option is to focus on market structure to avoid or eliminate buyer power itself.

III. CONTROL OF MARKET STRUCTURE IS CENTRAL TO CONTROL OF BUYER POWER

Because of the limited capacity of direct conduct-oriented controls to respond effectively to buyer power, competition policy should, whenever possible, employ strict rules to deter or prevent the creation of undue buyer power. Merger policy and policy toward buying groups or other collaborations among buyers are central to a competition policy that seeks to preserve and enhance the competitive process overall.

Naked cartelistic buying schemes should continue to be condemned—even if the parties can credibly claim the scheme holds down the prices they pay and so in some abstract economic sense increases overall economic welfare. Consistent with the goal of advancing the competitive process, the better option for oppressed buyers is to find other ways to circumvent the power of a dominant seller. Buyers in general have the resources and incentives to engage in such efforts. It bears emphasis here that the buyers of concern are those using the purchased goods as inputs for other products or for sale in their retailing operations. When buyer resistance is ineffective, the better policy choice would be to restructure the buying industry rather than allow a cartel.

Legitimate buying groups should generally be allowed. These are valid joint ventures that can provide efficiencies and countervailing power for buyers. But at the same time, they can create serious longer term risks to the competitive process. The current relaxed structural standards for judging such activity need to be revisited and made stricter, especially with respect to the relative size of such groups. The central point of the analysis is that producers need multiple buyers and in most circumstances buyers can get the transactional and scale efficiencies of joint buying at levels that do not create significant risks for the competitive process. Chapter 7 suggests that buying groups that take more than about 20 percent of any commodity can create significant buyer power concerns and should be subject to a presumption of illegality.

Mergers are another means by which buying markets become concentrated. Here too, there has been a long-term failure of public policy to identify and challenge mergers that create undue concentration on the buying side—even in the countries with the most advanced competition policy systems. As Chapter 8 has shown, mergers that create significant buyer concentration can substantially increase the risk of harm to the competitive process. As with buyer groups, the risks to competition arise at lower market shares and involve both unilateral and collective risks of exploitive and exclusionary conduct.

Competition agencies should focus more attention on the buyer side of the market—especially in those industries in which the upstream supply market consists of many small businesses. As explained in Chapter 8, there are particular challenges in defining relevant buying markets because of the elasticities of both supply and demand. This is why buyer-side merger analysis calls for appropriate metrics and analytic methods. Moreover, the empirical data from a variety of examples of abuses of buyer power show that effective buyer-side markets require five or more competitors. Hence, the presumption of illegality should be invoked at lower thresholds with respect to a merger that increases buyer-side concentration.

These standards should create no significant, long-term efficiency concerns in large economies. However, in smaller economies, there will be a much greater potential that economies of scale and scope will be lost in the effort to retain a sufficiently viable buying market. In such contexts, to protect the workability of the competitive buying market or at least ensure equal and fair treatment of suppliers, enforcement agencies will have to examine closely the options for constraints on a buyer's discretion.

IV. THE SCOPE OF THE PROBLEM OF BUYER POWER

The impact of buyer power will vary depending on market facts, particularly the extent to which there is elasticity in either supply or demand of any particular input. Increased buyer power is a source of concern regardless of the size of the producer(s) relative to the powerful buyer. Traditionally, the primary focus has been on the large buyer facing many small suppliers. Agriculture, groceries and employment (particularly of professional athletes, doctors and computer software engineers) fit that framework. It is likely, however, that this focus is, in significant part, a consequence of the limited concern for abuses of buyer power. The foregoing contexts are the ones in which abuse is most obvious.

A comprehensive review of examples of exploitation of buyer power reveals that it can occur in a wide range of markets for inputs and branded goods. In markets with relatively few buyers, buyer power can be abused even when buyers and sellers are evenly matched in size. The presence of strong buyers excuses mergers that increase seller power, which excuses mergers that increase buyer power. Highly concentrated markets are the result. Buyers and sellers then have incentives to restrict entry at both levels and to exploit both upstream and downstream markets.

Additionally, the analysis here shows that increasing concentration at any buying level creates more buyer power as the number of producers decreases. Favored producers have a greater ability to exploit their own powerless, upstream suppliers. The potential for upstream harm differentiates buyer power from seller power. Downstream exploitation results in overcharges that may be passed on down the distribution chain, but the fact of exploitation is evident in the first transaction. On the buying side, when both producers and buyers are substantial, the increased producer power resulting from buyer concentration can result in upstream harm without any visible impact on transactions between them. The producer with enhanced upstream power will be able to offer its buyer lower prices because it has exploited the power created by the elimination of its direct competition. The adverse competitive effects can occur at a stage of the production process one or more steps removed from the buying market in which the structure has changed. It is essential in assessing mergers or buying groups to look beyond the buyer-seller relationship to determine whether the buyer power created by a merger or buying group harms multiple levels of commerce.

Longer run concerns about innovation and choice also require a more comprehensive analysis of changes in buying-side market structure. These changes adversely affect the dynamics of markets by reducing, unnecessarily, the number of alternative decision makers, which affects the social-political power of enterprises and results in market structures that are prone to stultification and decreased flexibility.

The greatest danger to the competitive process arises from allowing unnecessarily concentrated markets—on either the buying or selling side—to arise. Once created they are likely to become entrenched. Even if an increase in buyer power appears to create limited short-term risks, a consistent public policy that rejects unjustified and excessive concentration will best preserve and protect the overall market process.

V. THE DISCONNECT BETWEEN GLOBAL BUYER POWER AND NATIONAL COMPETITION LAW

A recurring example of abusive buyer power is the exploitation of developing countries by buyers located in developed countries.[3] Buyers that merge or create buying groups domestically increase their power in their home countries. But if they deal in imported goods, the harms they cause primarily affect the countries in which they buy. The jurisdictional problem is self-evident.

Competition policy agencies in developed nations cannot point to harm in their domestic markets that results from this exploitation. If anything, consumers in the home country share some of the exploitation through lower prices. Even if an agency was convinced that the long-run public interest in a workably effective global economy was unduly threatened by

---

[3] A similar problem exists on the selling side of some global markets in which producers in the developed world overcharge buyers in both the developed and developing world. The emergence of a global economy has created major gaps in the effective enforcement of competition law and policy.

buyer practices, mergers or buying groups, it might not have the jurisdictional power to address extraterritorial harm.[4]

Conversely, developing countries face equally daunting challenges. First, they need the institutional capacity to identify and analyze the harmful effects of buyer power. In a concentrated buying market, a developing economy is likely to incur serious losses, but powerful buyers will have a mutual interest in deterring the enforcement of competition law. Second, thcy would need extraterritorial jurisdiction to reach the foreign exploiter, which raises important issues of *in personam* jurisdiction.[5] Even if a developing country has jurisdiction, a buyer might simply withdraw from that market and purchase its needs from other countries. The problems are even greater if the competitive concern arises from a merger among buyers or a buying group that has achieved undue buyer power. It is very likely that only the host country can effectively control these situations, but the host nation may lack both the incentive and legal authority to do so. And the developing country is unlikely to have standing to pursue its competitive concerns under the host country's competition law.

Thus, conduct that harms the global economy falls into an enforcement gap that arises from the lack of an effective global competition law enforcement system. The creation of a global agency to enforce a consensus of competition law has been proposed, but it is both politically and administratively implausible.

The experience of the European Union (EU) and other regional trade groups suggests that regional enforcement may be a more practical—if less than complete—solution. The larger the market area covered by such a group, the more effective enforcement is likely to be. Global enterprises cannot afford to be precluded from operating in significant markets. Thus, in 2001, the EU was able to block the merger of General

---

4 A buyers' cartel would arguably be subject to challenge as per se illegal; the absence of adverse effects in the home market would not then be relevant.

5 For example, De Beers sold its diamonds to American buyers in transactions outside the United States. Because DeBeers did not do business in the United States, it was impossible for American antitrust enforcers to exercise personal jurisdiction over the company. Hence, the court in *United States v General Electric Co.* rejected the government's theory of a price fixing conspiracy because DeBeers, General Electric's alleged co-conspirator, was not served and its records could not be obtained. 869 F. Supp. 1285 (S.D. Ohio 1994). A decade later, when it decided to enter the American market, De Beers had to resolve the case because the indictment was still outstanding. It pled guilty to price fixing, confirming the government's original theory. Plea Agreement, *United States v De Beers Centenary AG*, No. CR-2-94-019 (S.D. Ohio July 13, 2004), available at https://www.justice.gov/atr/case-document/plea-agreement-136.

Electric and Honeywell despite the fact that both were American enterprises, because their businesses required access to EU markets.[6] Joint competition enforcement regimes are emerging in a number of regions, formed as byproducts of regional trade agreements.[7] It is uncertain how effective these regimes will be in dealing with conventional competition issues, let alone the more complex and less developed concerns with buyer power. But compared to national authorities, these agencies may have the institutional capacity and jurisdictional power to provide greater oversight.

Another option has emerged for countries not in a trading group to coordinate their competition enforcement policies. In 2016, the BRICS (Brazil, the Russian Federation, India, China and South Africa) set up a system of consultation to coordinate their competition law enforcement.[8] Under this system, even if the primary adverse effects of a merger, agreement or unilateral practice affected only *some* of the countries, collective enforcement would be more likely to be effective. This is particularly true when enforcement requires only a single action such as blocking a merger or dissolving a monopolist. Remedies that involve continued oversight would be harder to enforce collectively, especially if some of the conduct occurs in countries not part of the enforcement group.

It is not the mission of this book to solve the problem of creating an effective global competition enforcement regime. But given the global impact of buyer power, it is important to acknowledge that absent some effective supranational enforcement policy, there is a significant and continuing gap between necessary policies and rules for dealing with buyer power and the capacity to enforce those rules effectively.

---

[6] Case COMP/M.2220, *General Electric/Honeywell* (Comm'n Decision July 3, 2001), available at http://ec.europa.eu/competition/mergers/cases/decisions/m2220_en.pdf.

[7] See, eg, Press Release, Trademark East Africa, 'EAC Competition Authority to Start Operations in July' (16 June 2016), available at https://www.trademarkea.com/news/eac-competition-authority-to-start-operations-in-july/.

[8] See Memorandum of Understanding between the Competition Authorities of the Federative Republic of Brazil, the Russian Federation, the Republic of India, the People's Republic of China and the Republic of South Africa on Cooperation in the Field of Competition Law and Policy (19 May 2016), available at http://www.cade.gov.br/noticias/membros-do-brics-firmam-memorando-de-cooperacao-na-area-de-politica-de-defesa-da-concorrencia/mou-brics-assinado-002.pdf.

VI. CONCLUSION

Robust, consistent and globally comprehensive enforcement policies with respect to mergers and buying groups are the best way to protect a workably competitive buying market. Control of extant monopsonistic markets is difficult and problematic for the reasons explained earlier. Merger and buyer group controls cannot protect markets entirely from undue buyer concentration. However, they can go a long way toward reducing the risks. There will always be Walmarts, Amazons and similar enterprises that grow internally and achieve substantial buyer power. Competition policy can never achieve perfection. But all countries must participate in a collective effort to establish and enforce rules that constrain the dangerous, but avoidable, creation of buyer power. The goal must be to preserve as much workable competition as possible on the buying as well as the selling side of the market.

Index